THE COMPLETE HANDBOOK OF PRO BASKETBALL

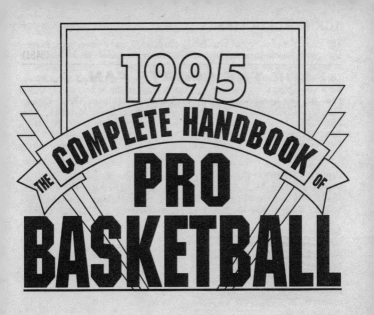

1995

THE COMPLETE HANDBOOK OF PRO BASKETBALL

EDITED BY

ZANDER HOLLANDER

AN ASSOCIATED FEATURES BOOK

Ⓞ

A SIGNET BOOK

ACKNOWLEDGMENTS

The game of switch begins even before the draft . . . and it never ends. Players are moving to new teams as you read this. Printing deadlines make it impossible to be as up-to-date as today's newspaper. But here it is, the 21st edition of *The Complete Handbook of Pro Basketball*. For helping to meet the deadline, we acknowledge contributing editor Eric Compton, the writers on the facing page and Lee Stowbridge, Phyllis Hollander, Linda Spain, David Kaplan, Deb Brody, Jerry Todd, the NBA's Alex Sachare, Brian McIntyre, Peter Steber, Matt Winick, Marty Blake and the team publicity directors, the CBA's Brent Meister, Elias Sports Bureau, Dot Gordineer of Libra Graphics, and Bill Foley, Shā Lee-Carmichael and the crew at Westchester Book Composition.

Zander Hollander

PHOTO CREDITS: Cover—Noren Trotman. Inside photos—Malcolm Emmons, Ira Golden, Michael Hirsch, Vic Milton, Mitch Reibel, NBC-TV, Wide World, UPI and the NBA club and college photographers, including Mike Maicher, Rich Mukai, Matthew West, Harry Blomberg and Mitchell Layton.

SIGNET
Published by the Penguin Group
Penguin Books USA Inc., 375 Hudson Street,
New York, New York 10014, U.S.A.
Penguin Books Ltd, 27 Wrights Lane,
London W8 5TZ, England
Penguin Books Australia Ltd, Ringwood,
Victoria, Australia
Penguin Books Canada Ltd, 10 Alcorn Ave.,
Toronto, Ontario, Canada M4V 3B2
Penguin Books (N.Z.,) Ltd, 182-190 Wairau Road,
Auckland 10, New Zealand

Penguin Books Ltd, Registered Offices:
Harmondsworth, Middlesex, England

First Signet Printing, November 1994

10   9   8   7   6   5   4   3   2   1

CONTENTS

HAKEEM FULFILLS THE DREAM
- By Fran Blinebury 6

BILL WALTON: FROM "GRATEFUL DEAD" TO ALIVE ON THE TUBE • By Bob Rubin.. 16

THE ECSTASY AND THE AGONY OF JOHN STARKS • By Clifford Brown 24

REGGIE MILLER: SUDDENLY A SUPERSTAR • By Conrad Brunner 32

INSIDE THE NBA
- By Fred Kerber & Scott Howard-Cooper.. 42

Dallas Mavericks.......	48	Atlanta Hawks	214
Denver Nuggets	62	Boston Celtics	227
Golden State Warriors..	74	Charlotte Hornets	241
Houston Rockets	86	Chicago Bulls..........	253
Los Angeles Clippers...	100	Cleveland Cavaliers.....	265
Los Angeles Lakers	112	Detroit Pistons	279
Minnesota Timberwolves	124	Indiana Pacers.........	290
Phoenix Suns	136	Miami Heat............	304
Portland Trail Blazers...	150	Milwaukee Bucks	316
Sacramento Kings	163	New Jersey Nets.......	326
San Antonio Spurs.....	176	New York Knicks	339
Seattle SuperSonics....	189	Orlando Magic.........	353
Utah Jazz	202	Philadelphia 76ers	367
		Washington Bullets	379

NBA College Draft 392
NBA Statistics 402
NBA Schedule 418
NBC-TV Games 428
TNT Games 429
TBS Games 431

Editor's Note: The material herein includes trades and rosters up to the final printing deadline.

HAKEEM FULFILLS THE DREAM

By FRAN BLINEBURY

The last shot had gone up and the last rebound had come down in the 1994 NBA Finals. At one end of the floor Hakeem Olajuwon squeezed the basketball to his chest as the final seconds ran off the clock, then jogged the length of the court and leaned back against the press table to watch the scene unfold.

As the joyful celebration of the Houston Rockets' first championship raged around him—kissing, hugging, tears, screams of relief—the man who did more than anyone else to make it all possible sat there quietly, alone with the ball and his thoughts and drank it all in like the champagne that would come later.

"I want to remember this," he said. "I want to remember my teammates at this moment, the excitement, the season, the play-offs. If you wrote a book, you couldn't write it any better than this."

If you wrote a book about this amazing story, it would most likely begin: "Once upon a time . . . ."

It was a modern-day fairytale with a fantasy finish. When the Rockets put the New York Knicks down for good, 90-84, in Game 7 of the toughest, grittiest, most defensive NBA Final series in history, it put the perfect cap on a season that was like none other.

It was a dream season. It was Hakeem the Dream's season. He became the first player in history to be named the regular-

Fran Blinebury is a columnist for the Houston Chronicle *who has seen the Dream fulfilled, from the early days of college to the NBA championship.*

He conquered the world . . . and now faces second decade.

season Most Valuable Player, Defensive Player of the Year, MVP of the NBA Finals and also win the title.

It is a tale that began 14 years ago when a towering African teen-ager stepped off a plane from Lagos, Nigeria, and first set foot in a new land with new customs that would change his life forever.

It has been an eventful journey filled with career success and sometimes disappointment, but it has also been a path of personal change and spiritual reawakening that has produced a 31-year-old man who has his game and his life in near-perfect order.

"If I never played another basketball game after today, I would be forever grateful for the success I've had in this game," Olajuwon said. "People have to learn to look at things for what they have, not what they haven't been given.

"What I have is 10 years in the NBA with a lot of accomplishments. I have a comfortable life, and if I don't achieve anything more in basketball than what I have today, that's more than enough."

This incredible journey could hardly have been envisioned on the day he unfolded his long body from the back of a taxi that delivered him from Houston Intercontinental Airport to the University of Houston campus.

"I remember the first time I saw Hakeem and I couldn't have imagined then that all of this would happen," said the Portland Trail Blazers' Clyde Drexler, a perennial NBA All-Star and former college teammate of Olajuwon. "But once I saw how hard he worked and how he lived, I figured he would eventually become a pretty good player. I figured that people would learn who he was."

Indeed.

On a shining New York morning in the middle of the championship battle with his career-long nemesis Patrick Ewing of the Knicks, Olajuwon was sitting in a two-room midtown Manhattan hotel suite, basking in the glory of his unofficial arrival as a celebrity of the highest ranking.

The night before, he had made a roundly successful talk-show debut as a guest on "Late Show With David Letterman" and then paid a visit to the "Charlie Rose Show" and was part of a roundtable discussion group that included noted economist John Kenneth Galbreath.

He has become such a white-hot commodity these days that the likes of entrepreneur Donald Trump and wife Marla had taken the limo ride to Madison Square Garden to watch him play. He was the guest of honor at a dinner party at the suburban home of

Olajuwon vs. Ewing: Only one, Hakeem, could take it all.

Ahmad and Phylicia Rashad. He has begun marketing his own "Dream Line" of men's clothing—*smart, casual* is how he describes it—and Olajuwon has even had a sandwich named after him at the legendary Carnegie Deli.

But on this morning, there is a moment when his attention is distracted by the headline on the front page of the *New York Daily News*: "O.J. Grilled in Slaying of Ex-Wife."

"Fame," said Olajuwon, shaking his head. "It can cause as much trouble as it can cause good. That is why you cannot get too wrapped up in the outside things in your life. You cannot put all of your efforts into becoming a celebrity or making a great deal of money.

"I am not saying these things are bad. But you cannot let them become the focus. You taste them, and you enjoy the journey. But you must keep a solid foundation in your life."

Olajuwon's life is so solid, so celebrated now, that it is almost hard to recall the shy, timid young man who arrived in Houston seeking only an education.

For so many years, immigrants came to this place from across the ocean in search of the American Dream. They traveled here like cattle, they passed through Ellis Island, and, in some cases, they have given up the names with which they were born just to get a toehold in the land of opportunity. They toiled in sweatshops and lived and worked in the most unbearable conditions, suffering indignities in return for nothing more than hope. Many of their ancestors came here in chains.

Now, here is Olajuwon. He is not simply living the dream. He is Hakeem the Dream.

"It is humbling," he said. "I never imagined that it would be like this. So good. So full."

He was like every other Nigerian child of his generation, growing up with a sense of pride in the traditions and values of his homeland, but always with one eye on someday leaving Lagos and coming to America to make it on his own. It is a trend that began in the 1950s when large oil deposits were discovered in Nigeria, almost overnight transforming it from an underdeveloped nation into a rich country. It quickly became a status symbol for affluent families to send their children abroad for their education.

Olajuwon's parents, Salaam and Akibe, ran a successful cement-making business in Lagos, but following in those family footsteps was never a consideration.

"The first time I thought about leaving Nigeria, I was about eight or nine years old," he said. "At that time, I didn't understand the significance of going to school overseas or what it meant to

Patrick Ewing topped Olajuwon in 1984 NCAA's.

come to America. All we knew as kids was that every time somebody announced that they were going to study overseas, a big party would take place. They would hold a celebration.

"At that point, the person who was leaving hadn't accomplished anything yet. But it was a point of honor just that they had been accepted to study in another country. Their parents were proud. They were going to America. That meant they were a success. Many of those people are driving taxicabs now or trying to get jobs. But that doesn't change things at home. They are in America, so they are a success."

Olajuwon's older brother, Yemi, attended college in England. But by the time Hakeem was of age, the United States was the destination of choice for upwardly mobile Nigerians.

The irony, of course, of his appearance against the Knicks in the NBA Finals and his long-awaited ascendancy to the pinnacle of his career is that New York is the place Olajuwon landed on the plane from Lagos 14 years ago.

Having been a member of the Nigerian national team and played in the All-African Games in 1980, Olajuwon had been recommended to several U.S. colleges by an American coach who was working overseas. Thus, Olajuwon disembarked from the plane carrying a list of five U.S. colleges he planned to visit. St. John's University in Queens, N.Y. was at the top of the list.

However, it was a cold day in New York when Olajuwon arrived. Too cold. So he stayed for only three hours, jumped on the next plane to Houston and never left.

"The fact that I did end up living in Houston played a big part in my ability to succeed," Olajuwon said. "Not only was it the right school for me, the right basketball program at the time that needed a big man in the middle, but the city was right. It is a big city, but not as big as New York. It is not as cold as New York, either in climate or attitude.

"Houston was the place where I could learn the game playing against Moses Malone and all of the other NBA stars at Fonde Rec Center, and then I was lucky that the Rockets were able to draft me and I never had to leave."

Olajuwon did, however, have to toil 10 long years with often mediocre Rocket teams before he was able to complete the climb to the top that culminated with the MVP season and the championship.

They were growing times and sometimes difficult times. Olajuwon came into the NBA after three straight trips to the NCAA Final Four with the University of Houston. But he had never won a championship and that final roadblock was erected by Ewing in

1984, when Houston met Georgetown for the NCAA title and Olajuwon was saddled with defeat again.

As a young player in the NBA, he showed exceptional athletic ability, but also flashes of a fiery temper that frequently burned referees and fans and even his own teammates. After the Rockets advanced to the NBA Finals in 1986 and lost to the Boston Celtics, he expected to compete for the brass ring so many more times. But it took eight years and a maturation process until he finally got the chance to become the MVP.

His parents visited annually from Nigeria, but never during the basketball season and therefore never got to see him play in person.

"My father knows about the game and understands it," Olajuwon said. "I always sent my parents tapes of our games from the time I came into the NBA. But I would only send them tapes of games that we won. So my parents thought I should have been MVP for years. They thought we were undefeated. It wasn't until CNN came along and started to give NBA scores all around the world that my parents realized we lost sometimes."

His athletic career began as a soccer goalie and the thought comes that he could have made his American sports debut in the 1994 World Cup as a member of the Nigerian team if Olajuwon had stayed with his first love.

"I love soccer," he said. "It is a wonderful game. But I could never have played in the World Cup."

How could anybody score against a 7-foot goalie?

"Low shots," said a grinning Olajuwon.

His humor is warm and his smile is engaging and that is a side of his personality that has came forth only in recent years after Olajuwon made a summertime pilgrimage to Mecca and made a recommitment to his Muslim faith. He says his spiritual beliefs have enabled him to deal better with the ups and downs of being a professional athlete.

It was Olajuwon's faith that helped him get through a most difficult time in 1992 when, locked in a contract dispute with management, the Rockets charged him with faking a hamstring injury and suspended him. Olajuwon responded by asking the club to trade him and he spent the offseason of 1992 working out and expecting to start over again with a new team.

But since the Rockets could not come up with a trade they felt was acceptable, a new season began under new head coach Rudy Tomjanovich and eventually the problems was resolved when Olajuwon was given a new $25-million contract that will keep him with the club until 1999.

While his faith has given Olajuwon inner peace, his joy comes

"Akeem" with coach Guy Lewis, Phi Slama Jama gang.

from his six-year-old daughter, Abisola, who lives with her mother, Leta Spencer, in Southern California. Olajuwon and Spencer never married, but they enjoy a close relationship in which Abisola is the center.

"So innocent, so happy, so beautiful," he said.

Beautiful, too, was the 1993-94 season in which Olajuwon finally climbed all the way to the top of his profession. A year earlier many felt he was more deserving of the MVP award than the winner, Charles Barkley, and Olajuwon began his year as if determined to prove his believers right.

He was the dominant player in the league from the start, leading the Rockets to an NBA record-tying 15 consecutive victories to open the season. The 15th win, so fittingly, came in Madison Square Garden against the Knicks in a preview of the championship dogfight that would come to pass seven months later.

Olajuwon averaged 27.3 points per game in the regular season, 11.9 rebounds, 3.7 blocked shots and 3.6 assists. He held off challenges for the MVP award from David Robinson of San An-

MVP Hakeem the Dream has reason to beam.

tonio and Shaquille O'Neal of Orlando. His Rockets held off the Spurs in a late-season race for the Midwest Division title and forged their championship character in a second-round playoff series with Phoenix. The Suns won the first two games in Houston and the Rockets were on the ropes. But Olajuwon led a stunning comeback that produced a seventh-game victory in the series and propelled the Rockets toward their ultimate showdown with Ewing and the Knicks.

It was grueling, it was grinding, it was debilitating as the Rocket and Knicks—with Olajuwon and Ewing as centerpieces—stood like heavyweight fighters in the center of the ring and took their best shots. Through seven arduous games, through seven mentally exhausting battles.

Until finally Olajuwon held that ball so close to his chest, leaned back against the courtside press table and stared at the scene with a sense of wonderment.

"Champion," he said. "I have always wanted to be called a champion."

1994: Bill Walton in his analyst's finery at NBC-TV.

BILL WALTON:
From "Grateful Dead"
To Alive on the Tube

By BOB RUBIN

Until he was 28, Bill Walton stuttered badly and was extremely reluctant to speak in public. Now, at 42, it seems like the big

1977: Leading the way to Portland's one NBA title.

redhead (and Deadhead) is making up for lost time. You can't shut him up.

Walton's lengthy comments at his 1993 induction into the Basketball Hall of Fame prompted the NBA's Brian McIntyre to remark, tongue firmly in cheek, that Big Red was the first honoree whose speech was longer than his career.

Last season Walton's gigs as an analyst included NBC's ''NBA Showtime,'' hosted by Bob Costas, halftime at the NBA playoffs

---

Always close to the NBA scene, Bob Rubin is a sports columnist on the Miami Herald.

and calling the games for the Los Angeles Clippers and UCLA Bruins.

"I like to work," he says. "I want to broadcast them all. When it comes down to the championship, and the executive producer looks up and down his roster, I want him to say, 'Walton, get in there and get the job done.' That's the kind of broadcaster I want to be."

It's no coincidence that Walton likens broadcasting to playing. The principles that govern both are the same to him. "I was incredibly fortunate to play for Hall-of-Famers such as John Wooden, Jack Ramsay, Lenny Wilkens and K.C. Jones," he says. "They taught me that basketball is no different than life, that it takes the same to succeed in both: hard work, preparation and enthusiasm.

"When they coached me, they weren't coaching me just to be a better basketball player, but to be a better person and more productive worker. So I take those lessons and apply them to whatever I'm doing."

If Walton is not yet considered to be among the best broadcasters in the business, he certainly has earned a reputation for being among the most outspoken. He says what he thinks without concern about offending, sort of a hoops version of football's Bob Trumpy. For example, Walton called the Michigan Wolverines' Fab Five "all-time underachievers."

In 1993 he criticized the idea of Michael Jordan and Charles Barkley playing golf together on offdays during the NBA Finals, saying a player must work up an intense dislike of his foe when it's all on the line. Such provocative commentary is rare on the network level, especially coming from a former player.

Walton shrugs. "I don't think I'm controversial at all," he says. "I've always been mainstream. I just learned at an early age from my parents—who were my greatest teachers—to think for myself, to question authority, and to speak my mind. If someone throws a good pass, I'll say it. If someone isn't getting it done, I'll say it. I don't know any other way."

Let's say NBA commissioner David Stern stepped aside for a day and appointed Walton to run the shop. What changes would he make?

"Obviously, things are great the way they are, but they could be better," Walton says. "I'd like to see more players stay in college [for four years]—I'm not a big fan of coming out early. I'd like to see a higher level of officiating; officials should be paid more, and the quality of their work should be upgraded. If I were an official, I'd be really strict on traveling violations, three-second

1975: Dog-sitting for activist Jack Scott's "Sigmund."

calls and offensive fouls."

What? Eliminate traveling? That's traditional. Some players would have to restrict their whole game. "They're smart, and they're good," says commissioner Walton. "They'd adjust quickly."

Wait, there's more. "I'm for letting defenses do whatever they want," Walton says. "Let them play zones or anything they else they want. I think the players, teams and coaching are good enough where you don't have to legislate against the defense to ensure the offensive stars will remain stars."

Most people would have snickered and scoffed if, back during Walton's All-American days at UCLA, someone had predicted that one day he would be seen as a sportscaster all over America's airwaves. At that time he was aloof in his dealings with the media—and that was on a good day.

"There were two reasons," Walton says. "Because of my stuttering, I couldn't communicate my thoughts easily, and I was unwilling to give any information to the other team. I was never going to provide opponents with any insights into my thinking about the game, about them, about anything. So I wasn't very cooperative.

"Coach Wooden said it was our choice whether or not we wanted to deal with the media. Frankly, my desire was to be a college student, and I enjoyed it tremendously. I regret now not having a better relationship with the media, but I couldn't. With everything that was happening, I would have spent so much time dealing with that. I wouldn't have been able to enjoy myself like I did."

With his ponytail, his hippie garb and his allegiance to the Grateful Dead and various liberal causes, Walton was considered a member of the counterculture, both at UCLA and during his early years with the Portland Trail Blazers. His current three-piece suit, buttoned-down persona would seem to represent a 180-degree shift in style and philosophy—but Walton doesn't buy that premise.

"I've always been mainstream," he says again. "I just have a different uniform these days. It includes makeup, and who would have ever believed that?"

Walton's bass voice flows freely and smoothly, but that wasn't always the case. At one time, his pronounced stutter hurt him deeply.

"It was devastating to me personally and professionally," he says. "The inability to get my thoughts out and communicate in a coherent manner left me feeling trapped, helpless. It was maybe the greatest moment of my life when I learned to communicate without being terrified. Marty Glickman gave me the keys to getting over the stuttering, and I have such a great feeling of appreciation of him.''

Walton and Glickman, a legendary sportscaster based in New York, were brought together by Dr. Ernie Vandeweghe, who knew both. As a player for the Knicks in the early '50s, Vandeweghe went way back with Glickman, and he got to know Walton through his son, former pro Kiki Vandeweghe.

Glickman visited Ernie Vandeweghe in California one summer, and they wound up spending a day with Walton aboard his boat in the waters of his hometown of San Diego. The conversation got around to broadcasting, speech and Walton's problem.

''The most important thing I told Bill was that he had to express thoughts in a patient, deliberate manner and not let his head get ahead of his tongue,'' Glickman said. ''He had to learn to discipline himself to say things in their order of importance and keep the rest in his head.

''You can't say it all at once. I was well aware of it because it was a problem for me at the start of my career, and a problem for a lot of ex-jocks who go into broadcasting. You see a hundred things happening and the temptation is to try to explain it all, but you've got two to three hours to say what you see.''

Glickman is the first to admit his advice was hardly earth-shaking. ''It was simple,'' he said, ''but I know I hadn't thought it through, and apparently he hadn't, either. He had the capacity to accept it and apply it. It was more Bill's doing than mine.''

Two other veteran announcers, Pat O'Brien of CBS and Charlie Jones of NBC, gave Walton's broadcasting career a boost. A fellow resident of Southern California, Jones remains Walton's confidante and mentor. ''Charlie has helped me the way my coaches did; teaches me everything. We talk all the time, see each other as much as possible. He's my man.''

As a player, Walton was the man. He led UCLA to an 86-4 record and two national championships. He was named College Player of the Year three times and NCAA Tournament MVP twice. In the 1973 title game against Memphis State, he turned in one of the greatest individual performances in college basketball history when he sank 21 of 22 shots from the floor and scored 44 points en route to victory.

Nobody's perfect, but that night Walton and the Bruins approached it. ''We came very close to playing the game John Wooden dreamed for us,'' Walton says. ''He always talked about us competing against an ideal opponent. Forget the people you're actually playing against—get out there and play as if the person you're up against is the best ever.

"It all came together for us that night. Our guards had 23 assists between them, so it wasn't like I was getting the ball and going one-on-one. The ball was really moving. We had a beautiful team. It was such a joy to be part of it."

Speaking of perfection, 86-4 comes pretty close, too. "Coach Wooden had created an atmosphere in which we were expected to win," Walton says. "We spent all our time believing we were the best, practicing like we were the best, and then performing like the best."

"My most vivid memories are the four games we lost. They were terrible. Embarrassing. I still have nightmares about them."

Though a succession of foot injuries limited Walton's pro career to 468 games in 13 years—three of which he was forced to sit out completely—he was dominant when healthy, so much so he made the Hall of Fame in his first year of eligibility. He led the Trail Blazers to a championship in 1977, was named the NBA's Most Valuable Player the next season and won the league's Sixth Man Award as a member of the championship Celtics of '86.

Walton says the thrill of winning a championship never varies—"I was fortunate enough to win on every level, from grade school on, and there's no different whatsoever between sixth grade and the NBA." But he admits the title with the Celtics was special because it came after everyone, including Big Red himself, thought he was finished.

"My career had gone so bad for so many years," he says. "When you're a good player coming up, you think everything's always going to be perfect. With all the injuries, frustrations and disappointments I had, to contribute to a championship team and play with Hall-of-Famers like Larry Bird, Dennis Johnson, Robert Parish and Kevin McHale—yes, it was very special."

Walton could have dwelled on what might have been had he stayed healthy his whole career, anguished over how many other championships he might have been part of. He could have railed against the basketball gods.

He didn't.

"You do the best you can with what you have," he says. "It comes back to the parallels between basketball and life. You have to have a good foundation, and my physical foundation, meaning my feet, just wasn't strong enough. The opportunity for regret and bitterness is always there, but I was able to move on.

"You can't live in the past or feel sorry for yourself. I've got a beautiful framed photograph of the Grateful Dead in my house.

1973: All-Everything at UCLA in the Wooden era.

They're very good friends and they all signed it. One wrote across one of the drum skins, 'Never look back.'

"I don't. You've got to move on, go for tomorrow."

THE ECSTASY AND THE AGONY OF JOHN STARKS

By CLIFTON BROWN

John Starks did not retire. He did not spend the offseason in seclusion. And when he dozed off to sleep, he did not wake up in a cold sweat, dreaming about missed jumpers.

After shooting 2-for-18 in Game 7 of the NBA Finals, Starks faced the ugly truth that he failed miserably in the biggest game of his life. And it wasn't easy. He shouldered much of the blame for costing the Knicks their first championship since 1973. For weeks after the Knicks' loss to the Houston Rockets, Starks saw the look of pity in the eyes of those who offered condolences. He heard the comments. He read the criticism. And he knew that many people, especially Knicks' fans, would never understand how Starks could have played so badly in a game that meant so much.

Yet to know John Starks is to know a survivor. He has overcome an impoverished childhood to earn more money than he ever imagined. Despite being overlooked in the NBA draft and playing in the CBA, he has become a bonafide star, coming off his best season as one of the game's premier shooting guards.

After a few days of feeling sorry for himself and reliving Game 7 over and over, Starks was back in the gym, just one week after the Finals ended. There was no sense looking back anymore. So much more could be gained by looking ahead. After all, Starks is still only 29. The Knicks are still contenders. And to Starks,

As beat man on the Knicks for The New York Times, *Clifton Brown has been an eyewitness to the roller-coaster odyssey of John Starks.*

John Starks responds to foul call vs. Bulls in playoffs.

helping the Knicks win that elusive championship is the only way to soothe the pain of Game 7.

"I'll be a better player because of what happened, and we'll be a better team," said Starks from his offseason home in Tulsa, Okla. "We're still hungry. I'm still hungry. I feel like my best years are still ahead, so there's no sense going back over what happened. You have to be strong. If not, stuff that happens in this game can drive you crazy."

Of course, some people think the Knicks' volatile shooting guard is half-crazy anyway. What other player has been ejected from a game for head-butting? How many times have you seen Starks kick a scorer's table, or yell at an official, an opponent, or even one of his own teammates?

Starks' feistiness is part of what makes him one of the league's most charismatic players. He wants the ball with the game on the line. He is a tenacious defender. He can beat you with three-point shots, electrifying drives to the basket, by making a steal, by taking a charge.

He is one of those rare players who can take over a game, at any time, which is the main reason why Pat Riley refused to bench Starks in Game 7, even though he kept missing, and missing, and missing—shooting 0-for-11 from three-point range. So many times, Riley had seen Starks shake off a terrible shooting game to make clutch shots, to carry the team to victory. So Riley, who had won with Starks so many times, was also willing to lose with him. With each missed shot, the despair on Starks' face became more apparent, but if given another chance, Riley said he would have coached Game 7 the same way.

"You go up with your players and you go down with them," said Riley, who has won four championships as a coach doing just that. "The guy is fearless. He is one of the great competitors I have been around in my life, and I love him dearly for that competitive nature of his. He's a tough kid, and he'll eventually be able to lick these wounds, get over it, and learn from it."

Indeed, Starks is determined not to make Game 7 the defining moment of his career. Had it happened during the regular season, or even earlier in the playoffs, few people would've remembered. For Starks, it is simply another albatross to shake, another obstacle to be overcome. And perseverance is one of his greatest assets.

While Starks has been criticized for his temper and for his sometimes out-of-control play, few guards today have the impact on a game that Starks has. He averaged 19 points per game during the regular season, second on the team behind Patrick Ewing; he had eight games of 30 points or more, and 23 games of 20 points or more. Starks missed the final 23 regular-season games after

Starks drives in traffic vs. Pacers in playoffs.

undergoing arthroscopic knee surgery, but he returned coura-geously in the playoffs and helped the Knicks to the brink of a championship.

If the Knicks offered Starks for trade bait, all 26 other NBA teams would likely call. But the Knicks have no plans to part with Starks, who signed a four-year contract extension in 1992 that pays him an average of $1.2 million per season—a bargain in today's market.

"John Starks plays with so much heart and so much energy that a lot of coaches and general managers wish they had someone who played with his kind of passion and desire," said Dave Check-etts, the Knicks' president. "It's something you can't teach. It's something you can't coach. He's a guy who has worked hard and beaten the odds. I've seen some players come and go who had more talent, but they didn't play as hard, they didn't work as hard, and they didn't care as much as John does."

It is fitting that Starks has become a proficient three-point shooter, because he was a literally a long shot to make the NBA, not to mention to become a star. Few things in life have come easily for him. He grew up poor in Tulsa, the third of seven children raised by his mother, Irene, and his grandmother, Callie West. His father, also named John, left the family when Starks was three. Times were tough. Often money and meals did not stretch far enough. Starks lost count of how many times his family moved during his childhood.

Most of the people who watch Starks on television with a remote control in one hand and a cold beer in the other have no idea what he overcame to get to where he is. Starks wasn't even a big-name high school star in Tulsa. In fact, he only played one year of high-school basketball, because his family needed extra money, and Starks had to work while his buddies played.

"I had more important things to worry about than basketball at the time, like feeding myself," he said. "I started working in the 10th grade. I always loved the game, but I still just played mostly in the parks. Finally, it was my older brother, Vincent, who told me that I should try to go to school, that I might be able to get a scholarship."

But Starks' college experience became a four-school odyssey through Oklahoma, as he searched for a scholarship and respect. He started at Rogers State College, but he was cut from the team. Next came Northern Oklahoma College, where he had a good year. But he still wasn't offered a scholarship for the following season, and Starks could not afford another year of tuition, so he left.

It was after that season that Starks had perhaps his most publicized odd job—working at a Safeway grocery store for $3.35 per hour. Starks will never forget the experience, because he worked with people who encouraged him to go back to school, to reach for his dream before he ended up working at Safeway for the rest of his life.

Starks listened. He enrolled at Oklahoma Junior College, where he landed the elusive scholarship, and after one strong season, he finally played at a major college, Oklahoma State University. Starks' path was set. He vowed to play in the NBA one day, and to do whatever it took to get there.

How dedicated was he? While Starks was attending Oklahoma Junior College, a game was rescheduled at the last minute, moved to the same day that Starks married his wife, Jacqueline. Did Starks miss the game? Are you kidding? He left the wedding reception early, his wife sitting beside him in the passenger seat, and they burned rubber to the game, which was about 100 miles away.

"I think the biggest thing my wife was worried about was my driving," said Starks, recalling the incident with a laugh. "She knew I had a tendency to put the pedal to the metal. But she never complained. She has always supported me, stuck by my dream, and I've always appreciated that."

When he talks about his wife and two children, six-year-old John Jr. and his three-year-old daughter, Chelsea, Starks becomes sentimental and soft-spoken. It is a side that the general public rarely sees. He is one of the quietest Knick players. You will rarely find Starks hanging out in the Big Apple, checking out the nightspots or mingling with celebrities. Starks would rather be home with his family in Tulsa or in their playing-season home in Connecticut, watching a movie, playing with kids, or listening to one of his favorite CD's.

But something happens to Starks when he steps on the court. He even surprises himself when he watches videotapes of things he has done throughout his career. Competition brings out the fire in Starks, perhaps because of his background, and the experience of having to fight for virtually everything he has accomplished. Starks has a burning desire to succeed, and he will never forget that many expected him to fail. If you want to compete against Starks, be ready to come with everything that you have.

"When it comes to winning, well, something just goes off inside of me." Starks said. "I leave it between the lines. You should hear some of the things people say when they meet me on the street. They say stuff like, 'You're a nice guy, I can't believe it.' It's like they're shocked. The only image they have of me is from what they see on the court. Away from it, I'm nothing like that at all. But on the court, well, I've had my moments."

Indeed he has. While playing for Cedar Rapids in the CBA in 1990, he was suspended for bumping a referee. In a 1992 playoff game against the Bulls, Starks clotheslined Scottie Pippen on a fastbreak, and Pippen was fortunate to escape injury. He once threw a cup of water at Mark Jackson, then of the Clippers, during a game.

Then there was the infamous head-butting of Reggie Miller in a 1993 playoff game—a foolish act which led to Starks being ejected. And the most controversial play involving Starks occurred in March 1993, when he was fined $5,000 for a flagrant foul against Kenny Anderson of the Nets. Anderson suffered a broken wrist on the play, an injury that has bothered Anderson ever since.

Starks has insisted that he did not try to injure Anderson intentionally, and replays indicated as much. But controversy seems to follow Starks, whether he asks for it or not. He even got in trouble during the finals—fined $10,000 by the NBA for

Advice from Oklahoma State's Len Hamilton in 1987-88.

skipping the interview session before Game 7.

"If I had known I was going to be fined that much, I definitely would have said SOMETHING," Starks said, laughing. "I just felt I had already said everything that needed to be said, and I wanted to concentrate on getting ready for the game. Guess I learned an expensive lesson.

"All those things are part of the game, and they get blown out of proportion sometimes. Anyone who knows me knows that I would never attempt to injure another player. But I still have to do my job."

And Starks believes his job is not done. He still works on his game with the zest of someone who is trying to prove himself, one of those exceptional players who seem to get better every year. His three-point shooting has improved. His ball-handling has improved. What will Starks add to his game next?

"I'm not saying, but believe me, I've been working on something," Starks said. "All the great players added something to their game every year. Michael Jordan, Magic Johnson, Larry Bird—they didn't just sit back and stay with what they had. They added something new. I want to be just like that.

"I'll always work hard because of the things I've been through. There are always young players coming up, anxious to take your job. You have to stay one step ahead."

Certainly, the respect Starks longed for has come his way. He was cut after one season with the Golden State Warriors, but after playing one CBA year with Cedar Rapids during the 1989-90 season, the Knicks signed Starks as a free agent and he quickly established himself as a vital part of the team.

Starks' memorable battle with Jordan during the 1993 playoffs cemented Starks as a national figure. As Jordan said during that playoff series, "I don't remember when he was in the CBA. I don't remember when he came into the league. But I know he's here now."

Indeed, Starks has arrived, and the best may be yet to come. Starks' teammates stuck by him after the Game 7 episode, knowing that they never would have reached that point without him.

"There's no reason for John to blame himself at all," said the Knicks' Charles Smith. "We don't blame anyone. He had a tough night. So what? He was crushed like the rest of us."

But Starks never stays down for long. He remains perhaps the most popular Knick among the fans. His toughness is unquestioned. Once, during a game against Utah, Starks suffered a broken nose in the first quarter, then returned to the game wearing a face mask and made his next six shots. And he has also emerged as a team leader. He called a players-only meeting in his hotel room in Indianapolis prior to Game 6 of the Eastern Conference finals against the Pacers, a game the Knicks had to win. Then Starks went out and backed up his words, scoring 26 points and leading the Knicks to victory.

Starks nearly won the championship for the Knicks in Game 6 of the Finals, scoring 16 points in the fourth quarter and nearly leading New York to a dramatic comeback win. But Starks' potential game-winning three-pointer that could have won a championship for New York was blocked by Hakeem Olajuwon, sending the series to Game 7. And the rest, as they say, is history.

That was the final chapter of last season, but Starks is ready to write another. People have counted him out before, but Starks has always found a way. And no matter what the future holds, Starks is certain that he will be heard from again—with a bang.

"I'm not an old man, and we're not an old team," Starks said. "There are some young teams coming up who are ready to challenge us, but we'll be back. We want a ring. And I'm going to do whatever I can to help us get it."

REGGIE MILLER: SUDDENLY A SUPERSTAR

By CONRAD BRUNNER

He has cultivated an outlandish image, yet it could not be more different than the reality of his soft-spoken personality.

He is among the game's greatest scoring guards, yet he chafes when described as a scorer.

He seems one moment to crave the spotlight, the next to shrink from its heat.

They are the dichotomies of NBA fame now facing Reggie Miller, who finds himself a sudden superstar.

He carried the Indiana Pacers to within seconds of a trip to the NBA Finals, torturing the New York Knicks in a compelling seven-game semifinal series. The defining moment came in Game 5, when Miller sucked the life out of Madison Square Garden with a 25-point fourth quarter to carry the Pacers from a 12-point deficit to a 93-86 victory.

Through it all, he used filmmaker and rabid Knicks' fan Spike Lee as his foil, taunting him after every basket and giving Lee the choke sign after a 26-foot three-pointer that put the Pacers into the lead.

Though Miller averaged 30.5 points in the final four games of the series, he was involved in the two plays that produced the team's defeat in Game 7. With the Knicks up, 91-90, in the closing seconds, Miller came off a screen and thought he was open, committing himself to a jump shot. But when Charles Oakley stepped

---

Entering his seventh season covering the Pacers for the Indianapolis News, *Conrad Brunner has gotten to know both Reggie Millers, the public and the private.*

From braces on his legs...to footloose and fancy.

into his face, the promising shot was reduced to a mere lob that did not draw iron.

The ball wound up in the hands of John Starks. When Miller rushed over and shoved an already off-balance Starks, who toppled to the floor, official Mike Mathis called it a flagrant foul with 2.8 seconds left. There would be no more last chance for Miller's valiant Pacers.

Asked if he had ever hurt more, Miller could not come up with words. He looked down, shook his head twice, then broke down in tears.

Normally, a weeping opponent would serve as raw meat for the piranhas of the New York press. Not so in this case. With his performance, Miller had earned the right to cry.

This year, he hopes to finish the season with a championship celebration.

"We were 30 seconds away from playing Houston in the NBA Finals," Miller said. "The taste of winning is in all of our mouths. We know what it takes to get to the next level . . . We're definitely going to be back."

A player who had spent most of his career in someone's shadow finally has stepped into the light.

His basketball-playing sister Cheryl, who had shone at USC and as the leader of the 1984 Olympic gold-medal team, was always the greater star. When Miller came to the Pacers out of UCLA as the 11th pick in the 1987 draft, the selection was booed by a local populace that thought they wanted Indiana University's Steve Alford.

With the Pacers, he first toiled in the background while Chuck Person hogged the headlines, more with his outlandish behavior than his performance. Then, Detlef Schrempf stepped ahead of him into the starring role.

Person and Schrempf are long since gone. It is now Miller time.

His statistics (10,879 points, tops in franchise history) are the most prolific, his contract ($3.25 million) the fattest, his celebrity (most recently as a member of Dream Team II) the greatest and his personality (read on) the strongest.

During the playoffs, he went out of his way to cultivate an image totally askew to his true personality: that of an outlaw, a rebel, a player who loves to be loathed in every arena but his own.

"That's a bunch of malarkey," said coach Larry Brown. "Reggie's as nice a kid as you'd ever want to know."

For the Pacers' first-round series with the Orlando Magic, Miller made his fashion statements: a bandanna on the head for

Sister Cheryl Miller set the pace all the way.

Reggie was second in the NBA in FT pct.

practice, augmented by hip sunglasses for interviews. He stuck with it, and bandannas became a staple for Market Square Arena crowds.

Miller sees himself as the antisocial director for a team that has historically been left off the national media's A-list.

"This ain't a very nice team to like," Miller said. "We have a lot of attitudes on this team and if they don't like us, who cares, as long as we come to play every night. We're not worried about people liking us. It's the last thing on our minds.''

Like him or not, Miller commands attention.

When he took a pass 30 feet from the basket in the closing seconds of Game 1 of the first round in Orlando, three defenders ran at him. This left Byron Scott, who happens to rank third on the all-time list of playoff three-pointers made, wide open for a trey in the corner.

In technical parlance, the best way to describe that particular strategem would be, ''Oops.''

That shot enabled the team to do what it had never done before: win a playoff series.

Miller did not make the shot, but he made the play.

It was something of a role reversal for Miller, one of the league's most productive postseason scorers. For his career, he has averaged nearly a full five points more than his 19.3-point regular-season average.

To call him a scorer, though, would be an insult to Miller. He has worked hard to improve his overall game, primarily on defense, and it was reflected in the postseason.

In 16 playoff games, Miller outscored the opposing starter at shooting guard every time. Orlando's Nick Anderson, Atlanta's Stacey Augmon and Starks combined to average just 12.3 points on 41.4 percent shooting against Miller (who averaged 23.2 points and shot 44.8 percent).

''They won't recognize that,'' Miller said. ''The first impression is the last impression. All they remember is the jump shot.''

He has made many worth remembering, particularly in the playoffs. As a result, he has become a focal point of derision on the road, a fairly exclusive honor reserved for players who pose a serious threat.

''It's great. It's fantastic,'' said Miller. ''I love when they're chanting 'Reg-gie' or 'Cher-yl.' I encourage that. Maybe sometimes that's why I do things, just to rub 'em the wrong way.

''It's the best feeling anyone could feel. You guys don't know what it feels like to me to be booed, to be cursed at, have my name changed, hear little kids chanting my name because they're taught that from adults.

''I love it. It's the best. It's the odds of being the underdog, 12 vs. 16,000. We're supposed to lose, supposed to get hammered. To come in and kick some behind, that's what it's all about. I love being the underdog. It's the best feeling. I don't like playing at home. I'd rather play all my games on the road.''

It sounds strange, to be sure, but it runs consistent with Miller's personality. From the beginning of life, he fought against the odds.

CHALLENGING CHILDHOOD

Early in his life, Miller could only hope that one day he'd have the skill to be called for walking.

Born (Aug. 24, 1965, Riverside, Cal.) with pronated hips that caused severely splayed feet (instead of both pointing north, one foot went due east, the other due west) and an open-chest cavity. Miller's parents were told by doctors not to expect him ever to walk unassisted.

He spent the first four years of his life wearing braces on both legs. His only mobility came with crutches or a wheelchair.

The treatment for the open-chest cavity, though not as severe, was no less traumatic for a child.

"I had to eat liver twice a day, every day, till I was five," he said, shaking his head at the memory. "That's why you can't get me anywhere near liver today."

Now, he can joke about it. Then, it was much more serious.

"I just remember Cheryl always being by my side," he said. "She couldn't pronounce my name, so she called me 'Ready.' That became my nickname in the family."

His recovery and subsequent rise to basketball fame left an indelible mark on Cheryl, now the women's basketball coach at USC.

"I want Reggie to talk to my players one day about the work ethic, because he's a prime example," she told the *Los Angeles Times*. "You know, at one point Reggie was 6-7 and 160 pounds and all kinds of people told him he'd never be able to play college ball.

"Reggie never argued with anyone about it, he just worked. Those people who told him he couldn't play; when they were getting out of bed in the morning, Reggie had been shooting for two or three hours. And when they went to bed, he was still shooting."

He was, no doubt, making up for the lost time of his childhood. The braces came off when he was five. He didn't take to the court, he said, "for another four or five years" because he was too busy having fun hanging out with his brothers and sisters.

"I was just happy to be able to go out and play," he said, "instead of staying in the house all the time with my mom and the dog."

Though his story of perseverance is inspirational, Miller has chosen to keep it largely private.

"I really don't talk about it," he said, almost at a whisper. "There's not much for people to know."

For most lifetimes, that would've been challenge enough.
For Miller, it was only the first.

TEAM MILLER

Though he got a late start, he soon gained ground in an athletic family. Cheryl may have been the best woman player ever. His brother Darrell caught for the California Angels. And sister Tammy played volleyball at Cal State-Fullerton.

Initially, Reggie chose baseball.

"We would've all said he would be a major-league baseball player," said Saul, father and captain of Team Miller. "All of the boys played baseball, but Reggie exceeded them all, including Darrell. As a 12-year-old in Little League, he batted over .500 and was a pitcher who no one could hit. High school coaches were licking their chops."

He didn't exactly stray from basketball, keeping his jump shot sharp on the family's backyard court. As he grew into competitive play, Miller found himself motivated by the constant action and the roar of the crowd.

By his sophomore year at Riverside Poly High, Miller was committed to basketball.

But it wasn't easy.

As good as he became, he wasn't even the best in his family.

On the night of his first high-school start, the sophomore came home elated after scoring 39 points. The same night, Cheryl scored 105 for the girls' team.

When Cheryl chose USC, Reggie opted for UCLA. He was starting to seek his own spotlight.

Even there, Miller found his best wasn't enough to satisfy everyone. He scored 2,095 points, still good for third on the school's all-time list. He was a three-time John Wooden Award winner. And the Bruins won their first Pacific-10 Conference championship in years.

But at UCLA, the standards are higher. Anything short of a national championship is failure. The frustration got to Miller. As the team leader he was the focal point for media criticism. He developed a negative image that most certainly hurt his draft status.

When the Pacers drafted him, it should've been a joyous occasion for Miller. Instead, he was haunted by boos from Hoosier fans who sought the squeaky-clean, but marginally talented Alford.

Once again, Miller had to prove himself.

SHOOTING STAR

It didn't take long for Miller to prove the Pacers right. In his first year, he averaged 10 points and broke Larry Bird's record for three-pointers by a rookie (61).

The team struggled, though, failing to make the playoffs his first two years. His breakthrough came in the 1989-90 season, when Miller averaged a career-best 24.6 points and made the All-Star team.

No longer just a three-point shooter, Miller's game had expanded with slashing drives to the basket and a trademark move known as "the floater"—when he fakes an opponent into the air, drives past, leans under and softly flips the ball into the hoop.

The Pacers returned to the playoffs in 1990 but were swept out of the first round by Detroit. Two consecutive first-round losses to Boston were followed by a 3-1 loss to New York in 1993.

Entering last season, the team was reconstructed largely around Miller. Gone were two primary scorers, Person and Schrempf.

Miller looked around the locker room and quickly knew what he had to do. If the team was to accept coach Larry Brown's defensive philosophy, it had to start with Miller.

His personal life had settled with marriage to model-actress Marita Stavrou the previous summer. Now, his professional life would bring a similar maturation process.

"When they made the trade [sending Schrempf to Seattle for Derrick McKey], I really knew then it was all going to change for me, and there was no one else I could rely on. It was just me," Miller said. "There was no more Chuck, no more Det, no more Micheal Williams.

"I knew I was going to be out there by myself, so I was the one that was going to have to sacrifice the points. I was going to be the one that moved the basketball. I was going to be the one that had to get on guys out there. I knew that was what they were looking for.

"I had to accept it. If I didn't, we wouldn't have been 47-35 and the fifth seed. No way. There was no way I could be selfish."

Miller's greatest growth has been his role within the team. The responsibility of leadership was thrust upon him and he accepted it willingly.

"That's not really for me to say," Miller said. "That has to come from others. I've done some things, I've tried, but maybe I've done them wrong. I don't know."

In Brown's eyes, Miller has done little wrong.

"I don't think he'll ever be the kind of guy who's vocal in that

Reggie was drafted 11th out of UCLA in 1987.

way,'' Brown said, ''but the fact that he cares so much never goes unnoticed.''

In fact, it may have gotten him the kind of notice he always has wanted: official certification as one of the world's greatest players as a member of USA Basketball's Dream Team II.

''I don't know of many guys who are more of a winner than he,'' said Brown. ''The thing that has impressed me more about Reggie every day I'm with him is that he's completely unselfish.

''You're proud of a lot of things that went on [with the team] but I admire him and what he's done. He's let everybody know he'll make sacrifices on the court, he'll do whatever it takes to win. That's infectious, when your best player has that mentality.

''Reggie is a winner. The nicest thing is he's finally gotten recognition as one of the best players.''

But Reggie, ever seeking the championship ring, insists, ''There's nothing that can replace winning.''

INSIDE THE NBA

By FRED KERBER
and
SCOTT HOWARD-COOPER

PREDICTED ORDER OF FINISH

ATLANTIC	CENTRAL	MIDWEST	PACIFIC
New York	Atlanta	Houston	Seattle
Orlando	Indiana	Utah	Phoenix
New Jersey	Charlotte	Denver	Golden State
Miami	Chicago	San Antonio	Portland
Boston	Cleveland	Dallas	L.A. Lakers
Philadelphia	Milwaukee	Minnesota	Sacramento
Washington	Detroit		L.A. Clippers

EASTERN CONFERENCE: Indiana
WESTERN CONFERENCE: Seattle
CHAMPION: Seattle

Fool us once, shame on you. Fool us twice, shame on us.

But we're going to pick Seattle to win it all in the NBA this season anyway.

Sure, so many picked the Sonics going into the playoffs last season. Why not? The Sonics had everything going for them: home court to the end through a league-high 63 victories; a defense that

---

Free-swinging Fred Kerber is the veteran NBA beat man for the New York Post *and his forthright counterpart Scott Howard-Cooper follows the Lakers for the* Los Angeles Times. *Howard-Cooper wrote the Western Conference, Kerber the Eastern Conference and the introduction after an overtime confrontation with Howard-Cooper.*

No. 1 pick: Glenn Robinson, Boilermaker turned Buck.

made getting the ball across halfcourt comparable to scaling Everest. So what happened?

Well, there were the Denver Nuggets in the first round. But, according to coach George Karl, there was team harmony that made the chemistry as wonderful as that of a garden variety street gang.

Still, we're going with the Sonics. Name it—other than a title ring and a stud center—and on paper they have it. They can shoot, they can score, they can rebound and they can defend. And they can do it nine deep on the bench.

Despite the league's fourth most productive offense, the Sonic strength is a suffocating pressure. Led by Gary Payton and third guard Nate McMillan, the Sonics had 1,053 steals last season, just six shy of the all-time record. Inside, Shawn Kemp, Michael Cage (alas, he jumped to the Cavs) and Sam Perkins led an impressive rebounding corps that ignited the Sonic break. So the Sonics are the pick to wipe out the bitter memory of the first-round reversal against Denver.

Which means the defending champion Rockets will be watching the Finals at home. Houston outlasted all others, the last being the New York Knicks in the Finals.

In the East, the Knicks will be challenged to return to the conference finals for a third straight year. They'll have virtually the same cast but are hoping rookie Monty Williams can supply some much needed offense at forward. But the Knicks, despite Patrick Ewing in the middle and the wildly inconsistent but potentially explosive John Starks outside notwithstanding, simply can't score enough. No one defends better than the Knicks. But virtually everyone shoots better. So who's the pick in the East? How about the other conference finalist of a year ago, the Indiana Pacers?

Yes, Virginia, they do play basketball in Indiana other than in Bloomington. And Larry Brown's Pacers served notice last season with a terrific second half plus a lively playoff showing that included the ouster of Shaquille O'Neal and the Magic in three straight games, an upset of Atlanta in the second round and then a grueling, but ultimately disappointing, seven-game series with the Knicks. The difference this year? Mark Jackson.

Add Jackson, the wondrously talented point guard, to a cast that includes the game's purest shooter, Reggie Miller, two Davis guys named Dale and Antonio who board with the best and a potentially damaging, though erratic, Rik Smits at center and all the Pacers really need is some offense at forward to be considered strong favorites. Even without the added scorer, figure Brown finds a way.

In the Atlantic, the Knicks will rule again for a third straight year behind Pat Riley's blood, sweat and more blood and more sweat work-ethic regimen. They'll be pushed by the Orlando Magic, a year older and a year better with Shaq and Anfernee Hardaway, and now (assuming legal resolution) blessed with Hor-

No. 2 in draft, Cal's Jason Kidd will soar with Mavs.

ace Grant. In New Jersey, the hope is Butch Beard can continue what the departed Chuck Daly started, armed with Derrick Coleman and Kenny Anderson. Miami is basically the same team that met first-round playoff defeat.

At the bottom of the Atlantic, Boston, Philadelphia and Washington hope their rebuilding processes can switch into hyper-speed and maybe land a playoff spot. But with the powerful Central Division figuring to grab possibly five of the playoff berths again in the East, it will be tough. Boston should get better with the addition of Dominique Wilkins, but ironically it may hurt in the long run. Maybe they'll be good enough to make the playoffs, but won't be bad enough to get a choice lottery pick.

Philly is a long shot if Shawn Bradley continues developing, stays healthy and if John Lucas can infuse the same emotion he did in San Antonio. In Washington, much is in place for a future run but the two most important spots, point guard and center, are the biggest worries facing new coach Jim Lynam, who moved over from the 76ers' GM post. In Boston, the once proud Celtics hope their final season in hallowed Boston Garden isn't another mess. The Celtics were devastated last season by the tragic death of Reggie Lewis and have begun rebuilding with first-rounder Eric Montross.

In the Central, Indiana will challenge Atlanta's defending-champ status and the Charlotte Hornets will make some noise. Atlanta gave up aging superstar Wilkins for a younger star in Danny Manning last season and although they tied the franchise record with 57 victories, it just wasn't the same. Atlanta will be in the 50-victory category again and could repeat in the division. But the playoffs should be another matter.

Charlotte made a major pickup in landing defensive whiz assistant coach John Bach from Chicago. And the Hornets will score, providing Larry Johnson and Alonzo Mourning sidestep the injury problems of last year. Johnson, with back woes, is the bigger concern. If he goes down again, the Hornets will be so-so, a playoff-spot contender at best.

Chicago could be the most intriguing Central story. At press time, the Bulls had lost Grant and Scott Williams to free agency and Scottie Pippen was on the trading block. Lose those three and lose all hope.

Cleveland won 47 games despite some devastating injuries, especially to Brad Daugherty. The Cavs will be an ever-present danger again, but on a regular-season nightly basis, not as a threat to the title. Milwaukee landed the lottery prize in Glenn Robinson and will add him to last season's stud rookie Vin Baker and an impressive one-two point guard tandem in Eric Murdock and Lee

Mayberry as their rebuilding continues. They'll battle it out to avoid the Central cellar with Detroit, entering Year One Without Isiah Thomas.

In the Midwest, figure the Rockets to repeat behind reigning MVP Hakeem Olajuwon and the erratic Vernon Maxwell. The Rockets should play enough defense, score enough points to win the division—but not enough to take the Western Conference.

After the Rockets, the Midwest looks wide open. Utah was devoid of a first-round pick and will bring back the same cast that includes All-Stars Karl Malone and John Stockton. And even with in-season acquisition Jeff Hornacek around for a full season, there doesn't seem to be enough to vault the Jazz to the top. Denver, the pick as last season's surprise team, turned in the shocker of the playoffs with the Seattle upset. They'll be troublesome again with Dikembe Mutombo, the frightening defensive presence in the middle, and LaPhonso Ellis, the ever-improving forward. If the Nuggets get consistent point-guard play, plus continued effort from Brian Williams, they could end up second in the Midwest.

Figure San Antonio, minus Lucas, for fourth, David Robinson or not. The Spurs could again have the NBA's top scorer (Robinson) and top rebounder (Dennis Rodman) but it won't be enough. Dallas is searching for respectability under Dick Motta, back again in the coaching ranks, and with all the high draft choices—Jimmy Jackson, Jamal Mashburn in '93 and last June's pick, Jason Kidd—there's a strong rebuilding framework. The Timberwolves tried to re-locate to New Orleans with new owners but were denied. There's some individual talent, but not enough depth even with first-rounder Donyell Marshall. Giving Seattle the best run in the Pacific should be Phoenix, with Charles Barkley back for at least one more season and with Danny Manning aboard. They lost out in the conference semis to Houston. This time, they could make it to the conference finals behind their high-powered offense—before losing out to Seattle.

In Golden State, there's plenty of scoring, plenty of excitement. But there's also the age-old Don Nelson cry: no legit center, despite the presence of reigning Rookie of the Year Chris Webber, whose unhappiness with his coach was well-documented. Portland will battle the age factor as new coach P.J. Carlesimo, fresh from the college ranks, tries to delay the oncoming collapse.

The Lakers are stuck in transition and sought help through the free-agent market. The Kings will welcome back Bobby Hurley from his near-fatal accident but still need more help for Mitch Richmond to contend for the playoffs. And on the other side of Los Angeles, the Clippers will continue bumbling along, losing one star after another to bad trades or free agency.

DALLAS MAVERICKS

TEAM DIRECTORY: Owner/Pres.: Donald Carter; Chief Oper. Off./GM: Norm Sonju; Dir. Player Personnel: Keith Grant; Dir. Media Services: Kevin Sullivan; Coach: Dick Motta; Asst. Coaches: Brad Davis, Kip Motta. Arena: Reunion Arena (17,502). Colors: Blue and green.

SCOUTING REPORT

SHOOTING: The shots belong to two people: Jim Jackson, who had more than any guard in the league last season, and Jamal Mashburn. Together, they took 39.8 percent of their team's tries, so together they must share the blame of the Mavericks going just .432 from the field, easily the worst in the NBA. Jackson had a .445 success rate, while Mashburn was just .406 as a rookie. Neatness counts.

The future, however, remains bright. Jackson is aggressive in coming down the lane and can slowly back in smaller shooting guards. Mashburn puts the ball on the floor and shoots from the outside, as the 299 three-point attempts attest. He just needs to shoot better from the outside now.

PLAYMAKING: We have a hard time feeling sorry for the Mavericks for not getting the first pick in the draft even though they had the worst record. The pity will go to the opposition if Jason Kidd turns out to be as good as expected in joining Mashburn and Jackson to form a most promising core.

Fat Lever was commendable in his brief role as the bridge between the old guard (Derek Harper) and the new (Kidd), with an assist-to-turnover ratio of 2.4-1 when finally healthy last season. Lever's biggest contributions now can be in tutoring the rookie.

REBOUNDING: They are in the middle of the pack, encouraging enough for such a bad team but more so considering the possibilities. The Mavericks can be even better if two key performers are in place this season: Terry Davis and Sean Rooks. Davis averaged 9.9 and 9.3 rebounds a game the previous two seasons before missing all but 15 games of 1993-94 because of injury. Rooks contributed 5.5 per outing in just 26.7 minutes, meaning he can be a factor with extended minutes.

So it was perhaps a surprise the Mavericks were able to tread water so well last season without Davis. The credit goes to his

No rookie scored more points than Jamal Washburn.

replacement, Popeye Jones, who stepped in as a rookie to average 7.5 a game while getting nearly half his boards on the offensive end.

DEFENSE: A club without a force inside—the 44 blocked shots by Rooks was the worst team-high in the league—did what it had

MAVERICK ROSTER

No. Veterans	Pos.	Ht.	Wt.	Age	Yrs. Pro	College
U-19 Tony Campbell	F-G	6-7	215	32	10	Ohio State
43 Terry Davis	F-C	6-10	250	27	5	Virginia Union
U-40 Greg Dreiling	C	7-1	250	30	8	Kansas
30 Lucious Harris	G	6-5	190	23	1	Long Beach State
35 Donald Hodge	C	7-0	233	25	3	Temple
24 Jim Jackson	G	6-6	220	24	2	Ohio State
54 Popeye Jones	F	6-8	250	24	1	Murray State
U-23 Tim Legler	G	6-4	200	27	4	LaSalle
U-21 Fat Lever	G	6-3	175	34	11	Arizona State
32 Jamal Mashburn	F	6-8	240	21	1	Kentucky
45 Sean Rooks	C	6-10	250	25	2	Arizona
34 Doug Smith	F	6-10	238	25	3	Missouri
U-33 Randy White	F	6-8	249	26	5	Louisiana Tech
U-20 Morlon Wiley	G	6-4	192	28	6	Long Beach State
44 Lorenzo Williams	F-C	6-9	200	25	2	Stetson

U-unrestricted free agent

Rd. Rookies	Sel. No.	Pos.	Ht.	Wt.	College
1 Jason Kidd	2	G	6-3	205	California
1 Tony Dumas	19	G	6-4	190	Missouri-KC
2 Deon Thomas	28	F	6-7	238	Illinois

to do. The Mavericks compensated for that shortcoming by forcing 17.4 turnovers, up from 15.5 from the season before, and setting a franchise record for steals and opposition turnovers. That's noteworthy considering the success of the Mavericks of the late 1980s, and combined with the fact that they made the second-biggest improvement in the NBA in scoring defense, a cut from 114.5 to 103.8.

The counter is that the .499 shooting-percentage-against was 26th among the 27 teams, ahead of only Washington. Opponents used the lane as a target, getting the ball inside for easy shots with regularity, something that will continue to happen until the Mavericks prove they can stop the big men.

OUTLOOK: With Dick Motta calling the shots again, the Mavericks are tying to rebuild from the bottom for the second time—the first time, when they were an expansion team, and now, when they are a bad team. This is the right way to go about it, starting with Jackson, Mashburn and Kidd, with another lottery pick on the way after this season.

MAVERICK PROFILES

JIM JACKSON 24 6-6 220   Guard

Big-time player in the making . . . After lengthy holdout limited him to only 28 games as a rookie, he not only played all 82 in second campaign but set team record with 3,066 minutes . . . Mitch Richmond and Latrell Sprewell were the only guards in the entire league to score more points . . . Only five guards had more rebounds . . . Has started every game he has played since the Mavericks took him No. 4 overall out of Ohio State in 1992 . . . All-American as a Buckeye . . . He and teammate Jamal Mashburn tied for 18th in the NBA in scoring . . . Strength gives a lot of guards trouble inside on defense . . . Shooting percentage made a nice jump from first to second seasons, but still needs to get better . . . Born Oct. 14, 1970, in Toledo, Ohio . . . Made $2 million.

Year	Team	G	FG	FG Pct.	FT	FT Pct.	Reb.	Ast.	TP	Avg.
1992-93	Dallas	28	184	.395	68	.739	122	131	457	16.3
1993-94	Dallas	82	637	.445	285	.821	388	374	1576	19.2
	Totals	110	821	.433	353	.804	510	505	2033	18.5

SEAN ROOKS 25 6-10 250   Center

Piqued everyone's curiosity by going from second-round pick in 1992 to a promising rookie season, but then was beset by injuries in second campaign . . . Battled stress fracture in left foot before returning for a strong December, then a sprained ankle before returning to close the season on a high note . . . In 29 starts, he averaged 13.5 points and 5.8 rebounds in just 30.4 minutes while shooting .518, all good numbers for someone not getting a ton of time . . . Led Mavericks in shooting and blocked shots . . . Arizona product was born Sept. 9, 1969, in New York . . . Dallas took him No. 30 in the '92 draft . . . Made $488,000.

Year	Team	G	FG	FG Pct.	FT	FT Pct.	Reb.	Ast.	TP	Avg.
1992-93	Dallas	72	368	.493	234	.602	536	95	970	13.5
1993-94	Dallas	47	193	.491	150	.714	259	49	536	11.4
	Totals	119	561	.492	384	.641	795	144	1506	12.7

JAMAL MASHBURN 21 6-8 240   Forward

His 19.2 points a game last season was tops among all rookies . . . That also tied teammate Jim Jackson for No. 18 overall in the league . . . Getting this guy at No. 4 says a lot about the top of the 1993 draft . . . Plays outside and inside and can put the ball on the floor . . . "He's the most well-rounded rookie I've seen this year," Detroit's Joe Dumars said during the season. "(Chris) Webber and (Anfernee) Hardaway are going to be great players. But even at the time of the draft, I thought Jamal had the most potential." . . . Former Net coach Chuck Daly goes one better, saying Mashburn reminds him a lot of Larry Bird . . . That's getting ahead of things, but gives you an idea of what people think of his talent . . . The knock is that he shot just .406 and was too selfish at times . . . Born Nov. 29, 1972, in New York, and was the second-youngest player in the league behind Webber . . . Played college ball at Kentucky . . . Made $2.033 million.

Year	Team	G	FG	FG Pct.	FT	FT Pct.	Reb.	Ast.	TP	Avg.
1993-94	Dallas	79	561	.406	306	.699	353	266	1513	19.2

DOUG SMITH 25 6-10 238   Forward

The longer he is around, the less he plays . . . Are Mavericks trying to tell him something? . . . Slipped to an average of 21.3 minutes last season, his third since coming out of Missouri as the No. 6 pick . . . Did start 42 times at power forward, including 36 straight . . . Best game was Feb. 4 versus the Lakers when he had 36 points in 40 minutes . . . Has made nice improvement from the line in his three years since coming out of Missouri . . . Now needs to do the same in other parts of his game . . . Born Sept. 17, 1969, in Detroit . . . Made $1.65 million.

Year	Team	G	FG	FG Pct.	FT	FT Pct.	Reb.	Ast.	TP	Avg.
1991-92	Dallas	76	291	.415	89	.736	391	129	671	8.8
1992-93	Dallas	61	289	.434	56	.757	328	104	634	10.4
1993-94	Dallas	79	295	.435	106	.835	349	119	698	8.8
	Totals	216	875	.428	251	.780	1068	352	2003	9.3

LAFAYETTE (FAT) LEVER 34 6-3 175   Guard

He played 81 games. He played 81 games. He played 81 games . . . We repeat, he played 81 games . . . That is not a misprint . . . After making a combined 35 appearances over the previous three seasons because of injuries, he did not miss a game to injury in 1993-94 . . . The only contest he missed, Dec. 16, was because of the DNP-CD, the first of his career . . . Became the starting point guard for the final 53 games when Derek Harper was traded to the Knicks . . . Still has something left . . . Finished first in the league in steal-to-turnover ratio and was 11th in steals . . . In eighth place on the NBA's all-time steals list . . . Went into summer as unrestricted free agent . . . Originally No. 11 pick by Portland in 1982 but is best-known for his days as a Nugget . . . Born Aug. 18, 1960, in Pine Bluff, Ark., and attended Arizona State . . . Made $2.202 million.

Year	Team	G	FG	FG Pct.	FT	FT Pct.	Reb.	Ast.	TP	Avg.
1982-83	Portland	81	256	.431	116	.730	225	426	633	7.8
1983-84	Portland	81	313	.447	159	.743	218	372	788	9.7
1984-85	Denver	82	424	.430	197	.770	411	613	1051	12.8
1985-86	Denver	78	468	.441	132	.725	420	584	1080	13.8
1986-87	Denver	82	643	.469	244	.782	729	654	1552	18.9
1987-88	Denver	82	643	.473	248	.785	665	639	1546	18.9
1988-89	Denver	71	558	.457	270	.785	662	559	1409	19.8
1989-90	Denver	79	568	.443	271	.804	734	517	1443	18.3
1990-91	Dallas	4	9	.391	11	.786	15	12	29	7.3
1991-92	Dallas	31	135	.387	60	.750	161	107	347	11.2
1992-93	Dallas				Injured					
1993-94	Dallas	81	227	.408	75	.765	283	213	555	6.9
	Totals	752	4244	.447	1783	.771	4523	4696	10433	13.9

RON (POPEYE) JONES 24 6-8 250   Forward

Always had the nickname, but made a real name for himself last season . . . Rockets drafted him out of Murray State in 1992, but he didn't come to the NBA until they traded him to Dallas in the summer of '93 for Eric Riley . . . In what was officially his rookie season, Jones finished third among all first-year players in rebounding average, his 7.5 trailing only Chris Webber and Vin Baker . . . The 605 total boards also broke the Mavericks' rookie team mark held by Sam Perkins . . . Played in the rookie All-Star Game . . . Led Dallas with 11 double-

doubles . . . Twice grabbed 12 offensive rebounds . . . Born July 17, 1970, in Martin, Tenn . . . .Made $275,000.

Year	Team	G	FG	FG Pct.	FT	FT Pct.	Reb.	Ast.	TP	Avg.
1993-94	Dallas	81	195	.479	78	.729	605	99	468	5.8

TONY CAMPBELL 32 6-7 215   Forward-Guard

His stay in Dallas figures to be short . . . Arrived Jan. 6 along with a future No. 1 draft pick in the deal that sent Derek Harper to New York . . . Played 41 games, then headed into the summer as an unrestricted free agent . . . Went from one of the best teams to the worst and bolstered bench scoring by averaging 9.7 points in just 20.4 minutes . . . Former Ohio State star began NBA career as No. 20 pick by the Pistons in 1984 . . . Won two championship rings while a reserve with the Lakers . . . Went to Teaneck High School in New Jersey, the same school that produced commissioner David Stern . . . Born May 7, 1962, in Gainesville, Fla. . . . Made $1.702 million.

Year	Team	G	FG	FG Pct.	FT	FT Pct.	Reb.	Ast.	TP	Avg.
1984-85	Detroit	56	130	.496	56	.800	89	24	316	5.6
1985-86	Detroit	82	294	.484	58	.795	236	45	648	7.9
1986-87	Detroit	40	57	.393	24	.615	58	19	138	3.5
1987-88	L.A. Lakers	13	57	.564	28	.718	27	15	143	11.0
1988-89	L.A. Lakers	63	158	.458	70	.843	130	47	388	6.2
1989-90	Minnesota	82	723	.457	448	.787	451	213	1903	23.2
1990-91	Minnesota	77	652	.434	358	.803	346	214	1678	21.8
1991-92	Minnesota	78	527	.464	240	.803	286	229	1307	16.8
1992-93	New York	58	194	.490	59	.678	155	62	449	7.7
1993-94	N.Y.-Dal.	63	227	.443	94	.783	186	82	555	8.8
	Totals	612	3019	.458	1435	.786	1964	950	7525	12.3

TIM LEGLER 27 6-4 200   Guard

His fourth season in the NBA was also the first full season of the NBA . . . The 79 games in 1993-94 was more than the three years before that combined during bit parts with Phoenix, Denver and Utah . . . Originally came to Dallas on a 10-day contract, but turned that into a full-time job . . . Not always an accurate shooter—he's .428 lifetime—but a shooter . . . Was No. 7 in the league in three-point shooting on March 23 before 5-for-23 nosedive over the final 17 games dropped him to No. 23 . . . Has come off the bench for all 109 games of his Dallas career. Only Steve Alford, at 112 games, went longer in team history without a start . . . No. 3 in club history in career three-point accuracy and No. 4 in free-throw percentage . . . Undrafted out of LaSalle . . . Born Dec. 26, 1966, in Washington, D.C. . . . Made $250,000.

Year	Team	G	FG	FG Pct.	FT	FT Pct.	Reb.	Ast.	TP	Avg.
1989-90	Phoenix	11	11	.379	6	1.000	8	6	28	2.5
1990-91	Denver	10	25	.347	5	.833	18	12	58	5.8
1992-93	Utah-Dal.	33	105	.436	57	.803	59	46	289	8.8
1993-94	Dallas	79	231	.438	142	.840	128	120	656	8.3
	Totals	133	372	.428	210	.833	213	184	1031	7.8

TERRY DAVIS 27 6-10 250   Forward-Center

Just looking for some elbow room . . . He came back from a career-threatening elbow injury last season, but not far enough to make it a complete success . . . Originally shattered the bone in his left (shooting) arm in a May 2, 1993, car accident in hometown of South Boston, Va. Made it back to play in two preseason games, but went on the injured list before the start of the regular season . . . Activated Jan. 5 and played 15 of the next 16 games, starting the last four at center . . . Was a free-agent find for the Mavericks in the summer of 1991 . . . Averaged 9.9 and 9.3 rebounds the next two seasons . . . Slipped to 4.9 in 19.1 minutes in 1993-94, with an asterisk for the injury . . . Undrafted out of Virginia Union in 1989 before hooking on with Miami . . . Born June 17, 1967, in South Boston, Va . . . .Made $1.2 million.

Year	Team	G	FG	FG Pct.	FT	FT Pct.	Reb.	Ast.	TP	Avg.
1989-90	Miami	63	122	.466	54	.621	229	25	298	4.7
1990-91	Miami	55	115	.487	69	.556	266	39	300	5.5
1991-92	Dallas	68	256	.482	181	.635	672	57	693	10.2
1992-93	Dallas	75	393	.455	167	.594	701	68	955	12.7
1993-94	Dallas	15	24	.407	8	.667	74	6	56	3.7
	Totals	276	910	.466	479	.607	1942	195	2302	8.3

RANDY WHITE 26 6-8 249   Forward

Didn't exactly have a contract drive in 1993-94 . . . Played in just 18 games because of a sore right knee . . . That was his momentum heading into the summer when the former lottery pick would become a free agent . . . Maybe Mavericks should have kept him in the opening lineup; they won all three times he started . . . Then again, maybe the Mavericks never should have drafted him No. 8 in 1989 in the first place . . . Ranks among all-time franchise leaders in games (ninth), offensive rebounds (ninth), shots (10th) and steals (10th) . . . Born Nov. 4, 1967, in Shreveport, La., and stayed close to home to star at Louisiana Tech . . . Dismissed all the talk about being the next Karl Malone, another power player from La. Tech. Now we know why . . . Made $922,000.

Year	Team	G	FG	FG Pct.	FT	FT Pct.	Reb.	Ast.	TP	Avg.
1989-90	Dallas	55	93	.369	50	.562	173	21	237	4.3
1990-91	Dallas	79	265	.398	159	.707	504	63	695	8.8
1991-92	Dallas	65	145	.380	124	.765	236	31	418	6.4
1992-93	Dallas	64	235	.435	138	.750	370	49	618	9.7
1993-94	Dallas	18	45	.402	19	.576	83	11	115	6.4
	Totals	281	783	.401	490	.707	1366	175	2083	7.4

LUCIOUS HARRIS 23 6-5 190   Guard

The choice for the Mavericks with the first pick of the second round in the 1993 draft was between Lucious Harris and Nick Van Exel . . . Kind of shocking they made the wrong decision, huh? . . . While Van Exel started for the Lakers and made the all-rookie second team, Harris averaged 15.1 minutes and showed he needs to get tougher . . . Ten pounds or so of bulk would do it . . . Poor finisher; too slow on shot release . . . But a very hard worker, so don't be surprised if he makes strides in second season . . . Also proved to be a better defender than expected . . . Born Dec. 18, 1970, in Los Angeles and attended nearby Cal State-Long Beach . . . Made $350,000.

Year	Team	G	FG	FG Pct.	FT	FT Pct.	Reb.	Ast.	TP	Avg.
1993-94	Dallas	77	162	.421	87	.731	157	106	418	5.4

GREG DREILING 30 7-1 250   Center

Career backup also probably started on a new path last season . . . He will become a big guy for hire, bouncing around on free-agent deals . . . There's always a market for someone 7-1 who only turns 31 in the opening week of the season . . . Mavericks brought him in on a one-year deal to provide size and experience to thin frontcourt . . . With Sean Rooks and Terry

Davis out for extended stretches, he started 19 times for a team on a youth movement and appeared in each of the first 28 games . . . Then headed into the offseason as an unrestricted free agent again . . . His seven seasons with Indiana is second only to Vern Fleming (10) and Herb Williams (eight) for longevity . . . Standout at Kansas when the Jayhawks played in the 1986 Final Four at Reunion Arena . . . Pacers took him in the second round a few months later . . . Born Nov. 7, 1963, in Wichita, Kan . . . .Made $300,000.

Year	Team	G	FG	FG Pct.	FT	FT Pct.	Reb.	Ast.	TP	Avg.
1986-87	Indiana	24	16	.432	10	.833	43	7	42	1.8
1987-88	Indiana	20	8	.471	18	.692	17	5	34	1.7
1988-89	Indiana	53	43	.558	43	.672	92	18	129	2.4
1989-90	Indiana	49	20	.377	25	.735	87	8	65	1.3
1990-91	Indiana	73	98	.505	63	.600	255	51	259	3.5
1991-92	Indiana	60	43	.494	30	.750	96	25	117	2.0
1992-93	Indiana	43	19	.328	8	.533	66	8	46	1.1
1993-94	Dallas	54	52	.500	27	.711	170	31	132	2.4
	Totals	376	299	.477	224	.671	826	153	824	2.2

MORLON WILEY 28 6-4 192   Guard

His stints with the Mavericks are like a "Rocky" movie . . . Another sequel is always just around the corner . . . Had two stints last season alone, one in training camp and one after signing March 31 . . . In between, he spent time with Grand Rapids and Quad City of the CBA and had a 10-day contract with Miami when Bimbo Coles went out with a dislocated finger . . . Played four games with the Heat, 12 with the Mavericks . . . Dallas brought him into the NBA as a second-round pick out of Cal State-Long Beach in 1988 . . . Teammates like him because he is unselfish . . . Great locker-room guy . . . Poor shooter . . . Born Sept. 24, 1966, in New Orleans . . . Made $250,000.

Year	Team	G	FG	FG Pct.	FT	FT Pct.	Reb.	Ast.	TP	Avg.
1988-89	Dallas	51	46	.404	13	.813	47	76	111	2.2
1989-90	Orlando	40	92	.442	28	.737	52	114	229	5.7
1990-91	Orlando	34	45	.417	17	.680	17	73	113	3.3
1991-92	Orl.-S.A.-Atl.	53	83	.430	24	.686	81	180	204	3.8
1992-93	Atl.-Dal.	58	96	.378	17	.654	91	181	263	4.5
1993-94	Mia.-Dal.	16	9	.310	0	.000	10	23	21	1.3
	Totals	252	371	.409	99	.707	298	647	941	3.7

DONALD HODGE 25 7-0 233   Center

We double-checked, and he was on the team last season . . . No one averaged less than his 8.6 minutes an outing . . . Should be thankful that Doug Smith, Sean Rooks and Terry Davis had injuries; otherwise, he would have seen even less action . . . Went 30 minutes on Opening Night, which obviously made an impression on then-coach Quinn Buckner. Hodge played 20-plus minutes only two more times the rest of the season . . . To think this is the same guy who led the Mavericks with 79 appearances the season before . . . Temple product was born Feb. 25, 1969, in Washington, D. C . . . . Dallas got him with the 33rd choice in 1991 . . . Made $845,000.

Year	Team	G	FG	FG Pct.	FT	FT Pct.	Reb.	Ast.	TP	Avg.
1991-92	Dallas	51	163	.497	100	.667	275	39	426	8.4
1992-93	Dallas	79	161	.403	71	.683	294	75	393	5.0
1993-94	Dallas	50	46	.455	44	.846	95	32	136	2.7
	Totals	180	370	.446	215	.703	664	146	955	5.3

LORENZO WILLIAMS 25 6-9 200   Forward-Center

Played with four teams in 1993-94 if you include exhibitions . . . Opened with Celtics, where he finished the season before, before being the last cut in training camp . . . Signed by Magic on Nov. 30 and waived Dec. 2 . . . Signed by Hornets nine days later and waived on Jan. 5 . . . On to Rockford of the CBA . . . Reached Dallas, finally, in February with a pair of 10-day contracts before being signed for the rest of the season . . . Also has played in U.S. Basketball League and the Global Basketball Assn . . . . His 6.1 rebounds in the 34 games with the Mavericks was second-best on the team, behind only the 7.5 by Popeye Jones . . . Averaged 19.9 minutes, considerable time for a journeyman, and had 11 starts at center . . . Born July 15, 1969, in Ocala, Fla . . . . Undrafted out of Stetson.

Year	Team	G	FG	FG Pct.	FT	FT Pct.	Reb.	Ast.	TP	Avg.
1992-93	Char.-Orl.-Bos.	27	17	.472	2	.286	55	5	36	1.3
1993-94	Orl.-Char.-Dal.	38	49	.445	12	.429	217	25	110	2.9
	Totals	65	66	.452	14	.400	272	30	146	2.2

THE ROOKIES

JASON KIDD 21 6-3 205   **Guard**
The best point guard to come out since Magic Johnson . . . Says who? Magic Johnson . . . Left Cal after sophomore year, but that was enough time to be named Pacific-10 Conference Player of the Year and an All-American . . . Mavericks took him with the second pick, adding to the lottery-based foundation of Jimmy Jackson (1992) and Jamal Mashburn ('93) . . . Born March 23, 1973, in San Francisco.

TONY DUMAS 22 6-4 190   **Guard**
The public didn't know him at Missouri-Kansas City, but the scouts surely did . . . Mavericks got him at No. 19 to back up Jim Jackson at shooting guard . . . Ranked 11th in the nation in scoring as a junior (23.8) and seventh as a senior (26.0) . . . But what was that .421 from the field last season? . . . Born Aug. 25, 1972, in Chicago.

DEON THOMAS 23 6-7 238   **Forward**
All-time leading scorer in Illinois history was the first pick of the second round, No. 28 overall . . . Joins Kareem Abdul-Jabbar and Steve Johnson as the only players in NCAA history to have shot better than .600 with more than 800 field goals made . . . The free-throw line apparently was out of his range—he had just a .661 success rate over the four seasons . . . Consistent scorer in spite of that . . . Born Feb. 24, 1971, in Chicago.

COACH DICK MOTTA: Back in the saddle again . . . Coached the Mavericks their first seven years in the league . . . That's only part of a resume that includes 22 seasons and 856 wins in the regular season, fourth-best all-time . . . Only Red Auerbach (938), Lenny Wilkens (926) and Jack Ramsay (864) have more victories . . . Career record: 856-863 (.498) . . . The only coach in the league to ever guide two teams to four consecutive seasons of improved wins . . . Won a world championship

Jim Jackson was No. 3 in points scored by guards.

with the 1977-78 Bullets . . . Mavericks don't want to hear anything about how they hired a retread, seeing as how they made a bold move with unproved Quinn Buckner, and look where that got them . . . Says he wanted to be a coach since he was 13 years old; seems like he has been . . . Won Idaho high-school title in 1959 with Jazz assistant Phil Johnson as his star player . . . Spent six years at Weber State before joining the NBA with Chicago in 1968-69 . . . Won Coach of the Year in the third of his eight seasons with the Bulls . . . Moved on to Bullets for four years before coming to Dallas as one of the architects of an expansion team that grew into one of the league's best . . . Tried to give the same boost to Sacramento Kings, but that ended in disappointment 25 games into the third season . . . Born Sept. 3, 1931, in Midvale, Utah.

GREATEST PLAYER

Roy Tarpley, who elevated the team to new heights, is the could-have-been. Also the maybe-still-will-be, though no one is holding their breath. That leaves three players to choose from: Mark Aguirre, Rolando Blackman and Derek Harper.

The vote here is for Blackman in a very close race. He scored nearly 3,000 more points than the next closest Maverick, Aguirre. He was a four-time all-star, more than anyone else in team history. And, of the six times Dallas was in the playoffs during his tenure, Blackman raised his scoring average from the regular season on four of those occasions.

Aguirre, meanwhile, had terrific years while leading the Mavericks in scoring average six straight campaigns, breaking 25 points a game in four of those, and he produced in the playoffs. Harper is easily No. 1 in steals and tops in assists while also holding the No. 3 spot in points.

ALL-TIME MAVERICK LEADERS

SEASON

Points: Mark Aguirre, 2,330, 1983-84
Assists: Derek Harper, 634, 1987-88
Rebounds: James Donaldson, 973, 1986-87

GAME

Points: Mark Aguirre, 49 vs. Philadelphia, 1/28/85
Assists: Derek Harper, 18 vs. Boston, 12/29/88
Rebounds: James Donaldson, 27 vs. Portland (3 OT), 12/29/89

CAREER

Points: Rolando Blackman, 16,643, 1981-92
Assists: Derek Harper, 4,790, 1983-94
Rebounds: James Donaldson, 4,589, 1985-92

DENVER NUGGETS

TEAM DIRECTORY: Owner: Comsat; Pres.: Tim Leiweke; GM: Bernie Bickerstaff; Dir. Pub. Rel.: TBA; Coach: Dan Issel; Asst. Coaches: Gene Littles, Mike Evans. Arena: McNichols Sports Arena (17,171). Colors: Gold, blue and red.

SCOUTING REPORT

SHOOTING: The Paul Westhead era, the days of the offense on an autobahn, couldn't be more distant if his teams used a red, white and blue ball and played against the Tams and Squires. These are the new Nuggets, when shooting is sometimes more of an obligation than a priority. Even though Dikembe Mutumbo was second in shooting, Mahmoud Abdul-Rauf has proved to be a scorer and LaPhonso Ellis could someday approach the 20-point plateau, only seven teams had fewer attempts.

The Nuggets should take their own advice when it comes to three-pointers. They had the NBA's worst percentage in 1993-94, even with players like Abdul-Rauf and Reggie Williams. Then again, this would be the same Abdul-Rauf who went 42 of 133 (.316) and the same Williams who was 64 of 230 (.278). Fans in the baseline seats at McNichols Arena should have to sign insurance waivers.

The Nuggets should just be thankful Ellis provides some semblance of a post game. Mutumbo, despite his league ranking, was fifth on the team in attempts and, though getting better, is still too clumsy with the ball around the basket to be a real offensive threat.

PLAYMAKING: Abdul-Rauf may have been the leading scorer each of the last two seasons, but don't bronze this spot for him. Come to think of it, don't even write in his name in ink as the point guard, considering the comments about his leadership abilities from GM Bernie Bickerstaff: "I guarantee you if we had somebody in the backcourt who understood the game, we wouldn't have any problems." Ouch.

Bickerstaff promised to address the situation in the offseason. His reminder will be staring at the chart that showed the Nuggets finishing next-to-last in assist-to-turnover ratio for the second year in a row.

Shot-block leader Dikembe Mutombo was No. 2 in FG pct.

REBOUNDING: Mutumbo and Ellis provide a good one-two, enough to knock the Nuggets into a tie for 10th last season by percentage, even though they both slipped slightly from 1992-93. Credit goes to Brian Williams, who contributed 5.6 boards a game in just 18.8 minutes. Imagine if Rodney Rogers, the '93 lottery pick who plays both forward spots, starts to rebound like in college.

DEFENSE: Not much about the Nuggets got attention until the first round of the playoffs, when they pulled one of the greatest

NUGGET ROSTER

No.	Veterans	Pos.	Ht.	Wt.	Age	Yrs. Pro	College
3	Mahmoud Abdul-Rauf	G	6-1	150	25	4	Louisiana State
U-43	Kevin Brooks	F	6-8	200	25	3	SW Louisiana
20	LaPhonso Ellis	F	6-8	240	24	2	Notre Dame
21	Tom Hammonds	F	6-9	223	27	5	Georgia Tech
4	Darnell Mee	G	6-5	177	23	1	Western Kentucky
55	Dikembe Mutombo	C	7-2	250	28	3	Georgetown
14	Robert Pack	G	6-2	190	25	3	USC
42	Mark Randall	F	6-9	245	27	3	Kansas
7	Alvin Robertson	G	6-4	208	32	10	Arkansas
54	Rodney Rogers	F	6-7	260	23	1	Wake Forest
23	Bryant Stith	G	6-5	208	23	2	Virginia
8	Brian Williams	F	6-11	260	25	3	Arizona
34	Reggie Williams	G-F	6-7	195	30	7	Georgetown

R-restricted free agent

Rd.	Rookies	Sel. No.	Pos.	Ht.	Wt.	College
1	Jalen Rose	13	G-F	6-6	210	Michigan

upsets by beating Seattle. But if anything did, this should have been it. Or as coach Dan Issel noted: "Every coach tries to exploit his team's strength. And for us, our strength is defense."

There is plenty of evidence to support his claim. The Nuggets of 1993-94 may have been the best defensive unit in the 27-year history of the franchise that goes back to the ABA. The Mutombo-led group shattered the team record for blocked shots and became the first to hold the opposition to less than 100 points, at 98.7. No. 1 in many of the Denver record books, they weren't too bad compared to their current peers, either, finishing second only to New York in shooting-percentage-against.

OUTLOOK: Bickerstaff was only partially right. The Nuggets could probably use some veteran leadership at any position, not just point guard, considering that when they went into the playoffs last spring, Williams and backup point guard Robert Pack were the only people on the team with previous postseason experience. On the other hand, that showing against the SuperSonics, and the subsequent series against Utah before falling in Game 7 on the road, may have provided those intangibles.

One other thing about the playoffs of '94: It branded the Nuggets as one of the teams to watch this season. Let's see how they do now that the pressure is on.

NUGGET PROFILES

DIKEMBE MUTOMBO 28 7-2 250   Center

The best defender in the league . . . Says who? . . . Says Mutombo . . . Campaigned to be named Defensive Player of the Year by saying: "I deserve it. If I don't get it, I will tell the league to kiss my rear end." . . . Speaks five languages, but apparently is unaware of the word "modesty" . . . Then he finished third in the balloting behind Hakeem Olajuwon and David Robinson . . . "The league can go to hell," came the response . . . Not so much a great defender, per se, as a defensive force because of shot-blocking . . . Led NBA in that category, finished second in shooting percentage and tied for sixth in rebounding . . . Became club leader in career blocks . . . First Nugget to ever block 300 shots in a season . . . Starred at Georgetown before Denver picked him No. 4 in 1991 . . . Born June 25, 1966, in Kinshasa, Zaire . . . Made $3 million.

Year	Team	G	FG	FG Pct.	FT	FT Pct.	Reb.	Ast.	TP	Avg.
1991-92	Denver.........	71	428	.493	321	.642	870	156	1177	16.6
1992-93	Denver.........	82	398	.510	335	.681	1070	147	1131	13.8
1993-94	Denver.........	82	365	.569	256	.583	971	127	986	12.0
	Totals	235	1191	.520	912	.637	2911	430	3294	14.0

LaPHONSO ELLIS 24 6-8 240   Forward

Trying to break into the upper echelon of power forwards . . . Will have to try harder . . . Didn't build enough off very promising rookie campaign . . . "LaPhonso came in and underestimated what it was going to take the second time around," Nugget general manager Bernie Bickerstaff said. "He thought the second year was going to be easier when it's really a lot harder." . . . Finished second on the team in scoring and rebounding . . . No. 5 pick in the 1992 draft after standout career at Notre Dame that includes leaving as school's all-time leader in blocked shots . . . Named to all-rookie team in '93 . . . Born May 5, 1970, in East St. Louis, Ill. . . . Made $2.161 million.

Year	Team	G	FG	FG Pct.	FT	FT Pct.	Reb.	Ast.	TP	Avg.
1992-93	Denver.........	82	483	.504	237	.748	744	151	1205	14.7
1993-94	Denver.........	79	483	.502	242	.674	682	167	1215	15.4
	Totals	161	966	.503	479	.709	1426	318	2420	15.0

MAHMOUD ABDUL-RAUF 25 6-1 150   Guard

Magic Johnson says the former Chris Jackson has the quickest release he has ever seen... He's also one of the best anyone has ever seen from the free-throw line... Had streaks of 81 (second-longest in history), 57 and 63 without a miss... Joins Bill Sharman as the only players in NBA history with three runs of 50 or more... Abdul-Rauf's .956 fell just short of the all-time single-season mark of .958 by Calvin Murphy in 1980-81... Played at about 160 pounds two years ago, then dropped 10 pounds last season. Very noticeable in legs, but Nuggets were concerned he was too light... Still led team in scoring for second straight season... Has more tenure in Denver uniform than any player on the roster, having come aboard as the No. 3 pick in 1990 out of LSU... Born March 9, 1969, in Gulfport, Miss.... Made $1.825 million.

Year	Team	G	FG	FG Pct.	FT	FT Pct.	Reb.	Ast.	TP	Avg.
1990-91	Denver	67	417	.413	84	.857	121	206	942	14.1
1991-92	Denver	81	356	.421	94	.870	114	192	837	10.3
1992-93	Denver	81	633	.450	217	.935	225	344	1553	19.2
1993-94	Denver	80	588	.460	219	.956	168	362	1437	18.0
	Totals	309	1994	.439	614	.921	628	1104	4769	15.4

RODNEY ROGERS 23 6-7 260   Forward

If he's your third forward, you have a good pair of starting forwards... No. 9 pick made a very good impression his rookie season... Can shoot from outside or put the ball on the floor, though he needs to get more consistent (see: .439)... Started 14 times... At his size, he can be tough for some defenders to handle at small forward... Atlantic Coast Conference Player of the Year and second-team All-American as a junior at Wake Forest... Turned pro after that... Played for the Olympic development squad that scrimmaged the Dream Team in the summer of 1992... Born June 20, 1971, in Durham, N.C.... Made $1.2 million.

Year	Team	G	FG	FG Pct.	FT	FT Pct.	Reb.	Ast.	TP	Avg.
1993-94	Denver	79	239	.439	127	.672	226	101	640	8.1

REGGIE WILLIAMS 30 6-7 195   Guard-Forward

The same guy who once bounced from the Clippers to the Cavaliers to the Spurs to the Nuggets in rapid-fire succession is now looked upon as a team leader . . . Co-captain . . . He was a free agent with everything to prove when Denver signed him in January of 1991 . . . Today, he's about to climb into the top 10 on the Nuggets' all-time scoring list . . . Could become even more effective if he would stay around at least 47% or 48% from the field . . . Left Georgetown as school's all-time leading scorer and was a member of the 1984 NCAA championship team . . . Big East Player of the Year as a senior . . . High-school teammates in Baltimore with Muggsy Bogues, David Wingate and the late Reggie Lewis . . . Born March 5, 1964, in Baltimore . . . Made $1.258 million.

Year	Team	G	FG	FG Pct.	FT	FT Pct.	Reb.	Ast.	TP	Avg.
1987-88	L.A. Clippers	35	152	.356	48	.727	118	58	365	10.4
1988-89	L.A. Clippers	63	260	.438	92	.754	179	103	642	10.2
1989-90	LAC-Clev.-S.A.	47	131	.388	52	.765	83	53	320	6.8
1990-91	S.A.-Den.	73	384	.449	166	.843	306	133	991	13.6
1991-92	Denver	81	601	.471	216	.803	405	235	1474	18.2
1992-93	Denver	79	535	.458	238	.804	428	295	1341	17.0
1993-94	Denver	82	418	.412	165	.733	392	300	1065	13.0
	Totals	460	2481	.437	977	.786	1911	1177	6198	13.5

BRYANT STITH 23 6-5 208   Guard

Wonder what it sounded like . . . Wonder what it sounded like as he zoomed past Mark Macon to become the starting shooting guard . . . Macon had already lost his spot in the opening lineup by the time he was traded to Detroit . . . Virginia product took it from there and joined Dikembe Mutombo as the only Nuggets to start all 82 games . . . Also tied Mutombo for team lead in minutes (2,853) . . . Few shooting guards are less of a threat from behind the three-point line . . . Had only nine attempts back there all last season . . . In addition to gaining some range, he needs to raise shooting percentage . . . Strong, tough player, but teams will play way off and beg him to launch from the perimeter until

he proves he can be dangerous . . . No. 13 pick in the 1992 draft
. . . Born Dec. 10, 1970, in Emporia, Va. . . . Made $1.1 million.

Year	Team	G	FG	FG Pct.	FT	FT Pct.	Reb.	Ast.	TP	Avg.
1992-93	Denver	39	124	.446	99	.832	124	49	347	8.9
1993-94	Denver	82	365	.450	291	.829	349	199	1023	12.5
	Totals	121	489	.449	390	.830	473	248	1370	11.3

ROBERT PACK 25 6-2 190   Guard

Continues to make teams sorry they didn't even
invite him to summer league for a look, let
alone not draft him . . . Seattle is especially
sorry . . . Great Game 5 against the SuperSonics
helped propel Nuggets to huge first-round upset
. . . He could still help Portland, which signed
the uninvited, undrafted point guard from USC
and eventually traded him to Nuggets early in
1992-93 for a second-round pick . . . Gets great penetration down
the lane . . . Problem is, he takes the ball down the middle, then
tries to pass out only after finding he has no shot, then is caught
under the basket . . . But he has proved he has a spot in the league
for the long haul . . . Finished second in the slam-dunk contest
despite being only 6-2 . . . That means you don't need us to say
he's a leaper . . . Not much of a shooter . . . Born Feb. 3, 1969, in
New Orleans.

Year	Team	G	FG	FG Pct.	FT	FT Pct.	Reb.	Ast.	TP	Avg.
1991-92	Portland	72	115	.423	102	.803	97	140	332	4.6
1992-93	Denver	77	285	.470	239	.768	160	335	810	10.5
1993-94	Denver	66	223	.443	179	.758	123	356	631	9.6
	Totals	215	623	.451	520	.772	380	831	1773	8.2

BRIAN WILLIAMS 25 6-11 260   Forward

A pretty good player when he plays . . . Well-
chronicled history of clinical depression has
taken most of the headlines since Orlando took
him 10th in the 1991 draft, but last season will
go a long way toward changing that . . . Nuggets got him by sending Todd Lichti and Anthony Cook to Orlando, then got nice returns
. . . Solid contributor off the bench . . . After
playing only 69 games his first two seasons out of Arizona because
of physical and emotional problems, he missed just two games
with Denver because of heel injury . . . No. 2 on the team in

blocked shots and No. 3 in total rebounds . . . Father, Gene Williams, an original member of the Platters, sang the national anthem before one Nugget game . . . Born April 6, 1969, in Fresno, Cal. . . . Made $1.244 million.

Year	Team	G	FG	FG Pct.	FT	FT Pct.	Reb.	Ast.	TP	Avg.
1991-92	Orlando	48	171	.528	95	.669	272	33	437	9.1
1992-93	Orlando	21	40	.513	16	.800	56	5	96	4.6
1993-94	Denver	80	251	.541	137	.649	446	50	639	8.0
	Totals	149	462	.533	248	.665	774	88	1172	7.9

TOM HAMMONDS 27 6-9 223   Forward

When he left Georgia Tech in 1989, just before Washington used the ninth pick to draft him, Tech coach Bobby Cremins tagged him as "the hardest-working player I've ever had." . . . That didn't translate into success in the NBA— he bounced from the Bullets to Charlotte, then to Denver as a free agent in February 1993 . . . Nuggets like his versatility and athleticism . . . A fourth or fifth forward in most places . . . Has played both spots, but mostly is not big enough to play power forward and not quick enough to play small forward . . . Won a gold medal as part of the U.S. team at the 1986 world championships . . . Born March 27, 1967, in Crestview, Fla. . . . Made $600,000.

Year	Team	G	FG	FG Pct.	FT	FT Pct.	Reb.	Ast.	TP	Avg.
1989-90	Washington	61	129	.437	63	.643	168	51	321	5.3
1990-91	Washington	70	155	.461	57	.722	206	43	367	5.2
1991-92	Washington	37	195	.488	50	.610	185	36	440	11.9
1992-93	Char.-Den.	54	105	.475	38	.613	127	24	248	4.6
1993-94	Denver	74	115	.500	71	.683	199	34	301	4.1
	Totals	296	699	.472	279	.656	885	188	1677	5.7

ALVIN ROBERTSON 32 6-4 208   Guard

Coming off the season that wasn't . . . Went on the injured list Nov. 29 with lower back problems and stayed there entire season . . . Nuggets hoped he would provide some veteran leadership, but it didn't happen because of the injury . . . Opened with Detroit and was traded to Denver on Nov. 19 for Mark Macon and Marcus Liberty . . . Trade had something to do with his putting his hands around the neck of Piston exec Billy McKinney . . . Headed into the offseason facing the possibility of retirement because of the ongoing back problems . . . Has led the league in steals three times and is No. 2 on the all-time career list in that category . . . Originally the No. 7 pick by San Antonio in the 1984 draft after starring at Arkansas . . . Born July 22, 1962, in Barberton, Ohio . . . Made $2.458 million.

Year	Team	G	FG	FG Pct.	FT	FT Pct.	Reb.	Ast.	TP	Avg.
1984-85	San Antonio	79	299	.498	124	.734	265	275	726	9.2
1985-86	San Antonio	82	562	.514	260	.795	516	448	1392	17.0
1986-87	San Antonio	81	589	.466	244	.753	424	421	1435	17.7
1987-88	San Antonio	82	655	.465	273	.748	498	557	1610	19.6
1988-89	San Antonio	65	465	.483	183	.723	384	393	1122	17.3
1989-90	Milwaukee	81	476	.503	197	.741	559	445	1153	14.2
1990-91	Milwaukee	81	438	.485	199	.757	459	444	1098	13.6
1991-92	Milwaukee	82	396	.430	151	.763	350	360	1010	12.3
1992-93	Mil.-Det.	69	247	.458	84	.656	269	263	618	9.0
1993-94	Det.-Den.					Injured				
	Totals	702	4127	.478	1715	.748	3724	3606	10164	14.5

DARNELL MEE 23 6-5 177   Guard

Nagging leg injury took a big chunk out of his rookie season . . . Hurt left leg during training camp, played in 25 of 30 games, then reaggravated it Jan. 2. Went on the injured list with a stress fracture nine days later and stayed on the shelf for the better part of three months . . . Saw action in 13 of the final 18 outings, even if it was spot duty . . . No. 34 pick by Warriors before being traded that day to Nuggets for Josh Grant . . . Finished fourth in the nation in steals as a senior at Western Kentucky . . . Led Hilltoppers to Sun Belt Conference championship and round of 16 in the NCAA tournament . . . Born Feb. 11, 1971, in Cleveland, Tenn. . . . Made $150,000.

Year	Team	G	FG	FG Pct.	FT	FT Pct.	Reb.	Ast.	TP	Avg.
1993-94	Denver	38	28	.318	12	.444	35	16	73	1.9

MARK RANDALL 27 6-9 245   Forward

Grew a nice-looking goatee . . . So much for his 1993-94 accomplishments . . . Played 155 minutes after being signed as a free agent with the season about a month old . . . Biggest run was when he played in seven of the 14 February outings . . . In Heat camp before being waived, he then joined Rapid City of CBA before Nuggets called . . . Best known for college career, during which he led Kansas to the NCAA championship game as a senior . . . Bulls took him at No. 26 from there . . . Medical redshirt when Jayhawks won title in 1988 . . . Played for long-time NBA assistant coach Mack Calvin at Cherry Creek High in Englewood, Colo. . . . Born Sept. 30, 1967, in Edina, Minn.

Year	Team	G	FG	FG Pct.	FT	FT Pct.	Reb.	Ast.	TP	Avg.
1991-92	Chi.-Minn.	54	68	.456	32	.744	71	33	171	3.2
1992-93	Minn.-Det.	37	40	.500	16	.615	55	11	97	2.6
1993-94	Denver	28	17	.340	22	.786	22	11	58	2.1
	Totals	119	125	.448	70	.721	148	55	326	2.7

THE ROOKIE

JALEN ROSE 21 6-6 210   **Guard-Forward**
Nuggets got the versatile Michigan product with the 13th pick . . . His game figures to be better suited for the pros than college because he will have more opportunities to create off the dribble and with a free-flowing style . . . Can play both spots in the backcourt and small forward, but is a little thin to play there on defense against most people . . . Listed at 6-8, but measured at 6-6 at the pre-draft camp . . . Needs to become more consistent with outside shot . . . Born Jan. 20, 1973, in Detroit.

COACH DAN ISSEL: At a time when Nuggets should have been tense in their first playoff appearance, his easy-going nature made as big an impact as any play he called . . . Result was first-round win over Seattle, one of the biggest upsets in playoff history, before Denver pushed Utah to the limit the next series . . . That's quite an impact for a guy at the end of his second season of coaching at any level . . . Nuggets have improved by 18 games in those two campaigns . . . The 42-40 finish last year marked the first time they finished over .500 since 1989-90 . . . Career mark is 78-86 (.476) . . . Already popular in Denver because of great success as a player . . . In 15 years as a pro, he missed only 24 games . . . His 27,482 points trailed only Kareem Abdul-Jabbar, Wilt Chamberlain, Julius Erving and Moses Malone on the NBA/ABA scoring list . . . Nuggets' all-time scoring leader when he retired in 1985 and now is second to Alex English . . . Inducted into the Hall of Fame in 1983 . . . Set 23 school records while playing for legendary Adolph Rupp at Kentucky . . . Pro career started nearby with the ABA's Kentucky Colonels, where he spent five years and was a member of the 1975 championship team . . . Went to the vaunted Baltimore Claws before he was sold to Nuggets . . . Born Oct. 25, 1948, in Geneva, Ill.

Mahmoud Abdul-Rauf reigns as king of foul-shooters.

GREATEST PLAYER

Denver was the English countryside for years, ruled by a lanky forward who spent 11 seasons with the Nuggets, eight as an All-Star. Only once during that time did Alex English average less than 21 points a game.

By the time he left, English was No. 1 on the club list in games, points and assists. He had four of the five highest single-season scoring averages, topped by 29.8 in 1985-86. His imprint was as great as his play.

Honorable mention goes to Dan Issel, the current coach, who had a Hall of Fame career that included finishing No. 2 in games played and No. 1 in rebounding. Likewise to the thrilling David Thompson, who averaged 24.1 points in seven seasons with the Nuggets, and former ABA stars Ralph Simpson and Byron Beck.

ALL-TIME NUGGET LEADERS

SEASON

Points: Spencer Haywood, 2,519, 1969-70 (ABA)
        Alex English, 2,414, 1985-86
Assists: Michael Adams, 693, 1990-91
Rebounds: Spencer Haywood, 1,637, 1969-70 (ABA)
        Dikembe Mutombo, 1,070, 1992-93

GAME

Points: David Thompson, 73 vs. Detroit, 4/9/78
Assists: Larry Brown, 23 vs. Pittsburgh, 2/20/72 (ABA)
        Lafayette Lever, 23 vs. Golden State, 4/21/89
Rebounds: Spencer Haywood, 31 vs. Kentucky, 11/13/69 (ABA)
        Jerome Lane, 25 vs. Houston, 4/21/91

CAREER

Points: Alex English, 21,645, 1979-90
Assists: Alex English, 3,679, 1979-90
Rebounds: Dan Issel, 6,630, 1975-85

GOLDEN STATE WARRIORS

TEAM DIRECTORY: Owner: Jim Fitzgerald; Pres.: Daniel Finnane; GM/Coach: Don Nelson; VP/Asst. GM: Al Attles; Dir. Scouting: Ed Gregory; Asst. Coaches: Donn Nelson, Paul Pressey, Bob Lanier; Dir. Media Rel.: Julie Marvel. Arena: Oakland Coliseum (15,025). Colors: Gold and blue.

SCOUTING REPORT

SHOOTING: Simply the best. Even without their point guard. Even with their leading scorer going just .433. Still No. 1 in the league, at .492. Imagine what happens when they start to click.

And what of Latrell Sprewell dipping from the .464 of his rookie campaign to .433? Oh, yeah, can't you just sense the panic coming from the Bay Area over his struggles on offense? All he can do is shoot the three-pointer one minute (a respectable .364 last season) and beat his man off the dribble to throw down a 150-decibel dunk the next. The compensation, percentagewise, came with Chris Webber's .552, good for fourth in the league.

Webber provides the inside scoring threat, though Chris Gatling is improving from the post. Ricky Pierce's arrival from Seattle and the addition of second-round pick Dwayne Morton, who has shown three-point potential, adds to an already potent outside game led by Sprewell, Chris Mullin and Keith Jennings, who shot just .404 overall but tied Mullin for the second-most attempts from behind the stripe.

PLAYMAKING: The results were better last season than they probably had a right to expect without Tim Hardaway: a franchise record for assists, No. 3 in the league in that category, and in the middle of the pack in assist-to-turnover ratio. Credit goes to the signing of Avery Johnson (now back in San Antonio) and the play of psuedo-point guards Sprewell and Billy Owens. In fact, the Warriors flourished under what was tabbed Point Spree, to the extent that it will remain a regular option when they want to go big, even with Hardaway back this season. "It's not gimmicky, it's very solid," coach Don Nelson says. "It makes us better at the halfcourt, it makes us tougher, it makes us better rebounders, and those are the kind of things you need in the playoffs."

A healthy Hardaway is one of the best in the business. From

Chris Webber made the mark as Rookie of the Year.

there, the options are many. The Warriors can go with either Point Spree, the big lineup, or small with Jennings. All those possibilities together makes this one of Nelson's most comforting areas.

REBOUNDING: It could be better. Wait a minute. It was better. They went from last in the league by percentage in 1989-90 all the way to 12th by 1992-93, then added Webber, then dropped back down to a tie for 18th last season.

Webber is not to blame, because he averaged 9.1 boards a game and will get even better; Owens contributed 8.1. Maybe this

WARRIOR ROSTER

No.	Veterans	Pos.	Ht.	Wt.	Age	Yrs. Pro	College
52	Victor Alexander	C-F	6-10	265	25	3	Iowa State
U-35	Jud Buechler	G-F	6-6	220	26	4	Arizona
25	Chris Gatling	F-C	6-10	230	27	3	Old Dominion
11	Josh Grant	F	6-10	225	27	1	Utah
44	Jeff Grayer	G-F	6-5	215	28	6	Iowa State
10	Tim Hardaway	G	6-0	195	27	5	Texas-El Paso
2	Keith Jennings	G	5-7	160	25	2	E. Tennessee State
17	Chris Mullin	F	6-7	215	31	9	St. John's
30	Billy Owens	F-G	6-9	225	25	3	Syracuse
15	Latrell Sprewell	G	6-5	190	24	2	Alabama
4	Chris Webber	F-C	6-10	250	21	1	Michigan
22	Ricky Pierce	G	6-4	215	35	12	Rice

U-unrestricted free agent

Rd.	Rookies	Sel. No.	Pos.	Ht.	Wt.	College
1	Carlos Rogers	11	F	6-10	220	Tennessee State
1	Clifford Rozier	16	F	6-10	235	Louisville
2	Dwayne Morton	45	F	6-6	190	Louisville

is where Clifford Rozier, the first-round pick, comes in. If not him, somebody had better.

DEFENSE: This has never been a forte, but the improvement is significant, from holding the opposition to less than 100 points only 14 times two years ago to 25 last season. How important was it? The Warriors were 23-2 (.920) in those games. The impact of Webber finishing ninth in blocked shots, while just a rookie, is obvious.

In all, the Warriors allowed 106.1 points a game, their best showing in 15 years. In shooting-percentage-against, they were 14th.

OUTLOOK: Nelson has made no secret of the fact that he loves this team, or at least this team when it's healthy, no small matter the last two years. That thought may even have played into his mind as he reportedly listened to offers from other clubs, and it is easy to understand why. A backcourt that goes three deep with the likes of Hardaway, Sprewell and Pierce? Webber, Mullin, Owens and, possibly, Rozier up front? You'd stay, too.

WARRIOR PROFILES

LATRELL SPREWELL 24 6-5 190   Guard

Remember when people ripped the Warriors for taking another guard with the 24th pick in the '92 draft? We don't hear too many of those comments now . . . Didn't deserve the votes he got for Most Improved Player, because he showed plenty the season before as a rookie . . . He did, however, deserve the votes for first-team All-NBA . . . Known for defensive prowess coming out of Alabama, but his offensive game can be spectacular with drives to the basket and three-pointers . . . His 21 points per game last season was 11th in the league, the 2.20 steals ninth, and no guard had more blocks . . . He did everything but come out of the game—his 3,533 minutes (43.1 per) was the most in the NBA in 16 years . . . Natural shooting guard, but handled the ball well when the Warriors went big . . . A steal at $700,000 . . . Born Sept. 8, 1970, in Milwaukee.

Year	Team	G	FG	FG Pct.	FT	FT Pct.	Reb.	Ast.	TP	Avg.
1992-93	Golden State	77	449	.464	211	.746	271	295	1182	15.4
1993-94	Golden State	82	613	.433	353	.774	401	385	1720	21.0
	Totals	159	1062	.445	564	.763	672	680	2902	18.3

BILLY OWENS 25 6-9 225   Forward-Guard

Became more of a point forward last season . . . Even in the big lineup, when Latrell Sprewell is considered the point guard, Owens initiated the offense about 60 percent of the time . . . Had pretty good company in joining Charles Barkley, Scottie Pippen, Christian Laettner and David Robinson as the only players to average better than 15 points, eight rebounds and four assists . . . Admits he didn't always have the right attitude the first two seasons, to the point that he would go through the motions if things weren't going his way . . . Kings drafted former Syracuse star No. 3 overall in 1991, then sent him to Warriors for package highlighted by Mitch Richmond . . . Born May 1, 1969, in Carlisle, Pa . . . . Made $2.414 million.

Year	Team	G	FG	FG Pct.	FT	FT Pct.	Reb.	Ast.	TP	Avg.
1991-92	Golden State	80	468	.525	204	.654	639	188	1141	14.3
1992-93	Golden State	37	247	.501	117	.639	264	144	612	16.5
1993-94	Golden State	79	492	.507	199	.610	640	326	1186	15.0
	Totals	196	1207	.513	520	.633	1543	658	2939	15.0

CHRIS MULLIN 31 6-7 215   Forward

His kingdom for a healthy season... Missed the first 20 games of 1993-94 after missing the final 36 games from the year before. When he did return, the .472 from the field was his worst showing since .463 as a rookie... Big problems were torn ligaments in right hand... After two surgeries, he still couldn't put his thumb and pinky together, but could use right hand almost as effectively as before... The most encouraging sign was the finish—he averaged 19 points and shot .511 over the final 27 games, 25 of which were starts... In the starting lineup 39 times in all... May be destined to become Warriors' sixth man... Fourth-leading scorer in franchise history since being taken seventh in the 1985 draft, out of St. John's... Born July 30, 1963, in Brooklyn, N.Y....Made $2.844 million.

Year	Team	G	FG	FG Pct.	FT	FT Pct.	Reb.	Ast.	TP	Avg.
1985-86	Golden State	55	287	.463	189	.896	115	105	768	14.0
1986-87	Golden State	82	477	.514	269	.825	181	261	1242	15.1
1987-88	Golden State	60	470	.508	239	.885	205	290	1213	20.2
1988-89	Golden State	82	830	.509	493	.892	483	415	2176	26.5
1989-90	Golden State	78	682	.536	505	.889	463	319	1956	25.1
1990-91	Golden State	82	777	.536	513	.884	443	329	2107	25.7
1991-92	Golden State	81	830	.524	350	.833	450	286	2074	25.6
1992-93	Golden State	46	474	.510	183	.810	232	166	1191	25.9
1993-94	Golden State	62	410	.472	165	.753	345	315	1040	16.8
	Totals	628	5237	.513	2906	.862	2917	2486	13767	21.9

TIM HARDAWAY 28 6-0 195   Guard

Went from being named to Dream Team II to a nightmare... Suffered a torn anterior cruciate ligament in his left knee during an Oct. 21 scrimmage at training camp and missed the entire season... Then had to miss World Championships over the summer... Early-summer progress report was that his rehabilitation was going well and that he should be at full strength for the start of camp... Because quickness is such a crucial part of his game, the effects of the knee injury will be watched closely... We know this much: Before going down, he was one of the best two or three point guards in game... Pro career began with such a sense of durability after he was drafted in the first round out of UTEP in 1989, as he missed just four of his first 304 outings

. . . Since then, he has been sidelined 98 of a possible 106 games . . . Born Sept. 1, 1966, in Chicago . . . Made $3.343 million.

Year	Team	G	FG	FG Pct.	FT	FT Pct.	Reb.	Ast.	TP	Avg.
1989-90	Golden State	79	464	.471	211	.764	310	689	1162	14.7
1990-91	Golden State	82	739	.476	306	.803	332	793	1881	22.9
1991-92	Golden State	81	734	.461	298	.766	310	807	1893	23.4
1992-93	Golden State	66	522	.447	273	.744	263	699	1419	21.5
1993-94	Golden State					Injured				
	Totals	308	2459	.464	1088	.770	1215	2988	6 355	20.6

CHRIS WEBBER 21 6-10 250   Forward-Center

The No. 1 draft pick was also the No. 1 rookie . . . Even after missing most of training camp following an appendectomy, he became the first rookie in NBA history to total at least 1,000 points, 500 rebounds, 250 assists, 150 blocks and 75 steals . . . Only three other players have ever done it: Kareem Abdul-Jabbar, Hakeem Olajuwon and David Robinson . . . Finished fourth in the league in shooting and ninth in blocked shots (2.16 per game) . . . Not bad for being the youngest player in the game . . . Celebrated his 21st birthday by going for 26 points, 18 rebounds, six assists and four blocks against the Clippers . . . Magic took former Michigan star first in the draft, then sent him to Golden State for Anfernee Hardaway and three first-round picks . . . Born March 1, 1973, in Detroit . . . Made $1.6 million.

Year	Team	G	FG	FG Pct.	FT	FT Pct.	Reb.	Ast.	TP	Avg.
1993-94	Golden State	76	572	.552	189	.532	694	272	1333	17.5

VICTOR ALEXANDER 25 6-10 265   Center-Forward

Still seems to lack toughness and every-night effort . . . That hasn't changed much since rookie season . . . "It's up to him to be a butt-kicker when he's in there and prove to us that he belongs," coach Don Nelson says . . . Hits medium-range jumpers consistently, so can force big centers outside to guard him . . . Set career high in shooting percentage last season . . . But what's with the .527 from the line? That's dreadful under any circumstances, but especially since it marked such a dramatic drop from his career .688 coming in . . . Born Aug. 31, 1969, in Detroit, and his 1993-94 best of 19 points came in front of hometown fans . . . Warriors took Iowa State standout with the 17th pick in 1991 . . . Made $1.16 million.

Year	Team	G	FG	FG Pct.	FT	FT Pct.	Reb.	Ast.	TP	Avg.
1991-92	Golden State	80	243	.529	103	.691	336	32	589	7.4
1992-93	Golden State	72	344	.516	111	.685	420	93	809	11.2
1993-94	Golden State	69	266	.530	68	.527	308	66	602	8.7
	Totals	221	853	.524	282	.641	1064	191	2000	9.0

JUD BUECHLER 26 6-6 220   Guard-Forward

Pizza delivery man . . . Got most of his time, what little there was, in closing moments of blowouts. Warriors needed to get to 120 points and win so fans would get a free pizza . . . Good practice player and good guy . . . Last on the team in average minutes (6.1) . . . Solid on fundamentals . . . Originally a second-round pick of Seattle in 1990, but never played for Super Sonics . . . Was with Nets and Spurs before Golden State picked him up as a free agent in December of 1991 . . . Member of the same Arizona teams that included the likes of Sean Elliott, Sean Rooks and Brian Williams . . . Born June 19, 1968, in San Diego . . . Made $375,000.

Year	Team	G	FG	FG Pct.	FT	FT Pct.	Reb.	Ast.	TP	Avg.
1990-91	New Jersey	74	94	.416	43	.652	141	51	232	3.1
1991-92	N.J.-S.A.-G.S. . . .	28	29	.408	12	.571	52	23	70	2.5
1992-93	Golden State	70	176	.437	65	.747	195	94	437	6.2
1993-94	Golden State	36	42	.500	10	.500	32	16	106	2.9
	Totals	208	341	.435	130	.670	420	184	845	4.1

RICKY PIERCE 35 6-4 215   Guard

Warriors acquired him, rookie Carlos Rogers and two 1995 second-round draft picks from Sonics for Sarunas Marciulionis and Byron Houston . . . His 51 appearances were his fewest since 1987-88 . . . Biggest problem was bone spurs, which eventually needed surgery March 18 and earned him a long stay on the injured list . . . Led Sonics in scoring first two full seasons after coming from Milwaukee in exchange for Dale Ellis before big dropoff last year . . . Great from the free-throw line and pretty good from the three-point line . . . As a matter of fact, one of the best ever on free throws . . . Sixth Man of the Year in 1987 and '90 while a Buck . . . Played at Rice under Mike Schuler and went to the NBA when Detroit made him the No. 18 pick in 1982 . . . Born Aug. 19, 1959, in Dallas . . . Made $2.1 million.

Year	Team	G	FG	FG Pct.	FT	FT Pct.	Reb.	Ast.	TP	Avg.
1982-83	Detroit	39	33	.375	18	.563	35	14	85	2.2
1983-84	San Diego	69	268	.470	149	.861	135	60	685	9.9
1984-85	Milwaukee	44	165	.537	102	.823	117	94	433	9.8
1985-86	Milwaukee	81	429	.538	266	.858	231	177	1127	13.9
1986-87	Milwaukee	79	575	.534	387	.880	266	144	1540	19.5
1987-88	Milwaukee	37	248	.510	107	.877	83	73	606	16.4
1988-89	Milwaukee	75	527	.518	255	.859	197	156	1317	17.6
1989-90	Milwaukee	59	503	.510	307	.839	167	133	1359	23.0
1990-91	Mil.-Sea.	78	561	.485	430	.913	191	168	1598	20.5
1991-92	Seattle	78	620	.475	417	.916	233	241	1690	21.7
1992-93	Seattle	77	524	.489	313	.889	192	220	1403	18.2
1993-94	Seattle	51	272	.471	189	.896	83	91	739	14.5
	Totals	767	4725	.500	2940	.877	1930	1571	12582	16.4

JEFF GRAYER 28 6-5 215   Guard-Forward

Never has lived up to expectations after Milwaukee picked him No. 13 overall in 1988 . . . The upside: He has proved to be durable after major knee injury during rookie season . . . Slow start to 1993-94 culminated with a .526 from the field, easily a career best . . . Has improved shooting percentage three straight years . . . The ability to play two positions is an asset, especially in Don Nelson's system . . . Member of 1988 Olympic team . . . Helped recruit fellow Warrior Victor Alexander to Iowa State . . . Attended high school with Glen Rice and NFL star Andre Rison . . . Warriors signed him as a free agent . . . Born Dec. 17, 1965, in Flint, Mich . . . . Made $715,000.

Year	Team	G	FG	FG Pct.	FT	FT Pct.	Reb.	Ast.	TP	Avg.
1988-89	Milwaukee	11	32	.438	17	.850	35	22	81	7.4
1989-90	Milwaukee	71	224	.460	99	.651	217	107	548	7.7
1990-91	Milwaukee	82	210	.433	101	.687	246	123	521	6.4
1991-92	Milwaukee	82	309	.448	102	.667	257	150	739	9.0
1992-93	Golden State	48	165	.467	91	.669	157	70	423	8.8
1993-94	Golden State	67	191	.526	71	.602	191	62	455	6.8
	Totals	361	1131	.462	481	.663	1103	534	2767	7.7

CHRIS GATLING 27 6-10 230   Forward-Center

Only caused Don Nelson to lose hair occasionally last season, which is a big improvement . . . Also made strides with his low-post offense and conditioning . . . Displaced Victor Alexander as the starting center in early March . . . Posted a career high in shooting and finished by going .617 the final 48 games . . . Led the Warriors in scoring and rebounding productivity—i.e., the numbers of points and boards per minute . . . Spent first two seasons alternating between blunders and energetic play . . . That's why they call him "Energizer." . . . Has trouble with bigger, wide-body centers . . . No. 16 pick in 1991 draft after playing at Old Dominion . . . Born Sept. 3, 1967, in Elizabeth City, N. C . . . .Made $1.12 million.

Year	Team	G	FG	FG Pct.	FT	FT Pct.	Reb.	Ast.	TP	Avg.
1991-92	Golden State	54	117	.568	72	.661	182	16	306	5.7
1992-93	Golden State	70	249	.539	150	.725	320	40	648	9.3
1993-94	Golden State	82	271	.588	129	.620	397	41	671	8.2
	Totals	206	637	.564	351	.670	899	97	1625	7.9

KEITH JENNINGS 25 5-7 160   Guard

Another munchkin makes an impact . . . Good range on shot; led Warriors in three-point shooting (.371) . . . Also No. 1 on the team in assist-to-turnover ratio (2.9-to-1) . . . Had injury-free season after missing 74 games in 1992-93 with torn knee ligament . . . Started twice . . . Often referred to by nickname "Mister" . . . Shortest player in franchise history . . . Southern Conference Player of the Year while at East Tennessee State. Also won the Francis Pomeroy Award as the best college player under 6 feet, but was not drafted . . . Warriors signed him as a free agent . . . Born Nov. 21, 1968, in Culpepper, Va . . . .Made $250,000.

Year	Team	G	FG	FG Pct.	FT	FT Pct.	Reb.	Ast.	TP	Avg.
1992-93	Golden State	8	25	.595	14	.778	11	23	69	8.6
1993-94	Golden State	76	138	.404	100	.833	89	218	432	5.7
	Totals	84	163	.424	114	.826	100	241	501	6.0

JOSH GRANT 27 6-10 225   Forward

The measuring stick may say he is one of the Warriors' big men, but his game says otherwise . . . Not a power player, but a shooter who happens to be tall . . . Averaged only 7.2 minutes and played more than 10 minutes 17 times . . . Twice named Western Conference Player of the Year, a feat all the more impressive considering there was a one-year interruption because of a knee injury . . . Also spent three years on a church mission in England, so he didn't enter the NBA until he was 26 . . . No. 43 pick by Denver, out of Utah, and traded to Warriors for Darnell Mee . . . Born Aug. 7, 1967, in Salt Lake City . . . Made $150,000.

Year	Team	G	FG	FG Pct.	FT	FT Pct.	Reb.	Ast.	TP	Avg.
1993-94	Golden State	53	59	.404	22	.759	89	24	157	3.0

THE ROOKIES

CARLOS ROGERS 23 6-10 220   Forward

Tennessee State product was drafted 11th by SuperSonics, but landed at Golden State with Ricky Pierce in trade that sent Sarunas Marciulionis and Byron Houston to Sonics . . . Runs the floor well and is aggressive on the boards . . . Needs to add about 15 or 20 pounds . . . Two-time Ohio Valley Conference Player of the Year . . . Only player in the country to rank in the top 15 in Division I last season in scoring, rebounding, shooting and blocked shots . . . Born Feb. 6, 1971, in Detroit.

CLIFFORD ROZIER 22 6-10 235   Forward

Probable lottery pick on talent, but he fell to No. 16 because most teams questioned his work ethic and approach . . . Began college career at North Carolina, then transferred to Louisville, where he was an All-American as a junior before coming out early . . . "He's got incredible power," Bucks scout Kim Hughes said. "He gets any post position he wants." . . . Now he has to get some post-up moves to go with that . . . Two-time Metro Conference Player of the Year was born Oct. 31, 1972, in Bradenton, Fla.

DWAYNE MORTON 23 6-6 190   **Forward**

Don Nelson adds a shooter and another Cardinal . . . Percentage declined from .578 to .531 to .480 during Louisville career, but former Mr. Basketball in Kentucky left as school's all-time leader in three-point percentage (.461) . . . Born Aug. 8, 1971, in Louisville and stayed in his hometown to play for the Cardinals . . . Went 45th, not long after Warriors took Louisville teammate Clifford Rozier in the first round.

COACH DON NELSON: Few coaches have had such a successful season and spent as much time defending  themselves . . . Without all-star Tim Hardaway and Sarunas Marciulionis, he went from 48 losses to 50 wins . . . One of those was his 800th career victory . . . That is a testament to his success as much as longevity—only Red Auerbach got there faster . . . Said he may look back on last season and remember it as the best he's had in 17 years in coaching . . . On the other hand, he faced heat after perceived squabbles with Chris Webber went public . . . Then Houston's Mario Elie, a former Warrior, blasted him for mistreating some players . . . "All of the sudden I can't coach and I'm going to get fired, but the only thing I've done is reprimand a couple young players who questioned my authority," Nelson said. "What's going on around here? Can you tell me, because I'm confused." . . . Somebody must like him, though. He was selected to coach Dream Team II at the World Championships . . . Bottom line: If he ever leaves the Warriors or is asked to leave, the Bay Bridge would overflow with people lining up to hire him . . . Being Coach of the Year three times (1983, '85, '92) with Golden State and Milwaukee tends to do that . . . Doubles as Warrior general manager . . . Won five NBA championships as a player after being a two-time All-American at Iowa . . . Chicago Zephyrs drafted him 19th in 1962, then sold him to the Lakers. Waived about two years later and signed by the Celtics for the bulk of his career . . . Born May 15, 1949, in Muskegon, Mich.

GREATEST PLAYER

The greatest player in Warriors' history isn't even among the top 10 in games played, and that is the only way not to vote for him: lack of longevity with the organization.

On the other hand, that makes Wilt Chamberlain's other rankings so much more impressive: No. 1 in career points; No. 1 in career scoring average, the 41.5 so daunting next to the 25.6 of second-place Rick Barry; No. 2 in rebounds; No. 1 in field goals made and No. 2 in attempted. He's also No. 1 with 333 consecutive games played, No. 1 with 26 trips to the 30-30 club, a mere 24 more than anyone else. And, of course, No. 1 here, there and everywhere with 100 points in a game, set in the spring of 1962 while a Philadelphia Warrior.

Barry was great. Nate Thurmond was a presence in the middle while playing more games than anyone. But Wilt was Wilt.

ALL-TIME WARRIOR LEADERS

SEASON

Points: Wilt Chamberlain, 4,029, 1961-62
Assists: Eric Floyd, 848, 1986-87
Rebounds: Wilt Chamberlain, 2,149, 1960-61

GAME

Points: Wilt Chamberlain, 100 vs. New York, 3/2/62
Assists: Guy Rodgers, 28 vs. St. Louis, 3/14/63
Rebounds: Wilt Chamberlain, 55 vs. Boston, 11/24/60

CAREER

Points: Wilt Chamberlain, 17,783, 1959-65
Assists: Guy Rodgers, 4,845, 1958-70
Rebounds: Nate Thurmond, 12,771, 1963-74

HOUSTON ROCKETS

TEAM DIRECTORY: Owner: Les Alexander; VP-Basketball Oper.: Bob Weinhauer; VP: Bus. Oper.: John Thomas; Dir. Media Inf.: TBA; Coach: Rudy Tomjanovich; Asst. Coaches: Carroll Dawson, Bill Berry, Larry Smith. Arena: The Summit (16,279). Colors: Red and gold.

SCOUTING REPORT

SHOOTING: Bombs away. The champion Rockets not only took the most-three-pointers in the league, 148 more than second-place Orlando, but so many that it constituted 19 percent of their shots while setting an NBA record for makes and attempts from behind the arc. By comparison, it was 16.5 percent for the Magic and 14.7 percent for third-place Phoenix. The problem is, Houston was strictly middle-of-the-pack with a .334 success rate, meaning they need to cut back some of the launches in NASA's neighborhood. As if that's an original thought.

To what extent it hurts them is open for debate. Hakeem Olajuwon still took more shots than anyone in the NBA (1,694) and finished 10th in percentage, at .528, with an arsenal of jump hooks, fallaways, spin moves and perimeter shots as far as 16 to 18 feet out. Combine that with Otis Thorpe going .561, good for third, and the Rockets were able to recover for a respectable .475 as a team.

PLAYMAKING: All eyes will be on coach Rudy Tomjanovich to see if he sticks with Kenny Smith as the starting point guard and continues to use Sam Cassell as the closer out of the bullpen or if he makes the switch and gives the majority of the minutes to Cassell. Either way, with Vernon Maxwell, the Rockets will have a three-guard rotation that reminds people of the Maxwell-Smith-Sleepy Floyd troika from a few years back. "All three guys are quick and can play either guard spot," Maxwell says. "We're sort of interchangeable out there, which provides us a lot of options."

So does having someone like Olajuwon, who has become so adept at passing out of the double-team from the post, usually to hit an open guard on the perimeter. Imagine how many shots he could have had if he got selfish with even a portion of those 287 assists. But he has become a much better player since being convinced a few years back that making the extra pass would be more important to the team than individual scoring statistics.

FG proficiency (third in NBA) goes with Otis Thorpe.

REBOUNDING: Two players get it done because two players have to get it done. Without any depth on the front line, something

ROCKET ROSTER

No.	Veterans	Pos.	Ht.	Wt.	Age	Yrs. Pro	College
1	Scott Brooks	G	5-10	165	29	6	Cal-Irvine
50	Matt Bullard	F	6-10	235	27	4	Iowa
10	Sam Cassell	G	6-3	195	24	1	Florida State
35	Earl Cureton	C	6-9	215	36	11	Detroit
17	Mario Elie	G	6-5	210	30	4	American Int'l.
7	Carl Herrera	F	6-9	225	27	3	Houston
25	Robert Horry	F	6-10	220	24	2	Alabama
21	Chris Jent	F	6-7	220	24	1	Ohio State
11	Vernon Maxwell	G	6-4	190	29	6	Florida
34	Hakeem Olajuwon	C	7-0	255	31	10	Houston
3	Richard Petruska	C	6-10	260	25	1	UCLA
42	Eric Riley	C	7-0	245	24	1	Michigan
–	Larry Robinson	G-F	6-5	180	26	4	Centenary
30	Kenny Smith	G	6-3	170	29	7	North Carolina
33	Otis Thorpe	F	6-10	246	32	10	Providence

Rd.	Rookies	Sel. No.	Pos.	Ht.	Wt.	College
2	Albert Burditt	53	F	6-7	230	Texas

they were hoping to address in the summer with a free-agent signing or trade, the Rockets could only ride the shoulders of Olajuwon (11.9) and Thorpe (10.6) so far. They finished 20th in the league in percentage. So much for that famous Pat Riley slogan, "No rebounds, no rings."

DEFENSE: Even with Olajuwon, the Defensive Player of the Year, they played second fiddle in this area in the NBA Finals, where most of the attention went to the Knicks and their physical style. The Rockets shouldn't have been bothered. Their peers around the league know all about the unit that just set a franchise record for the fewest points allowed in a season and allowed the opposition to shoot just .440, the third-best figure in the league.

OUTLOOK: Very good, unless you are trying to sell tickets or were hired before new owner Les Alexander arrived. For those people, hope for the best while working in a town that hasn't supported the Rockets like a title team and working for a boss who has made more turnovers in the front office than players did on the court. Those players are on much more envious ground, the defending champions with the No. 1 talent in the world. Very good, indeed.

ROCKET PROFILES

HAKEEM OLAJUWON 31 7-0 255   Center

MVP! MVP! MVP!... They chanted it at the Summit, and they were right... Defensive Player of the Year, too... Finished second in blocks, third in scoring, fourth in rebounding and 10th in shooting. It's the fourth time he has finished in the top 10 in four different categories ... Capped it all off by being named Finals MVP in a unanimous vote... Needs six offensive rebounds to pass Moses Malone for the franchise record and 51 points to break Calvin Murphy's scoring mark... Has averaged at least 11 rebounds in each of first 10 seasons. Only Wilt Chamberlain (14), Bill Russell (13), Elvin Hayes (12) and Bob Pettit (11) had better starts... No. 3 all-time in blocked shots behind only Mark Eaton and Kareem Abdul-Jabbar... Nine-time All-Star has been in the Western Conference starting lineup five times... Great agility for his size, with spin moves and fallaways that make him almost impossible to defend one-on-one... A Bayou City lifer since coming to the U.S. from native Nigeria, having attended Houston before the Rockets made him No. 1 pick in 1984... Born Jan. 21, 1963, in Lagos, Nigeria... Made $3.17 million.

Year	Team	G	FG	FG Pct.	FT	FT Pct.	Reb.	Ast.	TP	Avg.
1984-85	Houston	82	677	.538	338	.613	974	111	1692	20.6
1985-86	Houston	68	625	.526	347	.645	781	137	1597	23.5
1986-87	Houston	75	677	.508	400	.702	858	220	1755	23.4
1987-88	Houston	79	712	.514	381	.695	959	163	1805	22.8
1988-89	Houston	82	790	.508	454	.696	1105	149	2034	24.8
1989-90	Houston	82	806	.501	382	.713	1149	234	1995	24.3
1990-91	Houston	56	487	.508	213	.769	770	131	1187	21.2
1991-92	Houston	70	591	.502	328	.766	845	157	1510	21.6
1992-93	Houston	82	848	.529	444	.779	1068	291	2140	26.1
1993-94	Houston	80	894	.528	388	.716	955	287	2184	27.3
	Totals	756	7107	.516	3675	.705	9464	1880	17899	23.7

OTIS THORPE 32 6-10 246   Forward

Between the MVP showing of Hakeem Olajuwon and the second-half improvement of Robert Horry, he became something of the forgotten member of the Rocket frontcourt... Opponents would never make that mistake... Doesn't have any range on his shot, including the ones from behind that line about 15 feet out when defenders are not allowed to try and stop him . . . But is great runner for a power forward, someone who can get out on the wing and finish on the break . . . Has strength at the same time, enough to finish 15th in the league in rebounding last season with a career-best 10.6 a game . . . No. 3 in shooting and has ranked among the top five in each of the last three seasons . . . Eighth-best all-time in that category . . . Back to playing all 82 games after bruised kidney at the start of 1992-93 broke his streak of 542 consecutive appearances . . . First-round pick by Kansas City Kings in 1984 out of Providence . . . Rockets stole him from Sacramento for Rodney McCray and Jim Petersen in 1988 . . . Born Aug. 5, 1962, in Boynton Beach, Fla. . . . Made $2.428 million.

Year	Team	G	FG	FG Pct.	FT	FT Pct.	Reb.	Ast.	TP	Avg.
1984-85	Kansas City	82	411	.600	230	.620	556	111	1052	12.8
1985-86	Sacramento	75	289	.587	164	.661	420	84	742	9.9
1986-87	Sacramento	82	567	.540	413	.761	819	201	1547	18.9
1987-88	Sacramento	82	622	.507	460	.755	837	266	1704	20.8
1988-89	Houston	82	521	.542	328	.729	787	202	1370	16.7
1989-90	Houston	82	547	.548	307	.688	734	261	1401	17.1
1990-91	Houston	82	549	.556	334	.696	846	197	1435	17.5
1991-92	Houston	82	558	.592	304	.657	862	250	1420	17.3
1992-93	Houston	72	385	.558	153	.598	589	181	923	12.8
1993-94	Houston	82	449	.561	251	.657	870	189	1149	14.0
	Totals	803	4898	.554	2944	.693	7320	1942	12743	15.9

VERNON MAXWELL 29 6-4 190   Guard

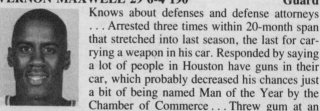

Knows about defenses and defense attorneys . . . Arrested three times within 20-month span that stretched into last season, the last for carrying a weapon in his car. Responded by saying a lot of people in Houston have guns in their car, which probably decreased his chances just a bit of being named Man of the Year by the Chamber of Commerce . . . Threw gum at an official after being ejected and then threw a cup of ice on the court . . . Everyone knows about his shooting, but he probably doesn't get enough credit for defense . . . Led Rockets in assists and steals in 1993-94 . . . Took nearly twice as many three-pointers as any Rocket, but his .298 success rate was only fourth among starters . . . Needs 16 more to pass Larry Bird for ninth on the all-time NBA list . . . Had four three-pointers in one quarter of Game 5 of the Western Conference finals against Utah . . . His biggest shot ever was a three-pointer that sealed the Game 7 win over New York for the title . . . Born Sept. 9, 1965, in Gainesville, Fla., and stayed close to attend Florida . . . Denver picked him in the second round in 1988 and rights were traded to San Antonio . . . Rockets paid cash to get him from Spurs in 1990 . . . Made $1.544 million.

Year	Team	G	FG	FG Pct.	FT	FT Pct.	Reb.	Ast.	TP	Avg.
1988-89	San Antonio	79	357	.432	181	.745	202	301	927	11.7
1989-90	S.A.-Hou.	79	275	.439	136	.645	228	296	714	9.0
1990-91	Houston	82	504	.404	217	.733	238	303	1397	17.0
1991-92	Houston	80	502	.413	206	.772	243	326	1372	17.2
1992-93	Houston	71	349	.407	164	.719	221	297	982	13.8
1993-94	Houston	75	380	.389	143	.749	229	380	1023	13.6
	Totals	466	2367	.412	1047	.729	1361	1903	6415	13.8

ROBERT HORRY 24 6-10 220   Forward

He's a Piston. He's a King. He's a Knick . . . Nope, still a Rocket . . . Rumors abounded last season . . . Actually was dealt with Matt Bullard to Detroit, only to be sent back after Sean Elliott failed his physical in Houston . . . May have been the best trade the Rockets never made . . . "He made us look pretty dumb . . . which is good," Rudy Tomjanovich said . . . The near-move served as his wake-up call . . . Became more aggressive on offense, the big knock on him before . . . Blossomed in time for the playoffs . . . Probably the best open-court player on the team . . . A 6-10 small forward makes him enough of a rarity, but to be a small forward who can also be a shot-blocker makes him even more unique . . . Rocket fans booed when he was picked 11th in 1992, even after he was named All-Southeastern Conference as a senior at Alabama . . . Born Aug. 25, 1970, in Andalusia, Ala. . . . Made $1.2 million.

Year	Team	G	FG	FG Pct.	FT	FT Pct.	Reb.	Ast.	TP	Avg.
1992-93	Houston	79	323	.474	143	.715	392	191	801	10.1
1993-94	Houston	81	322	.459	115	.732	440	231	803	9.9
	Totals	160	645	.466	258	.723	832	422	1604	10.0

KENNY SMITH 29 6-3 170   Guard

He isn't a true point guard and by the NBA Finals he was barely the starting point guard . . . Was in the opening lineup all seven games of the championship series, but got just 12 minutes more than backup Sam Cassell . . . Second on the team in assists to Vernon Maxwell during the regular season, but seventh in the league in three-point shooting . . . Also 10th best from the line . . . Joins Larry Bird and Jeff Hornacek as the only players in NBA history to finish in the top 10 in three-point and free-throw percentage three straight years . . . North Carolina product was originally the No. 6 pick in the 1987 draft by Sacramento and came to Rockets with Roy Marble for John Lucas and Tim McCormick . . . Born March 8, 1965, in Queens, N.Y. . . . Made $2.283 million.

Year	Team	G	FG	FG Pct.	FT	FT Pct.	Reb.	Ast.	TP	Avg.
1987-88	Sacramento.	61	331	.477	167	.819	138	434	841	13.8
1988-89	Sacramento.	81	547	.462	263	.737	226	621	1403	17.3
1989-90	Sac.-Atl.	79	378	.466	161	.821	157	445	943	11.9
1990-91	Houston	78	522	.520	287	.844	163	554	1380	17.7
1991-92	Houston	81	432	.475	219	.866	177	562	1137	14.0
1992-93	Houston	82	387	.520	195	.878	160	446	1065	13.0
1993-94	Houston	78	341	.480	135	.871	138	327	906	11.6
	Totals	540	2938	.485	1427	.826	1159	3389	7675	14.2

MARIO ELIE 30 6-5 210   Guard

One of the Rockets' most significant moves last year was easy to ignore at first: Elie from Portland for a second-round draft pick on Aug. 2 . . . But when he became the sixth man, someone who would average 24 minutes while playing two positions, no one could deny his eventual impact . . . Rejuvenated outside success gave the Rockets another three-point threat . . . Spent time at shooting guard and small forward . . . Had an option to become an unrestricted free agent in the summer. Must feel good about his chances on the open market—he turned down a four-year contract for about $6 million . . . One way or another is probably looking at nice raise after making $790,000 in 1993-94 . . . Attended high school for a year with Chris Mullin before going on to American International . . . Milwaukee made him a seventh-round pick from there . . . Born Nov. 26, 1963, in New York City.

Year	Team	G	FG	FG Pct.	FT	FT Pct.	Reb.	Ast.	TP	Avg.
1990-91	Phil.-G.S.	33	79	.497	75	.843	110	45	237	7.2
1991-92	Golden State	79	221	.521	155	.852	227	174	620	7.8
1992-93	Portland	82	240	.458	183	.855	216	177	708	8.6
1993-94	Houston	67	208	.446	154	.860	181	208	626	9.3
	Totals	261	748	.476	567	.854	734	604	2191	8.4

SAM CASSELL 24 6-3 195   Guard

Made nice progress in rookie season . . . By the end, he was getting the fourth-quarter minutes that once belonged to Scott Brooks . . . Rudy Tomjanovich even toyed with the idea at one stage of starting No. 24 over incumbent Kenny Smith at point guard . . . Had some big moments in the playoffs when he had 22 points and seven assists to help the Rockets win Game 7 of the Western Conference finals and when he scored the final seven points of Game 3 of the championship series to get Houston a victory . . . Words like ''fearless'' and ''gutsy'' seemed to come up a lot . . . Played in the rookie All-Star Game . . . Born Nov. 18, 1969, in Baltimore, another product from Dunbar High in that town . . . Went to Florida State and played in the same backcourt with Heisman Trophy winner Charlie Ward . . . Made $650,000.

Year	Team	G	FG	FG Pct.	FT	FT Pct.	Reb.	Ast.	TP	Avg.
1993-94	Houston	66	162	.418	90	.841	134	192	440	6.7

CARL HERRERA 27 6-9 225   Forward

Rockets' top inside reserve . . . Came up big during the Finals . . . He was the latest draft pick, but turned out to be the best player in the 1990 trade that sent him and Dave Jamerson to Houston in exchange for Alec Kessler . . . That was after Miami had picked him 10th . . . Started pro career in Spain after leaving the University of Houston, but got out of contract early to return to the U.S. to play for the Rockets in 1991 . . . First Venezuelan to play in the NBA and member of that country's 1992 Olympic team . . . Named among the top 100 most influential Hispanics in the United States by *Hispanic Business Magazine* . . . Not much of a scorer, but chooses shots wisely enough rank to No. 7 on the all-time franchise list for percentage . . . Born Dec. 14, 1966, in Trinidad . . . Made $1.1 million.

Year	Team	G	FG	FG Pct.	FT	FT Pct.	Reb.	Ast.	TP	Avg.
1991-92	Houston	43	83	.516	25	.568	99	27	191	4.4
1992-93	Houston	81	240	.541	125	.710	454	61	605	7.5
1993-94	Houston	75	142	.458	69	.711	285	37	353	4.7
	Totals	199	465	.508	219	.691	838	125	1149	5.8

SCOTT BROOKS 29 5-11 165   Guard

He was finishing last season when everyone else was just getting started . . . Opened in on-going role as Kenny Smith's fourth-quarter replacement at point guard, playing the entire final period 24 times with Rockets going 19-5 . . . Then Sam Cassell emerged in the second half and in time for the playoffs and Brooks fell out of the rotation . . . Barely played in the postseason . . . Still established career best for field-goal percentage . . . No. 2 on Rockets' all-time list for three-point percentage (.400) . . . Houston is 38-8 over two seasons when he plays the entire fourth quarter . . . Played at Texas Christian and then Cal-Irvine, but was not drafted . . . 76ers signed him as a free agent and he was befriended by Charles Barkley . . . Rockets got him from Minnesota in 1992 for a future second-round pick . . . Born July 31, 1965, in French Camp, Cal. . . . Made $525,000.

Year	Team	G	FG	FG Pct.	FT	FT Pct.	Reb.	Ast.	TP	Avg.
1988-89	Philadelphia	82	156	.420	61	.884	94	306	428	5.2
1989-90	Philadelphia	72	119	.431	50	.877	64	207	319	4.4
1990-91	Minnesota.	80	159	.430	61	.847	72	204	424	5.3
1991-92	Minnesota.	82	167	.447	51	.810	99	205	417	5.1
1992-93	Houston	82	183	.475	112	.830	99	243	519	6.3
1993-94	Houston	73	142	.491	74	.871	102	149	381	5.2
	Totals	471	926	.448	409	.850	530	1314	2488	5.3

ERIC RILEY 24 7-0 245   Center

Break glass in case of emergency . . . Played behind Hakeem Olajuwon . . . A few time zones behind . . . Rockets would usually go to a small lineup when Olajuwon went out, so Michigan product averaged just 4.7 minutes in 47 appearances . . . In the opening lineup twice, becoming team's first rookie starting center since Olajuwon in 1984-85 . . . Not on the playoff roster . . . Second-round pick by Dallas in 1993, then traded to Houston for Popeye Jones . . . Attended high school in Cleveland with future Heisman Trophy winner Desmond Howard . . . Born June 2, 1970, in Cleveland . . . Made $225,000.

Year	Team	G	FG	FG Pct.	FT	FT Pct.	Reb.	Ast.	TP	Avg.
1993-94	Houston	47	34	.486	20	.541	59	9	88	1.9

MATT BULLARD 27 6-10 235   Forward

Every guy who doesn't get drafted should hope to find his stability... Spent each of his first four pro seasons with the Rockets, who paid him $650,000 in 1993-94... Playing time was cut in half, so he didn't get nearly the three-point chances, but the .325 from behind the arc was still a worthwhile contribution while making three or more in a game seven times... He is No. 3 in franchise history at .362... His 91 three-pointers in 1992-93 broke Rick Barry's Rocket record for forwards... Part of the Robert Horry-Sean Elliott trade that got rescinded... Started college career at Colorado, then transferred to Iowa, where a knee injury before senior season scared off the pros... Born June 5, 1967, in West Des Moines, Iowa.

Year	Team	G	FG	FG Pct.	FT	FT Pct.	Reb.	Ast.	TP	Avg.
1990-91	Houston	18	14	.452	11	.647	14	2	39	2.2
1991-92	Houston	80	205	.459	38	.760	223	75	512	6.4
1992-93	Houston	79	213	.431	58	.784	222	110	575	7.3
1993-94	Houston	65	78	.345	20	.769	84	64	226	3.5
	Totals	242	510	.426	127	.760	543	251	1352	5.6

RICHARD PETRUSKA 25 6-10 260   Center

Sort of a practice player for the practice players... No Rocket averaged fewer than his 4.2 minutes a game... Got 35 of his minutes in two games the final week of the regular season, 57 minutes the other 20 appearances... Look at it as part of his postgraduate work after playing just two seasons in the United States, one at Loyola Marymount and the next at UCLA... Rockets liked enough of what they saw to take him with the 46th pick in 1993... Pac-10 Conference Newcomer of the Year as a senior... Played for Czechoslovakian National team in 1987 and '88... Born Jan. 25, 1969, in Levice, Slovakia... Made $150,000.

Year	Team	G	FG	FG Pct.	FT	FT Pct.	Reb.	Ast.	TP	Avg.
1993-94	Houston	22	20	.435	6	.750	31	1	53	2.4

CHRIS JENT 24 6-7 220   Forward

This is what's known as falling into a good situation... Was with Columbus of the CBA when Rockets called with a few weeks left in the regular season... Stop in Rapid City is also on resume... Aggressive play and ability to hit three-point shot won him a spot on the playoff roster from there... Reached double-digits in scoring in two of his three regular-season appearances and hit three three-pointers in one of the outings... Teammate of Jim Jackson at Ohio State, but was not drafted... All-Rookie in the CBA in 1992-93... Born Jan. 11, 1970, in Orange, Cal.

Year	Team	G	FG	FG Pct.	FT	FT Pct.	Reb.	Ast.	TP	Avg.
1993-94	Houston	3	13	.500	1	.500	15	7	31	10.3

EARL CURETON 36 6-9 215   Center

No one else can say they were teammates with Julius Erving, Magic Johnson, Isiah Thomas, Michael Jordan and Hakeem Olajuwon... Hadn't been in the NBA since Charlotte in 1991 when the Rockets signed him April 21, just in time to play two games and get a few minutes in the playoffs... Then got a second ring, the first coming as a 76er... Opened 1993-94 with CBA's Sioux City and Magic Johnson's touring all-star team... Spent the previous two seasons in France, Venezuela and Mexico... Went to Robert Morris, then the University of Detroit. Philadelphia took him in the third round from there... Born Sept. 3, 1957, in Detroit.

Year	Team	G	FG	FG Pct.	FT	FT Pct.	Reb.	Ast.	TP	Avg.
1980-81	Philadelphia	52	93	.454	33	.516	155	25	219	4.2
1981-82	Philadelphia	66	149	.487	51	.543	270	32	349	5.3
1982-83	Philadelphia	73	108	.419	33	.493	269	43	249	3.4
1983-84	Detroit	73	81	.458	31	.525	287	36	193	2.6
1984-85	Detroit	81	207	.484	82	.569	419	83	496	6.1
1985-86	Detroit	80	285	.505	117	.555	504	137	687	8.6
1986-87	Chi.-LAC	78	243	.476	82	.539	452	122	568	7.3
1987-88	L.A. Clippers	69	133	.429	33	.524	271	63	299	4.3
1988-89	Charlotte	82	233	.501	66	.537	488	130	532	6.5
1990-91	Charlotte	9	8	.333	1	.333	36	3	17	1.9
1993-94	Houston	2	2	.250	0	.000	12	0	4	2.0
	Totals	665	1542	.474	529	.539	3163	674	3613	5.4

LARRY ROBINSON 26 6-5 180   Guard-Forward

Second cousin of Robert Parish was only slightly related last season to the Rockets, too . . . Signed a pair of 10-day contracts and then for the rest of the season April 21, just in time to play 55 minutes in his six appearances . . . Not on the playoff roster . . . Spent most of 1993-94 with Yakima and Rapid City in the CBA, finishing fourth in that league in steals . . . Best known for his two stints with the Bullets after going undrafted out of Centenary . . . Has also played in France . . . Born Jan. 11, 1968, in Bossier City, La.

Year	Team	G	FG	FG Pct.	FT	FT Pct.	Reb.	Ast.	TP	Avg.
1990-91	Wash.-G.S.	36	62	.413	15	.556	51	35	139	3.9
1991-92	Boston	1	1	.200	0	.000	2	1	2	2.0
1992-93	Washington	4	6	.375	3	.600	3	3	15	3.8
1993-94	Houston	6	10	.500	3	.375	10	6	25	4.2
	Totals	47	79	.414	21	.525	66	45	181	3.9

THE ROOKIE

ALBERT BURDITT 22 6-7 230   Forward

Meet the Rockets' draft class . . . He's it, the No. 53 pick . . . Southwest Conference Defensive Player of the Year as a senior . . . All-time leading shot-blocker in Texas history and third in rebounds and shooting . . . In junior season, he was third in the nation in rebounding and had 19 in one game against eventual NCAA champion North Carolina before getting booted because of academic problems . . . Born May 15, 1972, in Austin, Tex.

COACH RUDY TOMJANOVICH: Guess he's happy now he

decided to become head coach . . . Originally didn't want to replace the fired Don Chaney for the final 30 games of 1991-92, even on an interim basis, preferring the relative security and obscurity as an assistant . . . Gave it a try, found he liked it and that the family could handle the pressures, so wanted the job on a permanent basis . . . Got it for 1992-93 and only guided the

Rockets to Midwest title and finished second to Pat Riley by one vote for Coach of the Year in a media vote. When papers voted for the same award with *The Sporting News*, he won . . . What to do for an encore? Took Rockets to their best record ever (58-24) and the championship . . . You mean everyone doesn't have 2½ years like this for openers in their first gig? . . . The rub is that Rudy T is so successful as a coach because he has done a 180 from so much of what he was as a player. Then, he was known for offense and never leading. Now, he stresses defenses and takes control . . . "His leadership qualities have really stunned me because I didn't know they were that strong," said Carroll Dawson, his No. 1 assistant and close friend. "I knew he had some that would probably come out, but he has been a leader and the guys believe in him." . . . Only nine coaches have reached 100 wins faster. He needed 150 games . . . Career: 129-65 . . . All 11 years as a player were spent with the Rockets, including five as an All-Star forward after he was the No. 2 pick overall in 1970. Team eventually retired his uniform No. 45 . . . Then spent two years as a Houston scout and the next nine as an assistant coach. That makes this his 25th consecutive season in the organization . . . Born Nov. 24, 1948, in Hamtramck, Mich., and went on to become an All-American at Michigan.

GREATEST PLAYER

He arrived as Akeem Olajuwon, changed to Hakeem Olajuwon and, somewhere along the line, also became the greatest of the Rockets.

Exactly when he zoomed past the likes of Moses Malone (24-point average in six seasons), Calvin Murphy and Elvin Hayes is not clear. What is known is that Olajuwon will continue to put distance between himself and the others because he shows no sign of slowing down, not after his glorious championship season.

While only fifth in games played, he already holds the team's career records for rebounds, steals and blocked shots, joining Sam Lacey of the Kings as the only other player in NBA history to be ranked No. 1 in franchise history in those three categories. Olajuwon also heads into this season needing only 51 points to break Murphy's scoring mark.

ALL-TIME ROCKET LEADERS

SEASON

Points: Moses Malone, 2,520, 1980-81
Assists: John Lucas, 768, 1977-78
Rebounds: Moses Malone, 1,444, 1978-79

GAME

Points: Calvin Murphy, 57 vs. New Jersey, 3/18/78
Assists: Art Williams, 22 vs. San Francisco, 2/14/70
        Art Williams, 22 vs. Phoenix, 12/28/68
Rebounds: Moses Malone, 37 vs. New Orleans, 2/9/79

CAREER

Points: Calvin Murphy, 17,949, 1970-83
Assists: Calvin Murphy, 4,402, 1970-83
Rebounds: Hakeem Olajuwon, 9,464, 1984-94

LOS ANGELES CLIPPERS

TEAM DIRECTORY: Owner: Donald Sterling; Exec. VP-Basketball Oper.: Elgin Baylor; Exec. VP: Andy Roeser; VP-Communications: Joe Safety; Coach: Bill Fitch. Arena: Los Angeles Sports Arena (16,005). Colors: Red, white and blue.

SCOUTING REPORT

SHOOTING: Long a weak spot, it took a curious turn last season when Mark Aguirre was in the top five in the league in three-point shooting and got cut to clear minutes for the impending return of John Williams. Come the end of the season, the Clippers were fifth-worst among all teams in three-point percentage. They weren't much better a step or two in front of the line, either.

This is a team that usually likes to drive so much they should play their games at rush hour. Ron Harper, should he return as a free agent, isn't bashful about launching from the outside, but is the first to admit that isn't his game. And now the team's leading scorer, Dominique Wilkins, is a Celtic. Loy Vaught, dependable on medium-range jumpers, might be the most consistent shooter from beyond 10 feet, especially coming off a season in which he went .537.

The Clippers have taken steps to improve the outside game. Again. On the heels of Reggie Williams, Bo Kimble, Randy Woods and, after one season, Terry Dehere, comes Lamond Murray, the first-rounder who was arguably the best shooter in the draft, to replace Wilkins. They also got another shooter in Eric Piatkowski, drafted by Indiana and then shipped to L.A. as part of the Pooh Richardson-Mark Jackson deal.

PLAYMAKING: Richardson replaces Jackson, who replaced Doc Rivers, who replaced Gary Grant, and the problem remains the same. The Clippers always commit too many turnovers, last season tying for the most in the league. How much does it hurt? They gave the ball away 18 times a night and lost nine games by three points or less.

REBOUNDING: This is what they get for losing their leading rebounder each of the previous two seasons, one in a trade that brought limited returns at best, and the other by free agency. They get last place, or in this case a tie for last place, in rebounding

Clippers traded for Nebraska's Eric Piatkowski (15).

CLIPPER PROFILES

RON HARPER 30 6-6 198   Guard

Inmate No. 2137488000 . . . Endeared himself to locals last season when he referred to his Clipper stint as being in prison . . . While most in Los Angeles would agree with the analogy, they don't have sympathy when it comes from someone making $4 million . . . Had even more bargaining power heading into the summer as an unrestricted free agent . . . The 20.1 marked his highest scoring average for a full season with the Clippers . . . That was also good for No. 15 in the league . . . Top rebounding guard in NBA...Co-captain...Came to Los Angeles from Cleveland along with a first-round draft pick that became Loy Vaught for Reggie Williams and Danny Ferry in what may be the greatest deal in Clipper history...Ohio guy all the way before the deal, having been born Jan. 20, 1964, in Dayton before playing college ball at Miami (Ohio) and being drafted No. 8 overall by Cavaliers in 1986.

Year	Team	G	FG	FG Pct.	FT	FT Pct.	Reb.	Ast.	TP	Avg.
1986-87	Cleveland	82	734	.455	386	.684	392	394	1874	22.9
1987-88	Cleveland	57	340	.464	196	.705	223	281	879	15.4
1988-89	Cleveland	82	587	.511	323	.751	409	434	1526	18.6
1989-90	Clev.-LAC.	35	301	.473	182	.788	206	182	798	22.8
1990-91	L.A. Clippers	39	285	.391	145	.668	188	209	763	19.6
1991-92	L.A. Clippers	82	569	.440	293	.736	447	417	1495	18.2
1992-93	L.A. Clippers	80	542	.451	307	.769	425	360	1443	18.0
1993-94	L.A. Clippers	75	569	.426	299	.715	460	344	1508	20.1
	Totals	532	3927	.452	2131	.726	2750	2621	10286	19.3

STANLEY ROBERTS 24 7-0 290   Center

He doesn't need another hurdle in his career, but one came along anyway...Has spent entire pro career, since Orlando took him 23rd in 1991, battling weight problems...Now he has a serious injury to come back from after suffering ruptured right Achilles tendon in 14th game last year...Clippers were 6-7 when he played, not counting that fateful night at the Sports Arena, and 21-48 the rest of the way...There's extra concern about his comeback because of the weight...Got down to about 295 pounds, management's target weight, but was reportedly in the 330-340 range heading into summer...Spent part of offseason with former teammate John Williams at weight-loss center...Magic picked former LSU star No. 23 in 1991, after he had played one season in Spain...Clippers got him in the summer of '92 as part of a three-team deal...Born Feb. 7, 1970, in Hopkins, S.C...Made $2.84 million.

Year	Team	G	FG	FG Pct.	FT	FT Pct.	Reb.	Ast.	TP	Avg.
1991-92	Orlando	55	236	.529	101	.515	336	39	573	10.4
1992-93	L.A. Clippers	77	375	.527	120	.488	478	59	870	11.3
1993-94	L.A. Clippers	14	43	.430	18	.409	93	11	104	7.4
	Totals	146	665	.520	239	.492	907	109	1547	10.6

LOY VAUGHT 26 6-9 240   Forward

We're still trying to figure this one out . . . How does someone go from being the starting power forward to being replaced by CBA claimer Harold Ellis despite nearly averaging a double-double and shooting well? . . . That marked a big step backward for potential-filled player who had waited for his chance behind Ken Norman and Danny Manning . . . Did finish sixth in the league in shooting at .537 . . . Loves doing the dirty work, but high percentage isn't just putbacks or chip shots as a last option in the offense . . . Has a nice touch out to 15 feet . . . Entering the second season of a four-year, $12-million deal he signed last summer that paid $1.225 million in 1993-94 . . . Starter on Michigan's 1989 NCAA championship team . . . Born Feb. 27, 1968, in Grand Rapids, Mich.

Year	Team	G	FG	FG Pct.	FT	FT Pct.	Reb.	Ast.	TP	Avg.
1990-91	L.A. Clippers	73	175	.487	49	.662	349	40	399	5.5
1991-92	L.A. Clippers	79	271	.492	55	.797	512	71	601	7.6
1992-93	L.A. Clippers	79	313	.508	116	.748	492	54	743	9.4
1993-94	L.A. Clippers	75	373	.537	131	.720	656	74	877	11.7
	Totals	306	1132	.510	351	.731	2009	239	2620	8.6

ELMORE SPENCER 24 7-0 270   Center

What do you mean he's the starting center? After playing all of 280 minutes the season before? Forced to step into the role 15 games into 1993-94 when Stanley Roberts went down with season-ending Achilles injury . . . In the opening lineup 62 of the 68 games the rest of the way . . . Got off to a fast start, but ultimately proved very inconsistent . . . Finished 14th in the league in blocked shots . . . This is a critical season for him to either prove he can contribute, even if only as a backup to Roberts, or force Clippers to find someone else for the role . . . They took him with the No. 25 pick in 1992 after he played at Georgia, Connors State (Okla.) JC and UNLV, in that order . . . Born Dec. 6, 1969, in Atlanta . . . Made $569,000.

Year	Team	G	FG	FG Pct.	FT	FT Pct.	Reb.	Ast.	TP	Avg.
1992-93	L.A. Clippers	44	44	.537	16	.500	62	8	104	2.4
1993-94	L.A. Clippers	76	288	.533	97	.599	415	75	673	8.9
	Totals	120	332	.534	113	.582	477	83	777	6.5

HAROLD ELLIS 23 6-5 221   Forward

Cut by the Clippers in training camp last season, then assured himself of never being an afterthought around these parts again . . . Came back Jan. 7 after playing with CBA's Quad City and made an impact . . . Made first start a week later, at Boston Garden no less, and had 29 points and five steals . . . That was the highest offensive output by a Clippers' rookie since Charles Smith in 1988 . . . Started 16 times in all and led team in steals 12 times . . . Coaches and teammates love his enthusiasm and hustle . . . Played some power forward, but basically a small forward . . . Division II Player of the Year in 1992 while at Moorhouse College in Georgia . . . Was not drafted and spent first pro year with Quad City . . . Born Oct. 7, 1970, in Atlanta.

Year	Team	G	FG	FG Pct.	FT	FT Pct.	Reb.	Ast.	TP	Avg.
1993-94	L.A. Clippers	49	159	.545	106	.711	153	31	424	8.7

GARY GRANT 29 6-3 195   Guard

Former starter and first-round draft pick has settled into his role as third guard . . . Good defender, but still turnover-prone . . . Finished 29th in the league in steals, which isn't anything spectacular until you realize he didn't even get 20 minutes a game . . . Would be a Top 15 guy as a full-timer . . . Clippers were 0-8 with him in the opening lineup last season . . . Went into summer waiting to see if team was going to pick up his option for 1994-95 after he made $1.1 million . . . They let former Michigan All-American become an unrestricted free agent last summer, didn't seem too concerned over the possibility of losing him, then re-signed him before training camp . . . His .855 from the line led the team and was a career best . . . Seattle drafted him No. 15 in 1988 and immediately shipped him to Clippers . . . Born April 21, 1965, in Canton, Ohio . . . Made $1.1 million last year.

Year	Team	G	FG	FG Pct.	FT	FT Pct.	Reb.	Ast.	TP	Avg.
1988-89	L.A. Clippers	71	361	.435	119	.735	238	506	846	11.9
1989-90	L.A. Clippers	44	241	.466	88	.779	195	442	575	13.1
1990-91	L.A. Clippers	68	265	.451	51	.689	209	587	590	8.7
1991-92	L.A. Clippers	78	275	.462	44	.815	184	538	609	7.8
1992-93	L.A. Clippers	74	210	.441	55	.743	139	353	486	6.6
1993-94	L.A. Clippers	78	253	.449	65	.855	142	291	588	7.5
	Totals	413	1605	.450	422	.763	1107	2717	3694	8.9

CHARLES (BO) OUTLAW 23 6-8 210   Forward

Probably the Clippers' best defender... On one of the most porous teams in the league, that means he'll get a long look this season... Good leaper... Limited offense because of limited range... Anything beyond a slam dunk is pushing it... Started in 14 of 37 appearances after being signed to a pair of 10-day contracts in February and then for the rest of the season ... Power forward mostly, but played some small forward... Undrafted out of Houston, where he was the Southwest Conference Player of the Year and twice named the best defensive player in the league... Was playing with Grand Rapids of CBA when Clippers called... Second-team All-CBA... Born April 13, 1971, in San Antonio.

Year	Team	G	FG	FG Pct.	FT	FT Pct.	Reb.	Ast.	TP	Avg.
1993-94	L.A. Clippers	37	98	.587	61	.592	212	36	257	6.9

TERRY DEHERE 23 6-4 190   Guard

Shooting problems, which tends to be a problem for shooting guard... If you think the .377 is bad, consider he was at just .366 heading into the last game before going 10-of-17... Has trouble shooting off the dribble... All-time leading scorer in Big East history after passing Chris Mullin during senior season at Seton Hall... Clippers picked him 13th after that and made him the backup to Ron Harper... Race horse Dehere is named after him... Lennox Dominique Dehere was born Sept. 12, 1971, in New York... Made $1.05 million.

Year	Team	G	FG	FG Pct.	FT	FT Pct.	Reb.	Ast.	TP	Avg.
1993-94	L.A. Clippers	64	129	.377	61	.753	68	78	342	5.3

RANDY WOODS 24 5-10 185   Guard

He's the throw-in for any attempted Clipper deal... They picked former LaSalle shooting guard No. 16 in 1992 and tried to make him a point guard... That transition has come with the same success rate as his shooting... Will need to win Most Improved Player award just to reach decent... Was third-string behind Mark Jackson and Gary Grant on his good days

... Averaged just 8.8 minutes last season ... Contract that paid $650,000 in 1993-94 still has three more years to run ... College teammate of Lionel Simmons ... Born Sept. 23, 1970, in Philadelphia.

Year	Team	G	FG	FG Pct.	FT	FT Pct.	Reb.	Ast.	TP	Avg.
1992-93	L.A. Clippers	41	23	.348	19	.731	14	40	68	1.7
1993-94	L.A. Clippers	40	49	.368	20	.571	29	71	145	3.6
	Totals	81	72	.362	39	.639	43	111	213	2.6

BOB MARTIN 25 7-0 255   Center

He's big and he hustles. That got his foot in the door ... Made team last season as a free agent with no NBA experience ... Was in Suns' camp the year before ... Spent 1992-93 with CBA's Rapid City ... Born Oct. 7, 1969, in Apple Valley, Minn., and stayed locally to play at Minnesota ... Left as Golden Gophers' all-time leader in games played and third-best shot-blocker ... Needs to improve offense ... Bad sign: shooting percentage drops every time he takes another step up, from .617 as a college senior to .504 in the CBA to .455 with Clippers ... Made $150,000.

Year	Team	G	FG	FG Pct.	FT	FT Pct.	Reb.	Ast.	TP	Avg.
1993-94	L.A. Clippers	53	40	.455	31	.608	117	17	111	2.1

JEROME (POOH) RICHARDSON 28 6-1 180   Guard

Pacers' Larry Brown is tough to please at point guard ... He left Richardson off the playoff roster and then traded him and Malik Sealy to the Clippers in deal that made Mark Jackson a Pacer ... Had suffered what was diagnosed as a calf bruise. Took too long coming back, so Pacer brass got antsy. Further exam revealed a stress fracture in lower right leg ... Adequate defender and decent shooter ... Confidence could be slipping though not on surface ... Only played in 37 games ... Better open-court player than in halfcourt. Given nature of playoffs, Pacers were in no rush to get him back ... Terrible free-throw shooter. Regressed, even in 37 games, to .610 after signs of life in first year with Indy . . . Pacers got him and Sam Mitchell from Minny for Chuck Person and Micheal Williams, Sept. 8, 1992 . . . Wolves' first-round pick at No. 10 in 1989 . . . Set Pac-10 assist record at UCLA . . . Born May 14, 1966, in Philadelphia . . . Made $1.694 million in first year of new deal.

Year	Team	G	FG	FG Pct.	FT	FT Pct.	Reb.	Ast.	TP	Avg.
1989-90	Minnesota	82	426	.461	63	.589	217	554	938	11.4
1990-91	Minnesota	82	635	.470	89	.539	286	734	1401	17.1
1991-92	Minnesota	82	587	.466	123	.691	301	685	1350	16.5
1992-93	Indiana	74	337	.479	92	.742	267	573	769	10.4
1993-94	Indiana	37	160	.452	47	.610	110	237	370	10.0
	Totals	357	2145	.467	414	.636	1181	2783	4828	13.5

MALIK SEALY 24 6-8 190   Forward

Don't give up the tie business . . . Designer-tie outfit may be better suited for the Pacers' 1992 first-rounder (No. 14) out of St. John's who shot .405 from the floor, .678 from the line and, in essence, fell off a cliff once the Pacers signed Byron Scott . . . So he wound up with the Clippers along with Pooh Richardson in the deal that sent Mark Jackson to the Pacers, who didn't even list him on playoff roster . . . No injury. Just no game . . . Began season as sixth man. Had 27-point, 10-rebound game Opening Night . . . Suffice it to say he didn't maintain pace . . . Decent defender, but slight build hurts . . . Really does produce some nice ties, though . . . If he ever developed a shot, he could be dangerous . . . Right now, the only person worried is Yves St. Laurent . . . He figured to flourish under Larry Brown with more motion. Didn't happen . . . Born Feb. 1, 1970, in the Bronx, N.Y. . . . Led Big East in scoring as senior . . . Made $1.023 million.

Year	Team	G	FG	FG Pct.	FT	FT Pct.	Reb.	Ast.	TP	Avg.
1992-93	Indiana	58	136	.426	51	.689	112	47	330	5.7
1993-94	Indiana	43	111	.405	59	.678	118	48	285	6.6
	Totals	101	247	.417	110	.683	230	95	615	6.1

THE ROOKIES

LAMOND MURRAY 21 6-6 220   Forward

The latest candidate to try and give the Clippers some outside shooting . . . He's also the guy to try and replace Dominique Wilkins as the starting small forward . . . 'Nique is his idol . . . Led

Pacific-10 Conference in scoring as a junior at 24.3 points a game before turning pro . . . Clippers grabbed him with the seventh pick . . . Cousin of Trail Blazers' Tracy Murray . . . Born April 20, 1973, in Pasadena, Cal.

ERIC PIATKOWSKI 24 6-6 215   Guard-Forward

He's been on the fast track since his senior season at Nebraska . . . Had a good showing then, but really intrigued teams starting with performances in the Big Eight tournament and then the Phoenix pre-draft camp, where he was named MVP . . . Pacers drafted him No. 15, then traded him to Clippers as part of Mark Jackson-Pooh Richardson deal . . . Can shoot and score in transition . . . Born Sept. 30, 1970, in Steubenville, Ohio.

COACH BILL FITCH: He drew the short straw this time . . .

Clips become the fifth stop of his pro coaching career; he's their ninth coach in the last 11 seasons . . . This will be his 22nd year in the NBA and 34th as a coach, starting with his alma mater, Coe College of Iowa, in 1958-59 . . . Went to North Dakota from there, then Bowling Green and Minnesota before moving to the pros . . . Has coached more NBA games (1,722) than anyone else . . . At 60, he's second-oldest in the league behind Dallas' Dick Motta (63) . . . Fifth-winningest in NBA history, although under .500 with 844-878 . . . Coach of the Year with Cleveland in 1976 and Boston in 1980 . . . What must have been appealing to the Clippers, other than that he would work for them, is that Fitch was at the helm (1) when the Cavaliers went from expansion to the playoffs; (2) when the Celtics went from winning 61 games the previous two seasons before his arrival to 61-21 the first campaign and an NBA title the second; and (3) when the Rockets went from 14 victories to the NBA Finals in his first three seasons . . . The last stop, New Jersey, resulted in the Nets' first playoff appearance in five years . . . He did have help: players like Austin Carr in Cleveland, Larry Bird in Boston, and Hakeem Olajuwon and Ralph Sampson in Houston . . . "Nobody took me a prisoner," he said of coming to the Clippers. "Nobody coerced me. I look at this as a fine opportunity. I've been in tougher situations than this." . . . Born May 19, 1934, in Davenport, Iowa.

GREATEST PLAYER

Once upon a time, this was an organization that included extended stardom, back before Los Angeles or San Diego or any nautical nickname.

In the days of the Buffalo Braves, two players stood out, Randy Smith and Bob McAdoo. This is where the choice gets tough. Smith was so good for so long, averaging 17.8 points over nine seasons, and he still holds the franchise record for points, assists and steals. McAdoo, however, was great for five years, the length of service being a slight deduction but still long enough.

McAdoo made the all-star team three times with the Braves, was the league MVP in 1974-75 and set the franchise record for rebounds. His 28.2 scoring average is second only to World B Free.

ALL-TIME CLIPPER LEADERS

SEASON

Points: Bob McAdoo, 2,831, 1974-75
Assists: Norm Nixon, 914, 1983-84
Rebounds: Swen Nater, 1,216, 1979-80

GAME

Points: Bob McAdoo, 52 vs. Seattle, 3/17/76
 Bob McAdoo, 52 vs. Boston, 2/22/74
 Charles Smith, 52 vs. Denver, 12/1/90
Assists: Ernie DiGregorio, 25 vs. Portland, 1/1/74
Rebounds: Swen Nater, 32 vs. Denver, 12/14/79

CAREER

Points: Randy Smith, 12,735, 1971-79, 1982-83
Assists: Randy Smith, 3,498, 1971-79, 1982-83
Rebounds: Bob McAdoo, 4,229, 1972-76

LOS ANGELES LAKERS

TEAM DIRECTORY: Owner: Jerry Buss; Exec. VP: Jerry West; GM: Mitch Kupchak; Dir. Pub. Rel.: John Black; Coach: Del Harris; Asst. Coaches: Bill Bertka, Larry Drew, Michael Cooper. Arena: The Great Western Forum (17,505). Colors: Royal purple and gold.

SCOUTING REPORT

SHOOTING: Let's put it this way: they took the second-most shots in the league last season and still came within a half-point of failing to average 100 for the first time since moving to Los Angeles. The 14.2 points per game by Vlade Divac was the lowest team-high among the 27 clubs. P.S. They weren't trying to play slow-down.

Of all the cold realities that these are new days around the Forum, this may have been the harshest, except, of course, the end result, that seat on the lottery stage. Part of the problem was bad breaks, with Anthony Peeler, their best creator, limited to only 30 games because of injury. The other part was bad shots, with Nick Van Exel taking 154 more attempts than anyone and going .394 from the field.

The production from center is fine, with Divac and backup Sam Bowie. It's even better at shooting guard, where Peeler, Doug Christie, Sedale Threatt and first-round pick Eddie Jones will battle for time and shots. What the Lakers need is big scoring from one the forwards.

PLAYMAKING: Van Exel showed nice improvement as the season went along, especially in using his terrific quickness to break down the defense, drive the lane and dish off. The counter to his shot selection was that he had an assist-to-turnover ratio of 3.2-1 while running an up-tempo offense as a rookie. That is an encouraging sign for the future for the Lakers, who had the third-fewest turnovers in the league.

An added dimension is that they can rely on the center for passing like few other teams. Actually, they can rely on the centers, because both Divac and Bowie hurt defenses from the high post even when they aren't scoring. The Lakers also have some depth for Van Exel with Threatt, the former starter, and, in a pinch, Christie, but a natural point guard as the backup is on the wish list.

No Kareem, but Vlade Divac led Lakers in boards, scoring.

REBOUNDING: A huge need. The loss of A.C. Green via free agency helped drop the Lakers from 20th by percentage in 1992-93 to 23rd last season, including 27th and last on the defensive end. It was a key factor why the term "running game" was usually an unsubstantiated allegation, even with Divac pulling his weight with 10.8 per game.

That would have been a good start, but the only help came from George Lynch, who, even at 6-7 and playing mostly small forward, proved he can be a factor, especially on the offensive boards. He finished at 5.8 an outing in 24.8 minutes a game,

LAKER ROSTER

No.	Veterans	Pos.	Ht.	Wt.	Age	Yrs. Pro	College
31	Sam Bowie	C	7-1	255	33	9	Kentucky
41	Elden Campbell	F-C	6-11	250	26	4	Clemson
8	Doug Christie	G-F	6-6	205	24	2	Pepperdine
12	Vlade Divac	C	7-1	250	26	5	Yugoslavia
U-53	James Edwards	F-C	7-1	252	28	17	Washington
R-40	Antonio Harvey	F	6-11	225	24	1	Pfeiffer
23	Reggie Jordan	G	6-4	200	26	1	New Mexico State
24	George Lynch	F	6-7	223	24	1	North Carolina
1	Anthony Peeler	G	6-4	212	24	2	Missouri
U-30	Kurt Rambis	F	6-8	215	36	13	Santa Clara
34	Tony Smith	G	6-4	205	26	4	Marquette
3	Sedale Threatt	G	6-2	185	33	11	W. Virginia Tech
R-9	Nick Van Exel	G	6-1	170	22	1	Cincinnati
42	James Worthy	F	6-9	225	33	12	North Carolina

R-restricted free agent
U-unrestricted free agent

Rd.	Rookies	Sel. No.	Pos.	Ht.	Wt.	College
1	Eddie Jones	10	G	6-6	190	Temple
2	Anthony Miller	39	F	6-8	255	Michigan State

including 7.6 in 32.5 minutes during a stretch of 44 consecutive starts. That leaves one culprit: Elden Campbell, c'mon down.

The Lakers would love to replace Campbell, inconsistent as ever, as the starting power forward after he averaged one more rebound than Lynch in about five more minutes. They hope some help will come from rookie Anthony Miller.

DEFENSE: This is where they need Campbell, because he finished 11th in the NBA in blocked shots despite those 29.6 minutes. Tony Smith is the best defender in the backcourt, but has no defined spot in the rotation, now more than ever. One of the reasons the Lakers liked Jones enough to take him with the 10th pick was because of his defense. No wonder it's an issue—the .476 by opponents was the seventh-highest mark in the league.

OUTLOOK: They needed a big free-agent signing in the summer and maybe even a significant trade. Otherwise, this remains a team of role players, enough guys you would like to have, but none that you'd want as the No. 1 talent.

LAKER PROFILES

VLADE DIVAC 26 7-1 250 Center

The most consistent Laker last season . . . No, seriously . . . Went from years of hit-and-miss play to emerge as one of the few bright spots on the team . . . Became the first person to lead the Lakers in scoring and rebounding the same season since Kareem Abdul-Jabbar in 1984-85 . . . Good hands . . . Nice spin moves from the low post, but ugly hook shot. It never looks the same twice in a row . . . Involved in charity activities to raise money for children of all ethnic backgrounds in his former Yugoslavia . . . Played five years of pro ball there before L.A. made him the 26th pick in the 1989 draft . . . Highest-paid Laker last season at $4.133 million . . . Born Feb. 3, 1968, in Prijepolje, Yugoslavia.

Year	Team	G	FG	FG Pct.	FT	FT Pct.	Reb.	Ast.	TP	Avg.
1989-90	L.A. Lakers	82	274	.499	153	.708	512	75	701	8.5
1990-91	L.A. Lakers	82	360	.565	196	.703	666	92	921	11.2
1991-92	L.A. Lakers	36	157	.495	86	.768	247	60	405	11.3
1992-93	L.A. Lakers	82	397	.485	235	.689	729	232	1050	12.8
1993-94	L.A. Lakers	79	453	.506	208	.686	851	307	1123	14.2
	Totals	361	1641	.510	878	.702	3005	766	4200	11.6

JAMES WORTHY 33 6-9 225 Forward

Retirement was a possibility as he went into the offseason . . . If that happens, he deserved a better sendoff than last season . . . A few nights he reminded people of Big Game James, but mostly it was a struggle . . . The .406 from the floor was easily a career low . . . Still got open enough with signature swoop through the lane or spin move from the blocks, but didn't convert enough . . . Has too much pride to struggle like that, or worse, again . . . Averaged 20 minutes in his 80 appearances, with two starts, both in the final week . . . Didn't go to the playoffs for the first time in his career . . . Team captain . . . Made $1.85 million last season and has two years left on the contract at $7.2

million and $5.15 million... Born Feb. 27, 1961, in Gastonia, N.C., and starred nearby at North Carolina.

Year	Team	G	FG	FG Pct.	FT	FT Pct.	Reb.	Ast.	TP	Avg.
1982-83	Los Angeles	77	447	.579	138	.624	399	132	1033	13.4
1983-84	Los Angeles	82	495	.556	195	.759	515	207	1185	14.5
1984-85	L.A. Lakers	80	610	.572	190	.776	511	201	1410	17.6
1985-86	L.A. Lakers	75	629	.579	242	.771	387	201	1500	20.0
1986-87	L.A. Lakers	82	651	.539	292	.751	466	226	1594	19.4
1987-88	L.A. Lakers	75	617	.531	242	.796	374	289	1478	19.7
1988-89	L.A. Lakers	81	702	.548	251	.782	489	288	1657	20.5
1989-90	L.A. Lakers	80	711	.548	248	.782	478	288	1685	21.1
1990-91	L.A. Lakers	78	716	.492	212	.797	356	275	1670	21.4
1991-92	L.A. Lakers	54	450	.447	166	.814	305	252	1075	19.9
1992-93	L.A. Lakers	82	510	.447	171	.810	247	278	1221	14.9
1993-94	L.A. Lakers	80	340	.406	100	.741	181	154	812	10.2
	Totals	926	6878	.521	2447	.769	4708	2791	16320	17.6

NICK VAN EXEL 22 6-1 170   Guard

Steal of the 1993 draft... A steal, period, at the minimum of $150,000... Lakers brought Cincinnati guard in for workout with No. 12 pick in mind, then found him still on the board at No. 37... Had more production than most first-round choices... Played in inaugural Rookie All-Star Game... His 123 three-pointers were the second-most ever by a rookie, falling two short of Dennis Scott's record... Two problems: He is a very streaky shooter and wouldn't back off when things were going badly. And, the point guard is supposed to distribute, not take 154 more shots than any teammate while going a disastrous .394 from the field... Good quickness allows him to break down defenses and penetrate... Born Nov. 27, 1971, in Kenosha, Wisc.

Year	Team	G	FG	FG Pct.	FT	FT Pct.	Reb.	Ast.	TP	Avg.
1993-94	L.A. Lakers	81	413	.394	150	.781	238	466	1099	13.6

ELDEN CAMPBELL 26 6-11 250   Forward

NBA ability, CBA approach... Teased Lakers again by going from great showing against Charles Barkley in 1993 playoffs to offseason conditioning program that added bulk to upper body by the start of training camp... Then got back on the see-saw... Started 74 of 76 appearances, but then-coach Randy Pfund wished he had a viable option... Leaping ability means he can be a shot-blocker, but the advantage is most noticeable when he goes up for a turnaround jumper. He gets up so much higher than the defender, clearing a path for an open shot . . . Led Lakers in blocks, but a 6-11 starting power forward should average more than 6.8 rebounds . . . Born July 23, 1968, in Inglewood, Cal. . . . Played college ball at Clemson before Lakers took him No. 27 in 1990 . . . Made $1.7 million.

Year	Team	G	FG	FG Pct.	FT	FT Pct.	Reb.	Ast.	TP	Avg.
1990-91	L.A. Lakers	52	56	.455	32	.653	96	10	144	2.8
1 991-92	L.A. Lakers	81	220	.448	138	.619	423	59	578	7.1
1992-93	L.A. Lakers	79	238	.458	130	.637	332	48	606	7.7
1993-94	L.A. Lakers	76	373	.462	188	.689	519	86	934	12.3
	Totals	288	887	.457	488	.652	1370	203	2262	7.9

ANTHONY PEELER 24 6-4 212   Guard

So much for the follow-up to an encouraging rookie season . . . Had two stints on the injured list, at the start and the end, not to mention missing much of training camp . . . The big problem was a stress fracture in the lower left leg that sidelined him for final 47 games . . . His 14.1 points still led Lakers in scoring most of the second half of the season before Vlade Divac passed him late . . . Averaged 17.5 points on the 17 occasions in which he played at least 30 minutes . . . A penetrator, but has shown he can also score from the outside . . . "Anthony is probably the most talented guy on the team," Magic Johnson said . . . No. 15 pick in 1992 after being named Big Eight Player of the Year at Missouri . . . Born Nov. 25, 1969, in Kansas City, Mo . . . . Made $910,000.

Year	Team	G	FG	FG Pct.	FT	FT Pct.	Reb.	Ast.	TP	Avg.
1992-93	L.A. Lakers	77	297	.468	162	.786	179	166	802	10.4
1993-94	L.A. Lakers	30	176	.430	57	.803	109	94	423	14.1
	Totals	107	473	.453	219	.791	288	260	1225	11.4

GEORGE LYNCH 24 6-7 223   Forward

He was as advertised . . . Not a star, like some teams might want from a 12th pick, but a solid and dependable worker . . . Buried at the end of the bench at the start of the season, getting his first DNP-CDs since grade school . . . Biggest problem is that he has power-forward skills in a small-forward body . . . Break came when Doug Christie went down with sprained ankle in early January ... Lynch flourished at small forward, and Christie never saw the starting job again ... Does his best work on offensive boards, getting more rebounds there than on defense ... Still played some fill-in power forward, but often overmatched there ... Good defender on perimeter ... Fundamentally sound ... Played on North Carolina's 1993 NCAA championship team ... Born Sept. 3, 1970, in Roanoke, Va ... Made $1.1 million.

Year	Team	G	FG	FG Pct.	FT	FT Pct.	Reb.	Ast.	TP	Avg.
1993-94	L.A. Lakers	71	291	.508	99	.596	410	96	681	9.6

DOUG CHRISTIE 24 6-6 205   Guard-Forward

The point guard of the future ... Check that. The small forward of the future. Check that. The shooting guard of the future ... He does have a future with those skills; it's just that no one is sure where ... Best-suited for shooting guard, which he says is his natural position ... Has had two fractured pro seasons after playing at Pepperdine, starting with lengthy rookie holdout with Seattle that forced the trade to the Lakers, where he became a point guard ... A sprained ankle kept him out a month of 1993-94, but starting the season as the opening small forward and finishing as a reserve off-guard made it even tougher ... He's great getting out on the break, but frustrates coaches by trying to make everything highlight-reel material, often causing needless turnovers ... Born May 9, 1970, in Seattle ... Made $1.445 million.

Year	Team	G	FG	FG Pct.	FT	FT Pct.	Reb.	Ast.	TP	Avg.
1992-93	L.A. Lakers	23	45	.425	50	.758	51	53	142	6.2
1993-94	L.A. Lakers	65	244	.434	145	.697	235	136	672	10.3
	Totals	88	289	.433	195	.712	286	189	814	9.3

SEDALE THREATT 33 6-2 185   Guard

Former starting point guard has fallen into his ideal role: third guard who can fill in at either spot in the backcourt ... Will handle the ball, but is first and foremost a shooter ... That would make him especially attractive to a playoff team looking for bench scoring ... Streaky ... Started 20 times, but, considering he was alongside Nick Van Exel, that made Lakers very small at guard ... Finished fourth in the league in free-throw shooting . . . Originally a sixth-round pick by Philadelphia in 1983 out of West Virginia Tech . . . Born Sept. 10, 1961, in Atlanta . . . Made $2.4 million.

Year	Team	G	FG	FG Pct.	FT	FT Pct.	Reb.	Ast.	TP	Avg.
1983-84	Philadelphia	45	62	.419	23	.821	40	41	148	3.3
1984-85	Philadelphia	82	188	.452	66	.733	99	175	446	5.4
1985-86	Philadelphia	70	310	.453	75	.833	121	193	696	9.9
1986-87	Phil.-Chi.	68	239	.448	95	.798	108	259	580	8.5
1987-88	Chi.-Sea.	71	216	.508	57	.803	88	160	492	6.9
1988-89	Seattle	63	235	.494	63	.818	117	238	544	8.6
1989-90	Seattle	65	303	.506	130	.828	115	216	744	11.4
1990-91	Seattle	80	433	.519	137	.792	99	273	1013	12.7
1991-92	L.A. Lakers	82	509	.489	202	.831	253	593	1240	15.1
1992-93	L.A. Lakers	82	522	.508	177	.823	273	564	1235	15.1
1993-94	L.A. Lakers	81	411	.482	138	.890	153	344	965	11.9
	Totals	789	3428	.487	1163	.820	1466	3056	8103	10.3

TONY SMITH 26 6-4 105   Guard

Top defensive guard on the team . . . Now if he had an offensive game to match . . . In the opening lineup for 31 of 73 games, but it's too hard for most teams to have a starting shooting guard going just .441 from the field . . . Lack of outside shot is biggest problem . . . It didn't help that he was shuttled between prominent and forgotten in an inconsistent rotation . . . Former No. 51 pick in 1990, he has proven he belongs in the league, even as a backup off-guard . . . Ideal role player . . . Athlete . . . Born June 14, 1968, in Wauwatosa, Wisc., and stayed locally to attend Marquette . . . Made $800,000.

Year	Team	G	FG	FG Pct.	FT	FT Pct.	Reb.	Ast.	TP	Avg.
1990-91	L.A. Lakers	64	97	.441	40	.702	71	135	234	3.7
1991-92	L.A. Lakers	63	113	.399	49	.653	76	109	275	4.4
1992-93	L.A. Lakers	55	133	.484	62	.756	87	63	330	6.0
1993-94	L.A. Lakers	73	272	.441	85	.714	195	148	645	8.8
	Totals	255	615	.441	236	.709	429	455	1484	5.8

SAM BOWIE 33 7-1 255   Center

Stop us if you've heard this one before: He missed most of the season with an injury . . . Sat out final 57 games with a sore knee that eventually needed arthroscopic surgery to remove bone chips . . . Amidst his well-chronicled medical history, he had never had a knee problem before . . . He came from New Jersey in exchange for Benoit Benjamin, which would have made him one of the most popular Lakers in itself, but then he made a big contribution in the 25 games . . . Nice passer from the post . . . Played with Vlade Divac in two-center alignment that proved a success . . . Former No. 2 selection overall with Portland in 1984 . . . Class act . . . Born March 7, 1961, in Lebanon, Pa . . . .Made $3.2 million.

Year	Team	G	FG	FG Pct.	FT	FT Pct.	Reb.	Ast.	TP	Avg.
1984-85	Portland	76	299	.537	160	.711	656	215	758	10.0
1985-86	Portland	38	167	.484	114	.708	327	99	448	11.8
1986-87	Portland	5	30	.455	20	.667	33	9	80	16.0
1987-88	Portland					Injured				
1988-89	Portland	20	69	.451	28	.571	106	36	171	8.6
1989-90	New Jersey	68	347	.416	294	.776	690	91	998	14.7
1990-91	New Jersey	62	314	.434	169	.732	480	147	801	12.9
1991-92	New Jersey	71	421	.445	212	.757	578	186	1062	15.0
1992-93	New Jersey	79	287	.450	141	.779	556	127	717	9.1
1993-94	L.A. Lakers	25	75	.436	72	.867	131	47	223	8.9
	Totals	444	2009	.453	1210	.747	3557	957	5258	11.8

ANTONIO HARVEY 24 6-11 225   Forward

In the summer of 1993, he was an undrafted rookie out of tiny Pfeiffer College, an NAIA school in North Carolina . . . A few months later, he not only made the Lakers but was the starting power forward on Opening Night because of an injury to Elden Campbell . . . That status didn't last, but Lakers like his potential and hope he's back . . . Needs to polish his game and bulk up his body . . . Gets pushed around too much by other power forwards . . . Raw, athletic shot-blocker likened by the Lakers to a young Larry Nance . . . Started college career at Southern Illinois, then went to Georgia, then to Pfeiffer . . . Born July 9, 1970, in Pascagoula, Miss . . . .Made $150,000.

Year	Team	G	FG	FG Pct.	FT	FT Pct.	Reb.	Ast.	TP	Avg.
1993-94	L.A. Lakers	27	29	.367	12	.462	59	5	70	2.6

KURT RAMBIS 36 6-8 215   Forward

His return meant 1993-94 wasn't a complete eyesore for Lakers' fans . . . One of the most popular players in team history came back as a free agent and averaged 12.7 minutes as a backup power forward . . . Member of four Laker championship teams during Showtime era before leaving as free agent . . . Made grunt work so famous he never got credit for actually having some talent . . . Took pride in doing the little things, like grabbing the ball as it came through the net quick enough to start a fastbreak . . . Went into the summer looking at retirement and a possible future in TV, but would also consider offers if the phone rings . . . Born Feb. 25, 1958, in Cupertino, Cal., and played at Santa Clara . . . Knicks drafted him with the 58th pick in 1980, but he went to Greece and joined the NBA with the Lakers . . . Made $400,000.

Year	Team	G	FG	FG Pct.	FT	FT Pct.	Reb.	Ast.	TP	Avg.
1981-82	Los Angeles	64	118	.518	59	.504	348	56	295	4.6
1982-83	Los Angeles	78	235	.569	114	.687	531	90	584	7.5
1983-84	Los Angeles	47	63	.558	42	.636	266	34	168	3.6
1984-85	L.A. Lakers	82	181	.554	68	.660	528	69	430	5.2
1985-86	L.A. Lakers	74	160	.595	88	.721	517	69	408	5.5
1986-87	L.A. Lakers	78	163	.521	120	.764	453	63	446	5.7
1987-88	L.A. Lakers	70	102	.548	73	.785	268	54	277	4.0
1988-89	Charlotte	75	325	.518	182	.734	703	159	832	11.1
1989-90	Char.-Phoe.	74	190	.509	82	.646	525	135	462	6.2
1990-91	Phoenix	62	83	.497	60	.706	266	64	226	3.6
1991-92	Phoenix	28	38	.463	14	.778	106	37	90	3.2
1992-93	Phoe.-Sac.	72	67	.519	43	.662	227	53	177	2.5
1993-94	L.A. Lakers	50	59	.518	46	.648	189	32	164	3.3
	Totals	854	1784	.534	991	.689	4927	915	4559	5.3

REGGIE JORDAN 26 6-4 200   Guard

Would be just another CBA guy trying to stick were it not for his background . . . Did not play basketball in high school or junior college until a coach noticed him in a pickup game . . . Ended up at New Mexico State and was named first-team All-Big West . . . CBA all-star in 1993 and '94 . . . Spent 2½ seasons in CBA after not getting drafted before making NBA debut with Lakers on 10-day deal . . . His jersey—Jordan No. 23— got more attention than he did until he went for 28 points in 25 minutes against the Jazz, earning him a contract for the rest of the season . . . The 22 second-half points were the most by any Laker in a half all season . . . Played some point, but mostly a shooting guard . . . Born Jan. 26, 1968, in Chicago.

Year	Team	G	FG	FG Pct.	FT	FT Pct.	Reb.	Ast.	TP	Avg.
1993-94	L.A. Lakers	23	44	.427	35	.686	67	26	125	5.4

THE ROOKIES

EDDIE JONES 23 6-6 190   **Guard**
The last thing the Lakers needed was another shooting guard, but they thought he was too good to pass up . . . Maybe the best athlete in the entire draft . . . Nice first step, great leaping ability and a slashing style going to the basket . . . Defense is a strength . . . Has drawn comparisons to former Laker player and current assistant coach Michael Cooper, both in appearance and for ability to play defense and throw down alley-oop passes . . . No. 10 pick after standout career at Temple . . . Born Oct. 20, 1971, in Toledo, Ohio.

ANTHONY MILLER 23 6-8 255   **Forward**
Warriors took him 39th, then traded power forward to Lakers a few days later for 1995 second-round pick . . . Lakers hope he will provide much-needed rebounding help . . . Finished third in the nation in shooting (.651) as a senior and is third on Michigan State's career list (.609) . . . Didn't become a regular starter until 1993-94 . . . Born Oct. 22, 1971, in Benton Harbor, Mich.

COACH DEL HARRIS: After going with untested Pat Riley, Mike Dunleavy and Randy Pfund, the Lakers go for a repeat performer . . . The surprise was that it's him, someone known for defense and a halfcourt approach . . . Reminds people he made reputation as a college coach by having teams that scored 100 points a game and says he can do the fastbreak thing, too, because he adapts to the personnel: "Pat Riley became categorized as a Showtime kind of coach. Now, he's doing just the opposite." . . . Makes sense . . . Has eight years experience with Milwaukee and Houston . . . Best season was 1980-81, when he guided Rockets to Western Conference title . . . Took over Bucks in the summer of 1987 and went 191-154, making playoffs all four years . . . In all, he failed to reach the postseason only once in the eight seasons . . . Consultant at Sacramento before taking Laker job . . . Longtime friend of Exec. VP Jerry West, which should help.

GREATEST PLAYER

We're supposed to pick a greatest *player*? A greatest first team would be tough enough with the Lakers, considering, it could be argued, six of the greatest dozen or so talents in NBA history have been with this franchise: Kareem Abdul-Jabbar, Elgin Baylor, Wilt Chamberlain, Magic Johnson, George Mikan and Jerry West.

Abdul-Jabbar is the greatest scorer ever. Chamberlain may have been the most dominant player ever, but his five seasons with the Lakers don't compare to the others, a strike against him in this balloting. Baylor's 27.4 career average is third best all-time, behind only Michael Jordan and Chamberlain. On and on.

So why do we pick Johnson? Because he was so versatile, so intelligent, so unselfish, was such a great passer and had such great court sense and leadership abilities. Among all that, it is even understandable to forget for a moment that no player in NBA history has more assists. All this from the guy who played point guard at 6-9 most of his career, yet was making the transition to forward at the end of his career and, in perhaps his most memorable game of all, decided to play a little center and led the Lakers to a win in the deciding game of the NBA Finals his rookie season.

ALL-TIME LAKER LEADERS

SEASON

Points: Elgin Baylor, 2,719, 1962-63
Assists: Earvin (Magic) Johnson, 989, 1990-91
Rebounds: Wilt Chamberlain, 1,712, 1968-69

GAME

Points: Elgin Baylor, 71 vs. New York, 11/15/60
Assists: Earvin (Magic) Johnson, 24 vs. Denver, 11/17/89
       Earvin (Magic) Johnson, 24 vs. Phoenix, 1/9/90
Rebounds: Wilt Chamberlain, 42 vs.Boston, 3/7/69

CAREER

Points: Jerry West, 25,192, 1960-74
Assists: Earvin (Magic) Johnson, 9,921, 1980-91
Rebounds: Elgin Baylor, 11,463, 1958-72

MINNESOTA TIMBERWOLVES

TEAM DIRECTORY: Owner: Glen Taylor; GM: Jack McCloskey; Asst. GM: Kevin McHale; Dir. Media Rel.; Kent Wipf; Coach: TBA. Arena: Target Center (19,006). Colors: Blue, green and silver.

(Editor's Note: The Timberwolves had not named a new coach at press time.)

SCOUTING REPORT

SHOOTING: They will only if you insist. Sidney Lowe's Timberwolves took the second-fewest shots in the league last season, just 19 more than Indiana, and beat out only Dallas to avoid last place in scoring. They addressed that problem in the draft by taking Donyell Marshall in the lottery, providing a nice nucleus of Christian Laettner, Isaiah Rider and Marshall that should average more than last year's 96.7 points, even with the departure of Chuck Person.

There is a minor counter-balance. The Timberwolves were No. 1 in free-throw percentage. Big deal? Big deal for a team that needs to win some games to gain respectability but is turnover-prone. The success from the line, with three prominent players going .810 or better, played a role in Minnesota going 6-8 in contests decided by three points or less, an encouraging figure for a bad club.

PLAYMAKING: A telling anecdote: In a game late last season at Miami Arena, the Timberwolves shot .643 the first quarter . . . and trailed by 19 points, 43-24. The problem was the 11 turnovers. That killed them that night and that killed them all of 1993-94, when no team committed more turnovers and only the L.A. Clippers committed as many.

Finding a cure for this season may not be as simple as replacing Micheal Williams with Chris Smith at point guard in the opening lineup, one possibility, or giving second-round pick Howard Eisley a chance for big minutes. The most turnover-prone of all the Timberwolves last season was Laettner.

REBOUNDING: The improvement can be charted. The Timberwolves finished 26th three seasons ago and 25th in 1992-93, then made the big jump to where 11 teams had a worse percentage last year. Especially encouraging was the tie for 12th on the offensive boards.

Slam-dunk winner J.R. Rider had fine debut as rookie.

The thing is, they have only one dependable person on the boards, Laettner, who has averaged 8.7 and 8.6 the last two campaigns at power forward. That makes this Item 2 on the things-to-do list after correcting the turnover problem.

TIMBERWOLF ROSTER

No.	Veterans	Pos.	Ht.	Wt.	Age	Yrs. Pro	College
U-41	Thurl Bailey	F	6-11	232	33	11	North Carolina State
40	Mike Brown	C	6-10	260	31	8	George Washington
R-23	Brian Davis	G-F	6-7	195	24	1	Duke
30	Tellis Frank	F-C	6-10	225	29	5	Western Kentucky
R-51	Andres Guibert	C	6-10	242	26	1	Cuba
R-7	Stanley Jackson	G	6-3	185	24	1	Ala.-Birmingham
21	Stacey King	C-F	6-11	250	27	5	Oklahoma
32	Christian Laettner	F	6-11	235	25	2	Duke
25	Marlon Maxey	F	6-8	250	25	2	Texas-El Paso
34	Isaiah Rider	G	6-5	215	23	1	UNLV
3	Chris Smith	G	6-3	191	24	2	Connecticut
5	Doug West	G-F	6-6	200	27	5	Villanova
24	Micheal Williams	G	6-2	175	28	6	Baylor

R-restricted free agent
U-unrestricted free agent

Rd.	Rookies	Sel. No.	Pos.	Ht.	Wt.	College
1	Donyell Marshall	4	F	6-8	210	Connecticut
2	Howard Eisley	39	G	6-2	180	Boston College

DEFENSE: Two of the top three individual performances of last season came against the Timberwolves and their big men: the 53 points by Shaquille O'Neal and the 50 points by David Robinson. Any more questions?

Feel free to find some encouragement, Minnesota fans. The Timberwolves were bad, but they did, after all, improve from the season before in points allowed and shooting-percentage-against. On the other hand, they're still not forcing turnovers, indicating someone needs to turn up the pressure.

OUTLOOK: With new ownership and the franchise set to remain in Minneapolis, this is good news for Twin Cities fans who have done a good job supporting a team that has gained a reputation as a brat pack. A new coach to replace the fired Sidney Lowe had not been named at press time.

The faithful should be rewarded with the start of something good in the Laettner-Rider-Marshall combo, but can't hope for anything more than beating out Dallas to avoid the cellar in the Midwest Division.

TIMBERWOLF PROFILES

CHRISTIAN LAETTNER 25 6-11 235   Forward

It's a shame that his attitude continues to get more attention than his ability, but Laettner is the one person who can do something about that... Few players draw such a mixed response at road games... He gets squeals from swooning girls and boos and derisive comments from others... Added the headband to his ensemble last season... Tough for opposing power forwards to handle because he can battle inside or work from the perimeter... Third among all forwards in assists at 4.4 a game, trailing only Chris Mullin and Charles Barkley... Only college player on Dream Team that steamrolled to gold medal at 1992 Barcelona Olympics... All-American at Duke before going No. 3 in the 1992 draft... Born Aug. 17, 1969, in Buffalo, N.Y. ... Made $2.73 million.

Year	Team	G	FG	FG Pct.	FT	FT Pct.	Reb.	Ast.	TP	Avg.
1992-93	Minnesota.......	81	503	.474	462	.835	708	223	1472	18.2
1993-94	Minnesota.......	70	396	.448	375	.783	602	307	1173	16.8
	Totals	151	899	.462	837	.811	1310	530	2645	17.5

ISAIAH (J.R.) RIDER 23 6-5 215   Guard

The Not-So-Easy Rider... His play drew attention, but so did his antics... Set club record for field goals made and attempted... Won NBA slam-dunk contest... So tough for defenders because he is strong and works inside but is also comfortable on the perimeter... Mano-a-mano block of Patrick Ewing dunk attempt was one of the highlights of the year... Made $2 million as the first installment of a seven-year contract UNLV product signed after being the fifth pick in the 1993 draft... Born March 12, 1971, in Oakland.

Year	Team	G	FG	FG Pct.	FT	FT Pct.	Reb.	Ast.	TP	Avg.
1993-94	Minnesota.......	79	522	.468	215	.811	315	202	1313	16.6

DOUG WEST 27 6-6 200   Guard-Forward

Arrival of Isaiah Rider cut about 1,000 minutes off his previous season, even though West played only eight fewer games... More significant drop was in shooting percentage... Moved from off-guard to become the starting small forward... Too good to get lost in the shuffle... Any team that has him running the break on the wing is in great shape... Leaper ... Lone holdover from the original Timberwolves... Broke Pooh Richardson's club record for career starts and minutes played ... Born May 27, 1967, in Altoona, Pa., and attended Villanova ... No. 38 pick by Wolves in 1989... Made $1.275 million.

Year	Team	G	FG	FG Pct.	FT	FT Pct.	Reb.	Ast.	TP	Avg.
1989-90	Minnesota.......	52	53	.393	26	.813	70	18	135	2.6
1990-91	Minnesota.......	75	118	.480	58	.690	136	48	294	3.9
1991-92	Minnesota.......	80	463	.518	186	.805	257	281	1116	14.0
1992-93	Minnesota.......	80	646	.517	249	.841	247	235	1543	19.3
1993-94	Minnesota.......	72	434	.487	187	.810	231	172	1056	14.7
	Totals	359	1714	.502	706	.808	941	754	4144	11.5

MICHEAL WILLIAMS 28 6-2 175   Guard

Timberwolves tied for last in the league in turnovers last season, so guess which point guard faces the possibility of losing his starting job this fall?... Williams finished 10th in assists, but Chris Smith still may push him for the spot ... Gets to the line a lot for a point guard, an indication that he has success in getting into the lane and drawing fouls... That can be as good as a basket because Baylor product set NBA record with 97 consecutive makes from the line... Strangely, he only finished 18th in the league in free-throw percentage... Timberwolves got him along with Chuck Person in Sept. 8, 1992, deal that sent Pooh Richardson and Sam Mitchell to Indiana... Born July 23, 1966, in Dallas... Made $2.075 million.

Year	Team	G	FG	FG Pct.	FT	FT Pct.	Reb.	Ast.	TP	Avg.
1988-89	Detroit.........	49	47	.364	31	.660	27	70	127	2.6
1989-90	Phoe.-Char.	28	60	.504	36	.783	32	81	156	5.6
1990-91	Indiana.........	73	261	.499	290	.879	176	348	813	11.1
1991-92	Indiana.........	79	404	.490	372	.871	282	647	1188	15.0
1992-93	Minnesota.......	76	353	.446	419	.907	273	661	1151	15.1
1993-94	Minnesota.......	71	314	.457	333	.839	221	512	971	13.7
	Totals	376	1439	.468	1481	.867	1011	2319	4406	11.7

THURL BAILEY 33 6-11 232   Forward

All that sitting last season was tough for such a dignified player . . . At least he had something to look forward to: heading into the summer as an unrestricted free agent . . . Feels he can still contribute to some team . . . Best in short stretches, as proved in 1993-94 . . . Had streak of 451 consecutive appearances snapped in 1993 . . . Has missed only 19 games in 11 pro seasons since Utah made him the seventh pick in 1983 . . . Timberwolves got him from the Jazz Nov. 25, 1991, in exchange for Tyrone Corbin . . . College teammate of coach Sidney Lowe at North Carolina State and starting forward on 1983 NCAA championship team . . . Born April 7, 1961, in Washington, D.C. . . . Made $1 million.

Year	Team	G	FG	FG Pct.	FT	FT Pct.	Reb.	Ast.	TP	Avg.
1983-84	Utah	81	302	.512	88	.752	464	129	692	8.5
1984-85	Utah	80	507	.490	197	.842	525	138	1212	15.2
1985-86	Utah	82	483	.448	230	.830	493	153	1196	14.6
1986-87	Utah	81	463	.447	190	.805	432	102	1116	13.8
1987-88	Utah	82	633	.492	337	.826	531	158	1604	19.6
1988-89	Utah	82	615	.483	363	.825	447	138	1595	19.5
1989-90	Utah	82	470	.481	222	.779	410	137	1162	14.2
1990-91	Utah	82	399	.458	219	.808	407	124	1017	12.4
1991-92	Utah-Minn.	84	368	.440	215	.796	485	78	951	11.3
1992-93	Minnesota.	70	203	.455	119	.838	215	61	525	7.5
1993-94	Minnesota.	79	232	.510	119	.799	215	54	583	7.4
	Totals	885	4675	.473	2299	.813	4624	1272	11653	13.2

STACEY KING 27 6-11 250   Center-Forward

Midseason trade that sent him from Chicago to Minnesota meant a big drop in the standings but a big increase in personal stature . . . Took advantage of his new beginning by posting increases in almost every statistical category . . . Became a focal part of the offense, something that never would have happened with the Bulls . . . Had some impressive stretches, like four consecutive double-doubles . . . Started 15 of 18 games with the Timberwolves, compared to 15 of 31 with the Bulls . . . Timberwolves would rather have him at power forward, but based on what they saw last spring they figure it wouldn't be the worst thing in the world if he opened at center this season . . . This is the closest he has come to living up to the promise of a No. 6 pick in 1989 . . . Born Jan. 29, 1967, in Lawton, Okla., and stayed close for college while starring at Oklahoma... Made $1.6 million.

Year	Team	G	FG	FG Pct.	FT	FT Pct.	Reb.	Ast.	TP	Avg.
1989-90	Chicago	82	267	.504	194	.727	384	87	728	8.9
1990-91	Chicago	76	156	.467	107	.704	208	65	419	5.5
1991-92	Chicago	79	215	.506	119	.753	205	77	551	7.0
1992-93	Chicago	76	160	.471	86	.705	207	71	408	5.4
1993-94	Chi.-Minn.	49	146	.428	93	.684	241	58	385	7.9
	Totals	362	944	.479	599	.717	1245	358	2491	6.9

CHRIS SMITH 24 6-3 191   Guard

The backup point guard the last two seasons may become the starting point guard this season ... At least he is expected to push Micheal Williams for the job... Timberwolves' second-round pick in 1992 continues to improve his stock... Started 16 times last season, mostly when Williams was hurt, and the team responded well... Averaged 11.6 points and 6.6 assists those 16 games... Already known as aggressive defender... Needs to become a better shooter than the .433 and .435 his first two seasons so defenses don't completely play off him and worry only about the pass... Born May 17, 1970, in Bridgeport, Conn., and played at Connecticut... Made $270,000.

Year	Team	G	FG	FG Pct.	FT	FT Pct.	Reb.	Ast.	TP	Avg.
1992-93	Minnesota.......	80	125	.433	95	.792	96	196	347	4.3
1993-94	Minnesota.......	80	184	.435	95	.674	122	285	473	5.9
	Totals	160	309	.434	190	.728	218	481	820	5.1

MARLON MAXEY 25 6-8 250   Forward

Heads into make-or-break season... Timberwolves are starting to run thin on patience... Inside player who makes good use of leaping ability to compensate for size deficit among power forwards... Probably the best offensive rebounder on the team... True athlete... Played freshman season at the University of Minnesota before transferring to Texas-El Paso, then returned to Minneapolis when Timberwolves made him the 28th pick in 1992... College teammate of Tim Hardaway and

Greg Foster at UTEP... Born Feb. 19, 1969, in Chicago... Made $375,000.

Year	Team	G	FG	FG Pct.	FT	FT Pct.	Reb.	Ast.	TP	Avg.
1992-93	Minnesota.......	43	93	.550	45	.643	164	12	231	5.4
1993-94	Minnesota.......	55	89	.533	70	.714	199	10	248	4.5
	Totals	98	182	.542	115	.685	363	22	479	4.9

MIKE BROWN 31 6-10 260   Center

The widebody is Timberwolves' most physical player and a good presence inside... Very limited offensive skills... Started 42 times, but best suited as a backup... That he played all 82 games isn't unusual. It's come to be expected from the George Washington product, who wasn't even drafted until the third round and then played a year in Italy before making the NBA... Has 463 consecutive appearances, the third-longest active streak in the league... The 1,921 minutes during 1993-94 marked a career high... Timberwolves sent Felton Spencer to Utah in the summer of '93 to get him... Inducted in GWU Hall of Fame last April... Born July 19, 1963, in East Orange, N.J. ... Made $1.375 million.

Year	Team	G	FG	FG Pct.	FT	FT Pct.	Reb.	Ast.	TP	Avg.
1986-87	Chicago	62	106	.527	46	.639	214	24	258	4.2
1987-88	Chicago	46	78	.448	41	.577	159	28	197	4.3
1988-89	Utah	66	104	.419	92	.708	258	41	300	4.5
1989-90	Utah	82	177	.515	157	.789	373	47	512	6.2
1990-91	Utah	82	129	.454	132	.742	337	49	390	4.8
1991-92	Utah	82	221	.453	190	.667	476	81	632	7.7
1992-93	Utah	82	176	.430	113	.689	391	64	465	5.7
1993-94	Minnesota.......	82	111	.427	77	.653	447	72	299	3.6
	Totals	584	1102	.458	848	.697	2655	406	3053	5.2

TELLIS FRANK 29 6-10 225   Forward-Center

Free-agent signee made the team last season on hustle and aggressive play... Long after Golden State used the 14th pick in the 1987 draft to get him, he's still looking for offensive skills to improve... Has a hard time knocking shots down and even finishing... In the opening lineup for 11 of 67 outings... This is his second stint with the Timberwolves... In addition to playing with three NBA teams, he has also had two trips to play in Italy... Attended Western Kentucky... Made $200,000... Born April 26, 1965, in Gary, Ind.

Year	Team	G	FG	FG Pct.	FT	FT Pct.	Reb.	Ast.	TP	Avg.
1987-88	Golden State	78	242	.428	150	.725	330	111	634	8.1
1988-89	Golden State	32	34	.374	39	.765	61	15	107	3.3
1989-90	Miami	77	278	.458	179	.765	385	85	735	9.5
1991-92	Minnesota	10	18	.545	10	.667	26	8	46	4.6
1993-94	Minnesota	67	67	.419	54	.711	220	57	188	2.8
	Totals	264	639	.439	432	.741	1022	276	1710	6.5

BRIAN DAVIS 24 6-7 195   Guard-Forward

The 68 appearances in 1993-94 would seem to indicate he was an integral part of the team—except that his average of 5.5 minutes per game was the second-lowest among all Timberwolves... And that was even with the three starts, all early in the season... Used mostly in defensive situations and blowouts... Even if offense isn't his game, he still needs to do better than .317 from the field as a swingman if he hopes to stick anywhere in the league... Roommates with Christian Laettner at Duke and part of two NCAA championship clubs... Phoenix picked him 48th in 1992, then cut him in training camp... Played in France last season before Minnesota brought him back to the NBA at the $150,000 minimum... Born June 21, 1970, in Atlantic City, N.J.

Year	Team	G	FG	FG Pct.	FT	FT Pct.	Reb.	Ast.	TP	Avg.
1993-94	Minnesota	68	40	.317	50	.735	55	22	131	1.9

ANDRES GUIBERT 26 6-10 242   Center

Will have to make a big contribution for his future to be anywhere as interesting as his past... Will have to make the 1994-95 Timberwolves first... A member of the Cuban national team who defected to Puerto Rico last summer... Left behind parents and two sisters and played with San Juan Capitals... First Cuban to play in the NBA... Management is intrigued, but he may go to Spain without even trying training camp if he sees the NBA chances as limited... Unpolished, but handles the ball very well for a big man and runs the floor... Aggressive in going after blocks . . . Pronounced ON-draz Ge-BEART . . . Born Oct. 28, 1968, in Cuba.

Year	Team	G	FG	FG Pct.	FT	FT Pct.	Reb.	Ast.	TP	Avg.
1993-94	Minnesota.	5	6	.300	3	.500	16	2	15	3.0

STANLEY JACKSON 24 6-3 185   Guard

Probably the second-best athlete on the team last season behind Isaiah Rider, but suffers because he's a tweener . . . Too small to be a regular at shooting guard, too inexperienced at handling the ball and running the offense . . . Timberwolves at least wanted him back for summer league so he could work on those areas . . . Signed rookie free-agent contract for $150,000 after going undrafted out of Alabama-Birmingham . . . Did catch some eyes by being named to the all-tournament team at the Portsmouth Invitational . . . UAB's all-time career leader in steals and fifth in scoring . . . Born Oct. 14, 1970, in Tuskegee, Ala.

Year	Team	G	FG	FG Pct.	FT	FT Pct.	Reb.	Ast.	TP	Avg.
1993-94	Minnesota.	17	17	.515	3	1.000	27	16	38	2.2

THE ROOKIES

DONYELL MARSHALL 21 6-8 210   Forward

Has been compared to a young Connie Hawkins . . . Certainly has the same body, tall and wiry . . . Shaky showing in NCAA tournament didn't stop Timberwolves from taking him at No. 4 . . . They want to put Connecticut product at small forward . . . Big East Conference Player of the Year and All-American before foregoing senior season to turn pro . . . Born May 18, 1973, in Reading, Pa.

HOWARD EISLEY 21 6-2 180   Guard

Some had Boston College point guard going in the first round, but Timberwolves got him with the No. 30 pick, which could make for a nice pickup . . . Led Eagles in assists and improved scoring all four years in college . . . Teammate of Bill Curley, who went 22nd to the Spurs . . . Set Eagles' record with 126 games played . . . Born Dec. 4, 1972, in Detroit.

T-Wolves keep hoping for more from Christian Laettner.

GREATEST PLAYER

Unlike other teams, where length of service is given heavy consideration, we don't have to worry about that with the Timberwolves because no one has longevity. So we can pick Christian Laettner, even though he has all of two seasons of NBA experience.

We pick him, simply, because he is their greatest player. The stats will catch up soon enough; he should become the No. 1 rebounder this season barring significant injury and the No. 1 scorer sometime soon after. Until then, keep in mind that he is a power forward with all-star potential, plays some center in a pinch, and would be coveted by every general manager if they didn't spend so much time shaking their heads about his attitude.

There are a few names ahead of Laettner for Timberwolves' career leaders, mostly Tony Campbell and Pooh Richardson. But Laettner leads all in talent.

ALL-TIME TIMBERWOLF LEADERS

SEASON

Points: Tony Campbell, 1,903, 1989-90
Assists: Jerome Richardson, 734, 1990-91
Rebounds: Christian Laettner, 708, 1992-93

GAME

Points: Tony Campbell, 44 vs. Boston, 2/2/90
Assists: Sidney Lowe, 17 vs. Golden State, 3/20/90
　　　　　Pooh Richardson, 17 vs. Washington, 3/13/92
Rebounds: Todd Murphy, 20 vs. L.A. Clippers, 1/2/90

CAREER

Points: Tony Campbell, 4,888, 1989-92
Assists: Jerome Richardson, 1,973, 1989-92
Rebounds: Sam Mitchell, 1,455, 1989-92

PHOENIX SUNS

TEAM DIRECTORY: Pres./CEO: Jerry Colangelo; Senior VP: Cotton Fitzsimmons; VP-Dir. Player Personnel; Dick Van Arsdale; VP-Dir. Pub. Rel.: Tom Ambrose; Dir. Media Rel.: Julie Fie; Coach: Paul Westphal; Asst. Coaches: Lionel Hollins, Scotty Robertson. Arena: America West (19,000). Colors: Purple, orange and copper.

SCOUTING REPORT

SHOOTING: Gone are the days when the Suns were known as a track team, even though they can still run with the best of 'em. Here are the days when the three-point shot is a primary weapon, to the extent that only Houston and Orlando had more attempts last season. "That line's not out there for decoration," Danny Ainge says. "You're supposed to use it." So they do, mainly Dan Majerle, Charles Barkley and Ainge. First-round pick Wesley Person should fit right in.

The Suns led the league by averaging 108.2 points not only because they have a lot of people who score, but because they have some terrific marksmen. Cedric Ceballos was hardly the primary option among the starters, probably ahead of only centers Oliver Miller and Mark West (now gone to the Pistons) when everyone was healthy, but he contributed 19.1 points largely because he shot .535. Miller and West combined for 741 attempts, only sixth on the team if they were one person, but went .609 and .566, respectively. They are more potent with the arrival of Danny Manning as a free agent.

PLAYMAKING: The Suns had the fourth-best assist-to-turnover ratio in the league, second in the Western Conference, and not just because of Kevin Johnson, though that's a good place to start. Johnson finished fifth in the league in assists at 9.5 a game while committing just 3.5 turnovers. Frank Johnson, the backup who played 70 games, was better than 2-1. Duane Cooper would have been solid for a third-stringer had he not blown out his knee.

Barkley is another reason they succeed in this area because the ball is in his hands so often, much of the time on the post with a double- or triple-team running at him. That he is so effective in whipping passes back out is one reason why Majerle can break the NBA record for three-pointers in a season. Barkley himself has bought into this theory so well that his 385 assists in 1992-

Sir Charles is back, hopefully without aching back.

93, before his 1993-94 was hampered by injuries, were more than he ever had in any of the eight seasons in Philadelphia, despite sometimes playing hundreds more minutes. Manning, meanwhile, is one of the best ball-handling big men in the league.

REBOUNDING: Three years ago, they finished 15th in the league by percentage, and people pegged this as a problem area. Two years ago, after Barkley and Miller arrived, they jumped to ninth. Finally, last year, still with no one taller than 6-10 getting significant minutes, they climbed all the way to a tie for fourth.

So no one talks about this as a problem area anymore. The main reason is the two primary acquisitions each of the previous two summers: Barkley in 1992 and A.C. Green in '93. Barkley averaged 10.2 rebounds in 1993-94 despite playing with a bad back and a bad leg, two things that hinder jumping. When he was unable to play, Green filled in by getting 9.2 a game. The hidden

SUN ROSTER

No.	Veterans	Pos.	Ht.	Wt.	Age	Yrs. Pro	College
22	Danny Ainge	G	6-5	185	35	13	Brigham Young
34	Charles Barkley	F	6-5	252	31	10	Auburn
23	Cedric Ceballos	F-G	6-7	225	25	4	Cal-Fullerton
–	Duane Cooper	G	6-1	185	25	2	USC
45	A.C. Green	F	6-9	225	31	9	Oregon State
3	Frank Johnson	G	6-1	180	36	10	Wake Forest
7	Kevin Johnson	G	6-1	190	28	7	California
35	Joe Kleine	C	7-0	271	32	9	Arkansas
27	Malcolm Mackey	F-C	6-11	248	24	1	Georgia Tech
9	Dan Majerle	G	6-6	220	29	6	Central Michigan
–	Danny Manning	F	6-10	234	28	6	Kansas
R-25	Oliver Miller	C	6-9	280	24	2	Arkansas
0	Jerrod Mustaf	F	6-10	245	24	4	Maryland
2	Elliot Perry	G	6-0	160	25	2	Memphis State

R-restricted free agent

Rd.	Rookies	Sel. No.	Pos.	Ht.	Wt.	College
1	Wesley Person	23	G	6-5	195	Auburn
2	Antonio Lang	29	F	6-8	205	Duke
2	Charles Claxton	50	C	6-11	265	Georgia
2	Anthony Goldwire	52	G	6-1	182	Houston

factor was Ceballos, who averaged 6.5 boards from small forward in just 30.2 minutes.

DEFENSE: They still surrender too many easy baskets. How many? Only seven teams had a more porous shooting-percentage-against than the Suns' .474, and all seven were in the lottery. The strange thing is that the drop from 17th the season before came as Miller started to develop as a shot-blocker—he finished eighth despite playing just 25.9 minutes, ahead of more-publicized intimidators like Chris Webber, Shawn Kemp and Derrick Coleman.

OUTLOOK: Much better after Barkley announced he would return for 1994-95. Much, much better after Manning announced he would sign. If Barkley's back holds up, Paul Westphal's Suns will be as they have been, contenders for the title.

SUN PROFILES

CHARLES BARKLEY 31 6-5 252 Forward

Welcome return after an offseason conditioning program . . . Struggled to recover from a torn tendon above the knee and sore back . . . Went stretches without usual jumping ability and quickness . . . That meant he played as if he was only 6-8 instead of the usual 6-11 . . . The back has been ongoing problem . . . Was great again when it mattered, in the playoffs . . . His 56 points against Golden State tied the third-highest offensive output ever in the postseason and his 38 points were the most ever for a first half . . . Coach Paul Westphal says he's the Suns' best defender at any position . . . Coming off worst shooting season of his career (.495) . . . Leading vote-getter for All-Star Game, but did not play because of knee injury . . . Starred at Auburn, was a 1992 Olympian and the 1992-93 MVP . . . Philadelphia drafted the round mound of rebound and traded him to Suns two seasons ago for Jeff Hornacek, Andrew Lang and Tim Perry . . . Born Feb. 20, 1963, in Leeds, Ala. . . . Made $3.25 million.

Year	Team	G	FG	FG Pct.	FT	FT Pct.	Reb.	Ast.	TP	Avg.
1984-85	Philadelphia	82	427	.545	293	.733	703	155	1148	14.0
1985-86	Philadelphia	80	595	.572	396	.685	1026	312	1603	20.0
1986-87	Philadelphia	68	557	.594	429	.761	994	331	1564	23.0
1987-88	Philadelphia	80	753	.587	714	.751	951	254	2264	28.3
1988-89	Philadelphia	79	700	.579	602	.753	986	325	2037	25.8
1989-90	Philadelphia	79	706	.600	557	.749	909	307	1989	25.2
1990-91	Philadelphia	67	665	.570	475	.722	680	284	1849	27.6
1991-92	Philadelphia	75	622	.552	454	.695	830	308	1730	23.1
1992-93	Phoenix	76	716	.520	445	.765	928	385	1944	25.6
1993-94	Phoenix	65	518	.495	318	.704	727	296	1402	21.6
	Totals	751	6259	.562	4683	.734	8734	2957	17530	23.3

KEVIN JOHNSON 28 6-1 190 Guard

Disappointed at not originally being selected to Dream Team II before eventually getting a spot when Isiah Thomas went down with an injury . . . Took it out on the rest of the league . . . Finished No. 5 in assists (9.5) and No. 15 in steals (1.87) and would have been No. 16 in scoring and tops among all point guards (20.0) but fell three games short of the minimum qualifications . . . Earned third all-star berth . . . One of only six players in NBA history to record a triple-double with steals . . . Suns' all-time assist leader says he will retire when contract expires in three seasons . . . Chosen in the 1986 baseball draft by Oakland A's . . . Chosen in the first round in 1987 NBA draft, out of California, by Cavaliers . . . They traded him during rookie season to Suns along with Mark West, Tyrone Corbin and picks for Larry Nance, Mike Sanders and pick . . . Born March 4, 1966, in Sacramento . . . Made $2.3 million.

Year	Team	G	FG	FG Pct.	FT	FT Pct.	Reb.	Ast.	TP	Avg.
1987-88	Clev.-Phoe.	80	275	.461	177	.839	191	437	732	9.2
1988-89	Phoenix	81	570	.505	508	.882	340	991	1650	20.4
1989-90	Phoenix	74	578	.499	501	.838	270	846	1665	22.5
1990-91	Phoenix	77	591	.516	519	.843	271	781	1710	22.2
1991-92	Phoenix	78	539	.479	448	.807	292	836	1536	19.7
1992-93	Phoenix	49	282	.499	226	.819	104	384	791	16.1
1993-94	Phoenix	67	477	.487	380	.819	167	637	1340	20.0
	Totals	506	3312	.494	2759	.837	1635	4912	9424	18.6

DAN MAJERLE 29 6-6 220   Guard

Remember when he was known for driving dunks, those explosive inside moves that earned him the nickname "Thunder"? . . . The same guy set an NBA record last season with 192 three-pointers, breaking Vernon Maxwell's mark of 172, set in 1990-91 . . . The problem is, he finished 20th in accuracy for the second season in a row and dropped to a career-low .418 overall . . . Has missed just two games the last three seasons and seven the last four seasons . . . Good defender who can match up with big guards and small forwards . . . Member of Dream Team II and was on the 1988 Olympic team that won a bronze medal . . . Central Michigan product was so unknown that local fans booed when Suns picked him 14th in 1988 draft . . . Born Sept. 9, 1965, in Traverse City, Mich . . . .Made $2.975 million.

Year	Team	G	FG	FG Pct.	FT	FT Pct.	Reb.	Ast.	TP	Avg.
1988-89	Phoenix	54	181	.419	78	.614	209	130	467	8.6
1989-90	Phoenix	73	296	.424	198	.762	430	188	809	11.1
1990-91	Phoenix	77	397	.484	227	.762	418	216	1051	13.6
1991-92	Phoenix	82	551	.478	229	.756	483	274	1418	17.3
1992-93	Phoenix	82	509	.464	203	.778	383	311	1388	16.9
1993-94	Phoenix	80	476	.418	176	.739	349	275	1320	16.5
	Totals	448	2410	.451	1111	.747	2272	1394	6453	14.4

A.C. GREEN 31 6-9 225   Forward

Only his address changed . . . Joined Suns as a free agent for 1993-94 after eight seasons with the Lakers . . . Didn't miss any games, hit the boards, never stopped working . . . Ho-hum . . . Scoring average was a career high and rebounding average was second-best . . . Ran streak of consecutive regular-season appearances to 649, the longest active run and the sixth-longest in league history . . . Next up: Harry Gallatin at 682 . . . By that time, he should be even richer . . . Signed five-year, $15.2-million contract that paid $1.885 million in 1993-94 and has since signed a revised contract reportedly worth $25 million for five years. . . . Initials A.C. do not stand for anything . . . Born Oct. 4, 1963, in Portland, Ore., and stayed close to home to attend Oregon State before Lakers took him in the first round in 1985.

Year	Team	G	FG	FG Pct.	FT	FT Pct.	Reb.	Ast.	TP	Avg.
1985-86	L.A. Lakers	82	209	.539	102	.611	381	54	521	6.4
1986-87	L.A. Lakers	79	316	.538	220	.780	615	84	852	10.8
1987-88	L.A. Lakers	82	322	.503	293	.773	710	93	937	11.4
1988-89	L.A. Lakers	82	401	.529	282	.786	739	103	1088	13.3
1989-90	L.A. Lakers	82	385	.478	278	.751	712	90	1061	12.9
1990-91	L.A. Lakers	82	258	.476	223	.738	516	71	750	9.1
1991-92	L.A. Lakers	82	382	.476	340	.744	762	117	1116	13.6
1992-93	L.A. Lakers	82	379	.537	277	.739	711	116	1051	12.8
1993-94	Phoenix	82	465	.502	266	.735	753	137	1204	14.7
	Totals	735	3117	.506	2281	.747	5899	865	8580	11.7

CEDRIC CEBALLOS 25 6-7 225   Forward-Guard

Richard Dumas is more expendable than ever because this is the small forward the Suns can count on . . . Missed the first 29 games of 1993-94 with a stress fracture in the left foot, then returned to finish sixth in the league in shooting and record a career-best 19.1 scoring average . . . That jump of nearly seven points earned him some votes for Most Improved Player . . . The progression continues . . . Played just one season of varsity basketball in high school, went to junior college before moving to Cal State-Fullerton, hardly a big stage, and barely made the second round of the 1990 draft at No. 49 overall . . . The Suns have gotten a nice return on their investment . . . Still best known for winning the slam-dunk title in 1992 with his hocus-pocus stunt

... Born Aug. 2, 1969, on the island of Maui in Hawaii ... Made $2 million.

Year	Team	G	FG	FG Pct.	FT	FT Pct.	Reb.	Ast.	TP	Avg.
1990-91	Phoenix	63	204	.487	110	.663	150	35	519	8.2
1991-92	Phoenix	64	176	.482	109	.736	152	50	462	7.2
1992-93	Phoenix	74	381	.576	187	.725	408	77	949	12.8
1993-94	Phoenix	53	425	.535	160	.724	344	91	1010	19.1
	Totals	254	1186	.529	566	.714	1054	253	2940	11.6

OLIVER MILLER 24 6-9 280   Center

The Too-Big O ... Lost his starting job and minutes after his weight went over 290 pounds again ... Suns set a 280-pound limit ... Admitted he let the team, the coach and himself down ... Those always seem to be the most prominent numbers, those on the scale, but there are others ... Finished eighth in the league in blocked shots, even at 6-9 ... Also would have been No. 1 in field-goal accuracy (.609) but fell 23 attempts shy of qualifying minimum ... Started in 30 of his 69 appearances ... Arkansas product was born April 6, 1970, in Fort Worth, Tex .... Suns took him with 22nd pick in 1992 draft ... Made $672,000.

Year	Team	G	FG	FG Pct.	FT	FT Pct.	Reb.	Ast.	TP	Avg.
1992-93	Phoenix	56	121	.475	71	.710	275	118	313	5.6
1993-94	Phoenix	69	277	.609	80	.584	476	244	636	9.2
	Totals	125	398	.561	151	.637	751	362	949	7.6

FRANK JOHNSON 36 6-1 180   Guard

Role decreased only slightly with Suns last season, but was still around much longer than he expected when he signed as a free agent in October 1992 ... He had just spent three years in Italy and was figuring to retire after getting cut in camp ... Then Kevin Johnson went down with an injury two days later ... He was brought back and hasn't left since ... Rewarded with jump from $140,000 salary in 1992-93 to $500,000 last campaign ... Started five times in 1993-94 ... No relation to Kevin Johnson ... Older brother, Eddie, once played in the NBA

... Starred at Wake Forest before opening pro career with Bullets ... Born Nov. 23, 1958, in Weirsdale, Fla.

Year	Team	G	FG	FG Pct.	FT	FT Pct.	Reb.	Ast.	TP	Avg.
1981-82	Washington......	79	336	.414	153	.750	147	380	842	10.7
1982-83	Washington......	68	321	.408	196	.751	178	549	852	12.5
1983-84	Washington......	82	392	.467	187	.742	184	567	982	12.0
1984-85	Washington......	46	175	.489	72	.750	63	143	428	9.3
1985-86	Washington......	14	69	.448	38	.704	28	76	176	12.6
1986-87	Washington......	18	59	.461	35	.714	30	58	153	8.5
1987-88	Washington......	75	216	.434	121	.812	121	188	554	7.4
1988-89	Houston.......	67	109	.443	75	.806	79	181	294	4.4
1992-93	Phoenix........	77	136	.436	59	.776	113	186	332	4.3
1993-94	Phoenix........	70	134	.448	54	.783	82	148	324	4.6
	Totals	596	1947	.439	990	.760	1025	2476	4937	8.3

DANNY MANNING 28 6-10 234   Forward

He's what's new under the Sun, a free-agent signee from the Hawks ... Began last season with Clippers and was traded for Dominique Wilkins and conditional first-rounder in February ... Played 26 games with Hawks, averaged 15.7 points, 6.5 rebounds, 3.3 assists and 1.8 steals ... Hawks were 20-9 after he arrived (he missed three games with illness) ... A solid, steady all-around player but not nearly the superstar his hype says ... Added 994 points as a Clip before trade. Became Clips' all-time scorer ... Had career highs in points (43), rebounds (18) assists (10) and steals (7) last season ... Led Hawks in playoff scoring (20.0) but despite good numbers, lagged against Pacers in Eastern semis ... Made $3.25 million in final year of pact ... Born May 17, 1966, in Hattiesburg, Miss.... Two-time first-team All-American, 1987 and '88 ... MVP of '88 NCAA tourney when he led Kansas to national title ... Father Ed played nine pro years with six teams.

Year	Team	G	FG	FG Pct.	FT	FT Pct.	Reb.	Ast.	TP	Avg.
1988-89	L.A. Clippers.....	26	177	.494	79	.767	171	81	434	16.7
1989-90	L.A. Clippers.....	71	440	.533	274	.741	422	187	1154	16.3
1990-91	L.A. Clippers.....	73	470	.519	219	.716	426	196	1159	15.9
1991-92	L.A. Clippers.....	82	650	.542	279	.725	564	285	1579	19.3
1992-93	L.A. Clippers.....	79	702	.509	388	.802	520	207	1800	22.8
1993-94	LAC-Atl..........	68	586	.488	228	.669	465	261	1403	20.6
	Totals	399	3025	.516	1467	.738	2568	1217	7529	18.9

DANNY AINGE 35 6-5 185   Guard

No, that big fall didn't come because millions of Americans want to push him off a cliff... Dropped all the way to .417 from the field, the lowest since his rookie campaign with Celtics, and .328 on three-pointers... Heads into the final year of three-year deal he signed when Suns lured him away from Portland as a free agent... That doesn't have to mean it's the final year of his career... Even with diminished skills, he's worth plenty to some team because of those quote-unquote intangibles ... Everyone hates that fiery spirit until he is playing for their team... Could fit in several situations, either with championship contender looking for an insurance policy or a young club wanting someone to show youngsters the ropes... Trails only Dale Ellis for career three-pointers made and Michael Adams for three-pointers attempted... Second-round pick by Boston in 1981 after starring at Brigham Young... Born March 17, 1959, in Eugene, Ore....Made $1.69 million.

Year	Team	G	FG	FG Pct.	FT	FT Pct.	Reb.	Ast.	TP	Avg.
1981-82	Boston	53	79	.357	56	.862	56	87	219	4.1
1982-83	Boston	80	357	.496	72	.742	214	251	791	9.9
1983-84	Boston	71	166	.460	46	.821	116	162	384	5.4
1984-85	Boston	75	419	.529	118	.868	268	399	971	12.9
1985-86	Boston	80	353	.504	123	.904	235	405	855	10.7
1986-87	Boston	71	410	.486	148	.897	242	400	1053	14.8
1987-88	Boston	81	482	.491	158	.878	249	503	1270	15.7
1988-89	Bos.-Sac.	73	480	.457	205	.854	255	402	1281	17.5
1989-90	Sacramento	75	506	.438	222	.831	326	453	1342	17.9
1990-91	Portland	80	337	.472	114	.826	205	285	890	11.1
1991-92	Portland	81	299	.442	108	.824	148	202	784	9.7
1992-93	Phoenix	80	337	.462	123	.848	214	260	947	11.8
1993-94	Phoenix	68	224	.417	78	.830	131	180	606	8.9
	Totals	968	4449	.469	1571	.849	2659	3989	11393	11.8

JOE KLEINE 32 7-0 271   Center

At least he got $650,000... He sure didn't get much playing time as third-string center behind Oliver Miller and Mark West... A just-in-case free-agent signing by Suns last summer... Averaged only 11.5 minutes, the fewest of his career that started as a No. 6 pick by Sacramento out of Arkansas... Also coming off low-rebound season... 1984 Olympian... No speed, but will step out about 10 or 12 feet for short jumpers...

Born Jan. 4, 1962, in Colorado Springs, Colo . . . . Played on same Arkansas team as Alvin Robertson, Scott Hastings and Darrell Walker.

Year	Team	G	FG	FG Pct.	FT	FT Pct.	Reb.	Ast.	TP	Avg.
1985-86	Sacramento......	80	160	.465	94	.723	373	46	414	5.2
1986-87	Sacramento......	79	256	.471	110	.786	483	71	622	7.9
1987-88	Sacramento......	82	324	.472	153	.814	579	93	801	9.8
1988-89	Sac.-Boston	75	175	.405	134	.882	378	67	484	6.5
1989-90	Boston.........	81	176	.480	83	.830	355	46	435	5.4
1990-91	Boston.........	72	102	.468	54	.783	244	21	258	3.6
1991-92	Boston.........	70	144	.491	34	.708	296	32	326	4.7
1992-93	Boston.........	78	108	.404	41	.707	346	39	257	3.3
1993-94	Phoenix........	74	125	.488	30	.769	193	45	285	3.9
	Totals	691	1570	.461	733	.793	3247	460	3882	5.6

JERROD MUSTAF 25 6-10 245   Forward

Was on the injured list at the end of the season because of tendinitis in his knee . . . May have been left off the playoff roster even if he were healthy . . . His offensive strength is his post game . . . Future in doubt . . . Came to Suns in the fall of 1991 as part of the Xavier McDaniel deal with New York . . . Born Oct. 28, 1969, in Whiteville, N.C . . . . Maryland product was No. 17 pick by Knicks in 1990 . . . Made $1.074 million.

Year	Team	G	FG	FG Pct.	FT	FT Pct.	Reb.	Ast.	TP	Avg.
1990-91	New York.......	62	106	.465	56	.644	169	36	268	4.5
1991-92	Phoenix........	52	92	.477	49	.690	145	45	233	4.5
1992-93	Phoenix........	32	57	.438	33	.623	83	10	147	4.6
1993-94	Phoenix........	33	30	.357	13	.591	55	8	73	2.2
	Totals	179	285	.449	151	.648	452	99	721	4.0

DUANE COOPER 25 6-1 185   Guard

Played 23 games with Phoenix before blowing out his knee . . . Underwent reconstructive surgery . . . Suns signed him as a free agent after he was cut by the Lakers at the end of camp . . . Like coach Paul Westphal, he came out of the USC backcourt . . . Left school as all-time leader in games played and was second in assists . . . Point guard who needs to get better at making decisions, especially on the run . . . If the Suns don't want to bring him back this season, he should hook on with someone ... Born June 25, 1969, in Benton Harbor, Mich.... Made $250,000.

Year	Team	G	FG	FG Pct.	FT	FT Pct.	Reb.	Ast.	TP	Avg.
1992-93	L.A. Lakers	65	62	.392	25	.714	50	150	156	2.4
1993-94	Phoenix	23	18	.439	11	.733	9	28	48	2.1
	Totals	88	80	.402	36	.720	59	178	204	2.3

ELLIOT PERRY 25 6-0 160   Guard

Went from the CBA to making Suns' playoff roster... Arrived Jan. 22 on a 10-day contract after injuries to Kevin Johnson and Danny Ainge... Signed for the rest of the season Feb. 11... Jitterbug-quick... Only player in Metro Conference history to compile more than 2,000 points and 500 assists... That was while at Memphis State, where he was tough to miss. He was skinny 6-footer wearing goggles and throwing down slam dunks... L.A. Clippers brought him into the NBA as a second-round pick in 1991... Has also played with LaCrosse of the CBA ... Born March 28, 1969, in Memphis, Tenn.

Year	Team	G	FG	FG Pct.	FT	FT Pct.	Reb.	Ast.	TP	Avg.
1991-92	LAC-Char	50	49	.380	27	.659	39	78	50	2.5
1993-94	Phoenix	27	42	.372	21	.750	39	125	105	3.9
	Totals	77	91	.376	48	.696	78	203	155	2.0

MALCOLM MACKEY 24 6-11 248   Forward-Center

Decent skills, indecent work ethic... Suns disappointed with his approach after using their first-round pick last season to get him... He'll have to get it in gear or else they will be disappointed, period... Not on the playoff roster ... Finished the season on the injured list because of tendinitis in his knees... Made $550,000... Left Georgia Tech as the all-time leader in games played and rebounds and was second-leading shot-blocker, behind only John Salley... No. 27 pick in '93... Born July 11, 1970, in Chattanooga, Tenn.

Year	Team	G	FG	FG Pct.	FT	FT Pct.	Reb.	Ast.	TP	Avg.
1993-94	Phoenix	22	14	.378	4	.500	24	1	32	1.5

Kevin Johnson achieved rare triple-double in steals.

THE ROOKIES

WESLEY PERSON 23 6-5 195   Guard

Chuck's younger brother . . . Doesn't have the same mouth, but can shoot, too . . . With Suns planning to move Dan Majerle back to small forward, he will have a chance to start right away . . . Third on Auburn's all-time scoring list, behind only Chuck Person and Mike Mitchell . . . May have been the best shooter in the draft, but lasted until Suns took him at No. 23 . . . Born March 28, 1971, in Crenshaw, Ala.

ANTONIO LANG 22 6-8 205 Forward

One of the few guys who can go to a championship contender and still probably end up losing more games as a rookie than in four years of college... Won NCAA titles with Duke in 1991 and '92 and played in a third championship game... Shot .523 or better all four seasons... No. 29 selection despite averaging double-figure points just once, the 12.5 as a senior... Born May 15, 1972, in Columbia, S.C.

CHARLES CLAXTON 23 6-11 265 Center

Left Georgia after junior year... Suns picked him 50th from there ... Finished fourth in the Southeastern Conference in blocked shots and sixth in rebounding, but had better scoring and shooting numbers as a sophomore... Started all but two games as a Bulldog ... Born Dec. 13, 1970, in St. Thomas, Virgin Islands.

ANTHONY GOLDWIRE 23 6-1 182 Guard

Add him to the list of guys who will compete for the few minutes available as backup point guard... In just two years at Houston, after spending the previous two at a JC, he climbed to ninth on Cougars' all-time assist list... Southwest Conference newcomer of the year as a junior... Born Sept. 6, 1971, in West Palm Beach, Fla.

COACH PAUL WESTPHAL: Did he just have the coaching  version of the sophomore jinx?... Suns went from 62 wins and a trip to the NBA Finals in 1992-93 to 56 wins and a second-round elimination... Injuries hurt, but there were other developments... Team president Jerry Colangelo suggested he was too mellow, so Westphal became more vocal and demonstrative on the sideline... Reached 100-win plateau after just 140 games... Red Auerbach, Pat Riley and Bill Russell are the only coaches to get there faster... Career: 118-46 (.720)... Spent 12 years in the NBA after starring at USC... First-round selection by Celtics in 1972 and spent three seasons in Boston... Traded to Suns, where he played five years... Led team in scoring every season, topped by the 25.2 mark in 1977-78, and made all-star team four times... Finished career with Seattle and New York ... Suns retired his uniform No. 44 in 1989... Began coaching career with one year at Southwestern College and one at Grand

Canyon College, both in Arizona, before joining Cotton Fitzsimmons' staff . . . Was an assistant for four seasons before getting the promotion . . . Born Nov. 30, 1950, in Torrance, Calif.

GREATEST PLAYER

Sorry, Charlie. You may be the greatest player ever to wear a Suns' uniform, but that is different than being the greatest Suns player ever, the difference being more than semantics. It's too difficult to go with someone who has been with the organization only two years so far, even if those did produce one MVP season and scoring averages of 25.6 and 21.6 points.

Charles Barkley can dominate in most areas, just not this one. Not when someone like Paul Westphal was around, averaging 20.6 points over five seasons. The biggest challenge comes from Walter Davis, who holds the team record with 15,666 points.

In truth, several Suns could have been named the greatest, including current standout Kevin Johnson. Another few years and he may get the title without hesitation. Meanwhile, don't forget Dick Van Arsdale or Connie Hawkins, who also had their uniform numbers retired.

ALL-TIME SUN LEADERS

SEASON

Points: Tom Chambers, 2,201, 1989-90
Assists: Kevin Johnson, 991, 1988-89
Rebounds: Paul Silas, 1,015, 1970-71

GAME

Points: Tom Chambers, 60 vs. Seattle, 3/24/90
Assists: Gail Goodrich, 19 vs. Philadelphia, 10/22/69
Rebounds: Paul Silas, 27 vs. Cincinnati, 1/18/71

CAREER

Points: Walter Davis, 15,666, 1977-88
Assists: Kevin Johnson, 4,719, 1987-94
Rebounds: Alvan Adams, 6,937, 1975-88

PORTLAND TRAIL BLAZERS

TEAM DIRECTORY: Governor: Paul Allen; Pres.: Harry Glickman; VP-Player Personnel: Brad Greenburg; Dir. Sports Communications: John Lashway; Coach: P.J. Carlesimo; Asst. Coaches: Rick Carlisle, Dick Harter. Arena: Memorial Coliseum (12,888). Colors: Red, black and white.

SCOUTING REPORT

SHOOTING: Just try to get them to stop. The Trail Blazers took 111 more shots than any other team last season, meaning they played about an extra game and a half on offense. In this case, more is not better, though, because they shot just .454—20th best in the league. Boston was much better. The L.A. Clippers were more accurate. Minnesota and Philadelphia beat them out.

To understand exactly how bad the Trail Blazers are in this area, consider the showing of 1993-94 was an *improvement* of four spots from the previous season. That's what you get when leading scorer Clifford Robinson shoots .457, No. 2 contributor Clyde Drexler makes just .428 and Terry Porter, who tried more three-pointers than anyone, goes .416 overall.

They need to get better. Either that or focus on the positives of Buck Williams shooting .555 and Tracy Murray winning the three-point title and just keep hoping they can still win by outgunning people.

PLAYMAKING: This is one way they can compensate for the poor showing. Only five teams committed fewer turnovers, an encouraging stat for a team that likes to push the ball, with Rod Strickland's assist-to-turnover ratio just below 3-1. He was even better when the reins were turned over on a permanent basis. The Trail Blazers can also be comforted by the presence of Porter, the former starter at point guard who now supplies the depth. Most teams would love that kind of insurance policy.

REBOUNDING: It's still a strength. Only New York and San Antonio had better percentages last season, and the Trail Blazers were the best in the West on the defensive boards and tied for second overall. They just do it a strange way—shooting guard Drexler averaged practically the same number of rebounds (6.5) as primary center Robinson (6.7).

Multi-purpose Clifford Robinson paced Blazers in scoring.

The strength of the strength, of course, is Williams, who turns 35 in March but played last season like someone just hitting his stride. That 10.4 average came in 32.5 minutes, better numbers than kids like Rony Seikaly, Clarence Weatherspoon and Tom Gugliotta had with more time.

TRAIL BLAZER ROSTER

No.	Veterans	Pos.	Ht.	Wt.	Age	Yrs. Pro	College
2	Mark Bryant	F-C	6-9	245	29	6	Seton Hall
22	Clyde Drexler	G	6-7	232	32	11	Houston
24	Chris Dudley	C	6-11	240	29	7	Yale
44	Harvey Grant	F	6-9	225	29	6	Oklahoma
25	Jerome Kersey	F	6-7	225	32	10	Longwood
31	Tracy Murray	F	6-7	228	23	2	UCLA
30	Terry Porter	G	6-3	195	31	8	Wis.-Stevens Pt.
35	Kevin Thompson	C	6-11	260	23	1	North Carolina State
3	Clifford Robinson	F-C	6-10	225	27	5	Connecticut
26	James Robinson	G	6-2	180	24	1	Alabama
1	Rod Strickland	G	6-3	185	28	6	DePaul
35	Kevin Thompson	C	6-11	260		1	North Carolina State
52	Buck Williams	F	6-8	225	34	13	Maryland

Rd.	Rookies	Sel. No.	Pos.	Ht.	Wt.	College
1	Aaron McKie	17	G	6-4	209	Temple
2	Shawnelle Scott	43	F-C	6-10	250	St. John's

DEFENSE: The defense has everything to do with the offense, now more than ever because it must start a running game that does not ignite as easily as in the past. The defense needs to get stops since it's tough to run when you're taking the ball from the bottom of the net all the time. As Rick Adelman observed last season before being fired: "We're not the same team we were three years ago, when we had two of the best finishers in the league in Clyde and Jerome [Kersey]. We're not able to run as well now. But if we defend, we still can get out on the break." Adelman's goal was to keep opponents around .450, but the Trail Blazers allowed a poor .469. That was the third straight season the shooting percentage-against has increased.

OUTLOOK: P.J. Carlesimo takes over as coach with a difficult path ahead. This is a team whose window of opportunity appears to have closed, a group that is sliding backwards and doesn't have many options for brakes. Carlesimo, as coach and infusion of new energy, may be the best solution.

TRAIL BLAZER PROFILES

CLYDE DREXLER 32 6-7 222   Guard

Hopes for a healthy season and figures everything else will fall in line from there . . . Missed about a month last season with a sprained ankle and said it took about half the campaign to get back to 100% mentally . . . This was after missing 33 games the year before with hamstring and knee problems . . . The encouraging part to 1993-94 was that he finished well, averaging 24.1 points in April . . . Second-best rebounding guard in NBA behind Ron Harper, and No. 1 at offensive end . . . Eight-time all-star, three-time All-Star Game starter . . . All-time club leader in 11 of 17 categories . . . Portland took him with 14th pick in 1983 after he starred with Hakeem Olajuwon on U. of Houston team that went to Final Four twice . . . Born June 22, 1962, in New Orleans . . . Made $1.578 million.

Year	Team	G	FG	FG Pct.	FT	FT Pct.	Reb.	Ast.	TP	Avg.
1983-84	Portland	82	252	.451	123	.728	235	153	628	7.7
1984-85	Portland	80	573	.494	223	.759	476	441	1377	17.2
1985-86	Portland	75	542	.475	293	.769	421	600	1389	18.5
1986-87	Portland	82	707	.502	357	.760	518	566	1782	21.7
1987-88	Portland	81	849	.506	476	.811	533	467	2185	27.0
1988-89	Portland	78	829	.496	438	.799	615	450	2123	27.2
1989-90	Portland	73	670	.494	333	.774	507	432	1703	23.3
1990-91	Portland	82	645	.482	416	.794	546	493	1767	21.5
1991-92	Portland	76	694	.470	401	.794	500	512	1903	25.0
1992-93	Portland	49	350	.429	245	.839	309	278	976	19.9
1993-94	Portland	68	473	.428	286	.777	445	333	1303	19.2
	Totals	826	6584	.480	3591	.786	5105	4725	17136	20.7

CLIFFORD ROBINSON 27 6-10 225   Forward-Center

He went from Cliff to Clifford, but retained the versatility and the talent . . . Plays all three positions on the frontline . . . Creates great match-up possibilities when Trail Blazers use him at small forward . . . Of his 64 starts, 61 were at center . . . His 20.1 points a game was No. 1 on the team and No. 15 in the league . . . Made All-Star Game for the first time . . . Owns the fifth-longest active streak with 410 consecutive games and has participated in every regular-season and playoff game since rookie debut in 1989 . . . Blazers got Connecticut product with a second-round pick, No. 36 overall, making him one of league's biggest steals in recent years . . . Former Sixth Man of the Year . . . Born Dec. 16, 1966, in Albion, N.Y. . . . Made $2.336 million.

Year	Team	G	FG	FG Pct.	FT	FT Pct.	Reb.	Ast.	TP	Avg.
1989-90	Portland	82	298	.397	138	.550	308	72	746	9.1
1990-91	Portland	82	373	.463	205	.653	349	151	957	11.7
1991-92	Portland	82	398	.466	219	.664	416	137	1016	12.4
1992-93	Portland	82	632	.473	287	.690	542	182	1570	19.1
1993-94	Portland	82	641	.457	352	.765	550	159	1647	20.1
	Totals	410	2342	.455	1201	.678	2165	701	5936	14.5

BUCK WILLIAMS 34 6-8 225   Forward

That's Mr. President to you . . . Elected as players' point man in the union during All-Star Weekend . . . Only one achievement in an eventful, upbeat season from a personal standpoint . . . Answered talk that he might be slowing down by averaging 10.4 rebounds and shooting .555 . . . Would have been one of the most coveted unrestricted free agents this summer, but signed a two-year contract extension, with a Blazer option for a third, in final month of regular season . . . Reportedly worth about $2.5 million annually after making $5.05 million in 1993-94 . . . No truth to the rumor that he will now be known as Bucks Williams . . . Has missed just five out of a possible 410 games in five years as a Blazer . . . Portland sent Sam Bowie and a No. 1 pick to Nets to get him in 1989 . . . Attended Maryland . . . Born March 8, 1960, in Rocky Mount, N.C.

Year	Team	G	FG	FG Pct.	FT	FT Pct.	Reb.	Ast.	TP	Avg.
1981-82	New Jersey	82	513	.582	242	.624	1005	107	1268	15.5
1982-83	New Jersey	82	536	.588	324	.620	1027	125	1396	17.0
1983-84	New Jersey	81	495	.535	284	.570	1000	130	1274	15.7
1984-85	New Jersey	82	577	.530	336	.625	1005	167	1491	18.2
1985-86	New Jersey	82	500	.523	301	.676	986	131	1301	15.9
1986-87	New Jersey	82	521	.557	430	.731	1023	129	1472	18.0
1987-88	New Jersey	70	466	.560	346	.668	834	109	1279	18.3
1988-89	New Jersey	74	373	.531	213	.666	696	78	959	13.0
1989-90	Portland	82	413	.548	288	.706	800	116	1114	13.6
1990-91	Portland	80	358	.602	217	.705	751	97	933	11.7
1991-92	Portland	80	340	.604	221	.754	704	108	901	11.3
1992-93	Portland	82	270	.511	138	.645	690	75	678	8.3
1993-94	Portland	81	291	.555	201	.679	843	80	783	9.7
	Totals	1040	5653	.554	3541	.663	11364	1452	14849	14.4

ROD STRICKLAND 28 6-3 185   Guard

Voted Trail Blazers' MVP last season by teammates . . . Led team in assists, steals and minutes and played all 82 games . . . No. 6 in the league in assists . . . Averaged 9.0 overall, but 9.6 while starting the final 58 games . . . Portland is 57-36 (.613) with him in the starting lineup the last two seasons . . . Trail Blazers got one of the game's best penetrators as an unrestricted free agent in the summer of 1992 after San Antonio renounced his rights . . . There should have been drug tests all around in the Spurs' front office . . . He may have been the problem child, but don't let him go for nothing . . . Had standout career at DePaul before Knicks used 19th pick in 1988 to draft hometown product . . . Born July 11, 1966, in Bronx, N.Y., and grew up playing basketball with future pros Mark Jackson and Kenny Smith . . . Made $1.56 million.

Year	Team	G	FG	FG Pct.	FT	FT Pct.	Reb.	Ast.	TP	Avg.
1988-89	New York	81	265	.467	172	.745	160	319	721	8.9
1989-90	N.Y-S.A.	82	343	.454	174	.626	259	468	868	10.6
1990-91	San Antonio	58	314	.482	161	.763	219	463	800	13.8
1991-92	San Antonio	57	300	.455	182	.687	265	491	787	13.8
1992-93	Portland	78	396	.485	273	.717	337	559	1069	13.7
1993-94	Portland	82	528	.483	353	.749	370	740	1411	17.2
	Totals	438	2146	.472	1315	.716	1610	3040	5656	12.9

JEROME KERSEY 32 6-7 225   Forward

Was the starter for most of the previous seven seasons before falling behind Harvey Grant and Tracy Murray on the depth chart in 1993-94 . . . Declining minutes at small forward led to frustration . . . ''I want out of here and you can quote me on that,'' he said. ''I can't take any more of this.'' . . . Apparently he'll have to; that contract will be tough to move . . . Played at least 25 minutes only once after the all-star break . . . Started just six times, including only three after the first week of the season . . . Scoring average has dropped six straight years . . . Second on Trail Blazers' all-time list for games played and blocked shots, third in rebounding and steals and fifth in scoring . . . Born June 26, 1962, in Clarksville, Va., and became a success story after being picked in the second round in 1984 from tiny Longwood College in Virginia . . . Made $2.94 million.

Year	Team	G	FG	FG Pct.	FT	FT Pct.	Reb.	Ast.	TP	Avg.
1984-85	Portland	77	178	.478	117	.646	206	63	473	6.1
1985-86	Portland	79	258	.549	156	.681	293	83	672	8.5
1986-87	Portland	82	373	.509	262	.720	496	194	1009	12.3
1987-88	Portland	79	611	.499	291	.735	657	243	1516	19.2
1988-89	Portland	76	533	.469	258	.694	629	243	1330	17.5
1989-90	Portland	82	519	.478	269	.690	690	188	1310	16.0
1990-91	Portland	73	424	.478	232	.709	481	227	1084	14.8
1991-92	Portland	77	398	.467	174	.664	633	243	971	12.6
1992-93	Portland	65	281	.438	116	.634	406	121	686	10.6
1993-94	Portland	78	203	.433	101	.748	331	75	508	6.5
	Totals	768	3778	.480	1976	.696	4822	1680	9559	12.4

TERRY PORTER 31 6-3 195   Guard

Is he the weapon who last season was among the league leaders in three-point and free-throw accuracy or the guy who struggled while shooting .416, easily a career low? . . . That about sums up his 1993-94 . . . Former all-star lost starting job to Rod Strickland and became third guard, the guy who can fill in at either spot in the backcourt . . . In some ways, that makes him a victim of his own versatility . . . Made for a frustrating situation . . . Never was a true point guard and never claimed to be . . . Third in career assists among all active players . . . Born April 8, 1963, in Milwaukee and made a name for himself at Wisconsin-Stevens Point before Trail Blazers used the 24th pick in 1985 to get him . . . Made $2.5 million.

Year	Team	G	FG	FG Pct.	FT	FT Pct.	Reb.	Ast.	TP	Avg.
1985-86	Portland	79	212	.474	125	.806	117	198	562	7.1
1986-87	Portland	80	376	.488	280	.838	337	715	1045	13.1
1987-88	Portland	82	462	.519	274	.846	378	831	1222	14.9
1988-89	Portland	81	540	.471	272	.840	367	770	1431	17.7
1989-90	Portland	80	448	.462	421	.892	272	726	1406	17.6
1990-91	Portland	81	486	.515	279	.823	282	649	1381	17.0
1991-92	Portland	82	521	.461	315	.856	255	477	1485	18.1
1992-93	Portland	81	503	.454	327	.843	316	419	1476	18.2
1993-94	Portland	77	348	.416	204	.872	215	401	1010	13.1
	Totals	723	3896	.473	2497	.850	2539	5186	11018	15.2

HARVEY GRANT 29 6-9 225   Forward

At least the Blazers got something for Kevin Duckworth... Beyond that, Grant's contributions were minimal... Three seasons after receiving consideration for the league's Most Improved Player award, he went the other way and posted career low in shooting percentage (.460) and averaged only 10.4 points... Went into the summer with an option to become an unrestricted free agent, but that seemed unlikely coming off this season and knowing that he had several years left on guaranteed contract... Loves to shoot along baseline and will go as far as 20 feet out on perimeter... Twin brother is Horace of the Magic ... Born July 4, 1965, in Augusta, Ga.... Played college ball at Oklahoma before Bullets took him No. 12 overall in 1988... Made $2.429 million.

Year	Team	G	FG	FG Pct.	FT	FT Pct.	Reb.	Ast.	TP	Avg.
1988-89	Washington......	71	181	.464	34	.596	163	79	396	5.6
1989-90	Washington......	81	284	.473	96	.701	342	131	664	8.2
1990-91	Washington......	77	609	.498	185	.743	557	204	1405	18.2
1991-92	Washington......	64	489	.478	176	.800	432	170	1155	18.0
1992-93	Washington......	72	560	.487	218	.727	412	205	1339	18.6
1993-94	Portland........	77	356	.460	84	.641	351	107	798	10.4
	Totals	442	2479	.480	793	.725	2257	896	5757	13.0

TRACY MURRAY 23 6-7 228   Forward

How to succeed at small forward without a lot of quickness: outshoot everyone... No player, at any position, had more success on three-pointers last season... Became the seventh Trail Blazer to lead the league in an individual category... Still, that didn't make him a regular focus of the offense—he averaged 12.4 minutes and had 16 DNP-CDs... Shot almost as well from behind the arc (.459) as overall (.470)... First-round pick by San Antonio in 1992, but then was traded to Milwaukee and Portland within weeks... Trail Blazers sent Alaa Abdelnaby to Bucks to get UCLA product... Born July 25, 1971, in Los Angeles... Made $942,000.

Year	Team	G	FG	FG Pct.	FT	FT Pct.	Reb.	Ast.	TP	Avg.
1992-93	Portland........	48	108	.415	35	.875	83	11	272	5.7
1993-94	Portland........	66	167	.470	50	.694	111	31	434	6.6
	Totals	114	275	.447	85	.759	194	42	706	6.2

MARK BRYANT 29 6-9 245   Forward-Center

Started 10 times, including nine in a row at center before giving way to Clifford Robinson . . . Probably best-suited to be a power forward . . . Best part of offensive game is mid-range jumper . . . Has bulk to play on the low post, but not much of an offensive game to go with it . . . Can get out and run, too . . . He led Seton Hall to its first-ever NCAA tournament berth while earning All-Big East honors in 1988 . . . Trail Blazers made him the 21st overall pick from there and he went right into the Opening Night starting lineup . . . Only seven Portland players have ever done that . . . Born April 25, 1965, in Glen Ridge, N.J. . . . Made $1.3 million.

Year	Team	G	FG	FG Pct.	FT	FT Pct.	Reb.	Ast.	TP	Avg.
1988-89	Portland	56	120	.486	40	.580	179	33	280	5.0
1989-90	Portland	58	70	.458	28	.560	146	13	168	2.9
1990-91	Portland	53	99	.488	74	.733	190	27	272	5.1
1991-92	Portland	56	95	.480	40	.667	201	41	230	4.1
1992-93	Portland	80	186	.503	104	.703	324	41	476	6.0
1993-94	Portland	79	185	.482	72	.692	315	37	442	5.6
	Totals	382	755	.486	358	.673	1355	192	1868	4.9

JAMES ROBINSON 24 6-2 180   Guard

A leaper who needs to prove he can also be a shooter . . . Whether he plays point guard or off-guard, he will have to raise last season's .365 from the field . . . Averaged just 11.6 minutes, but did score 13 points a game when he started in place of Terry Porter against Charlotte, New York and Seattle in January . . . Participated in slam-dunk contest at All-Star Weekend . . . Would be heading into rookie season now, but left Alabama after junior season . . . Trail Blazers used their 1993 first-round pick, No. 21 overall, to take him . . . First-team All-SEC and led Crimson Tide in scoring three straight years . . . Born Aug. 31, 1970, in Jackson, Miss . . . Basketball star in high school also set Mississippi record in the 300-meter intermediate hurdles . . . Made $650,000.

Year	Team	G	FG	FG Pct.	FT	FT Pct.	Reb.	Ast.	TP	Avg.
1993-94	Portland	58	104	.365	45	.672	78	68	276	4.8

CHRIS DUDLEY 29 6-11 240   Center

Much ado about nothing... It turned out that way because of the Nov. 9 fractured ankle that kept him out 76 games... Had two screws placed in the ankle during surgery... Made it back far enough to be included on the Trail Blazers' playoff roster... A year ago at this time, he was one of the most talked-about players in the league... His one-year escape clause as part of a free-agent deal became the test case for the league... As it turned out, that spent more time in the courts than Dudley spent on the court... Especially productive on the offensive boards... Originally a fourth-round pick by Cleveland in 1987... Yalie... Grandfather, Guilford Dudley, was ambassador to Denmark under Presidents Nixon and Ford... Born Feb. 22, 1965, in Stamford, Conn....Made $790,000.

Year	Team	G	FG	FG Pct.	FT	FT Pct.	Reb.	Ast.	TP	Avg.
1987-88	Cleveland	55	65	.474	40	.563	144	23	170	3.1
1988-89	Cleveland	61	73	.435	39	.364	157	21	185	3.0
1989-90	Clev.-N.J.	64	146	.411	58	.319	423	39	350	5.5
1990-91	New Jersey	61	170	.408	94	.534	511	37	434	7.1
1991-92	New Jersey	82	190	.403	80	.468	739	58	460	5.6
1992-93	New Jersey	71	94	.353	57	.518	513	16	245	3.5
1993-94	Portland	6	6	.240	2	.500	24	5	14	2.3
	Totals	400	744	.404	370	.451	2511	199	1858	4.6

KEVIN THOMPSON 23 6-11 260   Center

Could still be in Blazers' plans despite averaging just 4.1 minutes as a rookie while missing most of the season with phantom injuries... Didn't play after Jan. 11... There is a chance he will be with the team again this season... Positive attitude helps his chances... Good skills from the low post, with good passing abilities and decent moves... Left North Carolina State as all-time leader in shooting percentage (.588) and second in blocks (150)... Trail Blazers picked him 48th in 1993... Born Feb. 7, 1971, in Winston-Salem, N.C....Made $150,000.

Year	Team	G	FG	FG Pct.	FT	FT Pct.	Reb.	Ast.	TP	Avg.
1993-94	Portland	14	6	.429	1	.500	13	3	13	0.9

THE ROOKIES

AARON McKIE 22 6-4 209   **Guard**
Just in case Clyde Drexler and Terry Porter start to show their age
at the same time . . . Went No. 17, seven picks after Temple teammate Eddie Jones . . . Played shooting guard and still led the Owls
in rebounding as a senior . . . Averaged 39.2 out of a possible 40
minutes a game . . . Atlantic-10 Conference Player of the Year as
a junior . . . Born Oct. 2, 1972, in Philadelphia.

SHAWNELLE SCOTT 22 6-10 250   **Forward-Center**
Can score from the post . . . Portland took him 43rd hoping for
some depth inside . . . Led St. John's in scoring and rebounding
as a junior, when he was named second team All-Big East . . .
Improved scoring average all four seasons, peaking at 16 points
per game in 1993-94 . . . Poor free-throw shooter . . . Born June
16, 1972, in New York.

COACH P.J. CARLESIMO: One of the biggest names in

college basketball tries to make the switch to
the NBA . . . First time ever in the pros, but
does have experience with the best players in
the world as assistant coach to Chuck Daly for
the 1992 Olympic Dream Team . . . That team
debuted, coincidentally, in Portland for the
Tournament of the Americas . . . Spent the last
12 years at Seton Hall, where he went 212-166
(.561) . . . Highlights were leading the Pirates to their first-ever
appearance in the NCAA tournament (1988) and then a trip to the
championship game in 1989 . . . Consensus Coach of the Year that
season . . . Four-year letterman at Fordham began his coaching
career at New Hampshire College in 1975-76, where he also was
athletic director, then left after one season to take over at Wagner
College, where he eventually became AD again . . . The next
move, in 1982, was to Seton Hall . . . Lifetime: 291-270 . . . Active
in USA Basketball, having coached in the World University
Games, Goodwill Games and World Championships, in addition
to the Barcelona Olympics . . . Born May 30, 1949, in Scranton,
Pa., the oldest of 10 children.

Still going strong, Buck Williams launches 14th season.

GREATEST PLAYER

The greatest is still pretty darn good. Clyde Drexler arrived as the 14th pick in the 1983 draft and quickly began to run down Trail Blazers' records with the same ferocity as if he was running a fastbreak. He was at 17.2 points by the second year, 18.5 the third, 21.7 the third.

It was his presence as an emerging star, as much as the lure of Kentucky center Sam Bowie, that prompted Portland to pass on Michael Jordan in the '84 draft. You can second-guess that move, but there is no denying what Drexler has done in his 11 seasons, starting with the fact that he is No. 1 in 11 of 17 of the team's career statistical categories and second in three others.

Honorable mention goes to Bill Walton, Maurice Lucas, Dave Twardzik, Larry Steele, Lloyd Neal and Geoff Petrie, all of whom had their jerseys retired.

ALL-TIME TRAIL BLAZER LEADERS

SEASON

Points: Clyde Drexler, 2,185, 1987-88
Assists: Terry Porter, 831, 1987-88
Rebounds: Lloyd Neal, 967, 1972-73

GAME

Points: Geoff Petrie, 51 vs. Houston, 1/20/73
        Geoff Petrie, 51 vs. Houston, 3/16/73
Assists: Rod Strickland, 20 vs. Phoenix, 4/4/94
Rebounds: Sidney Wicks, 27 vs. Los Angeles, 2/26/75

CAREER

Points: Clyde Drexler, 17,136, 1984-94
Assists: Terry Porter, 5,186, 1985-94
Rebounds: Clyde Drexler, 5,105, 1984-94

SACRAMENTO KINGS

TEAM DIRECTORY: Managing General Partner: Jim Thomas; Pres.: Rick Benner; VP-Basketball Oper.: Geoff Petrie; Dir. Player Personnel: Jerry Reynolds; Dir. Media Rel.: Travis Stanley; Coach: Garry St. Jean; Asst. Coaches: Eddie Jordan, Mike Bratz. Arena: ARCO Arena (17,317). Colors: Purple, silver and black.

The challenge: Can courageous Bobby Hurley make it back?

SCOUTING REPORT

SHOOTING: They had the fifth-worst percentage in the league and may be facing even tougher times. There was a strong possibility heading into the summer that Wayman Tisdale would not be re-signed, which would create a nice salary slot but a vacuum on offense. If that happens, the Kings could be left with only two people who made at least half their shots in either of the last two seasons: center Duane Causwell in 1992-93 and center Olden Polynice in 1993-94.

Either way, Mitch Richmond will be the main man. Though his .445 from the field was hardly overwhelming, defenses must contend with a shooting guard who is strong enough to post up and consistent enough from the outside to finish seventh in the league in three-point accuracy. The offense goes through him so much that Dallas' Jim Jackson was the only guard to get more attempts.

The Kings want to run, but they need to run more, or run better. They were sixth in the seven-team Pacific Division in shot attempts, which, combined with the poor percentage, did them in. The 101.1 points won't cut it on a club that, without a defensive presence, needs to outscore people to win.

PLAYMAKING: The expected return of Bobby Hurley from the near-fatal car accident will make this one of the most watched spots in all the NBA, but the attention doesn't figure to faze a guy who seemed to be in the Final Four every other week. The Kings would be happy if he just picked up as if Dec. 12 never happened, when he was leading all rookies in assists. Then the 6.1 average would climb in no time. Spud Webb is there for depth and the just-in-case role that he played so well last season.

REBOUNDING: Harold Pressley in 1986. Kenny Smith in '87. Ricky Berry in '88. Pervis Ellison in '89. Lionel Simmons in '90. Billy Owens in '91. Walt Williams in '92. Hurley in '93. Only once in the eight drafts prior to 1994 did the Kings use their first pick on a big man, and Ellison never panned out in Sacramento, even though rebounding has long been a problem.

They made up for that in a big way this summer. No. 1 selection Brian Grant is pegged as the power forward of the future. Second-rounder Michael Smith is the Big East's all-time leading rebounder by average and second in total boards. Lawrence Funderburke, the third forward to come in the draft, led Ohio State in rebounding as a senior.

KING ROSTER

No. Veterans	Pos.	Ht.	Wt.	Age	Yrs. Pro	College
45 Randy Breuer	C	7-3	260	34	11	Minnesota
3 Randy Brown	G	6-3	190	26	3	New Mexico State
31 Duane Causwell	C	7-0	240	26	4	Temple
7 Bobby Hurley	G	6-0	165	23	1	Duke
51 Mike Peplowski	F-C	6-11	270	24	1	Michigan State
– Olden Polynice	C	7-0	250	29	7	Virginia
2 Mitch Richmond	G	6-5	215	29	6	Kansas State
22 Lionel Simmons	F	6-7	210	25	4	LaSalle
– LaBradford Smith	G	6-3	205	25	3	Louisville
– Andre Spencer	F	6-6	220	30	2	Northern Arizona
23 Wayman Tisdale	F	6-9	260	30	9	Oklahoma
4 Anthony Webb	G	5-7	133	31	9	North Carolina State
42 Walt Williams	F-G	6-8	230	24	2	Maryland
– Trevor Wilson	F	6-8	215	26	2	UCLA

Rd. Rookies	Sel. No.	Pos.	Ht.	Wt.	College
1 Brian Grant	8	F	6-8	254	Xavier
2 Michael Smith	35	F	6-7	230	Providence
2 Lawrence Funderburke	51	F	6-8	230	Ohio State

DEFENSE: Grant has been described as a tenacious defender, so the Kings are counting on his impact here, too. They need any kind of impact inside, whether at center or power forward because only Dallas, Milwaukee and Washington allowed the opposition a higher shooting percentage. It was once thought that would be Causwell's role, but, through injuries and lost playing time, the best shot-blocker on the team has largely become a non-factor in that department.

OUTLOOK: They are still trying to reach puberty, having made one jump last season by avoiding another last-place finish in the Pacific Division. Still, they're not ready to make a big mark. Too many question marks.

Will Hurley be completely healthy? Will Tisdale be back to provide some scoring? Will Richmond and Lionel Simmons have to go it alone in that area? Will Grant and Polynice be able to make a difference on defense when so many others have not? Where will team representatives go for breakfast on the day of the lottery?

KING PROFILES

MITCH RICHMOND 29 6-5 215   Guard

Finally getting proper recognition as one of the top guards in the league... Arguably one of the two best shooting guards last season along with neighbor to the south, Latrell Sprewell... His 23.4 points was seventh-best in the NBA and the highest average by a King since Otis Birdsong in 1980-81... First King since Nate Archibald in 1975 to start an All-Star Game... So tough to defend because it's impossible to get a favorable matchup against him... Dependable shooter from outside (No. 7 in three-point shooting last season) and strong inside... Kings sent Billy Owens to Golden State to get him... Warriors picked him No. 5 in 1988 out of Kansas State and were rewarded with Rookie of the Year performance... Born June 30, 1965, in Ft. Lauderdale, Fla....Made $2.5 million.

Year	Team	G	FG	FG Pct.	FT	FT Pct.	Reb.	Ast.	TP	Avg.
1988-89	Golden State	79	649	.468	410	.810	468	334	1741	22.0
1989-90	Golden State	78	640	.497	406	.866	360	223	1720	22.1
1990-91	Golden State	77	703	.494	394	.847	452	238	1840	23.9
1991-92	Sacramento	80	685	.468	330	.813	319	411	1803	22.5
1992-93	Sacramento	45	371	.474	197	.845	154	221	987	21.9
1993-94	Sacramento	78	635	.445	426	.834	286	313	1823	23.4
	Totals	437	3683	.474	2163	.835	2039	1740	9914	22.7

WALT WILLIAMS 24 6-8 230   Forward-Guard

Wants to use a mulligan for last season... Went from being No. 7 pick in 1992 and a rookie campaign of great promises to a second year that mostly felt like broken promises... Got booed by fans... Spent time playing behind free-agent pickup Trevor Wilson, which caused frustration... Doesn't have greatest relationship with coach Garry St. Jean... Maybe that .390 from the field, .635 from the line and 132-145 assist-to-turnover ratio had something to do with it... Started four times, so his primary role was as sixth man... Very versatile... Born April 16, 1970, in Washington, D.C., and stayed locally to star at Maryland... Made $1.658 million.

Year	Team	G	FG	FG Pct.	FT	FT Pct.	Reb.	Ast.	TP	Avg.
1992-93	Sacramento	59	358	.435	224	.742	265	178	1001	17.0
1993-94	Sacramento	57	226	.390	148	.635	235	132	638	11.2
	Totals	116	584	.416	372	.695	500	310	1639	14.1

WAYMAN TISDALE 30 6-9 260 Forward

Continues to be a dependable scorer, but that doesn't mean his future is secure here . . . Went into the summer as an unrestricted free agent and Kings would like to use his $2.333-million salary towards another player . . . Still a potent offensive weapon, especially from the low post . . . Stopped being the primary offensive weapon when Mitch Richmond arrived, but has still averaged at least 16.6 points and shot .500 or better in each of the past three years . . . In short, he's still going strong after LaSalle Thompson has been reduced to a supporting role in Indiana and Randy Wittman has retired. Those are the two players the Kings traded to Pacers to get Tisdale . . . Indiana drafted the 1984 Olympian and three-time All-American at Oklahoma with the No. 2 pick in '85 . . . Born June 9, 1964, in Tulsa, Okla.

Year	Team	G	FG	FG Pct.	FT	FT Pct.	Reb.	Ast.	TP	Avg.
1985-86	Indiana	81	516	.515	160	.684	584	79	1192	14.7
1986-87	Indiana	81	458	.513	258	.709	475	117	1174	14.5
1987-88	Indiana	79	511	.512	246	.783	491	103	1268	16.1
1988-89	Ind.-Sac.	79	532	.514	317	.773	609	128	1381	17.5
1989-90	Sacramento	79	726	.525	306	.783	595	108	1758	22.3
1990-91	Sacramento	33	262	.483	136	.800	253	66	660	20.0
1991-92	Sacramento	72	522	.500	151	.763	469	106	1199	16.6
1992-93	Sacramento	76	544	.509	175	.758	500	108	1263	16.6
1993-94	Sacramento	79	552	.501	215	.808	560	139	1319	16.7
	Totals	659	4623	.510	1964	.762	4536	954	11210	17.0

ANTHONY (SPUD) WEBB 31 5-7 133 Guard

What role he has depends on how Bobby Hurley recuperates from his car crash . . . This much we do know for sure: He came up big last season, and that has nothing to do with his size . . . Was splitting time with Hurley before the accident and handled it like a pro . . . Unhappy but gracious during the transition to a younger point guard, he tried to help Hurley whenever possible . . . Played well in 62 starts after Hurley went out . . . Never a great ballhandler but still finished 12th in the league in assists . . . Relies heavily on beating people off the dribble to drive down the lane and take a pull-up jumper . . . Teammates with Nate McMillan and Vinny Del Negro at North Carolina State . . . Detroit used a fourth-round pick in 1985 to get him from there . . . Kings acquired him by sending Travis Mays to Hawks . . . Born July 13, 1963, in Dallas . . . Made $1.462 million.

Year	Team	G	FG	FG Pct.	FT	FT Pct.	Reb.	Ast.	TP	Avg.
1985-86	Atlanta	79	199	.483	216	.785	123	337	616	7.8
1986-87	Atlanta	33	71	.438	80	.762	60	167	223	6.8
1987-88	Atlanta	82	191	.475	107	.817	146	337	490	6.0
1988-89	Atlanta	81	133	.459	52	.867	123	284	319	3.9
1989-90	Atlanta	82	294	.477	162	.871	201	477	751	9.2
1990-91	Atlanta	75	359	.447	231	.868	174	417	1003	13.4
1991-92	Sacramento	77	448	.445	262	.859	223	547	1231	16.0
1992-93	Sacramento	69	342	.433	279	.851	193	481	1000	14.5
1993-94	Sacramento	79	373	.460	204	.813	222	528	1005	12.7
	Totals	657	2410	.456	1593	.835	1465	3575	6638	10.1

LIONEL SIMMONS 26 6-7 210 Forward

Has not turned out to be the star many (including us) expected after he came out of LaSalle as the No. 7 selection in 1990 . . . Hardly a bust, though, considering he has averaged 17 points over the first four seasons despite not being a great shooter . . . Very good rebounder for a small forward . . . Runs the court, but lack of great speed and athleticism holds him back from reaching that next level . . . Led team in steals, was second in rebounding and minutes, third in scoring and assists . . . Getting close to some all-time franchise records . . . Finished second to Derrick Coleman in Rookie of the Year balloting in 1991 . . . Left college as the third-leading scorer in NCAA history, behind only Pete Maravich and Freeman Williams . . . Born Oct. 14, 1968, in Philadelphia . . . Made $1.743 million.

Year	Team	G	FG	FG Pct.	FT	FT Pct.	Reb.	Ast.	TP	Avg.
1990-91	Sacramento	79	549	.422	320	.736	697	315	1421	18.0
1991-92	Sacramento	78	527	.454	281	.770	634	337	1336	17.1
1992-93	Sacramento	69	468	.444	298	.819	495	312	1235	17.9
1993-94	Sacramento	75	436	.438	251	.777	562	305	1129	15.1
	Totals	301	1980	.439	1150	.773	2388	1269	5121	17.0

OLDEN POLYNICE 29 7-0 250 Center

Have attitude, will travel . . . Teams love his enthusiasm when he arrives, then grow tired of it when he uses the same emotional level against them . . . Kings knew what they were getting when they sent Pete Chilcutt and future picks to Detroit to get him last February . . . Mainly, they knew they needed a center . . . Paid dividends by averaging 11.4 rebounds in 31 games

with Sacramento to finish fifth in the league in that category . . .
Also 13th in shooting . . . Bad hands . . . Came into the league as
No. 8 pick overall, by Chicago, in 1987 draft after career at
Virginia that included one trip to the Final Four . . . Born Nov.
21, 1964, in Port-au-Prince, Haiti . . . Made $850,000.

Year	Team	G	FG	FG Pct.	FT	FT Pct.	Reb.	Ast.	TP	Avg.
1987-88	Seattle	82	118	.465	101	.639	330	33	337	4.1
1988-89	Seattle	80	91	.506	51	.593	206	21	233	2.9
1989-90	Seattle	79	156	.540	47	.475	300	15	360	4.6
1990-91	Sea.-LAC	79	316	.560	146	.579	553	42	778	9.8
1991-92	L.A. Clippers.	76	244	.519	125	.622	536	46	613	8.1
1992-93	Detroit	67	210	.490	66	.465	418	29	486	7.3
1993-94	Det.-Sac.	68	346	.523	97	.508	809	41	789	11.6
	Totals	531	1481	.520	633	.561	3152	227	3596	6.8

BOBBY HURLEY 23 6-0 165   Guard

Dec. 12 . . . The Kings played the Clippers that
night at Arco Arena. Hurley had just started his
drive home. A car hit his truck . . . The medical
chart: eight hours of surgery to repair a torn
trachea tube that was severed from the main
airway to his left lung, a torn ligament in right
knee, multiple rib fractures, fractured left
shoulder, small compression fracture in the
mid-portion of his back . . . Despite it all, was scheduled to play
for Kings in summer league and join team in training camp . . .
Started first 19 games of 1993-94 at point guard, averaging 6.1
assists, tops among all rookies to that stage . . . No. 7 pick in the
draft after career at Duke highlighted by back-to-back national
championships and finishing as the NCAA's all-time assist leader
. . . Born June 28, 1971, in Jersey City, N.J. . . . Made $1.616
million.

Year	Team	G	FG	FG Pct.	FT	FT Pct.	Reb.	Ast.	TP	Avg.
1993-94	Sacramento.	19	54	.370	24	.800	34	115	134	7.1

TREVOR WILSON 26 6-8 215   Forward

Back in the league after two seasons in Spain
. . . Hard worker . . . Not much of a shooter,
which will hold back his chances of starting on
a regular basis at small forward . . . Good knack
for being around the ball inside . . . All in all,
a nice free-agent pickup . . . Began 1993-94
with the Lakers and was even in the Opening
Night starting lineup because of injuries . . .
Played five games with L.A. before going on the injured list. Did

not return before being waived in December . . . Kings signed him about a week later . . . Atlanta picked him in the second round in 1990 . . . Three-time All-Pacific-10 selection at UCLA, where he finished as the fourth-leading scorer in school history . . . Born March 16, 1968, in Los Angeles . . . Made $200,000.

Year	Team	G	FG	FG Pct.	FT	FT Pct.	Reb.	Ast.	TP	Avg.
1990-91	Atlanta	25	21	.300	13	.500	40	11	55	2.2
1993-94	LAL-Sac.	57	187	.482	92	.554	273	72	466	8.2
	Totals	82	208	.454	105	.547	313	83	521	6.4

RANDY BREUER 34 7-3 260   Center

He's still tall . . . He's still in the league . . . Sprained ankle limited him to 26 appearances while he played for the $150,000 minimum . . . Went on injured list Feb. 7 with the ankle injury and never came off . . . Has played just 38 games the last two seasons . . . Good chance he's heading to a fourth team in as many years this season . . . Kings signed him as a free agent just before 1993 training camp . . . Former first-round draft pick by Milwaukee in 1983 after standout career at Minnesota . . . Born Oct. 11, 1960, in Lake City, Minn.

Year	Team	G	FG	FG Pct.	FT	FT Pct.	Reb.	Ast.	TP	Avg.
1983-84	Milwaukee	57	68	.384	32	.696	109	17	168	2.9
1984-85	Milwaukee	78	162	.511	89	.701	256	40	413	5.3
1985-86	Milwaukee	82	272	.477	141	.712	458	114	685	8.4
1986-87	Milwaukee	76	241	.485	118	.584	350	47	600	7.9
1987-88	Milwaukee	81	390	.495	188	.657	551	103	968	12.0
1988-89	Milwaukee	48	86	.480	28	.549	135	22	200	4.2
1989-90	Mil.-Minn.	81	298	.429	126	.653	417	97	722	8.9
1990-91	Minnesota	73	197	.453	35	.443	345	73	429	5.9
1991-92	Minnesota	67	161	.468	41	.532	281	89	363	5.4
1992-93	Atlanta	12	15	.484	2	.400	28	6	32	2.7
1993-94	Sacramento	26	8	.308	3	.214	56	8	19	0.7
	Totals	681	1898	.467	803	.628	2986	616	4599	6.8

RANDY BROWN 26 6-3 190   Guard

Fourth or fifth guard . . . Good defender with quick hands and long arms . . . Will be even better when he's not as foul-prone . . . Played some at the point, but is moving more toward shooting guard . . . Lost some minutes as backup point guard to LaBradford Smith . . . So-so ballhandler . . . Played in the same high-school backcourt as former Jazz and Maverick

Walter Bond . . . Went to a JC in Texas from there before finishing college career as two-time All-Big West selection at New Mexico State . . . Kings used the No. 31 pick to draft him in 1991 . . . Born May 22, 1968, in Chicago . . . Made $550,000.

Year	Team	G	FG	FG Pct.	FT	FT Pct.	Reb.	Ast.	TP	Avg.
1991-92	Sacramento......	56	77	.456	38	.655	69	59	192	3.4
1992-93	Sacramento......	75	225	.463	115	.732	212	196	567	7.6
1993-94	Sacramento......	61	110	.438	53	.609	112	133	273	4.5
	Totals	192	412	.455	206	.682	393	388	1032	5.4

DUANE CAUSWELL 26 7-0 240   Center

Such a nice guy. When the Kings tried to trade him to Detroit last season, he volunteered info on his medical history to Piston doctors, so they flunked him . . . Those stress fractures in his feet are around even after they're gone . . . Showed some improvement toward the end of the season, so maybe it wasn't so bad that he stayed. Biggest area of improvement was in offensive moves around the basket . . . Best as a shot-blocker . . . Poor hands, so he tends to lose rebounds or balls inside . . . Tends to mope when he doesn't get the minutes . . . Averaged just 16.4 per game while starting eight times . . . College teammates with Tim Perry, Mark Macon and Donald Hodge at Temple . . . Kings took him No. 18 in 1990 from there . . . Born May 31, 1968, in Queens Village, N.Y . . . . Made $1.26 million.

Year	Team	G	FG	FG Pct.	FT	FT Pct.	Reb.	Ast.	TP	Avg.
1990-91	Sacramento......	76	210	.508	105	.636	391	69	525	6.9
1991-92	Sacramento......	80	250	.549	136	.613	580	59	636	8.0
1992-93	Sacramento......	55	175	.545	103	.624	303	35	453	8.2
1993-94	Sacramento......	41	71	.518	40	.588	186	11	182	4.4
	Totals	252	706	.532	384	.619	1460	174	1796	7.1

MIKE PEPLOWSKI 24 6-11 270   Forward-Center

Wildly popular in Sacramento because of his role in helping to rescue teammate Bobby Hurley after car wreck . . . He saw the crash, pulled over without knowing who was involved, then pulled Hurley out of the ditch and stayed close until the ambulance arrived . . . Gets huge ovations . . . That doesn't do much for his spot in the rotation, though . . . Reports were that owner Jim Thomas ordered Garry St. Jean to sit him in December. Thomas denies it . . . A big body who bangs inside . . . Kings figure that with his size he can be a decent backup center with time and coaching . . . Second-round selection in 1993 after being voted MVP at Michigan State . . . Born Oct. 15, 1970, in Detroit . . . Made $150,000.

Year	Team	G	FG	FG Pct.	FT	FT Pct.	Reb.	Ast.	TP	Avg.
1993-94	Sacramento......	55	76	.539	24	.545	169	24	176	3.2

LaBRADFORD SMITH 25 6-3 205   Guard

Former first-round washout with Bullets tries the other coast . . . Like so much of the Kings' backcourt, how much he gets to try may depend on Bobby Hurley's recovery . . . Provided depth at point guard behind Spud Webb after being signed in early December, two days after being cut by Washington, but that's not his natural position . . . Athletic . . . Tends to make a lot of mistakes . . . Pretty good rebounder for his size . . . Inconsistent shooter who one night will go 6-for-6 and the next 1-for-10 . . . Underwent minor knee surgery to repair cartilage the day after the season ended, but that was expected to be only a minor setback for summer . . . Former Louisville standout was the No. 19 pick in 1991 . . . Born April 3, 1969, in Bay City, Tex. . . . Made $940,000.

Year	Team	G	FG	FG Pct.	FT	FT Pct.	Reb.	Ast.	TP	Avg.
1991-92	Washington......	48	100	.407	45	.804	81	99	247	5.1
1992-93	Washington......	69	261	.458	109	.858	106	186	639	9.3
1993-94	Wash.-Sac.......	66	124	.405	63	.750	84	109	332	5.0
	Totals	183	485	.432	217	.813	271	394	1218	6.7

ANDRE SPENCER 30 6-6 220   Forward

Word association: U-Haul. Bekins. Andre Spencer . . . Undrafted out of Northern Arizona in 1986, he has played for Atlanta, Sacramento and Golden State in the NBA, five teams in the CBA and in Sweden, France and Israel . . . Began 1993-94 with Warriors before being waived in November. He hooked on with Rockford, then finished back in NBA when Kings signed him in March . . . They like his athleticism, but he needs to get more consistent . . . Had a couple of good showings . . . Attended high school in Los Angeles with Darryl Strawberry and former Clipper John Williams . . . Born July 20, 1964, in Dumas, Ark.

Year	Team	G	FG	FG Pct.	FT	FT Pct.	Reb.	Ast.	TP	Avg.
1992-93	Atl.-G.S.	20	73	.448	41	.759	81	24	187	9.4
1993-94	G.S.-Sac.	28	52	.441	55	.714	73	22	159	5.7
	Totals	48	125	.445	96	.733	154	46	346	7.2

THE ROOKIES

BRIAN GRANT 22 6-8 254   Forward
Made a big jump with showing in pre-draft camps, all the way to No. 8 overall . . . Kings hope he is the tenacious inside player they've been lacking on defense . . . Needs to prove he can bang hard to compensate for being a power forward without the height of some counterparts . . . Led Xavier in rebounding all four seasons and was named Midwestern Collegiate Conference Player of the Year as a junior and senior . . . Born March 5, 1972, in Columbus, Ohio.

MICHAEL SMITH 22 6-7 230   Forward
Has always done well on his boards . . . Providence product holds Big East record for career rebounding average (11.67) and is second in total rebounds (630) . . . Finished ninth in the nation in rebounding as a junior and 11th as a senior . . . Named most outstanding player of the Big East Tournament, which was won by Friars . . . Kings took him 35th . . . Born March 28, 1972, in Washington, D.C.

LAWRENCE FUNDERBURKE 23 6-8 230   Forward
Surprised he slipped so far . . . Not only the 51st pick overall, but the third forward taken by the Kings . . . Some teams may have been scared off by his surgeries on both knees before senior season . . . Started college career at Indiana before transferring to Ohio State after freshman year . . . Born Dec. 15, 1970, in Columbus, Ohio.

COACH GARRY ST. JEAN: Got the backhanded vote of

confidence from owner Jim Thomas about returning for this, his third season: "He's got the contract," Thomas said, "and I don't like to waste money." . . . How will St. Jean ever be able to contain his excitement over that backing? . . . Last season, he coached the Kings out of last place in the Pacific Division for the first time since 1988-89 . . . They beat the teams they should have, going 16-10 against sub-.500 opponents . . . Career mark is 53-111 (.323) . . . Four more wins and he'll pass Jerry Reynolds to become the winningest coach during the Sacramento era . . . As a King, you take the positives where you can find them . . . NBA assistant for 12 years, 10 on Don Nelson's staff, before Sacramento gave him first chance to be head coach . . . The other two years were with the Nets . . . Went to Eastern Conference finals three times as an assistant with the Bucks . . . Also has front-office experience as assistant director of player personnel at New Jersey and Milwaukee . . . Born Feb. 10, 1950, in Chicopee, Mass., and attended Springfield College in Massachusetts.

GREATEST PLAYER

The Big O was, and is, the One.

Back when there was something called the Cincinnati Royals, there was Oscar Robertson, the jewel of the franchise for 10 years while making the All-Star Game each season before being traded to Milwaukee. All he did in that stretch was *average* a triple-double in his second season and come close several other times, lead the league in assists six times, average 29.3 points and break the 30-point average barrier six times.

The franchise, which also once set down temporary roots in Rochester, later moved to Kansas City/Omaha and Sacramento, but no one ever entered Robertson's stratosphere, which is no great shock since few have in league history.

Among those who tried to come close were Nate Archibald (who in 1972-73 became the only player to lead the NBA in points and assists the same season), Sam Lacey (who has the longest tenure at 12 seasons) and future Hall of Famers like Jerry Lucas, Jack Twyman and Bob Davies.

ALL-TIME KING LEADERS

SEASON

Points: Nate Archibald, 2,719, 1972-73
Assists: Nate Archibald, 910, 1972-73
Rebounds: Jerry Lucas, 1,688, 1965-66

GAME

Points: Jack Twyman, 59 vs. Minneapolis, 1/15/60
Assists: Phil Ford, 22 vs. Milwaukee, 2/21/79
Oscar Robertson, 22 vs. New York, 3/5/66
Oscar Robertson, 22 vs. Syracuse, 10/29/61
Rebounds: Jerry Lucas, 40 vs. Philadelphia, 2/29/64

CAREER

Points: Oscar Robertson, 22,009, 1960-70
Assists: Oscar Robertson, 7,721, 1960-70
Rebounds: Sam Lacey, 9,353, 1971-82

SAN ANTONIO SPURS

TEAM DIRECTORY: Chairman: Robert F. McDermott; Pres./ CEO: Bob Coleman; VP-Basketball Oper.: Bob Bass; Exec. VP: Russ Bookbinder; Media Services Dir.: Dave Senko; Media Services Mgr.: Tom James; Coach: TBA. Arena: Alamodome (20,500). Colors: Metallic silver and black.

(Editor's Note: The Spurs had not named a new coach at press time.)

SCOUTING REPORT

SHOOTING: It is not a misprint. The Spurs really did have the league's leading scorer last season, David Robinson at 29.8 points a game, and still finished 20th out of 27 in team scoring at 100 even. It's not hard to see why—they took the third-fewest shots.

Robinson, of course, is marvelous. He runs the floor, can hit the medium-range jumper and has great quickness, if not great moves, from the post. Free-agent signee Chuck Person is dangerous as a three-point shooter. But that's it. Just one player who scored more than 15 points a game, even if Willie Anderson, coming off a series of operations on both legs, showed he had retained the ability to put the ball on the floor.

Whoever is the coach (none had been named by mid-July) will need to generate more offense. Or at least generate more chances for the offense.

PLAYMAKING: All anyone needs to know is that Robinson led the team in assists last season, which is more of an indicator of the Spurs' need than his versatility, even if he was No. 1 among all forwards or centers in that category. What makes it even more apparent is that they have chosen to bandage the problem instead of fixing it, shuffling the responsibility around from natural shooting guard Vinny Del Negro to unproven Lloyd Daniels to trading for Negele Knight and then finding he couldn't run the show either.

We would be confused, except this was the same team that let two consecutive starters, Rod Strickland and Avery Johnson, go for nothing as free agents. The Spurs couldn't have gotten anything in trade after determining they didn't want either player. Now, after passing on Charlie Ward and Howard Eisley in the draft, they have brought back Johnson as a free agent. They'd opted for another big man, Bill Curley of Boston College, whom they sent to Detroit to reacquire Sean Elliott.

David Robinson's 71-point game wrapped up scoring title.

REBOUNDING: This is a health issue. The coaching staff and front office that kept getting those 10-gallon headaches and ulcers over behavior and tardiness just needs to keep reminding themselves that the Spurs went from last place in offensive rebounding percentage in 1992-93 to first last season, thanks to Dennis Rodman. Is it worth it? Only they know for sure, but we know this much: 1. Local pharmacists love it because aspirin sales to front-office staff shot up. 2. The team that got so few attempts as it

SPUR ROSTER

No.	Veterans	Pos.	Ht.	Wt.	Age	Yrs. Pro	College
40	Willie Anderson	G	6-8	205	27	6	Georgia
U-35	Antoine Carr	F	6-9	255	33	10	Wichita State
34	Terry Cummings	F	6-9	245	33	12	DePaul
R-24	Lloyd Daniels	G	6-7	205	27	2	None
15	Vinny Del Negro	G	6-4	200	28	4	North Carolina State
–	Sean Elliott	F	6-8	215	26	5	Arizona
U-21	Eric Floyd	G	6-3	185	34	12	Georgetown
U-54	Jack Haley	C	6-10	250	30	6	UCLA
6	Avery Johnson	G	5-11	175	29	6	Southern
U-32	Negele Knight	G	6-1	182	27	4	Dayton
–	Chuck Person	F	6-8	225	30	8	Auburn
7	J.R. Reid	F	6-9	265	26	5	North Carolina
50	David Robinson	C	7-1	235	29	5	Navy
10	Dennis Rodman	F	6-8	210	33	8	SE Oklahoma State
R-20	Chris Whitney	G	6-0	170	23	1	Clemson

R-restricted free agent
U-unrestricted free agent

was, as noted above, may have gotten the same number of shots on goal as the Dutch soccer team without all of Rodman's offensive boards that led to second chances.

In all, he easily led the league for the third season in a row, this time at 17.3 a game, as the Spurs jumped from No. 19 overall to No. 1. Let's not forget the contributions of Robinson, whose 10.7 average was 14th, and Terry Cummings' 5.0 a game in just 19.2 minutes.

DEFENSE: The Spurs of gone-to-Philly John Lucas weren't much for pressuring the ball, easily forcing the fewest turnovers in the league. But with Robinson finishing third in blocked shots and Rodman still able to put the clamps on his assignment, big or small, this is a strong point. Only three teams were better in shooting percentage-against and the 94.8 points allowed was second to the Knicks.

OUTLOOK: Sure they will be good. But the Spurs are not going for good, they are going for the championship. They have the dominant player, the defense and the rebounding, all major pieces of the puzzle. So why is it that no one trusts them?

SPUR PROFILES

DAVID ROBINSON 29 7-1 235   Center

Always a star, he has climbed to the next level ... "Before, he was embarrassed to be great," ex-coach John Lucas said. "He isn't embarrassed any more." ... Won NBA scoring title by trashing the Clippers for 71 points on the final day of the regular season ... No player scored more in a game all season ... No player went to the line more ... First center to lead the league in scoring since Bob McAdoo in 1975-76 ... His 4.8 assists led the Spurs and was the most by any forward or center in the league ... Struggled in the playoffs ... No. 1 in something else: his salary of $5.74 million ... Great quickness ... Olympian in 1992 and 1988 ... No. 1 pick in 1987 out of Navy and, after completing his military obligation, Rookie of the Year in 1990 ... Born Aug. 6, 1965, in Key West, Fla.

Year	Team	G	FG	FG Pct.	FT	FT Pct.	Reb.	Ast.	TP	Avg.
1989-90	San Antonio	82	690	.531	613	.732	983	164	1993	24.3
1990-91	San Antonio	82	754	.552	592	.762	1063	208	2101	25.6
1991-92	San Antonio	68	592	.551	393	.701	829	181	1578	23.2
1992-93	San Antonio	82	676	.501	561	.732	956	301	1916	23.4
1993-94	San Antonio	80	840	.507	693	.749	855	381	2383	29.8
	Totals	394	3552	.527	2852	.738	4686	1235	9971	25.3

AVERY JOHNSON 29 5-11 175   Guard

Free-agent signee returned to Spurs after he ended up leading Warriors in assists and finishing fourth in steals and fifth in scoring and minutes ... His points, rebounds, steals and minutes were all career highs ... His .492 from the field was third-best among all point guards, trailing only John Stockton and Gary Payton ... Has a chance to become only the fourth player ever to improve scoring average over each of his first seven seasons as a pro. Alex English, Kevin McHale and Derek Harper are the others ... Made such an immediate impact with Warriors that teammates voted him as one of the tri-captains with Chris

Mullin and Tim Hardaway . . . Was not drafted after playing collegiately at Southern . . . Born March 25, 1965, in New Orleans.

Year	Team	G	FG	FG Pct.	FT	FT Pct.	Reb.	Ast.	TP	Avg.
1988-89	Seattle	43	29	.349	9	.563	24	73	68	1.6
1989-90	Seattle	53	55	.387	29	.725	43	162	140	2.6
1990-91	Den.-S.A.	68	130	.469	59	.678	77	230	320	4.7
1991-92	S.A.-Hou.	69	158	.479	66	.653	80	266	386	5.6
1992-93	San Antonio	75	256	.502	144	.791	146	561	656	8.7
1993-94	Golden State	82	356	.492	178	.704	176	433	890	10.9
	Totals	390	984	.476	485	.714	546	1725	2460	6.3

VINNY DEL NEGRO 28 6-4 200   Guard

Strange as it sounds after Spurs went 40-16 with him in the starting lineup, he's not a point guard . . . He's just the best they had last season . . . Solid player, though . . . Good shooter, but not a lot of range . . . Limit is about 16 feet . . . Nice pull-up jumper . . . Hard-nosed player . . . Finished third on the team in assists . . . Had minor role on the team before Dec. 26, then was moved into the opening lineup and took off . . . Has spent two seasons in San Antonio after signing as a free agent . . . Two seasons before that were in Italy, where teammates included current Bull Toni Kukoc . . . Selected by Sacramento in the second round in 1988 after playing at North Carolina State . . . Made $1.195 million.

Year	Team	G	FG	FG Pct.	FT	FT Pct.	Reb.	Ast.	TP	Avg.
1988-89	Sacramento	80	239	.475	85	.850	171	206	569	7.1
1989-90	Sacramento	76	297	.462	135	.871	198	250	739	9.7
1992-93	San Antonio	73	218	.507	101	.863	163	291	543	7.4
1993-94	San Antonio	77	309	.487	140	.824	161	320	773	10.0
	Totals	306	1063	.481	461	.851	693	1067	2624	8.6

DENNIS RODMAN 33 6-8 210   Forward

More colorful than ever . . . Only now, that means his hair, too . . . His 34 technical fouls led the league and his five flagrant fouls tied New York's Charles Oakley for No. 1 in the league . . . Ejected six times . . . Suspended three times, once at a crucial juncture of the playoffs . . . ''Dennis has to put the team first and the hype second,'' Spurs VP Bob Bass says

. . . Translation: They've about had it up to here with him . . . Spurs went into the offseason planning to concentrate on how to contain him . . . Management isn't too concerned about way he sets up own schedule, but it is concerned about his court antics . . . But he does produce . . . Led NBA in rebounding for third straight season . . . Had at least 20 rebounds 27 times . . . Born May 13, 1961, in Trenton, N.J . . . .Obtained from Detroit along with Isaiah Morris in exchange for Sean Elliott and David Wood . . . Pistons got him in second round in 1986 after career at Southeastern Oklahoma State . . . Made $2.45 million.

Year	Team	G	FG	FG Pct.	FT	FT Pct.	Reb.	Ast.	TP	Avg.
1986-87	Detroit	77	213	.545	74	.587	332	56	500	6.5
1987-88	Detroit	82	398	.561	152	.535	715	110	953	11.6
1988-89	Detroit	82	316	.595	97	.626	772	99	735	9.0
1989-90	Detroit	82	288	.581	142	.654	792	72	719	8.8
1990-91	Detroit	82	276	.493	111	.631	1026	85	669	8.2
1991-92	Detroit	82	342	.539	84	.600	1530	191	800	9.8
1992-93	Detroit	62	183	.427	87	.534	1132	102	468	7.5
1993-94	San Antonio	79	156	.534	53	.520	1367	184	370	4.7
	Totals	628	2172	.537	800	.587	7666	899	5214	8.3

WILLIE ANDERSON 27 6-8 205   Guard

The comeback is complete . . . Had no apparent problem with legs after missing the first 44 games of 1992-93 following a series of surgeries on both shins . . . Eventually had rods inserted into both legs . . . Returned for 1993-94, missed only two games for unrelated reasons and averaged 31.1 minutes an outing . . . Still had driving skills and spin moves down low . . . The problem was with consistency . . . Would have a good game every seven or eight . . . On the other hand, the .471 from the field marked significant improvement over the previous three seasons . . . Member of the 1988 Olympic team before joining the Spurs as the No. 10 pick in the draft and earning all-rookie honors . . . Attended Georgia . . . Born Jan. 8, 1967, in Greenville, S.C. . . . Made $2.075 million.

Year	Team	G	FG	FG Pct.	FT	FT Pct.	Reb.	Ast.	TP	Avg.
1988-89	San Antonio	81	640	.498	224	.775	417	372	1508	18.6
1989-90	San Antonio	82	532	.492	217	.748	372	364	1288	15.7
1990-91	San Antonio	75	453	.457	170	.798	351	358	1083	14.4
1991-92	San Antonio	57	312	.455	107	.775	300	302	744	13.1
1992-93	San Antonio	38	80	.430	22	.786	57	79	183	4.8
1993-94	San Antonio	80	394	.471	145	.848	242	347	955	11.9
	Totals	413	2411	.476	885	.784	1739	1822	5761	13.9

TERRY CUMMINGS 33 6-9 245   Forward

Had career lows in most every statistical category, but 1993-94 was far from disheartening ... He made it back, which made those 59 games an accomplishment ... Played only eight games the season before after suffering torn knee ligament ... Then proved the knee could hold up for the long haul ... Now there's that other prominent problem to deal with: age ... Former Rookie of the Year with San Diego Clippers is not much of a scorer anymore ... Shooting has fallen off ... But can still knock people off the blocks ... Banger ... Two-time all-star with Bucks ... Spurs sent Alvin Robertson and Greg Anderson to Milwaukee to get him in the summer of 1989 ... Clippers chose former DePaul star second in 1982 ... Born March 15, 1961, in Chicago ... Made $2.407 million.

Year	Team	G	FG	FG Pct.	FT	FT Pct.	Reb.	Ast.	TP	Avg.
1982-83	San Diego	70	684	.523	292	.709	744	177	1660	23.7
1983-84	San Diego	81	737	.494	380	.720	777	139	1854	22.9
1984-85	Milwaukee	79	759	.495	343	.741	716	228	1861	23.6
1985-86	Milwaukee	82	681	.474	265	.656	694	193	1627	19.8
1986-87	Milwaukee	82	729	.511	249	.662	700	229	1707	20.8
1987-88	Milwaukee	76	675	.485	270	.665	553	181	1621	21.3
1988-89	Milwaukee	80	730	.467	362	.787	650	198	1829	22.9
1989-90	San Antonio	81	728	.475	343	.780	677	219	1818	22.4
1990-91	San Antonio	67	503	.484	164	.683	521	157	1177	17.6
1991-92	San Antonio	70	514	.488	177	.711	631	102	1210	17.3
1992-93	San Antonio	8	11	.379	5	.500	19	4	27	3.4
1993-94	San Antonio	59	183	.428	63	.589	297	50	429	7.3
	Totals	835	6934	.487	2913	.711	6979	1877	16820	20.1

ANTOINE CARR 33 6-9 255   Forward

Didn't contribute much on the court, but remained an emotional leader ... Rah-rah type, with a twist: he barks and gets the fans to bark ... Thus the nickname "Big Dawg" and his role as founder of the Canine Club ... Ankle injury hampered him much of the first four months of last season ... Logged at least 20 minutes only five times ... All-American while at Wichita State, where he was teammates with Greg Dreiling, Cliff Levingston and Xavier McDaniel ... Went into summer as unrestricted free agent ... Originally a No. 8 pick by Detroit in 1983, but didn't come to terms with Pistons and was eventually traded to Hawks to begin NBA career ... Spurs sent Dwayne Schinztius and a second-round pick to Sacramento to get him ...

Born July 23, 1961, in Oklahoma City, Okla . . . Made $1.353 million.

Year	Team	G	FG	FG Pct.	FT	FT Pct.	Reb.	Ast.	TP	Avg.
1984-85	Atlanta	62	198	.528	101	.789	232	80	499	8.0
1985-86	Atlanta	17	49	.527	18	.667	52	14	116	6.8
1986-87	Atlanta	65	134	.506	73	.709	156	34	342	5.3
1987-88	Atlanta	80	281	.544	142	.780	289	103	705	8.8
1988-89	Atlanta	78	226	.480	130	.855	274	91	582	7.5
1989-90	Atl.-Sac.	77	356	.494	237	.795	322	119	949	12.3
1990-91	Sacramento	77	628	.511	295	.758	420	191	1551	20.1
1991-92	San Antonio	81	359	.490	162	.764	346	63	881	10.9
1992-93	San Antonio	71	379	.538	174	.777	388	97	932	13.1
1993-94	San Antonio	34	78	.488	42	.724	51	15	198	5.8
	Totals	642	2688	.510	1374	.775	2530	807	6755	10.5

NEGELE KNIGHT 27 6-1 182   Guard

Not the answer at point guard . . . That doesn't make him unique around these parts, just a reserve like in Phoenix . . . Once a hot property who could have brought a first-round pick, he was traded to San Antonio in last season's first week for a second-rounder . . . Played one game with Suns, then 64 with Spurs, including 18 starts . . . Made too many bad decisions and had stretches with a lot of turnovers . . . Has bad habit of trying to plow into the defense . . . Iffy jumper . . . Dayton product was 31st pick in 1990 draft . . . Born March 6, 1967, in Detroit . . . Made $469,000.

Year	Team	G	FG	FG Pct.	FT	FT Pct.	Reb.	Ast.	TP	Avg.
1990-91	Phoenix	64	131	.425	71	.602	71	191	339	5.3
1991-92	Phoenix	42	103	.475	33	.688	46	112	243	5.8
1992-93	Phoenix	52	124	.391	67	.779	64	145	315	6.1
1993-94	Phoe.-S.A.	65	225	.474	141	.810	103	197	595	9.2
	Totals	223	583	.443	312	.732	284	645	1492	6.7

J.R. REID 26 6-9 265   Forward

Where does he fit in? . . . Frustrated much of last season with uncertain rotation . . . Lost about five minutes a game from the previous campaign . . . We assume he didn't head the Dennis Rodman Welcoming Committee . . . Did develop a nice medium-range jump shot, from the 12-to-13-foot range . . . Played some small forward for the first time in his career . . . Joined current teammates David Robinson and Willie Anderson on 1988 Olympic team... Reunited after Spurs got him from Charlotte in December 1992 in exchange for Sidney Green, a No. 1 and a No. 2... Star at North Carolina before Hornets picked local hero No. 5 in 1989... Born March 31, 1968, in Virginia Beach, Va....Made $1.818 million.

Year	Team	G	FG	FG Pct.	FT	FT Pct.	Reb.	Ast.	TP	Avg.
1989-90	Charlotte	82	358	.440	192	.664	691	101	908	11.1
1990-91	Charlotte	80	360	.466	182	.703	502	89	902	11.3
1991-92	Charlotte	51	213	.490	134	.705	317	81	560	11.0
1992-93	Char.-S.A.	83	283	.476	214	.764	456	80	780	9.4
1993-94	San Antonio	70	260	.491	107	.699	220	73	627	9.0
	Totals	366	1474	.468	829	.708	2186	424	3777	10.3

LLOYD DANIELS 27 6-7 205   Guard-Forward

After the fanfare, the question marks remain ... Time continued to drop under ex-coach John Lucas... Got 30.6 minutes an outing when Jerry Tarkanian was coach for the first 19 games of rookie season, then 17.1 after Lucas took over, then 15.1 last season with Lucas ... Had five starts, three at guard and two at forward... Should be—needs to be—a better shooter than his .418 in the two seasons would indicate... Joined Spurs as a free agent after playing five years in the CBA, USBL, GBA and New Zealand... Left high school after junior season, by which time he had become a playground legend in New York City... Attended Mt. San Antonio College in suburban Los Angeles before transferring to UNLV, but never played for Tarkanian in college... Born Sept. 4, 1967, in Brooklyn, N.Y....Made $182,000.

Year	Team	G	FG	FG Pct.	FT	FT Pct.	Reb.	Ast.	TP	Avg.
1992-93	San Antonio	77	285	.443	72	.727	216	148	701	9.1
1993-94	San Antonio	65	140	.376	46	.719	111	94	370	5.7
	Totals	142	425	.418	118	.724	327	242	1071	7.5

ERIC (SLEEPY) FLOYD 34 6-3 185   Guard

Same player who once had two streaks of at least 300 consecutive appearances has now had minutes drop five consecutive seasons... Former all-star with Rockets came to Spurs as a free agent for a one-year deal at the $150,000 minimum... His .335 from the field was a team low... Inserted for defensive purposes when first wave couldn't stop opposing point guards . . . Career started as No. 13 pick of 1982 draft by New Jersey, but best known for years with Golden State and Houston . . . Had one of the best playoff games in NBA history as a Warrior on May 1, 1987, when he hit the Lakers for 51 points, including a record 29 in one quarter . . . Born March 6, 1960, in Gastonia, N.C., and played college ball at Georgetown.

Year	Team	G	FG	FG Pct.	FT	FT Pct.	Reb.	Ast.	TP	Avg.
1982-83	N.J.-G.S.	76	226	.429	150	.833	137	138	612	8.1
1983-84	Golden State	77	484	.463	315	.816	271	269	1291	16.8
1984-85	Golden State	82	610	.445	336	.810	202	406	1598	19.5
1985-86	Golden State	82	510	.506	351	.796	297	746	1410	17.2
1986-87	Golden State	82	503	.488	462	.860	268	848	1541	18.8
1987-88	G.S.-Hou..	77	420	.433	301	.850	296	544	1155	15.0
1988-89	Houston	82	396	.443	261	.845	306	709	1162	14.2
1989-90	Houston	82	362	.451	187	.806	198	600	1000	12.2
1990-91	Houston	82	386	.411	185	.752	159	317	1005	12.3
1991-92	Houston	82	286	.406	135	.794	150	239	744	9.1
1992-93	Houston	52	124	.407	81	.794	86	132	345	6.6
1993-94	San Antonio	53	70	.335	52	.667	70	101	200	3.8
	Totals	909	4377	.446	2816	.816	2440	5049	12063	13.3

SEAN ELLIOTT 26 6-8 215   Forward

Back to San Antonio in July deal that sent first-round draft pick Bill Curley to Pistons . . . Came from Spurs with David Wood for Dennis Rodman and Isaiah Morris on Oct. 1, 1993 . . . Acquired for scoring, he provided 885 points, 12.1 a game . . . Rodman had just 1,367 rebounds, 17.3 a game . . . Yeah, a real good deal . . . Pistons tried to send 1989 No. 3 overall pick to Houston for Robert Horry in midseason. Houston sent him back. And won a championship . . . Worst year of career, with an asterisk . . . In fairness, medication for kidney ailment left him woefully underconditioned for start . . . Made $1.807 million . . . Soft defender . . . Doesn't go inside enough . . . Born Feb. 2, 1968, in Tucson, Ariz. . . . Left Arizona as Pac-10's all-time scorer.

Year	Team	G	FG	FG Pct.	FT	FT Pct.	Reb.	Ast.	TP	Avg.
1989-90	San Antonio	81	311	.481	187	.866	297	154	810	10.0
1990-91	San Antonio	82	478	.490	325	.808	456	238	1301	15.9
1991-92	San Antonio	82	514	.494	285	.861	439	214	1338	16.3
1992-93	San Antonio	70	451	.491	268	.795	322	265	1207	17.2
1993-94	Detroit	73	360	.455	139	.803	263	197	885	12.1
	Totals	388	2114	.484	1204	.825	1777	1068	5541	14.3

CHUCK PERSON 30 6-8 225   Forward

Signed with Spurs in July after becoming unrestricted free agent when Timberwolves bought out remainder of his contract . . . Had 122 more three-point attempts than any Timberwolves' player . . . And still shoots his mouth off . . . Speaking about his diminished role in the spring, he said: ''They might as well tie my hands behind my back, leave me on the side of the road and feed me to the crows.'' They did worse . . . They made him show up and watch the games . . . He and Micheal Williams came to Timberwolves in September of 1992 from Indiana for Pooh Richardson and Sam Mitchell . . . Chuck Connors Person was named after TV's ''The Rifleman'' . . . Born June 27, 1964, in Brantley, Ala. . . . Former Auburn star made $2.156 million.

Year	Team	G	FG	FG Pct.	FT	FT Pct.	Reb.	Ast.	TP	Avg.
1986-87	Indiana.	82	635	.468	222	.747	677	295	1541	18.8
1987-88	Indiana.	79	575	.459	132	.670	536	309	1341	17.0
1988-89	Indiana.	80	711	.489	243	.792	516	289	1728	21.6
1989-90	Indiana.	77	605	.487	211	.781	445	230	1515	19.7
1990-91	Indiana.	80	620	.504	165	.721	417	238	1474	18.4
1991-92	Indiana.	81	616	.480	133	.675	426	382	1497	18.5
1992-93	Minnesota.	78	541	.433	109	.649	433	343	1309	16.8
1993-94	Minnesota.	77	356	.422	82	.759	253	185	894	11.6
	Totals	634	4659	.470	1297	.732	3703	2271	11299	17.8

CHRIS WHITNEY 23 6-0 170   Guard

Needs another season of seasoning . . . Lack of experience showed last season after Spurs drafted him in the second round . . . Had trouble penetrating against tough guards . . . Just a fair ballhandler . . . Has range on his jumper, but needs to do much better than the .305 from the field . . . Hasn't done better than .441 since leaving junior college . . . Did leave Clemson as the school's all-time leader in three-pointers despite playing only two years . . . Put on the injured list in March and was not on the playoff roster . . . Born Oct. 5, 1971, in Hopkinsville, Ky. . . . Made $150,000.

Year	Team	G	FG	FG Pct.	FT	FT Pct.	Reb.	Ast.	TP	Avg.
1993-94	San Antonio	40	25	.305	12	.800	29	53	72	1.8

JACK HALEY 30 6-10 250   **Center**

Same role, different team . . . Human victory cigar . . . Practice player who gave David Robinson good workouts . . . Consummate cheerleader . . . Opened training camp last year with Cavaliers before being cut before the start of the regular season. Was playing with Magic Johnson's barnstorming team when the Spurs called . . . Averaged 3.4 minutes in his 28 appearances . . . Originally fourth-round pick of Chicago in 1987 after playing at UCLA . . . Bounced to Europe and back to Bulls, then on to New Jersey, the Lakers, Cleveland and San Antonio . . . Born Jan. 27, 1964, in Long Beach, Cal. . . . Made $150,000.

Year	Team	G	FG	FG Pct.	FT	FT Pct.	Reb.	Ast.	TP	Avg.
1988-89	Chicago	51	37	.474	36	.783	71	10	110	2.2
1989-90	Chi.-N.J.	67	138	.398	85	.680	300	26	361	5.4
1990-91	New Jersey	78	161	.469	112	.619	356	31	434	5.6
1991-92	L.A. Lakers	49	31	.369	14	.483	95	7	76	1.6
1992-93	L.A. Lakers					Injured				
1993-94	San Antonio	28	21	.438	17	.810	24	1	59	2.1
	Totals	273	388	.431	264	.657	846	75	1040	3.8

GREATEST PLAYER

David Robinson is a superstar and so complete that he could average 10.7 rebounds and 3.31 blocked shots, things centers are supposed to do, while also leading the team in assists. He is a special player who will someday undoubtedly deserve this spot.

But to forget about George Gervin would be too shortsighted because the Ice Age wasn't all that long ago in San Antonio. Gervin was a brilliant offensive threat whose 23,602 career points only put him some 13,000 ahead of the closest persuer, James Silas. That translates into an average of 27.3 points over nine seasons with the NBA Spurs, including seven times of at least 25, four league scoring titles and nine All-Star Game appearances.

Gervin is even No. 1 in rebounds, though Robinson, barring injury, will pass his sometime this season. He will probably pass him in this category, too, but for now this spot still belongs to the original.

ALL-TIME SPUR LEADERS

SEASON

Points: George Gervin, 2,585, 1979-80
Assists: Johnny Moore, 816, 1984-85
Rebounds: Swen Nater, 1,279, 1974-75 (ABA)

GAME

Points: David Robinson, 71 vs. LA Clippers, 4/24/94
Assists: John Lucas, 24 vs. Denver, 4/15/84
Rebounds: Manny Leaks, 35 vs. Kentucky, 11/27/70 (ABA)

CAREER

Points: George Gervin, 23,602, 1974-85
Assists: Johnny Moore, 3,865, 1980-90
Rebounds: George Gervin, 4,841, 1974-85

SEATTLE SUPERSONICS

TEAM DIRECTORY: Chairman: Barry Ackerley; Pres./GM: Wally Walker; Dir. Pub. Rel: Cheri White; Coach: George Karl; Asst. Coaches: Bob Kloppenburg, Tim Grgurich, Terry Stotts. Arena: Tacoma Dome (16,296). Colors: Green and yellow.

Shawn Kemp made second-team All-NBA in his best season.

SCOUTING REPORT

SHOOTING: You know this is a different kind of team from the start. The point guard took 169 more shots than anyone else last season. Then there is the fact that their two most accurate three-point shooters are Nate McMillan and Sam Perkins, the former a part-time small forward and the latter a center and power forward. Most defenses aren't made for those kinds of matchups.

The SuperSonics don't take a ton of shots, just enough. They averaged 105.9 points a game in 1993-94 because they tied for fourth-best overall in percentage, including tied for second best in the Western Conference. That's even with Perkins slumping to .438 and Kendall Gill, the shooting guard, going for a career-low .443, the compensation being Shawn Kemp finishing fifth in the NBA at .538 and Gary Payton becoming a weapon from the outside.

Management was so comfortable with the number of shooters that they could trade Ricky Pierce for Sarunas Marciulionis, a swap of styles as well as teams. Pierce remains one of the biggest three-point threats in the league despite the number of last season, but Marciulionis' trademark is his driving style. What effect playing just 30 games the last two years will have is one of the things to watch this season.

PLAYMAKING: It would be enough if they just had Payton, who emerged in his fourth season to become one of the best point guards in the league. His value isn't measured in assists—just 6.0 in 1993-94—but durability, quickness and take-charge attitude.

But there is more. Gill, the shooting guard, began his pro career with Charlotte playing the point. McMillan is well-tested and at 6-5 allows for versatility in George Karl's lineup.

REBOUNDING: Most people would be happy with the showing of 1993-94: tied for 10th in rebounding percentage, including tied for fifth on the offensive boards. But that was a significant drop for the Sonics, who went No. 5 and tied for No. 2, respectively, the season before.

This becomes an even bigger area of concern with the free-agent departure to Cleveland of Michael Cage, best known for his hard-hat work with offensive rebounds. Someone will have to replace that. Perhaps it will be Byron Houston.

SUPERSONIC ROSTER

No.	Veterans	Pos.	Ht.	Wt.	Age	Yrs. Pro	College
U-17	Vincent Askew	G-F	6-6	235	28	5	Memphis State
U-44	Michael Cage	F-C	6-9	240	32	10	San Diego State
13	Kendall Gill	G	6-5	200	26	4	Illinois
–	Byron Houston	F	6-5	250	24	2	Oklahoma State
50	Ervin Johnson	C	6-11	245	26	1	New Orleans
40	Shawn Kemp	F	6-10	245	24	5	Trinity JC
R-35	Chris King	F	6-8	215	25	1	Wake Forest
45	Rich King	C	7-2	265	25	3	Nebraska
–	Sarunas Marciulionis	G	6-5	215	30	4	Lithuania
10	Nate McMillan	G-F	6-5	200	30	8	No. Carolina State
20	Gary Payton	G	6-4	190	26	4	Oregon State
14	Sam Perkins	C-F	6-9	245	33	10	North Carolina
U-55	Steve Scheffler	C	6-9	250	27	4	Purdue
U-11	Detlef Schrempf	F	6-10	230	31	9	Washington

R-restricted free agent
U-unrestricted free agent

Rd.	Rookies	Sel. No.	Pos.	Ht.	Wt.	College
2	Dontonio Wingfield	37	F	6-7	256	Cincinnati
2	Zeljko Rebraca	54	C	6-11	198	Yugoslavia

DEFENSE: Where it all begins. The SuperSonics don't try to beat people so much as suffocate them by taking several good one-on-one defenders and getting them to rely on each other with a switching, trapping attack. Credit goes to the coaching staff.

The only thing they didn't do last season was break the NBA record of 1,059 steals by the Suns, falling just short at 1,053. No team had a better steal-to-turnover ratio. McMillan, Payton and Gill were all in the top nine among individuals in that category. And no team forced more turnovers.

OUTLOOK: They could either win it all or implode. Or maybe both at the same time. We'd feel better about picking them to be the last team standing in mid-June if only they felt better about themselves. The offseason vibes were not good—president Bob Whitsett, the architect, leaving; nearly trading Kemp for Scottie Pippen; dealing Pierce.

The best advice: Hold on tight. It will either be a long ride or very bumpy.

SUPERSONIC PROFILES

SHAWN KEMP 24 6-10 245   Forward

Our little baby is all grown up . . . Entered the NBA at age 19 after never having played in college and is now among the best in the game . . . Oh, yeah. He turns only 25 in the first month of the season . . . Member of Dream Team II . . . Has played in the last two All-Star Games, the first SuperSonic to be picked in consecutive years since Jack Sikma in 1984-85 . . . Imagine the wreckage he could leave behind if he got more than 32.9 minutes of last season . . . Still averaged 18.1 points and 10.8 rebounds . . . All this for $800,000 . . . Signed through the end of 2002 . . . Born Nov. 26, 1969, in Elkhart, Ind., and attended Trinity Valley JC in Texas, but not long enough to play . . . Seattle got him from there with the 17th pick in 1989 draft, a let's-see-what-happens choice.

Year	Team	G	FG	FG Pct.	FT	FT Pct.	Reb.	Ast.	TP	Avg.
1989-90	Seattle	81	203	.479	117	.736	346	26	525	6.5
1990-91	Seattle	81	462	.508	288	.661	679	144	1214	15.0
1991-92	Seattle	64	362	.504	270	.748	665	86	994	15.5
1992-93	Seattle	78	515	.492	358	.712	833	155	1388	17.8
1993-94	Seattle	79	533	.538	364	.741	851	207	1431	18.1
	Totals	383	2075	.508	1397	.716	3374	618	5552	14.5

KENDALL GILL 26 6-5 200   Guard

And he thought things were tough in Charlotte playing with Alonzo Mourning and Larry Johnson . . . Played 10 more games in his first season as a SuperSonic compared to 1992-93, but only five more minutes . . . Said Orlando's Nick Anderson, a college teammate: "If he had to do it over again, he would have stayed in Charlotte. He doesn't like the minutes (in Seattle) at all." . . . Sonics sent Dana Barros, Eddie Johnson and what became a '94 lottery pick to Hornets to get Illinois product . . . Charlotte landed him with the No. 5 pick in the 1990 draft . . . Can handle the ball and play defense . . . Finished 14th in the league in steals . . . Born May 25, 1968, in Chicago . . . Made $2 million.

Year	Team	G	FG	FG Pct.	FT	FT Pct.	Reb.	Ast.	TP	Avg.
1990-91	Charlotte	82	376	.450	152	.835	263	303	906	11.0
1991-92	Charlotte	79	666	.467	284	.745	402	329	1622	20.5
1992-93	Charlotte	69	463	.449	224	.772	340	268	1167	16.9
1993-94	Seattle	79	429	.443	215	.782	268	275	1111	14.1
	Totals	309	1934	.454	875	.776	1273	1175	4806	15.6

GARY PAYTON 26 6-4 190   Guard

Finally, the game to back up the talk . . . Finally, the jumper to back up the month . . . His 1992-93 season was a step in the right direction, but last year was the giant step the SuperSonics had been waiting for since making him the No. 2 pick in 1990 . . . The ability to consistently hit from the outside, long a weak spot, has been a key factor in the improvement . . . How far has he come? The .504 in 1993-94 was the third-best among all guards, behind only John Stockton and Stacey Augmon . . . "He made them a true championship contender," Charles Barkley said in pushing Payton for MVP consideration. "He is the player that makes them go." . . . Member of 1994 All-Star team . . . Has missed just one game in four seasons since coming out of Oregon State . . . Born July 23, 1968, in Oakland . . . Made $2.383 million.

Year	Team	G	FG	FG Pct.	FT	FT Pct.	Reb.	Ast.	TP	Avg.
1990-91	Seattle	82	259	.450	69	.711	243	528	588	7.2
1991-92	Seattle	81	331	.451	99	.669	295	506	764	9.4
1992-93	Seattle	82	476	.494	151	.770	281	399	1110	13.5
1993-94	Seattle	82	584	.504	166	.595	269	494	1349	16.5
	Totals	327	1650	.481	485	.674	1088	1927	3811	11.7

DETLEF SCHREMPF 31 6-10 230   Forward

Home again, sort of . . . German native came to area to attend high school, starred in college at Washington, and was building a home in the Seattle area when he was traded from Pacers to SuperSonics a few days before the 1993-94 opener for Derrick McKey and Gerald Paddio . . . Versatile small forward started all but one of 81 appearances after being named Sixth Man of the Year in 1991 and '92 with Indiana and in 1992-93 was the only NBA player to finish in top 25 of scoring, rebounding and assists . . . Started at every position while at Washington, before Dallas took him with eighth pick in 1985 . . . Played on the 1984 (West Germany) and 1992 (unified Germany) Olympic teams . . . Born Jan. 21, 1963, in Leverkusen, Germany . . . Made $1.151 million.

Year	Team	G	FG	FG Pct.	FT	FT Pct.	Reb.	Ast.	TP	Avg.
1985-86	Dallas	64	142	.451	110	.724	198	88	397	6.2
1986-87	Dallas	81	265	.472	193	.742	303	161	756	9.3
1987-88	Dallas	82	246	.456	201	.756	279	159	698	8.5
1988-89	Dal.-Indiana	69	274	.474	273	.780	395	179	828	12.0
1989-90	Indiana.	78	424	.516	402	.820	620	247	1267	16.2
1990-91	Indiana.	82	432	.520	441	.818	660	301	1320	16.1
1991-92	Indiana.	80	496	.536	365	.828	770	312	1380	17.3
1992-93	Indiana.	82	517	.476	525	.804	780	493	1567	19.1
1993-94	Seattle	81	445	.493	300	.769	454	275	1212	15.0
	Totals	699	3241	.494	2810	.794	4459	2215	9425	13.5

NATE McMILLAN 30 6-5 200   Guard-Forward

One of the game's most underrated player continues to make an impact with the players, if not the fans . . . Has long been the SuperSonics' floor leader . . . Last season, he finished No. 1 in the league in steals and became the all-time franchise leader when he passed Fred Brown on March 17 . . . Now at 1,212 since joining the team as a second-round pick out of North Carolina State in 1986 . . . Already No. 1 in career assists . . . Only Brown and Jack Sikma have played more games in a Sonic uniform . . . George Karl's switching, trapping, defense-oriented system was made for his versatility . . . Plays point guard and small forward, so must be able to check both, too . . . Dangerous as a three-point shooter . . . Born Aug. 3, 1964, in Raleigh, N.C. . . . Made $890,000.

Year	Team	G	FG	FG Pct.	FT	FT Pct.	Reb.	Ast.	TP	Avg.
1986-87	Seattle	71	143	.475	87	.617	331	583	373	5.3
1987-88	Seattle	82	235	.474	145	.707	338	702	624	7.6
1988-89	Seattle	75	199	.410	119	.630	388	696	532	7.1
1989-90	Seattle	82	207	.473	98	.641	403	598	523	6.4
1990-91	Seattle	78	132	.433	57	.613	251	371	338	4.3
1991-92	Seattle	72	177	.437	54	.643	252	359	435	6.0
1992-93	Seattle	73	213	.464	95	.709	306	384	546	7.5
1993-94	Seattle	73	177	.447	31	.564	283	387	437	6.0
	Totals	606	1483	.451	686	.651	2552	4080	3808	6.3

SARUNAS MARCIULIONIS 30 6-5 215   Guard

Joined Sonics in July with Byron Houston in deal that brought Ricky Pierce and rookie Carlos Rogers to Golden State . . . Would like to pretend the last two seasons never happened, but he can be a major contributor, if the legs hold up . . . Suffered torn ligament in right knee during informal workout last September and missed all of 1993-94 . . . This after playing just 30 games the year before because of a fractured right leg and broken right ankle suffered before the season and, later, tendinitis of the right Achilles . . . The last time he went wire to wire, 1991-92, he was the league's top scoring reserve and finished second to Detlef Schrempf for Sixth Man of the Year . . . Specialty is putting the ball on the floor and driving to the basket . . . The first player from the former Soviet Union to sign with the NBA was born June 13, 1964, in Kaunas, Lithuania . . . Leading scorer for Soviet team that won 1988 Olympic gold medal and four years later led Lithuania to bronze medal . . . Made $1.9 million.

Year	Team	G	FG	FG Pct.	FT	FT Pct.	Reb.	Ast.	TP	Avg.
1989-90	Golden State	75	289	.519	317	.787	221	121	905	12.1
1990-91	Golden State	50	183	.501	178	.724	118	85	545	10.9
1991-92	Golden State	72	491	.538	376	.788	208	243	1361	18.9
1992-93	Golden State	30	178	.543	162	.761	97	105	521	17.4
1993-94	Golden State					Injured				
	Totals	227	1141	.528	1033	.771	644	554	333 2	14.7

SAM PERKINS 33 6-9 245   Center-Forward

Fighting for a spot in the rotation . . . Averaged 26.8 minutes and started 41 times . . . Another bad shooting season and people may start to get concerned, having gone .450 and .438 within the last three campaigns . . . Difficult matchup for opposing power forwards and centers because he can score from the post or step out to the three-point line . . . Went 7-for-7 from behind the arc Nov. 9 to tie an NBA record for most without a miss in a game . . . His 90 threes were the most by a SuperSonic since Dale Ellis in 1988-89 . . . Three-time All-American at North Carolina was Dallas' first pick, fourth overall, in 1984 . . . Went from Mavericks to Lakers as a free agent, then to Seattle when Benoit Benjamin and Doug Christie were sent to L.A. . . . Born June 14, 1961, in New York City . . . Made $3.587 million.

Year	Team	G	FG	FG Pct.	FT	FT Pct.	Reb.	Ast.	TP	Avg.
1984-85	Dallas	82	347	.471	200	.820	605	135	903	11.0
1985-86	Dallas	80	458	.503	307	.814	685	153	1234	15.4
1986-87	Dallas	80	461	.482	245	.828	616	146	1186	14.8
1987-88	Dallas	75	394	.450	273	.822	601	118	1066	14.2
1988-89	Dallas	78	445	.464	274	.833	688	127	1171	15.0
1989-90	Dallas	76	435	.493	330	.778	572	175	1206	15.9
1990-91	L.A. Lakers	73	368	.495	229	.821	538	108	983	13.5
1991-92	L.A. Lakers	63	361	.450	304	.817	556	141	1041	16.5
1992-93	L.A. Lakers-Sea.	79	381	.477	250	.820	524	156	1036	13.1
1993-94	Seattle	81	341	.438	218	.801	366	111	999	12.3
	Totals	767	3991	.473	2630	.814	5751	1370	10825	14.1

Gary Payton shot up in stats with hits from the outside.

VINCENT ASKEW 28 6-6 235   Guard-Forward

The only thing better than his play last season was the timing . . . Opened by frequently getting lost in the rotation and openly wondering about his future, then charged to the forefront as a key defender, just in time to head into the summer as an unrestricted free agent . . . Says assistant coach Bob Kloppenburg, the Sonics' defensive guru: "I've never had a more versatile defensive player than Vincent because he can play big or small. He wears you down." . . . Could be decent payday ahead for the guy who was once waived by 76ers and played a couple of seasons in the CBA and had a cup of coffee in Italy . . . Seattle spent only a second-round pick to get him from Sacramento in November 1992 . . . Made $525,000 in 1993-94 . . . Born Feb. 28, 1966, in Memphis, Tenn., and stayed home to play at Memphis State.

Year	Team	G	FG	FG Pct.	FT	FT Pct.	Reb.	Ast.	TP	Avg.
1987-88	Philadelphia	14	22	.297	8	.727	22	33	52	3.7
1990-91	Golden State	7	12	.480	9	.818	11	13	33	4.7
1991-92	Golden State	80	193	.509	111	.694	233	188	498	6.2
1992-93	Sac.-Sea.	73	152	.492	105	.705	161	122	411	5.6
1993-94	Seattle	80	273	.481	175	.829	184	194	727	9.1
	Totals	254	652	.482	408	.753	611	550	1721	6.8

ERVIN JOHNSON 26 6-11 245   Center

He has the name for greatness and some tools for decent success . . . Runs the floor . . . Quickness as a shot-blocker, the one part of the defense the SuperSonics are lacking . . . Best showing as a rookie was the 10 rebounds in just eight minutes Dec. 14 against Orlando . . . Had to be content with those cameos—he averaged just 6.2 minutes per outing . . . No. 23 pick of the 1993 draft didn't play high school basketball and then worked for 2½ years in a Baton Rouge, La., supermarket before enrolling at New Orleans in January 1989 . . . That's why he was older before ever playing a pro game than teammate Shawn Kemp was after five seasons . . . Progressed enough to be named Sun Belt Conference Player of the Year and third-team All-American by UPI as a senior . . . Born Dec. 21, 1967, in New Orleans . . . Made $617,000.

Year	Team	G	FG	FG Pct.	FT	FT Pct.	Reb.	Ast.	TP	Avg.
1993-94	Seattle	45	44	.415	29	.630	118	7	117	2.6

CHRIS KING 25 6-8 215 Forward

Dunking ability is a well-kept secret. Teammates say he isn't far behind Shawn Kemp... Didn't get much of a chance to show it off in games, with only 86 minutes in 15 sightings... Second-round pick in 1992, No. 45 overall, but spent first pro season in Spain... Returned for summer league and '93 training camp and stuck for the regular season... Four-year starter at Wake Forest, where he was one of only four players to total more than 1,600 points and 600 rebounds... Born July 24, 1969, in Newton Grove, N.C.... Made $150,000.

Year	Team	G	FG	FG Pct.	FT	FT Pct.	Reb.	Ast.	TP	Avg.
1993-94	Seattle	15	19	.396	15	.577	15	11	55	3.7

RICH KING 25 7-2 265 Center

Came back after missing practically all of 1992-93 with a stress fracture in his right foot, though it may have been hard to tell... Never played more than seven minutes in any of his 27 appearances last season... Sonics have been expecting him to emerge as a dependable backup center... No Nebraska player ever blocked more shots in a career and only two others had more rebounds... Heading into final season of his contract... Not on the playoff roster because of a sore back... No. 14 pick in the 1991 draft... Born April 4, 1969, in Omaha, Neb.... Made $700,000.

Year	Team	G	FG	FG Pct.	FT	FT Pct.	Reb.	Ast.	TP	Avg.
1991-92	Seattle	40	27	.380	34	.756	49	12	88	2.2
1992-93	Seattle	3	2	.400	2	1.000	5	1	6	2.0
1993-94	Seattle	27	15	.441	11	.500	20	8	41	1.5
	Totals	70	44	.400	47	.681	74	21	135	1.9

STEVE SCHEFFLER 27 6-9 250 Forward-Center

When people tell him to pick on someone his own size, they don't mean another 6-9 guy... Has strength most big centers would kill for... Uses it best in practice, when he bangs Shawn Kemp and others around so much they probably begin to look forward to games as a breather... Hardest worker on the court, hardest worker on the sidelines as a cheerleader... Big Ten

Player of the Year at Purdue in 1990, just before Charlotte picked him in the second round. Bounced from Hornets to Celtics to CBA's Quad City to Kings to Nuggets before SuperSonics got him as a free agent . . . Born Sept. 3, 1967, in Grand Rapids, Mich. . . . Made $170,000.

Year	Team	G	FG	FG Pct.	FT	FT Pct.	Reb.	Ast.	TP	Avg.
1990-91	Charlotte	39	20	.513	19	.905	45	9	59	1.5
1991-92	Sac.-Den.	11	6	.667	9	.750	14	0	21	1.9
1992-93	Seattle	29	25	.521	16	.667	36	5	66	2.3
1993-94	Seattle	35	28	.609	19	.950	26	6	75	2.1
	Totals	114	79	.556	63	.818	121	20	221	1.9

BYRON HOUSTON 24 6-5 250 — Forward

Came to Sonics with Sarunas Marciulionis in July deal that sent Ricky Pierce and rookie Carlos Rogers to the Warriors . . . Everyone notices the body . . . The 250 pounds on 6-foot-5 frame makes him look like a fire-plug . . . And he has a seven-foot wingspan that helps on defense . . . Started twice and the average of 12.2 minutes was a drop of about four a game from the season before . . . It's an even bigger fall considering he led the Warriors in games played in 1992-93 . . . Was on the floor Feb. 6 when the Warriors tied an NBA record by limiting the Bullets to seven points in the fourth quarter . . . No. 1 in points, rebounds and blocked shots by the time he left Oklahoma State in 1992 . . . Chicago took him with the last pick in the first round that year, then traded him to Warriors as part of a three-team deal that also included Dallas . . . Born Nov. 22, 1969, in Watonga, Kan. . . . Made $600,000.

Year	Team	G	FG	FG Pct.	FT	FT Pct.	Reb.	Ast.	TP	Avg.
1992-93	Golden State	79	145	.446	129	.665	315	69	421	5.3
1993-94	Golden State	71	81	.458	33	.611	194	32	196	2.8
	Totals	150	226	.450	162	.653	509	101	617	4.1

THE ROOKIES

DONTONIO WINGFIELD 20 6-7 256 — Forward

No one is quite sure what to expect . . . After finishing high school, he tore up his mother's kitchen, reportedly because she wouldn't let him use the car, and later pleaded guilty to one count of criminal damage to property and two counts of obstructing justice . . . Then enrolled at Cincinnati, but left after one year . . . No. 37 pick . . . Averaged 16 points and nine rebounds in that freshman season and was named Great Midwest Conference newcomer of the year . . . Born June 23, 1974, in Albany, Ga.

ZELJKO REBRACA 22 6-11 198   Center

The 76ers should have taken him to make Shawn Bradley look overweight . . . Is it possible something got lost in the translation, or does that 198 need to be converted from metric? . . . Serbian played for Partizan, the same club that produced Vlade Divac . . . MVP of the Yugoslavian League . . . Born April 9, 1972, in Prigrevica, Yugoslavia.

COACH GEORGE KARL: He's got everything under control

. . . Doesn't he? . . . Gives the plays and personalities plenty of rope, sometimes just enough to hang themselves . . . Such was the case with the shocking first-round playoff loss to Denver . . . Had that run-over-by-a-steam-roller look for the next few days . . . Second full season with the SuperSonics resulted in best record in franchise history (63-19) . . . His 145-61 mark in 2½ years is the highest winning percentage (.703) ever for the team . . . Career: 264-237 (.527) . . . Played college ball at North Carolina, then went on to San Antonio in the ABA and through the NBA merger . . . Point guard . . . Began sideline career with Spurs as an assistant to Doug Moe and became a head coach two years later with Montana of the CBA, where he was named Coach of the Year two of the three seasons . . . Made the jump to NBA as director of player acquisition for the Cavaliers in 1983 and a year later became coach. Fired late in 1985-86, he went to Warriors that fall . . . Next came stops with Albany of the CBA and Real Madrid of the Spanish League before the Sonics called . . . He replaced K.C. Jones and has quickly become one of the hottest coaching properties going . . . Has done a great job handling the bruised egos on a team where distribution of minutes has been focus of much attention, like All-Star Shawn Kemp getting just 32.9 . . . Wears feelings on his sleeve and gives straightforward answers to media questions . . . Born May 12, 1951, in Penn Hills, Pa.

GREATEST PLAYER

Let's figure someone is just keeping this seat warm until Shawn Kemp gets a few more seasons under his belt. The question then is who. The SuperSonics have had only two players make All-NBA first team, Spencer Haywood (twice) and Gus Williams, and only one, Slick Watts, to lead the league in a statistical category more than once.

We choose none of the above. The vote here is for Fred Brown, who joined Jack Sikma and Lenny Wilkens as having their uniforms retired but left other impressive numbers behind upon his retirement in 1984. Such as: No. 1 in team history in points (some 2,000 more than anyone), steals, games, shots made and attempted and minutes.

Wilkens is a Hall of Famer, though he played only four years in Seattle, and Sikma was durable. But Downtown Freddie Brown was uptown all the way.

ALL-TIME SUPERSONIC LEADERS

SEASON

Points: Spencer Haywood, 2,251, 1972-73
Assists: Lenny Wilkens, 766, 1971-72
Rebounds: Jack Sikma, 1,038, 1981-82

GAME

Points: Fred Brown, 58 vs. Golden State, 3/23/74
Assists: Nate McMillan, 25 vs. LA Clippers, 2/23/87
Rebounds: Jim Fox, 30 vs. Los Angeles, 12/26/73

CAREER

Points: Fred Brown, 14,018, 1971-84
Assists: Nate McMillan, 4,080, 1986-94
Rebounds: Jack Sikma, 7,729, 1977-86

UTAH JAZZ

TEAM DIRECTORY: Owner: Larry Miller; Pres.: Frank Layden; GM: R. Tim Howells; Dir. Baskerball Oper.: Scott Layden; VP-Pub. Rel.: David Allred; Dir. Media Services: Kim Turner; Coach: Jerry Sloan; Asst. Coaches: Phil Johnson, David Fredman, Gordon Chiesa. Arena: Delta Center (19,911). Colors: Purple, gold and green.

SCOUTING REPORT

SHOOTING: Utah still runs the best two-man game, the point guard with great passing skills and the post player who gets such deep position he is almost guaranteed to get a shot off unless the double-team comes very quickly. The John Stockton-Karl Malone staple propelled the Jazz to the sixth-best percentage in the league last season, with a twist. It was Stockton who led the way at .528, tops among all guards and No. 11 overall, while Malone dropped from the top 10 all the way down to No. 33.

Even at .497, though, Malone is still one of the most feared weapons, someone who can average 25.2 points despite the lowest shooting percentage since his rookie season because he can be a player going to the basket or someone with a soft touch on the fallaway. The trade that sent Jeff Malone to Philadelphia in exchange for Jeff Hornacek was significant if only because it gave the Jazz a second three-point option to go with Stockton. There were, after all, only three teams with fewer attempts from behind the arc.

PLAYMAKING: Even the greediest person would be content. The only debate on Stockton is whether he is the greatest point guard ever. Consider those seven straight assists titles and that he is bearing down on Magic Johnson for the record of career assists. Jay Humphries, though he finished 1993-94 as the starting shooting guard, has plenty of experience at the point. Hornacek began his pro career as the primary ball-handler in Phoenix. And that doesn't even begin to discuss John Crotty, a prospect the Jazz like.

It all meshes so well that the Jazz committed the second-fewest turnovers last season, bettered only by the Cleveland Cavaliers, and has the best assist-to-turnover ratio in the league. It's a safe bet Stockton, et al, will be great again.

John Stockton snaps Magic Johnson's assists mark this year!

REBOUNDING: The Jazz tried. Tried to get bigger and it still didn't help much—15th in rebounding percentage in 1992-93, a tie for 14th last season. Luther Wright came in the 1993 draft, but hardly played. Felton Spencer came in a trade from Minnesota and did contribute 8.3 rebounds a game. But that still wasn't enough to push a team that had Malone (11.5) into the top 10.

JAZZ ROSTER

No.	Veterans	Pos.	Ht.	Wt.	Age	Yrs. Pro	College
21	David Benoit	F	6-8	220	26	3	Alabama
20	Walter Bond	G	6-5	200	25	2	Minnesota
23	Tyrone Corbin	F	6-6	225	31	9	DePaul
25	John Crotty	G	6-1	185	25	2	Virginia
14	Jeff Hornacek	G	6-4	190	31	8	Ohio State
43	Stephen Howard	F	6-9	230	24	2	DePaul
6	Jay Humphries	G	6-3	200	32	10	Colorado
32	Karl Malone	F	6-9	256	31	9	Louisiana Tech
–	Bryon Russell	F	6-7	225	23	1	Cal-Long Beach
50	Felton Spencer	C	7-0	280	26	4	Louisville
12	John Stockton	G	6-1	175	32	10	Gonzaga
44	Luther Wright	C	7-2	270	23	1	Seton Hall

Rd.	Rookies	Sel. No.	Pos.	Ht.	Wt.	College
2	Jamie Watson	47	G-F	6-6	190	South Carolina

DEFENSE: This may have been one of the most comforting areas last season, when the Jazz did not collapse when playing without Mark Eaton, one of the biggest defensive factors of his era who missed the entire campaign with a back problem. If anything, it may have inspired his teammates not to rely on having a 7-4 backstop to compensate for any missed assignments when going for a steal because Utah climbed from eighth to third in steal-to-turnover ratio while Stockton finished fourth in steals.

It's not hard to imagine another improvement this season. Now, the Jazz will have familiarity on its side, an important factor in team defense, after having to work in critical elements like Spencer and Hornacek in 1993-94 while also making switches at small forward. As it was, Jerry Sloan's team was fifth best in shooting percentage-against and ninth best in scoring defense.

OUTLOOK: There is so much to like about this club, but why should we believe this season will be any different? Good, but not good enough to win it all. That frustration could re-ignite Malone, who got frustrated last year and won't be shy about hiding his feelings if things go south again.

JAZZ PROFILES

JOHN STOCKTON 32 6-1 175   Guard

Should reach the top of the mountain this season ... Needs 539 assists to pass Magic Johnson and become No. 1 all-time in that category ... That's about a half-season worth of work for someone to whom greatness has become routine ... Has led league in assists the last seven years and broken 1,000 six of those times ... No one else has ever done it more than twice ... Also finished fourth in league in steals in 1993-94, and no guard shot better than his .528, good for 11th overall ... Great hands, great vision, great tenacity ... Has missed only four games in the 10 years since the Jazz stole him with the 16th pick in 1984 ... Gold medalist in 1992 Olympics ... Born March 26, 1962, in Spokane, Wash., and went down the road to attend Gonzaga ... Made $2.4 million.

Year	Team	G	FG	FG Pct.	FT	FT Pct.	Reb.	Ast.	TP	Avg.
1984-85	Utah	82	157	.471	142	.736	105	415	458	5.6
1985-86	Utah	82	228	.489	172	.839	179	610	630	7.7
1986-87	Utah	82	231	.499	179	.782	151	670	648	7.9
1987-88	Utah	82	454	.574	272	.840	237	1128	1204	14.7
1988-89	Utah	82	497	.538	390	.863	248	1118	1400	17.1
1989-90	Utah	78	472	.514	354	.819	206	1134	1345	17.2
1990-91	Utah	82	496	.507	363	.836	237	1164	1413	17.2
1991-92	Utah	82	453	.482	308	.842	270	1126	1297	15.8
1992-93	Utah	82	437	.486	293	.798	237	1118	1239	15.1
1993-94	Utah	82	458	.528	272	.805	258	1031	1236	15.1
	Totals	816	3883	.512	2745	.822	2128	9383	10870	13.3

FELTON SPENCER 26 7-0 280   Center

Jazz: "You mean he wasn't always like this?" Timberwolves: "Don't we wish." ... If he was always like this—the 8.6 points and 8.3 rebounds last season—the Wolves never would have let him go for Mark Brown in the summer of '93 ... Jazz wanted to get a little younger and a little taller. If he stays near averaging a double-double, Jazz will also have a steal of a deal ... Timberwolves had run out of patience for No. 6 pick in 1990, especially as he seemed to be going backwards with every season ... Stepped into Mark Eaton's spot as the starting center for all 79 appearances ... Ended season on a high note with a strong showing in playoffs . . . Born Jan. 15, 1968, in Louisville, and attended Louisville . . . Made $1.581 million.

Year	Team	G	FG	FG Pct.	FT	FT Pct.	Reb.	Ast.	TP	Avg.
1990-91	Minnesota.	81	195	.512	182	.722	641	25	572	7.1
1991-92	Minnesota.	61	141	.426	123	.691	435	53	405	6.6
1992-93	Minnesota.	71	105	.465	83	.654	324	17	293	4.1
1993-94	Utah	79	256	.505	165	.607	658	43	677	8.6
	Totals	292	697	.482	553	.667	2058	138	1947	6.7

JAY HUMPHRIES 32 6-3 200   Guard

Benefitted from Jeff Malone getting traded almost as much as Jeff Hornacek . . . Took over as the starting shooting guard after the deal . . . Was in the opening lineup 19 times in all . . . Shot a career-low for second season in a row, but was a three-point threat by going .396 from behind the arc . . . Only .436 overall . . . Was never a great marksman . . . Can also play some at point guard . . . Started pro career after Phoenix took him 13th in 1984, then went to Milwaukee . . . Bucks sent him to Jazz along with Larry Krystkowiak for Blue Edwards, Eric Murdock and a first-round pick . . . Born Oct. 17, 1962, in Los Angeles and grew up near the Forum . . . Made $1.8 million.

Year	Team	G	FG	FG Pct.	FT	FT Pct.	Reb.	Ast.	TP	Avg.
1984-85	Phoenix	80	279	.446	141	.829	164	350	703	8.8
1985-86	Phoenix	82	352	.479	197	.767	260	526	905	11.0
1986-87	Phoenix	82	359	.477	200	.769	260	632	923	11.3
1987-88	Phoe.-Mil	68	284	.528	112	.732	174	395	683	10.0
1988-89	Milwaukee	73	345	.483	129	.816	189	405	844	11.6
1989-90	Milwaukee	81	496	.494	224	.786	269	472	1237	15.3
1990-91	Milwaukee	80	482	.502	191	.799	220	538	1215	15.2
1991-92	Milwaukee	71	377	.469	195	.783	184	466	991	14.0
1992-93	Utah	78	287	.436	101	.777	143	317	690	8.8
1993-94	Utah	75	233	.436	57	.750	127	219	561	7.5
	Totals	770	3494	.477	1547	.782	1990	4320	8752	11.4

KARL MALONE 31 6-9 256   Forward

Go ahead. Knock the battery off his shoulder. We dare you . . . Future Hall of Famer has been an all-star the last seven years . . . No. 1 in franchise history in points and rebounds and No. 3 in assists since Jazz took him with 13th pick in 1985 . . . Of concern: He once made great strides to go from horrible to decent on free throws, but the last two seasons he has started to slip. For someone who goes to the line so much, that becomes significant . . . Of greater concern: He's starting to become frustrated with failure to reach the Finals. That started to boil over during the '94 playoffs, when owner Larry Miller walked to the bench and yelled at Jerry Sloan to get a struggling Malone out of the game . . . And put who in, Larry? . . . Finished fifth in the league in scoring and eighth in rebounds last season . . . Dream Teamer was born July 24, 1963, in Summerfield, La., and attended Louisiana Tech . . . Made $3.081 million.

Year	Team	G	FG	FG Pct.	FT	FT Pct.	Reb.	Ast.	TP	Avg.
1985-86	Utah	81	504	.496	195	.481	718	236	1203	14.9
1986-87	Utah	82	728	.512	323	.598	855	158	1779	21.7
1987-88	Utah	82	858	.520	552	.700	986	199	2268	27.7
1988-89	Utah	80	809	.519	703	.766	853	219	2326	29.1
1989-90	Utah	82	914	.562	696	.762	911	226	2540	31.0
1990-91	Utah	82	847	.527	684	.770	967	270	2382	29.0
1991-92	Utah	81	798	.526	673	.778	909	241	2272	28.0
1992-93	Utah	82	797	.552	619	.740	919	308	2217	27.0
1993-94	Utah	82	772	.497	511	.694	940	328	2063	25.2
	Totals	734	7027	.525	4956	.719	8058	2185	19050	26.0

TYRONE CORBIN 31 6-6 225   Forward

Continues to bounce between starter and reserve at small forward, but he's always getting in one way or another . . . Has played 410 consecutive games, the fourth-longest active streak in the league . . . In the opening lineup 17 times, including the last 14 of the regular season after succeeding Bryon Russell . . . Came to Jazz from Minnesota in the opening month of 1991-92 in exchange for Thurl Bailey . . . Made jump from DePaul to NBA when Spurs drafted him in the second round in 1985 . . . That was the first of five pro stops . . . Born Dec. 31, 1962, in Columbia, S.C. . . . Made $1.4 million.

Year	Team	G	FG	FG Pct.	FT	FT Pct.	Reb.	Ast.	TP	Avg.
1985-86	San Antonio	16	27	.422	10	.714	25	11	64	4.0
1986-87	S.A.-Clev.	63	156	.409	91	.734	215	97	404	6.4
1987-88	Clev.-Phoe.	84	257	.490	110	.797	350	115	625	7.4
1988-89	Phoenix	77	245	.540	141	.788	398	118	631	8.2
1989-90	Minnesota	82	521	.481	161	.770	604	216	1203	14.7
1990-91	Minnesota	82	587	.448	296	.798	589	347	1472	18.0
1991-92	Minn.-Utah	80	303	.481	174	.866	472	140	780	9.8
1992-93	Utah	82	385	.503	180	.826	519	173	950	11.6
1993-94	Utah	82	268	.456	117	.813	389	122	659	8.0
	Totals	648	2749	.474	1280	.801	3561	1339	6788	10.5

JEFF HORNACEK 31 6-4 190 Guard

Someone up there must like him... Jazz rescued him from 76ers with Feb. 24 deal that sent Jeff Malone to Philadelphia... Immediately went from lottery to the playoffs... Had become used to the latter during years with Suns, who drafted him in the second round out of Iowa State in 1986... Started nine times in 27 games with Utah, but was mostly a third guard who played behind John Stockton and Jay Humphries... So many teams would kill to have him in their starting lineup... Said Rocket coach Rudy Tomjanovich after the deal: "If you look at the perfect player for their team, he's it. He's going to space the floor and open things up for that big guy (Karl Malone)."... Averaged 14.6 points with the Jazz... Second-leading scorer when he left Sixers... All-star in 1992... Born May 3, 1963, in Elmhurst, Ill.... Made $1.771 million.

			FG		FT				
Year	Team	G	FG	Pct.	FT	Pct.	Reb.	Ast.	TP	Avg.
1986-87	Phoenix	80	159	.454	94	.777	184	361	424	5.3
1987-88	Phoenix	82	306	.506	152	.822	262	540	781	9.5
1988-89	Phoenix	78	440	.495	147	.826	266	465	1054	13.5
1989-90	Phoenix	67	483	.536	173	.856	313	337	1179	17.6
1990-91	Phoenix	80	544	.518	201	.897	321	409	1350	16.9
1991-92	Phoenix	81	635	.512	279	.886	407	411	1632	20.1
1992-93	Philadelphia	79	582	.470	250	.865	342	548	1511	19.1
1993-94	Phil.-Utah	80	472	.470	260	.878	279	419	1274	15.9
	Totals	627	3621	.497	1556	.860	2374	3490	9205	14.7

BRYON RUSSELL 23 6-7 225 Forward

Nice fadeaway... Oops. That wasn't his jump shot... That was his rookie season... Made nice impact at the start, especially for someone drafted 45th... Named to the inaugural rookie All-Star Game... Then faded in the second half and lost job as starting small forward to Tyrone Corbin... In all, 48 of his 67 appearances were in the opening lineup... That says something about Jazz' scouting because he didn't even make All-Big West Conference at Cal-State-Long Beach... Lost count of how many people got his name wrong... He's Byron Russell in about half the NBA arenas... Even Rod Thorn botched it when announcing the Jazz' pick at the draft... Born Dec. 31, 1970, in San Bernardino, Cal.... Made $150,000.

			FG		FT				
Year	Team	G	FG	Pct.	FT	Pct.	Reb.	Ast.	TP	Avg.
1993-94	Utah	67	135	.484	62	.614	181	54	334	5.0

JOHN CROTTY 25 6-1 185 Guard

Jazz like him as a fourth or fifth guard . . . Now we'll see how much Jazz like him . . . Headed into offseason as a free agent after making $200,000 in 1993-94 . . . He impressed the team enough to sign him in September of '92 after an impressive showing at summer league . . . Had played in Global Basketball Assn. before that . . . Former Virginia standout was undrafted after joining Phil Ford and Kenny Smith as the only players in ACC history to compile at least 1,500 points and 600 assists . . . Born July 15, 1969, in Orange, N.J.

Year	Team	G	FG	FG Pct.	FT	FT Pct.	Reb.	Ast.	TP	Avg.
1992-93	Utah	40	37	.514	26	.684	17	55	102	2.6
1993-94	Utah	45	45	.455	31	.861	31	77	132	2.9
	Totals	85	82	.480	57	.770	48	132	234	2.8

LUTHER WRIGHT 23 7-2 270 Center

Rookie season, take II . . . First try at first campaign ended after only 15 appearances, including two starts, when he went on the injured list with personal problems headed by attention deficit disorder . . . Also showed as much immaturity as potential . . . Never rejoined the team, but by early summer appeared to have made great strides . . . Was working regularly with Jazz' strength coach after missing a ton of weight sessions before . . . If all continues to go well, Jazz figure him as backup to Felton Spencer at center this season . . . No. 18 pick in the '93 draft after playing just 64 games and two seasons at Seton Hall before departing after junior year . . . Passes well for a big man . . . Born Sept. 22, 1971, in Jersey City, N.J. . . . Made $650,000.

Year	Team	G	FG	FG Pct.	FT	FT Pct.	Reb.	Ast.	TP	Avg.
1993-94	Utah	15	8	.348	3	.750	10	0	19	1.3

DAVID BENOIT 26 6-8 220 Forward

He's not the answer at small forward, after all . . . Just part of the question. As in, "What happened?" . . . Started the final 23 games of 1992-93, but only 18 last season while shooting a career-low .385 and averaging 6.5 points . . . Missed 22 games early with a hamstring problem and never caught up . . . When Jerry Sloan replaced rookie Bryon Russell late, he went with Tyrone Corbin instead of Benoit... An athlete and a great leaper, but Jazz can only run the alley-oop play on the break so many times... Played college ball at Alabama, was not drafted and went to Spain for a year before Utah signed him as a free agent... Made $810,000... Born May 9, 1968, in Lafayette, La.

Year	Team	G	FG	FG Pct.	FT	FT Pct.	Reb.	Ast.	TP	Avg.
1991-92	Utah	77	175	.467	81	.810	296	34	434	5.6
1992-93	Utah	82	258	.436	114	.750	392	43	664	8.1
1993-94	Utah	55	139	.385	68	.773	260	23	358	6.5
	Totals	214	572	.431	263	.774	948	100	1456	6.8

WALTER BOND 25 6-5 200   Guard

A shooter, despite his percentage (.404) last season... Did go .352 on three-pointers... Jazz signed him as a free agent at the start of training camp at the $150,000 minimum after he spent the previous season with Mavericks ... He started in 38 of 54 appearances there and was getting big minutes. Then Jim Jackson signed, and Bond fell between the cracks... Spent 1991-92 with Wichita Falls in CBA... Played college ball at Minnesota, but was not drafted. Probably didn't help that his senior year was cut short by a stress fracture... Nephew of Walt Bond, first baseman with Indians, Colt .45s/Astros and Twins from 1960-67... Born Feb. 1, 1969, in Chicago.

Year	Team	G	FG	FG Pct.	FT	FT Pct.	Reb.	Ast.	TP	Avg.
1992-93	Dallas	74	227	.402	129	.772	196	122	590	8.0
1993-94	Utah	56	63	.404	31	.775	61	31	176	3.1
	Totals	130	290	.402	160	.773	257	153	766	5.9

STEPHEN HOWARD 24 6-9 230   Forward

What do you mean he went overseas and came back? Seriously? Most people didn't know he ever left... Jazz signed him as a free agent out of DePaul before 1992-93. He played. He was back for summer league. He left for Europe. He returned... When Jazz would not give him a guaranteed contract, he opted to go to Italy ... Landed back in Utah on March 8 and stuck around on playoff roster... But played only 53 minutes in his nine appearances during the regular season... Left college as Blue Demons' all-time leader in games (126) and free throws made

(528) and was fifth in scoring (1,691 points) and rebounds (883) ... Born July 15, 1970, in Dallas.

Year	Team	G	FG	FG Pct.	FT	FT Pct.	Reb.	Ast.	TP	Avg.
1992-93	Utah	49	35	.376	34	.642	60	10	104	2.1
1993-94	Utah	9	10	.588	11	.688	16	1	31	3.4
	Totals	58	45	.409	45	.652	76	11	135	2.3

THE ROOKIE

JAMIE WATSON 22 6-6 190   **Guard-Forward**
Utah's only draft pick, at No. 47 ... Averaged just 6.0 and 7.5 points first two seasons at South Carolina, then made a big jump to 14.7 and, finally, 18.1 ... No. 3 in school history in career steals and fourth in games played ... Born Feb. 23, 1972, in Elm City, N.C.

COACH JERRY SLOAN: He's supposedly spent years on the  bubble, but guess who has the second-longest tenure with his current club? ... Only Don Nelson has been with the Warriors longer than Sloan has been with the Jazz ... Is 304-171 in six years in Utah, an average of 52 wins per season ... That makes him the winningest coach in franchise history and includes two Midwest Division championships and twice setting the franchise record for victories in a season ... Has twice coached the Jazz to the Western Conference finals ... Spent three seasons as Bulls' coach ... Career: 397-293 ... Two-time all-star and six-time member of the all-defensive team during playing career with Baltimore and Chicago ... Came to the NBA after leading Evansville to a pair of Division II titles ... The definition of a hard-nosed player ... Bulls retired his uniform No. 4 and made him a scout when he retired in 1976. Took over as head coach in '79 ... Joined Jazz as a scout, then moved to the bench as an assistant to Frank Layden before 1984-85. When Layden retired Dec. 8, 1988, Sloan got the promotion ... A small-town guy at heart who still maintains a home in his native McLeansboro, Ill., which makes Salt Lake City seem like the concrete jungle ... Born March 14, 1946, in Louisville.

Faithful Karl Malone will deliver the mail for 10th season.

GREATEST PLAYER

We plead spineless. Short of flipping a coin, it is virtually impossible to break the tie—Karl Malone over John Stockton or John Stockton over Karl Malone?

They are both future Hall of Famers, in the elite at their respective positions for years, and so dominating in this franchise that a talent like Pete Maravich gets but a passing mention. Stockton holds the record for assists and steals, Malone for points and rebounds. Not only that, their success is co-dependant, making it all the more difficult to choose. It's become easier to split an atom than to split these two.

So, they were, are and always will be 1 and 1a, and it will be no different here.

ALL-TIME JAZZ LEADERS

SEASON

Points: Karl Malone, 2,540, 1989-90
Assists: John Stockton, 1,164, 1990-91
Rebounds: Len Robinson, 1,288, 1977-78

GAME

Points: Pete Maravich, 68 vs. New York, 2/25/77
Assists: John Stockton, 28 vs. San Antonio, 1/15/91
Rebounds: Len Robinson, 27 vs. Los Angeles, 11/11/77

CAREER

Points: Karl Malone, 19,050, 1985-94
Assists: John Stockton, 9,383, 1984-94
Rebounds: Karl Malone, 8,058, 1985-94

ATLANTA HAWKS

TEAM DIRECTORY: Pres.: Stan Kasten; GM: Pete Babcock; Dir. Pub. Rel.: Arthur Triche; Coach: Lenny Wilkens; Asst. Coaches: Dick Helm, Brian Winters. Arena: The Omni (16,510). Colors: Red, white and gold.

SCOUTING REPORT

SHOOTING: Well, they didn't have Dominique Wilkins to kick the ball into any more. They missed that. And they missed it in the playoffs. And now they don't have Danny Manning.

The Hawks are a below-average shooting team, ranking 17th last season. Only two players made it to 50 percent: Stacey Augmon, who gets much of his on layups, and Ennis Whatley, the backup point.

Manning was the obvious go-to guy in 'Nique's absence. Kevin Willis, with a fine array of post-up moves and a deft mid-range jumper, needs to keep carrying the burden. And Craig Ehlo must regain the accuracy on his perimeter bombs.

PLAYMAKING: Nothing wrong here with Mookie Blaylock leading the show. And with Lenny Wilkens preaching unselfishness, the Hawks moved the ball better than they had in eons.

But Manning's exceptional passing will take place in Phoenix and Willis still needs improvement if, and when, he draws a double-team on the blocks. The biggest concern may be the backup point guard. The Hawks have fingers crossed on rookie Gaylon Nickerson as a guy to perhaps replace Whatley, who served commendably, if not exceptionally, last season.

REBOUNDING: With Willis, the Hawks possessed one of the premier boarders in the game. And while everyone after him is capable, the Hawks were a bit lax—especially on the defensive glass. They outrebounded opponents by less than two a game.

Still, they hit the boards with a ferocity that made them the second-best offensive rebounding club (they ranked a so-so 15th on the defensive glass). The addition of Ken Norman, if he plays to potential and ability, will help big-time. But they simply must get more rebounding from the center position of Andrew Lang and Jon Koncak. Together, they got 678, a great one-player total. But by two?

Another board year for Kevin Willis, but also 19.1 ppg.

DEFENSE: They're coming off the greatest defensive season in Atlanta history (96.2 points allowed, .455 opponent shooting, eighth-best in the league after ranking 26th the previous season). And they might be better.

That was Wilkens' prime mission in his first year: to get this athletically gifted, vastly underachieving team to defend through a team concept. Players bought into it. Players won. Players kept it up. So there's no reason to regress. The guards are the key.

HAWK ROSTER

No.	Veterans	Pos.	Ht.	Wt.	Age	Yrs. Pro	College
2	Stacey Augmon	G	6-8	205	26	3	UNLV
10	Mookie Blaylock	G	6-1	185	27	6	Oklahoma
34	Doug Edwards	F	6-7	235	23	1	Florida State
U-3	Craig Ehlo	G	6-7	206	33	11	Washington State
U-33	Duane Ferrell	F	6-7	209	29	6	Georgia Tech
U-25	Paul Graham	F	6-6	200	26	3	Ohio
31	Adam Keefe	F	6-9	241	23	2	Stanford
32	Jon Koncak	C	7-0	250	31	9	SMU
28	Andrew Lang	C	6-11	250	28	6	Arkansas
–	Ken Norman	F	6-8	223	30	7	Illinois
41	Blair Rasmussen	C	7-0	250	31	8	Oregon
U-1	Ennis Whatley	G	6-3	170	32	8	Alabama
42	Kevin Willis	F-C	7-0	240	32	10	Michigan State

U-unrestricted free agent

Rd.	Rookies	Sel. No.	Pos.	Ht.	Wt.	College
2	Gaylon Nickerson	34	G	6-3	190	NW Oklahoma State

Atlanta comes right at you and pressures the ball with Blaylock, he of the pickpocket hands, and Augmon, he of the arms as long as the Atlantic coastline. While there is no single outstanding shot-blocker, Lang, Koncak and Willis all capably get their share.

OUTLOOK: Curiously, an improved team that led the Eastern Conference in victories might not even win its division.

That doesn't mean the Hawks won't be a force. Not as long as they have that backcourt combo committing daylight—or Omni nightlight—robbery. It's just that the Central Division, powerful last year, figures to be even stronger. Indiana improved with the addition of Mark Jackson. Cleveland is always tough. Chicago is Chicago.

The Hawks improved with the addition of Norman and added rookie Nickerson, another in the Blaylock-Augmon defensive pressure mold. But Dominique and Manning are gone and the Hawks lack only one element: that explosive, score-any-time-anywhere performer. Still, we're not talking chopped liver. But we may not be talking conference championship, either.

HAWK PROFILES

KEVIN WILLIS 32 7-0 235   Forward-Center

Next up for Lenny Wilkens: the common cold . . . He got this rebounder deluxe to rotate and defend. Sounds simple, but others tried and died . . . Another super statline season: 19.1 points, which was 19th best in NBA and 12.0 rebounds, which was third . . . Missed third straight 1,000-board season by 37 . . . So he had a career-high scoring and shot-blocking season . . . Left off All-Star team. Coaches, voters asked to submit to random testing . . . Want to talk consistency? He had 335 offensive boards for second straight season . . . Only Dennis Rodman, Shaquille O'Neal and Charles Oakley had more . . . After six years of adequate, hardly great play, burst into national consciousness with staggering rebounding season in 1991-92. Averaged 15.5 per, with games of 33 and 31 rebounds . . . Born Sept. 6, 1962, in Los Angeles . . . Michigan State, Class of 1984 . . . Hawks picked him 11th in '84 . . . Fashion design major, designs own clothing . . . Made $2.625 million.

Year	Team	G	FG	FG Pct.	FT	FT Pct.	Reb.	Ast.	TP	Avg.
1984-85	Atlanta	82	322	.467	119	.657	522	36	765	9.3
1985-86	Atlanta	82	419	.517	172	.654	704	45	1010	12.3
1986-87	Atlanta	81	538	.536	227	.709	849	62	1304	16.1
1987-88	Atlanta	75	356	.518	159	.649	547	28	871	11.6
1988-89	Atlanta					Injured				
1989-90	Atlanta	81	418	.519	168	.683	645	57	1006	12.4
1990-91	Atlanta	80	444	.504	159	.668	704	99	1051	13.1
1991-92	Atlanta	81	591	.483	292	.804	1258	173	1480	18.3
1992-93	Atlanta	80	616	.506	196	.653	1028	165	1435	17.9
1993-94	Atlanta	80	627	.499	268	.713	963	150	1531	19.1
	Totals	722	4331	.505	1760	.695	7220	815	10453	14.5

STACEY AUGMON 26 6-8 205   Guard

Mission accomplished . . . After his first two seasons, one rap on this former UNLV star's game was the need to finish stronger . . . Any stronger and he'd be Hercules . . . Shot .510 and easily was team's best at finishing what he, or others, started . . . That .510 was 18th best in the NBA, and a personal best . . . Career highs across the board . . . But forget offense a minute. Along with Mookie Blaylock, formed a fearsome defensive

Mookie Blaylock was NBA's third-leading stealer.

backcourt that helped the Hawks to 915 steals, one off the team record and second only to Seattle . . . He had 1.82 per, 16th best in the NBA . . . With Blaylock, he formed the East's most successful theft backcourt . . . Scoring down, but everything else was pretty much status quo in playoffs . . . Good offensive rebounding two guard . . . Range on shot another matter . . . No. 9 pick in 1991 . . . Born Aug. 1, 1968, in Pasadena, Cal. . . . Made $1.4 million.

Year	Team	G	FG	FG Pct.	FT	FT Pct.	Reb.	Ast.	TP	Avg.
1991-92	Atlanta	82	440	.489	213	.666	420	201	1094	13.3
1992-93	Atlanta	73	397	.501	227	.739	287	170	1021	14.0
1993-94	Atlanta	82	439	.510	333	.764	394	187	1212	14.8
	Totals	237	1276	.500	773	.727	1101	558	3327	14.8

JON KONCAK 31 7-0 250   Center

Okay, he's not Shaq or Hakeem or Patrick or David or Chief. But he's not Benoit Benjamin, either . . . Had strong, intense season . . . Anchored backline defense and actually took some outside shots . . . Hawks winning, fans not booing . . . Confidence grew . . . Still about 1,500 points a season away from being considered offensive . . . Had career-high 125 blocks . . . Rebounding slipped to 4.5. Musta been concentrating on that jumper . . . Throws some nice outlet passes, but we're not talking Wes Unseld . . . Is alleged to have participated in the playoffs . . . Actually, broke loose for 5.3 points per in postseason. But shooting and rebounding were nowhere . . . No. 5 pick in 1985 draft by Hawks out of SMU . . . Born May 17, 1963, in Cedar Rapids, Iowa . . . Earned $2.8 million, thanks to a $12.5-million offer sheet from Pistons five years ago. Contract still has two years.

Year	Team	G	FG	FG Pct.	FT	FT Pct.	Reb.	Ast.	TP	Avg.
1985-86	Atlanta	82	263	.507	156	.607	467	55	682	8.3
1986-87	Atlanta	82	169	.480	125	.654	493	31	463	5.6
1987-88	Atlanta	49	98	.483	83	.610	333	19	279	5.7
1988-89	Atlanta	74	141	.524	63	.553	453	56	345	4.7
1989-90	Atlanta	54	78	.614	42	.532	226	23	198	3.7
1990-91	Atlanta	77	140	.436	32	.593	375	124	313	4.1
1991-92	Atlanta	77	111	.391	19	.655	261	132	241	3.1
1992-93	Atlanta	78	124	.464	24	.480	427	140	275	3.5
1993-94	Atlanta	82	159	.431	24	.667	365	102	342	4.2
	Totals	655	1283	.473	568	.600	3400	682	3138	4.8

MOOKIE BLAYLOCK 27 6-1 185   Guard

And while we're talking about steals . . . One of greatest trades in Atlanta history . . . Gave up disgruntled, underachieving Rumeal Robinson to New Jersey Nov. 3, 1992. What'd they get in return? . . . Just an All-Star who set a franchise record with 212 steals . . . Hawks also had to take Roy Hinson (who went for Ken Norman) . . . Get a comment from the Brinks people . . . Career highs in minutes, field goals, rebounds, assists, blocks, steals, points and reasons to make Nets feel silly . . . Second year with 200 steals, had team-record six in one quarter vs. Minnesota, March 1. Also had seven in a half, eight in a game in that one . . . 10 games of at least 20 points . . . Third in NBA in steals (2.62) and third in assists (9.7)... 41 double-doubles, two triple-doubles... Hawks had best steal-turnover ratio in East ... Now, get the shot to threat level (.411 regular season, .340 in playoffs) and we'll talk All-NBA... Three-point range, though: second straight year with over 110 treys... Set franchise record with 23 assists vs. Jazz March 6, 1993... Born Mar. 20, 1967, in Garland, Tex.... Made $1.63 million... No. 12 pick by Nets in '89 out of Oklahoma... Real name: Daron Oshay Blaylock.

Year	Team	G	FG	FG Pct.	FT	FT Pct.	Reb.	Ast.	TP	Avg.
1989-90	New Jersey	50	212	.371	63	.778	140	210	505	10.1
1990-91	New Jersey	72	432	.416	139	.790	249	441	1017	14.1
1991-92	New Jersey	72	429	.432	126	.712	269	492	996	13.8
1992-93	Atlanta	80	414	.429	123	.728	280	671	1069	13.4
1993-94	Atlanta	81	444	.411	116	.730	424	789	1118	13.8
	Totals	355	1931	.416	567	.744	1362	2603	4705	13.3

KEN NORMAN 30 6-8 223   Forward

Nicknamed Snake, which is pretty much what Milwaukee residents call him all the time... Signed megabucks free-agent deal with Bucks July 7, 1993. Bigger disappointment than blind date that turns out to be a goat... He was supposed to be a cog around rebuilding. Was awful, fans got on him, he got on fans and Bucks gave him away to Hawks for Roy Hinson's salary June 22, 1994... Was supposed to be high scorer, tenacious defender... Wasn't... But Hawks figured a winning situation would change that. They're probably right... Gave great depth at forward... Born Sept. 5, 1964, in Chicago... Was Clips' all-time scoring leader... Don't get excited. Nobody good stays there too long... And his 6,432 points were passed by Danny Manning ... No. 19 pick in '87 out of Illinois... Did one year at Wabash Valley (Ill.)... Signed six-year, $16-million deal with Bucks. Got $1.51 million last season.

Year	Team	G	FG	FG Pct.	FT	FT Pct.	Reb.	Ast.	TP	Avg.
1987-88	L.A. Clippers	66	241	.482	87	.512	263	78	569	8.6
1988-89	L.A. Clippers	80	638	.502	170	.630	667	277	1450	18.1
1989-90	L.A. Clippers	70	484	.510	153	.632	470	160	1128	16.1
1990-91	L.A. Clippers	70	520	.501	173	.629	497	159	1219	17.4
1991-92	L.A. Clippers	77	402	.490	121	.535	448	125	929	12.1
1992-93	L.A. Clippers	76	498	.511	131	.595	571	165	1137	15.0
1993-94	Milwaukee	82	412	.448	92	.503	500	222	979	11.9
	Totals	521	3195	.494	927	.584	3416	1186	7411	14.2

CRAIG EHLO 33 6-7 206   Guard-Forward

After Lenny Wilkens picked Atlanta, it took just over a month to secure this Washington State, '83, product . . . Classic underrated player . . . Super sixth man. Can go up front, can go in backcourt . . . Played seven years for Wilkens in Cleveland . . . In keeping with Hawk team policy, set career high in steals (136) . . . A solid, vastly underrated defender. Too many recall the way Michael Jordan generally toasted him. Yeah, like Jordan didn't do that to everybody . . . Shot was off. Second-lowest in seven years. But he's still a deadly spot-up perimeter type . . . Good rebounder . . . Fifth straight year of double-figure scoring . . . 82 games for second straight year, third in four . . . Made $1.2 million . . . Sought $2 million . . . Born Aug. 11, 1961, in Lubbock, Tex. . . . Third-rounder by Rockets in '83 . . . Waived, played in CBA . . . Cavs signed him as free agent Jan. 13, 1987 . . . Hawks did same July 2, 1993.

Year	Team	G	FG	FG Pct.	FT	FT Pct.	Reb.	Ast.	TP	Avg.
1983-84	Houston	7	11	.407	1	1.000	9	6	23	3.3
1984-85	Houston	45	34	.493	19	.633	25	26	87	1.9
1985-86	Houston	36	36	.429	23	.793	46	29	98	2.7
1986-87	Cleveland	44	99	.414	70	.707	161	92	273	6.2
1987-88	Cleveland	79	226	.466	89	.674	274	206	563	7.1
1988-89	Cleveland	82	249	.475	71	.607	295	266	608	7.4
1989-90	Cleveland	81	436	.464	126	.681	439	371	1102	13.6
1990-91	Cleveland	82	344	.445	95	.679	388	376	832	10.1
1991-92	Cleveland	63	310	.453	87	.707	307	238	776	12.3
1992-93	Cleveland	82	385	.490	86	.717	403	254	949	11.6
1993-94	Atlanta	82	316	.446	112	.727	279	273	821	10.0
	Totals	683	2446	.460	779	.689	2626	2137	6132	9.0

DUANE FERRELL 29 6-7 209   Forward

Took his inside game outside and became one of Hawks' better perimeter threats . . . Problem was where to use him once Ken Norman arrived in offseason. Bench Danny Manning? . . . Thanks, Duane. Here's your hat. What's your hurry? . . . A free-agent find. Undrafted out of Georgia Tech in '88 . . . A useful, serviceable player . . . But whacked by inconsistency last season . . . Shot plunged from .485 to .397 in playoffs . . . Had a bunch of 10-dayers, stops in CBA before hooking up with Hawks as a free agent Nov. 2, 1990 . . . Solid-citizen type. A valuable sub, especially when he concentrates on the whole court . . . Born Feb. 28, 1965, in Baltimore, Md. . . . Made $1.025 million.

Year	Team	G	FG	FG Pct.	FT	FT Pct.	Reb.	Ast.	TP	Avg.
1988-89	Atlanta	41	35	.422	30	.682	41	10	100	2.4
1989-90	Atlanta	14	5	.357	2	.333	7	2	12	0.9
1990-91	Atlanta	78	174	.489	125	.801	179	55	475	6.1
1991-92	Atlanta	66	331	.524	166	.761	210	92	839	12.7
1992-93	Atlanta	82	327	.470	176	.779	191	132	839	10.2
1993-94	Atlanta	72	184	.485	144	.783	129	65	513	7.1
	Totals	353	1056	.489	643	.771	757	356	2778	7.9

PAUL GRAHAM 26 6-6 200   Forward

By season's end, probably figured he was an Asian-American. Saw DNP after his name more than any other Hawk, 60 times . . . Hey, somebody has to lead the team . . . A little too much playground for Mr. Wilkens . . . Shot selection from the Chris Morris Handbook . . . Minutes only dropped by 1,380 . . . Had been a regular for two years. Of course, Hawks did basically nothing in those two years . . . Free agent signed in '91 preseason . . . Undrafted out of Ohio University, 1989 . . . Played in Australia and did the CBA thing, too . . . Born Nov. 28, 1967, in Philadelphia . . . Made $600,000 . . . Could be steady contributor with more work . . . Nicknamed Snoop by grandparents because he was always snooping in their things . . . Now is that tale worth some playing time?

Year	Team	G	FG	FG Pct.	FT	FT Pct.	Reb.	Ast.	TP	Avg.
1991-92	Atlanta	78	305	.447	126	.741	231	175	791	10.1
1992-93	Atlanta	80	256	.457	96	.733	190	164	650	8.1
1993-94	Atlanta	21	21	.368	13	.765	12	13	58	2.8
	Totals	179	582	.448	235	.739	433	352	1499	8.4

ANDREW LANG 28 6-11 250   Center

Beginning to see the light: Defend, Andrew, defend. Block, Andrew, block . . . Clog, Andrew, clog . . . Doesn't get: Score, Andrew, score too much . . . Defensive force found spot on defensive team and took aspirations away from offensive end . . . Second on team in blocks. But still trying to control rejects. Looks nice, but ball ending up in stands isn't too helpful . . . Led team in scoring once. See? . . . 3.8 rebounds, which really is rotten considering size and minutes . . . Probably no one said: Board, Andrew, board . . . Methodical, position defender who's beginning to get that "help out" thing down . . . Signed as a free agent Sept. 7, 1993, and made $1.228 million after one year in Philly . . . Part of the Barkley deal. Came from Suns to Sixers with Jeff Hornacek and Tim Perry for Sir Charles June 17, 1992 . . . Was second-round pick of Suns out of Arkansas in 1988 . . . Born June 28, 1966, in Pine Bluff, Ark.

Year	Team	G	FG	FG Pct.	FT	FT Pct.	Reb.	Ast.	TP	Avg.
1988-89	Phoenix	62	60	.513	39	.650	147	9	159	2.6
1989-90	Phoenix	74	97	.557	64	.653	271	21	258	3.5
1990-91	Phoenix	63	109	.577	93	.715	303	27	311	4.9
1991-92	Phoenix	81	248	.522	126	.768	546	43	622	7.7
1992-93	Philadelphia	73	149	.425	87	.763	436	79	386	5.3
1993-94	Atlanta	82	215	.469	73	.689	313	51	504	6.1
	Totals	435	878	.498	482	.717	2016	230	2240	5.1

DOUG EDWARDS 23 6-7 235   Forward

Was supposed to be a coming-out party. Didn't even get to cut the cake . . . Rookie year contained 107 valuable minutes . . . Hurt lots, used lots less . . . Calf injury knocked him out of first 19 games . . . Was supposed to be a real force inside after being the 15th pick out of Florida State . . . Became best known as the target for Miami's Keith Askins' sucker punch in playoffs . . . Two-game playoff ban, $10,000 fine . . . Florida State's first ever with 1,500 points, 700 rebounds, 200 assists . . . Finalist for Wooden Award . . . Born Jan. 21, 1971, in Miami, Fla. . . . Made $650,000.

Year	Team	G	FG	FG Pct.	FT	FT Pct.	Reb.	Ast.	TP	Avg.
1993-94	Atlanta	16	17	.347	9	.563	18	8	43	2.7

ADAM KEEFE 23 6-9 241   Forward

Can you say "Bust," boys and girls? . . . Real nice guy going nowhere in Atlanta . . . Second year saw minutes more than halved (1,549 down to 763) . . . 1992 lottery pick from Stanford, No. 10 . . . Makes a nice tenth man, bad tenth pick . . . Showed some promise as a rookie. In second year, showed he knows how to move toward end of bench so the real players don't have to run so far to report in . . . Will bang inside . . . Did a creditable job rebounding: 201 in those scant minutes . . . Improved each year at Stanford, so there's hope . . . Born Feb. 22, 1970, in Irvine, Cal. . . . Made $1.2 million.

Year	Team	G	FG	FG Pct.	FT	FT Pct.	Reb.	Ast.	TP	Avg.
1992-93	Atlanta.........	82	188	.500	166	.700	432	80	542	6.6
1993-94	Atlanta.........	63	96	.451	81	.730	201	34	273	4.3
	Totals	145	284	.482	247	.710	633	114	815	5.6

ENNIS WHATLEY 32 6-3 180   Guard

Figured to be mere insurance, but Hawks had to cash in on the policy . . . Played in all 82 games, one start . . . Disappeared in playoffs . . . Nice guy, bad game . . . Just doesn't do any one thing well enough . . . Quickness gone, ball-handling suspect . . . These are not good attributes for a point guard . . . Spent 1992-93 in Israel . . . Has seen all or parts of eight NBA seasons in seven cities . . . Second time in Atlanta. Stopped off for five games in 1987-88 . . . Signed in '93 preseason as a minimum wage ($150,000) free agent . . . Born Aug. 11, 1962, in Birmingham, Ala. . . . Left Alabama after two years and was the No. 13 pick in the '83 draft by the Kansas City Kings, who traded his draft rights to Chicago.

Year	Team	G	FG	FG Pct.	FT	FT Pct.	Reb.	Ast.	TP	Avg.
1983-84	Chicago	80	261	.469	146	.730	197	662	668	8.4
1984-85	Chicago	70	140	.447	68	.791	101	381	349	5.0
1985-86	Clev.-Wash.-S.A.	14	15	.429	5	.500	14	23	35	2.5
1986-87	Washington......	73	246	.478	126	.764	194	392	618	8.5
1987-88	Atlanta.........	5	4	.444	3	.750	4	2	11	2.2
1988-89	L.A. Clippers.....	8	12	.364	10	.909	16	22	34	4.3
1991-92	Portland........	23	21	.412	27	.871	21	34	69	3.0
1993-94	Atlanta.........	82	120	.508	52	.788	99	181	292	3.6
	Totals	355	819	.469	437	.763	646	1697	2076	5.8

THE ROOKIE

GAYLON NICKERSON 25 6-3 190   Guard

All-tournament at Portsmouth Invitational . . . Good pressure defender who went through four colleges . . . Point guard led Oklahoma Intercollegiate Conference in scoring, assists and steals and was conference Player of the Year . . . Second-round pick, No. 34 overall out of Northwestern Oklahoma State . . . Born Feb. 5, 1969, in Oscela, Ark.

COACH LENNY WILKENS: Wasn't the problem in Cleveland . . . All he did was take a perennially underachieving team and lead them to the best record in the East . . . Came in the first day of camp and said simply, "Gentlemen, we will defend." And the Hawks did. In most ungentlemanly fashion as their pressure game became one of the NBA's most feared weapons . . . Signed five-year deal June 1, 1993 . . . In addition to tying the franchise-record 57 victories, he brought the Hawks to the Central Division title, an Atlanta-record 96.2 ppg yield for the first time EVER an Atlanta team was under 100 points . . . Hall of Famer and second-winningest coach ever achieved 900th coaching victory Feb. 2 . . . President of NBA Coaches Association . . . 21-year head-coaching regular-season record of 926-774 (.545). He'll pass Red Auerbach (938) this season . . . But the conference semis loss to Pacers took a lot of the lustre off season . . . Among all-time assist leaders with 3,285 in 15-year career . . . Front-office resume has titles of: player/coach (Seattle and Portland); Coach, Director of Player Personnel, VP, GM (Seattle) . . . A Dream Team assistant (the original Dreamers) . . . Players' coach. Quiet, dignified . . . Born Oct. 28, 1937, in Brooklyn, N.Y. . . . Providence College, '60. Drafted by Hawks on first round.

GREATEST PLAYER

For years, the question of the greatest Hawk was a no-brainer: Bob Pettit, the 20,000-point-plus scoring forward and two-time MVP who led the Hawks, then in St. Louis, to their only NBA title in 1958.

Times change. And the biggest change in Hawk history came when they obtained Dominique Wilkins in 1982. By the time he left the Hawks in last season's blockbuster trade, 'Nique had rewritten the team's record book. First in scoring, first in games, first in minutes and first in the hearts of Hawk fans. In addition to his all-time team-best 23,292 points, Wilkins tops the Hawk career list in steals (1,245), is fourth in blocks (588) and sixth in assists (2,321).

A strong case can be made for Pettit, who ranks respectably— in some cases, even above—Dominique in many categories. But no one ever in a Hawk uniform, be it in St. Louis or Atlanta, ever played with more flair and excitement than the "Human Highlight Film."

ALL-TIME HAWK LEADERS

SEASON

Points: Bob Pettit, 2,429, 1961-62
Assists: Glenn Rivers, 823, 1986-87
Rebounds: Bob Pettit, 1,540, 1960-61

GAME

Points: Dominique Wilkins, 57 vs. Chicago, 11/10/86
       Dominique Wilkins, 57 vs. New Jersey, 4/10/86
       Lou Hudson, 57 vs. Chicago, 11/10/69
       Bob Petitt, 57 vs. Detroit, 2/18/61
Assists: Mookie Blaylock, 23 vs. Utah, 3/6/93
Rebounds: Bob Pettit, 35 vs. Cincinnati, 3/2/58
       Bob Pettit, 35 vs. New York, 1/6/56

CAREER

Points: Dominique Wilkins, 23,292, 1982-94
Assists: Glenn Rivers, 3,866, 1983-91
Rebounds: Bob Pettit, 12,851, 1954-65

BOSTON CELTICS

TEAM DIRECTORY: Chairman: Paul Gaston; Vice-Chairmen: Paul Dupee, Stephen Schram, David Gavitt; Pres.: Red Auerbach; Exec. VP/GM: Jan Volk; Exec. VP/Dir. Basketball Oper.: M.L. Carr; VP-Marketing/Communications: Tod Rosensweig; Dir. Pub. Rel.: Jeff Twiss; Dir. Publications and Inf.: David Zuccaro; Coach: Chris Ford; Asst. Coaches: Don Casey, Jon Jennings, Dennis Johnson. Arena: Boston Garden (14,890) and Hartford Civic Center (15,239). Colors: Green and white.

SCOUTING REPORT

SHOOTING: No team can lose, in consecutive years, Larry Bird, Kevin McHale and Reggie Lewis and not be utterly overwhelmed.

Dino Radja: From Croatia to Celtic leader in points, boards.

The Celtics have made a partial comeback with the signing of Dominique Wilkins.

They managed to shoot their way to respectability (10th best in the league) and they'll be even better with 'Nique's low-post game. But there is no one of the star quality of Bird, McHale or Lewis.

The Celtics, despite Chris Ford's fervent up-tempo, take-it-inside hope, are basically a gang of perimeter shooters. It came down to two rookies, Acie Earl, shooting a team-best .522, and Dino Radja, one microstep behind at .521, who gave the Celtics anything resembling an inside presence. But after those two, it's 12 feet and beyond. Blue Edwards, acquired from Milwaukee, could provide some needed explosiveness, but in keeping with what has almost become team policy, he has tweener size at 6-4.

PLAYMAKING: If there is a Celtic strength, here it is. But there's an asterisk.

Dee Brown and Sherman Douglas settled in as the starting backcourt. Okay, Douglas is a point. Brown is a two with some point skills. Now the asterisk part. Where's the true drive-and-dish guy? And where, oh where, is the depth?

Answer to both: nowhere!

Douglas had a terrific season and racked up nice assist numbers, but he still isn't a break-down-the-defenses and take-it-inside guy. The Celtics' offense remains a basic tribute to jump-shot city. They were middle-pack 15th in assist-to-turnover ratio and lower-echelon 19th in total assists.

REBOUNDING: Always nice to have on your side. The Celtics used to. And the Celtics used to win.

They were 20th last season and could be even worse this time, unless first-round draftee Eric Montross proves to be an immediate NBA board stud. Radja led the rebounding brigade as a rookie and Robert Parish was second. Now Parish is gone and the Celtics are counting on the newly signed Pervis Ellison from the Bullets.

One of the Celtics' biggest problems comes from the bench, where just about everybody is 6-7 or under-bulked or game-kneed. And if they're tall, they're not too good. The Celtics used to crucify teams off the offensive glass.

DEFENSE: Oh, is that what they're supposed to be playing at the other end?

They did it at times. But those times were rare. Opponents shot .477, which was the third-lousiest mark in the East. There was,

CELTIC ROSTER

No.	Veterans	Pos.	Ht.	Wt.	Age	Yrs. Pro	College
R-4	Alaa Abdelnaby	F	6-10	240	26	4	Duke
7	Dee Brown	G	6-1	161	26	4	Jacksonville
20	Sherman Douglas	G	6-0	180	28	5	Syracuse
55	Acie Earl	F-C	6-10	240	24	1	Iowa
–	Blue Edwards	F-G	6-4	228	29	5	East Carolina
–	Pervis Ellison	C	6-10	225	27	5	Louisville
R-44	Rick Fox	G-F	6-7	231	25	3	North Carolina
U-34	Kevin Gamble	G-F	6-5	210	28	7	Iowa
–	Todd Lichti	G	6-4	206	27	5	Stanford
31	Xavier McDaniel	F	6-7	205	31	9	Wichita State
R-27	Jimmy Oliver	G	6-6	208	25	2	Purdue
40	Dino Radja	F	6-11	225	27	1	Croatia
45	Derek Strong	F	6-8	220	26	3	Xavier
R-50	Matt Wenstrom	C	7-1	250	23	1	North Carolina
–	David Wesley	G	6-0	190	23	1	Baylor
–	Dominique Wilkins	F	6-8	218	34	12	Georgia

R-restricted free agent
U-unrestricted free agent

Rd.	Rookies	Sel. No.	Pos.	Ht.	Wt.	College
1	Eric Montross	9	C	7-0	255	North Carolina

however, one constant to the Celtic defense: rotation breakdowns.

They entered the offseason with just four signed players (they quickly added a few, though), and one of them was the since-departed Parish. They had Eddie Pinckney for some added interior defense. And they traded him. Earl didn't impress from a toughness standpoint as a rookie. A healthy Ellison will add something to the shot-blocking corps.

OUTLOOK: The addition of Wilkins will make a difference. The Celtics now have a legitimate go-to scorer, but he can't score enough to carry this team to the top.

There are tweeners at every turn. No real muscle. And just who is running the show? Is it demigod Red Auerbach? Or senior executive vice president Dave Gavitt? Or newly appointed GM M.L. Carr?

Ford wants to run and he has less than a handful of players capable of doing so. It's only a matter of time before the fans start leaving Boston Garden (and in its final year, too). But why not? The leprechauns have already up and left.

CELTIC PROFILES

DOMINIQUE WILKINS 34 6-8 218   Forward

"I am a Celtic . . . a perfect fit for me," announced 'Nique after signing three-year, $10.9-million contract in July . . . How different this was from the day last February when the Hawks dealt him for Danny Manning . . . Finished fourth in the league in scoring and climbed to ninth on the all-time point list, second among active players . . . Comparisons: 24.4 points with Hawks and 29.1 with Clippers, 6.2 rebounds with Hawks and 7.0 with Clippers, 2.3 assists with Hawks and 2.2 with Clippers, 34.4 minutes with Hawks and 37.9 with Clippers . . . The Human Highlight Film hasn't reached the end of his reel . . . Born Jan. 12, 1960, in Sorbonne, France . . . Made $3,500,000.

Year	Team	G	FG	FG Pct.	FT	FT Pct.	Reb.	Ast.	TP	Avg.
1982-83	Atlanta	82	601	.493	230	.682	478	129	1434	17.5
1983-84	Atlanta	81	684	.479	382	.770	582	126	1750	21.6
1984-85	Atlanta	81	853	.451	486	.806	557	200	2217	27.4
1985-86	Atlanta	78	888	.468	577	.818	618	206	2366	30.3
1986-87	Atlanta	79	828	.463	607	.818	494	261	2294	29.0
1987-88	Atlanta	78	909	.464	541	.826	502	224	2397	30.7
1988-89	Atlanta	80	814	.464	442	.844	553	211	2099	26.2
1989-90	Atlanta	80	810	.484	459	.807	521	200	2138	26.7
1990-91	Atlanta	81	770	.470	476	.829	732	265	2101	25.9
1991-92	Atlanta	42	424	.464	294	.835	295	158	1179	28.1
1992-93	Atlanta	71	741	.468	519	.828	482	227	2121	29.9
1993-94	Atl-LAC	74	698	.440	442	.847	481	169	1923	26.0
	Totals	907	9020	.467	5455	.813	6295	2376	24019	26.5

DINO RADJA 27 6-11 225   Forward

The Celtics' best player last year . . . Now you know why they were in the lottery . . . It's not that he can't play, but when was the last time a rookie, a European rookie, was the best player for anybody? . . . Range to 18 feet . . . Good face-up and back-to-the-basket play . . . Nice hands, good interior passer . . . Yep, nothing wrong with him being a team leader . . . Now, there is something wrong with the Celtics in his view . . . Had visions of dynastic, 50-victory team . . . Found a deteriorating 50-defeat organization . . . Has an out after this season and may exercise it . . . Shot .521, 14th-best mark in NBA . . . Led team in rebounds and points . . . Had 36-point, 15-rebound effort, both personal bests, vs. Lakers March 4 . . . Celts' second-round pick, No. 40 overall, in 1989 . . . 1988 Olympic silver medalist for Yugoslavians. '92 silver medalist for Croatia . . . Favorable comparisons in game, not demeanor, to former Piston Bill Laimbeer . . . Born April 24, 1967, in Split, Croatia . . . Signed with Celts July 9, 1993 . . . Made $1.65 million.

Year	Team	G	FG	FG Pct.	FT	FT Pct.	Reb.	Ast.	TP	Avg.
1993-94	Boston	80	491	.521	226	.751	577	114	1208	15.1

ACIE EARL 24 6-10 240   Center

The next Chief . . . They hope . . . Sort of lacks Robert Parish's drive . . . At least off his rookie season, which was otherwise successful . . . Real happy-go-lucky sort . . . Doesn't realize the NBA is bigger than life and death. And in Boston, it's bigger than that . . . Must improve upper body and footwork . . . Tends to get pushed around . . . And those quick centers can be so, so, er, quick . . . Legit post player with 15-foot range . . . Transition defense? Must be a guard thing . . . Good interior defense, but Celts were looking for upwards of his 53 blocked shots . . . Brought around slowly with Parish's presence. But Chief won't be there . . . Personal best 15 points several times . . . Iowa's all-time shot-blocker with 365 . . . Celts took him No. 19 in '93 . . . Paid him $650,000 . . . Born June 23, 1970, in Peoria, Ill.

Year	Team	G	FG	FG Pct.	FT	FT Pct.	Reb.	Ast.	TP	Avg.
1993-94	Boston	74	151	.406	108	.675	247	12	410	5.5

XAVIER McDANIEL 30 6-7 205   Forward

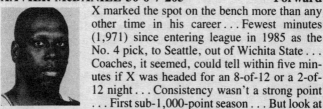

X marked the spot on the bench more than any other time in his career . . . Fewest minutes (1,971) since entering league in 1985 as the No. 4 pick, to Seattle, out of Wichita State . . . Coaches, it seemed, could tell within five minutes if X was headed for an 8-of-12 or a 2-of-12 night . . . Consistency wasn't a strong point . . . First sub-1,000-point season . . . But look at the minutes . . . Not so subtle signs his knees were achy again . . . All-Rookie team, sixth in offensive rebounding his first year . . . 68 minutes in five-OT game, one shy of record (set same night by Dale Ellis), Nov. 9, 1989, at Milwaukee... Went to Suns for Eddie Johnson and two first-rounders Dec. 7, 1990... Went from Suns to Knicks Oct. 1, 1991, for Trent Tucker, Jerrod Mustaf and two seconds... Signed with Celts as unrestricted free agent Sept. 10, 1992... Made $2.145 million... Born June 4, 1964, in Columbia, S.C.

Year	Team	G	FG	FG Pct.	FT	FT Pct.	Reb.	Ast.	TP	Avg.
1985-86	Seattle	82	576	.490	250	.687	655	193	1404	17.1
1986-87	Seattle	82	806	.509	275	.696	705	207	1890	23.0
1987-88	Seattle	78	687	.488	281	.715	518	263	1669	21.4
1988-89	Seattle	82	677	.489	312	.732	433	134	1677	20.5
1989-90	Seattle	69	611	.496	244	.733	447	171	1471	21.3
1990-91	Sea.-Phoe.	81	590	.497	193	.723	557	187	1373	17.0
1991-92	New York	82	488	.478	137	.714	460	149	1125	13.7
1992-93	Boston	82	457	.495	191	.793	489	163	1111	13.5
1993-94	Boston	82	387	.461	144	.676	400	126	928	11.3
	Totals	720	5279	.491	2027	.718	4664	1593	12648	17.6

SHERMAN DOUGLAS 28 6-0 180　　　　　Guard

One Boston writer summed up the Celtic-Douglas situation best: "He can give you 18 points, eight assists. But if you need that from him, you're not a good team."... And Celts needed it... Gave them a good year: third on team in scoring, first in assists. Shot .462, but regressed... Some in organization would love to get him a new zip code with his weighty contract that paid $2.3 million last year... Seventh in NBA in assists with 8.8 per... In proud, never-ending Syracuse tradition, was absolutely abysmal from the line (.641)... Career-high 21 assists vs. Kings Dec. 8. That tied for third-most ever by a Celt in regular-season game. Probably lost count with Bob Cousy a couple of times... Never has been a prototype point guard... But drove less for his shot than in past... Second-round pick to Miami in '89... To Celts for Brian Shaw Jan. 10, 1992... Left Syracuse as NCAA's all-time assist king... Born Sept. 15, 1966, in Washington, D.C.

Year	Team	G	FG	FG Pct.	FT	FT Pct.	Reb.	Ast.	TP	Avg.
1989-90	Miami	81	463	.494	224	.687	206	619	1155	14.3
1990-91	Miami	73	532	.504	284	.686	209	624	1352	18.5
1991-92	Mia.-Bos.	42	117	.462	73	.682	63	172	308	7.3
1992-93	Boston	79	264	.498	84	.560	162	508	618	7.8
1993-94	Boston	78	425	.462	177	.641	193	683	1040	13.3
	Totals	353	1801	.487	842	.661	833	2606	4473	12.7

DEE BROWN 26 6-1 161   Guard

Gee, sometimes you can't believe everything you hear. He said he wanted to get out of Boston. Then he goes and re-ups with long-term contract . . . Think it might have been posturing? By a pro athlete? . . . Career-best year, though some awful stretches of inconsistency . . . Set career scoring high twice: 35, then 40 points . . . Point guard-two guard question will follow him forever . . . Played off-guard most frequently . . . Shot .480 as his outside attempts fell a lot more than in past . . . Superbly gifted athlete . . . Former slam-dunk king ('91) . . . Two years removed from surgery to repair torn meniscus in left knee . . . Led team in steals, scoring . . . 10th in NBA at 2.03 steals per . . . Born Nov. 29, 1968, in Jacksonville, Fla. . . . No. 19 pick in 1990 out of Jacksonville . . . First name is DeCovan . . . Made $1.025 million.

Year	Team	G	FG	FG Pct.	FT	FT Pct.	Reb.	Ast.	TP	Avg.
1990-91	Boston	82	284	.464	137	.873	182	344	712	8.7
1991-92	Boston	31	149	.426	60	.769	79	164	363	11.7
1992-93	Boston	80	328	.468	192	.793	246	461	874	10.9
1993-94	Boston	77	490	.480	182	.831	300	347	1192	15.5
	Totals	270	1251	.466	571	.820	807	1316	3141	11.6

DAVID WESLEY 23 6-0 190   Guard

Didn't figure in 1994-95 Net blueprint and signed as free agent with Celtics in July . . . Had beaten out Nets' rookie Rex Walters for backup point . . . Has some quickness to harass and pressure . . . Usually infused a spark . . . Just fair, at best, in most offensive categories . . . Didn't handle pressure particularly well . . . CBA alum . . . Got $150,000 minimum for free-agent deal signed July 27, 1993 . . . Undrafted after one Juco year, three at Baylor . . . Born Nov. 14, 1970, in Longview, Tex.

Year	Team	G	FG	FG Pct.	FT	FT Pct.	Reb.	Ast.	TP	Avg.
1993-94	New Jersey	60	64	.368	44	.830	44	123	183	3.1

KEVIN GAMBLE 28 6-5 210   Guard-Forward

Kevin, this is the lane . . . Apparently, thinks driving is only done in an auto . . . Perimeter shooter dipped under .500 (way under, .458) for first time in four years . . . Had season highs of 26 points, eight assists in same game, at Philadelphia Jan. 10 . . . Three-point shooting way down. Went from 52 to 25 treys . . . Of course his minutes were off by nearly 700 . . . Made overtures about wanting to be elsewhere with unrestricted free agency beckoning . . . Another Celtic tweener . . . Defensive liability . . . As creative as cardboard . . . Born Nov. 13, 1965, in Springfield, Ill. . . . Went to Blazers on third round in '87 out of Iowa . . . Played in CBA and WBL . . . Also stopped off in the Phillipines. Presumably to do more than help Imelda Marcos shop for shoes . . . Leading CBA scorer when Celts signed him to free-agent deal Dec. 15, 1988 . . . Made $1.1 million.

Year	Team	G	FG	FG Pct.	FT	FT Pct.	Reb.	Ast.	TP	Avg.
1987-88	Portland	9	0	.000	0	.000	3	1	0	0.0
1988-89	Boston	44	75	.551	35	.636	42	34	187	4.3
1989-90	Boston	71	137	.455	85	.794	112	119	362	5.1
1990-91	Boston	82	548	.587	185	.815	267	256	1281	15.6
1991-92	Boston	82	480	.529	139	.885	286	219	1108	13.5
1992-93	Boston	82	459	.507	123	.826	246	226	1093	13.3
1993-94	Boston	75	368	458	103	.817	159	149	864	11.5
	Totals	445	2067	.518	670	.816	1115	1004	4895	11.0

ALAA ABDELNABY 26 6-10 240   Forward

It's always something. If it isn't mental, it's physical . . . Played 13 games . . . Out first 39 after back surgery Oct. 5. While recovering, underwent right knee arthroscope . . . Came back. Strained left calf. Sat. Came back. Sprained left ankle. Sat. Didn't bother coming back . . . Carefree attitude and reputed work ethic of a sloth have driven coaches crazy, back to Mike Krzyzewski at Duke . . . Once reported to scorer's table to sub. Without his shirt . . . Irksome part is he has talent. An NBA body. Good inside moves. Decent quickness . . . Three teams in four years says something . . . Celts really want this to work . . . Came from Bucks Dec. 4, 1992, for Jon Barry when Celts couldn't sign Barry . . . Born June 24, 1968, in Cairo, Egypt . . . Grew up in Bloomfield, N.J. . . . Drafted by Blazers No. 25 in 1990. They

sent him to Bucks for rights to Tracy Murray July 1, 1992...
Made $850,000.

Year	Team	G	FG	FG Pct.	FT	FT Pct.	Reb.	Ast.	TP	Avg.
1990-91	Portland	43	55	.474	25	.568	89	12	135	3.1
1991-92	Portland	71	178	.493	76	.752	260	30	432	6.1
1992-93	Mil.-Bos.	75	245	.518	88	.759	337	27	578	7.7
1993-94	Boston	13	24	.436	16	.640	46	3	64	4.9
	Totals	202	502	.500	205	.717	732	72	1209	6.0

RICK FOX 25 6-7 231   Guard-Forward

At least he comes to work... One of only two Celtics to play in all 82 games... Mae West Syndrome: When he's good, he's very good. When he's bad, he's like a bimbo... Had single-game career highs in points (33), assists (8) and rebounds (15)... Another complementary player... Lacks strength of a forward and ball-handling skills of a guard... Athletic, active. Can guard twos and smaller threes... Minutes virtually doubled from previous year. Sizeable stat gains followed... First name: Ulrick... Never missed a game in four years at North Carolina ... Majored in ''Radio, Television and Motion Pictures.''... Guess he's a future broadcaster. Or ''Jeopardy'' contestant... Mom, Diane, former Canadian Olympic high jumper... No. 24 on first round in '91... Born July 24, 1969, in Toronto... Made $755,000... Re-upped for four years and $5 million after season.

Year	Team	G	FG	FG Pct.	FT	FT Pct.	Reb.	Ast.	TP	Avg.
1991-92	Boston	81	241	.459	139	.755	220	126	644	8.0
1992-93	Boston	71	184	.484	81	.802	159	113	453	6.4
1993-94	Boston	82	340	.467	174	.757	355	217	887	10.8
	Totals	234	765	.468	394	.765	734	456	1984	8.5

THEODORE (BLUE) EDWARDS 29 6-4 228   F-G

One of the few bright spots in a dismal season for the Bucks... So they traded him. Had to, actually, to find a zillion dollars to sign Glenn Robinson... Came to Celts with Derek Strong for Ed Pinckney and second-round pick, Russian Andrei Fetisov, July 1... Solid performer, better in open court... Known for explosive dunks... But that size... Classic tweener with usual problems: too small for three, ball-handling insufficient for two . . . Gets exposed defensively by threes with any type of offensive game . . . Double-figure scorer, decent three-point shot . . . Jazz took him No. 21 out of East Carolina in '89 . . . Traded to Bucks with Eric Murdock and a first-rounder for Jay Humphries and Larry Krystkowiak June 24, 1992 . . . Immediate impact in Milwaukee. In first month, enjoyed week where he set career-high points three times, scoring 30, 31 and 32 (still his best, vs. Nuggets Nov. 15, 1992) . . . Made $1.5 million in first lap of five-year, $10-million extension . . . Born Oct. 31, 1965, in Washington, D.C.

Year	Team	G	FG	FG Pct.	FT	FT Pct.	Reb.	Ast.	TP	Avg.
1989-90	Utah	82	286	.507	146	.719	251	145	727	8.9
1990-91	Utah	62	244	.526	82	.701	201	108	576	9.3
1991-92	Utah	81	433	.522	113	.774	298	137	1018	12.6
1992-93	Milwaukee	82	554	.512	237	.790	382	214	1382	16.9
1993-94	Milwaukee	82	382	.478	151	.799	329	171	953	11.6
	Totals	389	1899	.508	729	.763	1461	775	4656	12.0

DEREK STRONG 26 6-8 220 Forward

Came to Celtics from Bucks with Blue Edwards in July 1 trade for Ed Pinckney . . . Led Milwaukee in rebounds per minute: one every 4.02, roughly 12 per 48 minutes . . . Lost playing time through emergence of Vin Baker . . . Did a nice job . . . Last name is his best asset . . . Good knack for the ball . . . Sixers made him a second-round pick in 1990 out of Xavier, where he was teammate of Tyrone Hill . . . Listed at 6-8. 6-6 more like it . . . Played in Spain and USBL in 1990-91 . . . Did time with Bullets and CBA, where he was MVP in 1993 . . . Bucks called in February 1992 . . . Made $420,000 . . . Born Feb. 9, 1968, in Los Angeles.

Year	Team	G	FG	FG Pct.	FT	FT Pct.	Reb.	Ast.	TP	Avg.
1991-92	Washington	1	0	.000	3	.750	5	1	3	3.0
1992-93	Milwaukee	23	42	.457	68	.800	115	14	156	6.8
1993-94	Milwaukee	67	141	.413	159	.772	281	48	444	6.6
	Totals	91	183	.419	230	.780	401	63	603	6.6

PERVIS ELLISON 27 6-10 225   Center

Is there anything left?... Celtics must think so ... They signed him as unrestricted Bullet free agent following season he began on injured list after summer surgery on both knees... Never got into a flow... Fewest games (47) since rookie year. And he missed lots in between... After return from IL, he played five games before knees began acting up again... Can show flashes of what made him the No. 1 pick overall for Sacramento out of Louisville in '89... Good rebounder and shot-blocker with solid low-post game and mid-range jumper at other end... Was averaging 9.9. points and 7.5 rebounds in March before going on IL in mid-month. Didn't return... MVP of NCAA Finals in '89, Louisville's title year... Three-way deal brought him from Kings to Bullets, who sent Jeff Malone to Jazz, June 25, 1990... Born April 3, 1967, in Savannah, Ga.... Made $2.3 million last year and reportedly signed six-year Celt contract for $12 million.

Year	Team	G	FG	FG Pct.	FT	FT Pct.	Reb.	Ast.	TP	Avg.
1989-90	Sacramento	34	111	.442	49	.628	196	65	271	8.0
1990-91	Washington	76	326	.513	139	.650	585	102	791	10.4
1991-92	Washington	66	547	.539	227	.728	740	190	1322	20.0
1992-93	Washington	49	341	.521	170	.702	433	117	852	17.4
1993-94	Washington	47	137	.469	70	.722	242	70	344	7.3
	Totals	272	1462	.513	655	.695	2196	544	3580	13.2

JIMMY OLIVER 25 6-6 208   Guard

He has a gun... Unfortunately, can't holster anybody else's gun. Not even a derringer... Real nice shooter with unlimited range... But too one-dimensional... Career-high 21 points vs. Sacramento Dec. 8... Minimum wage $150,000, free-agent since Oct. 4... Purdue, '91. All-Big Ten first-team as senior... Second-round pick of Cavs. Got into 27 games in 1991-92... Played with Pistons in '92 preseason, but ended up in CBA... Born July 12, 1969, in Menifee, Ark.

Year	Team	G	FG	FG Pct.	FT	FT Pct.	Reb.	Ast.	TP	Avg.
1991-92	Cleveland	27	39	.398	17	.773	27	20	96	3.6
1993-94	Boston	44	89	.416	25	.758	46	33	216	4.9
	Totals	71	128	.410	42	.764	73	53	312	4.4

All of Boston and the hoop world saluted Larry Bird.

MATT WENSTROM 24 7-1 250   Center

Gee, he can back up Eric Montross again... Was Montross' backup at North Carolina in '93 ... Spent most of season on injured list with (fill in the blank)... Expected to be injured lots this year with (fill in the blank)... 13th-Man Syndrome... Received 37 valuable minutes of experience... A big guy, takes up space. And not much money: got $150,000 minimum...
Born Nov. 4, 1970, in Minneapolis... Signed as free agent Sept. 30.

Year	Team	G	FG	FG Pct.	FT	FT Pct.	Reb.	Ast.	TP	Avg.
1993-94	Boston.........	11	6	.600	6	.600	12	0	18	1.6

THE ROOKIE

ERIC MONTROSS 23 7-0 255   Center

Wow. What a stunner. Boston taking a big white guy... Member of North Carolina's championship squad in 1993... Was the No. 9 overall pick... Two-time All-American second team... Led Tar Heels in field-goal percentage for three years... Fourth all-time Carolina shot-blocker... Born Sept. 23, 1971, in Indianapolis.

COACH CHRIS FORD: With four years in Boston, Ford ranks fourth in consecutive tenure behind only Don Nelson, Jerry Sloan and Phil Jackson . . . Four-year record of 187-141 (.570) . . . Last season was his first loser (32-50) . . . Still, has won two divisional titles with teams rapidly approaching, or reaching, the pits . . . Teams basically overachieved. Until last year . . . His most fundamental offensive concept: run. Down 30, up 20 or tied, run . . . Hasn't had a team of thoroughbreds, you know? . . . First and foremost, he preaches defense. Kind of hard to believe watching recent Celts get back . . . Not a taskmaster, but brutally honest. Sometimes, players get ticked at honesty . . . No-nonsense guy. Expects pros to behave like pros. What a novel concept . . . 10-year NBAer with Pistons and Celts . . . Detroit took him on second round, No. 17, in '72 out of Villanova . . . Went to Celts with second-rounder for Earl Tatum Oct. 19, 1978 . . . Member of Boston's '81 champs . . . Made first three-point shot in NBA history Oct. 12, 1979. Same game Larry Bird made his debut . . . Born Jan. 11, 1949, in Atlantic City, N.J.

GREATEST PLAYER

Pick the greatest Celtic ever? Why not just ask someone to pick the most perfect grain of sand on the beaches of Cape Cod? Russell, Cousy, Sharman, Havlicek, Cowens, Heinsohn, etc., etc. But two words make the job a little easier.

Larry Bird.

Yes, Bill Russell won more championships and was the backbone of the Celtic dynastic reign of terror in the '50s and '60s. But no Celtic ever played a more complete game than Larry Legend.

From the eye-popping touch passes to the jaw-dropping shooting, Bird was virtually in a class by himself. He and Magic Johnson revitalized not only their teams, but an entire league as well and nurtured it until the Jordans and Thomases and Barkleys came along.

His accomplishments would rival the entries in an encyclopedia. He played on three championship teams and ranks as the Celts' all-time leading playoff scorer. He was league MVP three years running, the Rookie of the Year in 1980, a 12-time All-Star, the only Celt ever to score 60 points in one game, the greatest

Celtic free-throw shooter ever and the team's No. 2 all-time scorer (behind John Havlicek). The candidates were many for the selection of Greatest Celtic Ever, but there was only one Larry Legend.

ALL-TIME CELTIC LEADERS

SEASON

Points: John Havlicek, 2,338, 1970-71
Assists: Bob Cousy, 715, 1959-60
Rebounds: Bill Russell, 1,930, 1963-64

GAME

Points: Larry Bird, 60 vs. Atlanta, 3/12/85
Assists: Bob Cousy, 28 vs. Minneapolis, 2/27/59
Rebounds: Bill Russell, 51 vs. Syracuse, 2/5/60

CAREER

Points: John Havlicek, 26,395, 1962-78
Assists: Bob Cousy, 6,945, 1950-63
Rebounds: Bill Russell, 21,620, 1956-69

CHARLOTTE HORNETS

TEAM DIRECTORY: Owner George Shinn; Pres.: Spencer Stolpen; Player Personnel Dir.: Dave Twardzik; Dir. Pub. Rel.: Harold Kaufman; Coach: Allan Bristow; Asst. Coaches: T.R. Dunn, Bill Hanzlik, John Bach. Arena: Charlotte Coliseum (23,698). Colors: Teal, purple and white.

Alonzo Mourning proved he is one fiery performer.

SCOUTING REPORT

SHOOTING: The Hornets' two best players, Alonzo Mourning and Larry Johnson, spent much of the season in the hospital ward. And still the Hornets ranked as the seventh-best shooting team in the league.

No one ever complained about the Hornets' ability to put points on the board. They possess one of the game's best shooters coming off the bench in Dell Curry. They have the post-ups of Mourning and Johnson. And another offensive incinerator in Hersey Hawkins. Michael Adams, acquired from the Bullets, isn't what he used to be, but there are still some treys left.

In Muggsy Bogues, the Hornets also possess a guy who can help make it all come together. Only two men averaged better than 10 assists in the NBA last season and Bogues was one of them, making him the leader in the East.

PLAYMAKING: Like we said, only two guys averaged over 10 assists. And one was Bogues. His penetrations drive defenses crazy and he has a superior ability to put the ball in the right guy's hands at the right time. He was the NBA's runaway leader in assist-turnover ratio at 4.56-1.

The injury situation in Charlotte last season was well documented. But ironically, the Hornets were a better passing team overall when Mourning and Johnson were out. Face it, they get paid in the millions. They get the ball, they're going to shoot. But without them, the Hornets were forced to find better shots, better options, and so the ball stayed in constant movement. If the Hornets can ever blend the two, they could be downright ornery. Add Adams to the mix here.

REBOUNDING: Nowhere was the absence of Johnson and, especially Mourning, more apparent than on the boards. Unless you want to count that silly won-lost thing.

Every year, the Hornets had improved their rebounding. But last year, they took a step back and placed just 15th overall. But it's to be expected, given the medical situation. They held their own on the defensive boards, but their second-chance baskets were next to non-existent. So give them time. But mainly, give them 'Zo, who will have a quality backup in free-agent Boston legend Robert Parish.

DEFENSE: For their virtual entire existence, the Hornets could sum up their defense in two words: a joke.

HORNET ROSTER

No.	Veterans	Pos.	Ht.	Wt.	Age	Yrs. Pro	College
–	Michael Adams	G	5-10	175	31	9	Boston College
25	Tony Bennett	G	6-0	175	25	2	UW-Green Bay
1	Tyrone Bogues	G	5-3	144	29	7	Wake Forest
U-40	Frank Brickowski	F-C	6-9	248	35	10	Penn State
24	Scott Burrell	F	6-7	218	23	1	Connecticut
30	Dell Curry	G-F	6-5	208	30	8	Virginia Tech
R-43	LeRon Ellis	C	6-10	240	25	2	Syracuse
44	Kenny Gattison	C-F	6-8	246	30	8	Old Dominion
3	Hersey Hawkins	G	6-3	190	28	6	Bradley
U-8	Eddie Johnson	F-G	6-7	215	35	13	Illinois
2	Larry Johnson	F	6-7	250	25	3	UNLV
33	Alonzo Mourning	C	6-10	240	24	2	Georgetown
00	Robert Parish	C	7-0	230	41	18	Centenary
U-20	Rumeal Robinson	G	6-2	195	27	4	Michigan
11	David Wingate	G-F	6-5	185	30	8	Georgetown

R-restricted free agent
U-unrestricted free agent

Rd.	Rookies	Sel. No.	Pos.	Ht.	Wt.	College
2	Darrin Hancock	38	G-F	6-5	205	Kansas

But this year, they can sum it up in two different words: John Bach.

Few, if any, additions could impact the Central Division with the importance of Charlotte landing Chicago's veteran assistant coach, a defensive mastermind. Only Washington was worse in the East defensively than the Hornets, who were wretched, giving up a ghastly 106.7 points. Reportedly, Bulls' GM Jerry Krause wanted Bach out. Well, Bach is. Krause will regret it.

Combine Allan Bristow's offensive penchant with Bach's defensive knack (assuming Bristow is wise enough to concede) and the Hornets, with a shot-blocking Mourning in the middle and a ball-stealing Bogues in the backcourt, could be a major headache this season.

OUTLOOK: It looked great last year. And look what happened. But it should work this time, especially with the presence of Parish, who will contribute in the intangibles as well as on the court. Mourning's injuries figure to be one-shot deals. Now, the big question is Johnson's health. If he makes it through in one anatomical piece, added to the addition of Bach, the Hornets could be a devastatingly potent and balanced team.

HORNET PROFILES

LARRY JOHNSON 25 6-7 250   Forward

Spent much of the year trying to do complicated things. Like stand upright . . . Lower back problem wasted his third pro season and makes both him and Hornets a major question . . . Missed 31 games after playing two full seasons . . . Hornets were 9-22 without him . . . Stat-line lows across the board, of course . . . Kept improving upon return. Then hit the wall . . . There's only so much conditioning you can do on your back . . . But he did score double figures in 16 of last 17 games . . . Still, aren't the Hornets happy they gave him an eight year, $68-million extension, bringing total package to 12 years and $84 million? . . . Dream Team II member . . . Hornets made him the No. 1 overall pick in the '91 draft . . . Has assumed superstar status. Won't talk to press before games . . . "Grandmama" in national shoe-ad campaign . . . When healthy, combines muscular inside game with ever-improving perimeter touch . . . Has the only three triple-doubles in Hornets' history . . . '91 College Player of Year at UNLV . . . NBA Rookie of the Year in 1992 . . . Born March 14, 1969, in Tyler, Tex. . . . Made $3.125 million.

Year	Team	G	FG	FG Pct.	FT	FT Pct.	Reb.	Ast.	TP	Avg.
1991-92	Charlotte	82	616	.490	339	.829	899	292	1576	19.2
1992-93	Charlotte	82	728	.526	336	.767	864	353	1810	22.1
1993-94	Charlotte	51	346	.515	137	.695	448	184	834	16.4
	Totals	215	1690	.510	812	.778	2211	829	4220	19.6

ALONZO MOURNING 24 6-10 240   Center

Temper, temper . . . Extraordinarily talented but volatile . . . Almost as many tantrums as points . . . With Hornets barely alive in playoff hunt, he was suspended one game for fighting . . . Hornets won, but it was stupid move . . . Led team in scoring, rebounding and blocks (3.13, fourth-best in NBA) despite sprained right ankle and torn left calf muscle . . . Missed 21 games with injury. Hornets were 5-16 . . . Named to All-Star team, but sat out with injury . . . Ended year with career-best 39 points, two off Johnny Newman's team mark . . . Back-to-back 36-point games in December . . . Dream Team II member . . . Became Hornets' all-time shot-blocker in his 49th game of rookie season. Has 459 in just 138 games . . . From Georgetown, like

Patrick Ewing and Dikembe Mutombo. Practices with them in summer . . . Big East Player of the Year, Defensive Player of the Year and tourney MVP in '92 . . . Born Feb. 8, 1970, in Chesapeake, Va. . . . Made $3.12 million.

Year	Team	G	FG	FG Pct.	FT	FT Pct.	Reb.	Ast.	TP	Avg.
1992-93	Charlotte	78	572	.511	495	.781	805	76	1639	21.0
1993-94	Charlotte	60	427	.505	433	.762	610	86	1287	21.5
	Totals	138	999	.509	928	.772	1415	162	2926	21.2

DELL CURRY 30 6-5 208   Guard-Forward

All the teams that had a chance to land his shot but didn't pull the trade trigger a few years back feel dumb . . . NBA Sixth Man Award winner . . . A shot that was forged on Olympus . . . Hit team-record six three-pointers in a game twice . . . His .402 trifecta shooting was 10th-best in NBA . . . Career-high 16.3 ppg, third-best on team . . . And it's all off the bench, of course . . . Has not started a game in three years . . . Not a great one-on-one defender, but he'll get some steals, block some shots . . . Incredible April. Shot .514, including .513 on treys. And averaged 17.4 ppg . . . No. 15 pick in '86 by Utah, from Virginia Tech . . . Went to Cavaliers in three-way deal before 1987-88 season, became a Hornet in '88 expansion draft . . . Born June 25, 1964, in Harrisonburg, Va. . . . Made $1.04 million.

Year	Team	G	FG	FG Pct.	FT	FT Pct.	Reb.	Ast.	TP	Avg.
1986-87	Utah	67	139	.426	30	.789	78	58	325	4.9
1987-88	Cleveland	79	340	.458	79	.782	166	149	787	10.0
1988-89	Charlotte	48	256	.491	40	.870	104	50	571	11.9
1989-90	Charlotte	67	461	.466	96	.923	168	159	1070	16.0
1990-91	Charlotte	76	337	.471	96	.842	199	166	802	10.6
1991-92	Charlotte	77	504	.486	127	.836	259	177	1209	15.7
1992-93	Charlotte	80	498	.452	136	.866	286	180	1227	15.3
1993-94	Charlotte	82	533	.455	117	..873	262	221	1335	16.3
	Totals	576	3068	.464	721	.852	1522	1160	7326	12.7

TYRONE (MUGGSY) BOGUES 29 5-3 144   Guard

Team MVP . . . See? You don't have to be 7-foot to be good. Or even 6-foot. 5-foot helps, though . . . Best pro season . . . Second in league with 10.1 assists per game . . . Career-best 10.8 ppg . . . Hornets' all-time assist leader, with six straight years with 600-plus . . . Twice tied his own franchise record with 19 assists in one game . . . His 4.56-to-1 assist-turnover ratio again led NBA. It was fifth time in six years he has done so . . . Single-game career-high points (24, at Philly, Feb. 7) and rebounds (10, at Detroit, March 25) . . . One of two original Hornets (Dell Curry is the other) . . . Very tough in trapping, pressure defense. Obviously, a liability in half-court defense . . . No. 12 pick by Bullets out of N.C. State in '87, he went to Charlotte in '88 expansion draft . . . Born Jan. 9, 1965, in Baltimore . . . MVP of Dunbar High '83 national championship team that also boasted Reggie Lewis, David Wingate and Reggie Williams . . . Made $900,000.

Year	Team	G	FG	FG Pct.	FT	FT Pct.	Reb.	Ast.	TP	Avg.
1987-88	Washington	79	166	.390	58	.784	136	404	393	5.0
1988-89	Charlotte	79	178	.426	66	.750	165	620	423	5.4
1989-90	Charlotte	81	326	.491	106	.791	207	867	763	9.4
1990-91	Charlotte	81	241	.460	86	.796	216	669	568	7.0
1991-92	Charlotte	82	317	.472	94	.783	235	743	730	8.9
1992-93	Charlotte	81	331	.453	140	.833	298	711	808	10.0
1993-94	Charlotte	77	354	.471	125	.806	313	780	835	10.8
	Totals	560	1913	.457	675	.797	1570	4794	4520	8.1

KENNY GATTISON 30 6-8 246   Center-Forward

Coach's delight . . . Tell him to run naked through stands for a win, he'd do it . . . Tireless worker and a good banger to wear down opposing centers . . . Team guy all the way. Player rep . . . Didn't have his best year, but stepped up when team was going bad. Averaged 10.5 points in games Larry Johnson missed . . . Shot over 50 percent for fifth straight year. Team's all-time field-goal percentage leader at .531 . . . Sun Belt Conference Player of the Year for Old Dominion in 1986 before Suns took him on third round . . . Missed 1987-88 with anterior cruciate ligament injury . . . After CBA stint, he came to Hornets as free agent in December 1989 . . . Born May 23, 1964, in Wilmington, N.C.

Year	Team	G	FG	FG Pct.	FT	FT Pct.	Reb.	Ast.	TP	Avg.
1986-87	Phoenix	77	148	.476	108	.632	270	36	404	5.2
1987-88	Phoenix					Injured				
1988-89	Phoenix	2	0	.000	1	.500	1	0	1	0.5
1989-90	Charlotte	63	148	.550	75	.682	197	39	372	5.9
1990-91	Charlotte	72	243	.532	164	.661	379	44	650	9.0
1991-92	Charlotte	82	423	.529	196	.688	580	131	1042	12.7
1992-93	Charlotte	75	203	.529	102	.604	353	68	508	6.8
1993-94	Charlotte	77	233	.524	126	.646	358	95	592	7.7
	Totals	448	1398	.524	772	.654	2138	413	3569	8.0

HERSEY HAWKINS 28 6-3 190   **Guard**

Think it's tough being No. 2? Try being No. 3 ... Third in scoring behind Larry Johnson and Alonzo Mourning ... So he had the lowest scoring output of his career (14.4) ... Flourished when Johnson and Mourning were out with injuries ... Tied Johnny Newman's team record with 41 points vs. Warriors Feb. 9 ... Quality shooter who needs help creating shot ... Fewest three-pointers since rookie year ... Durable. Only he and Dell Curry played in all 82 Hornet games. Has missed only seven games in six years ... 133 straight starts ... Set club record with 37 straight free throws ... Player of the Year in 1988 at Bradley, he was No. 6 pick of Clippers and landed in Philadelphia through three-team draft-night trade that involved Seattle ... Came to Hornets Sept. 3, 1993, for Dana Barros, Sidney Green and Greg Graham ... Born Sept. 29, 1966, in Chicago ... Made $2.4 million.

Year	Team	G	FG	FG Pct.	FT	FT Pct.	Reb.	Ast.	TP	Avg.
1988-89	Philadelphia	79	442	.455	241	.831	225	239	1196	15.1
1989-90	Philadelphia	82	522	.460	387	.888	304	261	1515	18.5
1990-91	Philadelphia	80	590	.472	479	.871	310	299	1767	22.1
1991-92	Philadelphia	81	521	.462	403	.874	271	248	1536	19.0
1992-93	Philadelphia	81	551	.470	419	.860	346	317	1643	20.3
1993-94	Charlotte	82	395	.460	312	.862	377	216	1180	14.4
	Totals	485	3021	.464	2241	.867	1833	1580	8837	18.2

MICHAEL ADAMS 31 5-10 175   **Guard**

Came to Hornets in summer trade for two second-round draft choices ... Not the explosive point guard he once was ... Last two years saw 68 and 55 treys. Had notched at least 125 three-pointers in five straight seasons ... Third on all-time three-point list with 906 trifectas in nine seasons ... Had NBA-record 10th four-point play Nov. 20 vs. Heat ... Tied career high with 11 rebounds vs. Hawks Dec. 11 ... Leading Bullet all-time in assist average (7.2) ... Third-round pick of Kings in 1985, out of Boston College. Waived ... Bullets signed, waived him in '86. Then re-signed him ... Traded with Jay Vincent for Darrell Walker and Mark Alarie in '87 to Denver ... Bullets got him back

in June 1991 in swap of first-rounders... Made $1.309 million
... Born Jan. 19, 1963, in Hartford, Conn.

Year	Team	G	FG	FG Pct.	FT	FT Pct.	Reb.	Ast.	TP	Avg.
1985-86	Sacramento......	18	16	.364	8	.667	6	22	40	2.2
1986-87	Washington......	63	160	.407	105	.847	123	244	453	7.2
1987-88	Denver.........	82	416	.449	166	.834	223	503	1137	13.9
1988-89	Denver.........	77	468	.433	322	.819	283	490	1424	18.5
1989-90	Denver.........	79	398	.402	267	.850	225	495	1221	15.5
1990-91	Denver.........	66	560	.394	465	.879	256	693	1752	26.5
1991-92	Washington......	78	485	.393	313	.869	310	594	1408	18.1
1992-93	Washington......	70	365	.439	237	.856	240	526	1035	14.8
1993-94	Washington......	70	285	.408	224	.830	183	480	849	12.1
	Totals	603	3153	.414	2107	.850	1849	4047	9319	15.5

FRANK BRICKOWSKI 35 6-9 248   Forward-Center

Strong complementary player... Now if he
only had some cartilage left to complement his
knees... Hornets were 20-7 in games where
he played with Alonzo Mourning and Larry
Johnson... Averaged 10.1 points and 4.5
boards in 28 games after Hornets got him from
Bucks Feb. 24 for Mike Gminski and a future
No. 1... Scored 23 points in first game as a
Hornet... Became unrestricted free agent, but Hornets indicated
they wanted him back... Tough inside banger, makes most of
somewhat limited offensive skills... Good, smart passer. His 222
assists were second among Eastern Conference centers... Born
Aug. 14, 1959, in Bayville, N.Y.... Earned $1.85 million...
Picked by Knicks on third round in 1981, out of Penn State...
Played in Italy, France and Israel. Came to NBA with Seattle in
'84... Did time with Lakers, Spurs and Bucks.

Year	Team	G	FG	FG Pct.	FT	FT Pct.	Reb.	Ast.	TP	Avg.
1984-85	Seattle	78	150	.492	85	.669	260	100	385	4.9
1985-86	Seattle	40	30	.517	18	.667	54	21	78	2.0
1986-87	LAL-S.A.........	44	63	.508	50	.714	116	17	176	4.0
1987-88	San Antonio	70	425	.528	268	.768	483	266	1119	16.0
1988-89	San Antonio	64	337	.515	201	.715	406	131	875	13.7
1989-90	San Antonio	78	211	.545	95	.674	327	105	517	6.6
1990-91	Milwaukee	75	372	.527	198	.798	426	131	942	12.6
1991-92	Milwaukee	65	306	.524	125	.767	344	122	740	11.4
1992-93	Milwaukee	66	456	.545	195	.728	405	196	1115	16.9
1993-94	Mil.-Char........	71	368	.488	195	.768	404	222	935	13.2
	Totals	651	2718	.521	1430	.742	3225	1311	6882	10.6

DAVID WINGATE 30 6-5 185   Guard-Forward

Around for his defense . . . And with the shape his knees are in, he's happy to be around, period . . . Started 36 of his 50 appearances . . . But knees made extended minutes iffy . . . A good guy to have if he's healthy . . . Had preseason knee surgery on left knee, his second operation in five months . . . Missed first 31 games . . . Had career-high 13 rebounds Feb. 7 at Philly . . . Left Georgetown in '86 as school's third all-time leading scorer . . . Born Dec. 15, 1963, in Baltimore . . . Another Dunbar High alumnus . . . Made $570,000 . . . Drafted on second round by Sixers in 1986 . . . Traded to Spurs Aug. 28, 1989, in the Maurice Cheeks-Johnny Dawkins deal . . . Waived, did a free-agent year with Bullets . . . Signed with Hornets as free agent, Nov. 18, 1992.

Year	Team	G	FG	FG Pct.	FT	FT Pct.	Reb.	Ast.	TP	Avg.
1986-87	Philadelphia	77	259	.430	149	.741	156	155	680	8.8
1987-88	Philadelphia	61	218	.400	99	.750	101	119	545	8.9
1988-89	Philadelphia	33	54	.470	27	.794	37	73	137	4.2
1989-90	San Antonio	78	220	.448	87	.777	195	208	527	6.8
1990-91	San Antonio	25	53	.384	29	.707	75	46	136	5.4
1991-92	Washington	81	266	.465	105	.719	269	247	638	7.9
1992-93	Charlotte	72	180	.536	79	.738	174	183	440	6.1
1993-94	Charlotte	50	136	.481	34	.667	134	104	310	6.2
	Totals	477	1386	.450	609	.739	1141	1135	3413	7.2

ROBERT PARISH 41 7-0 230   Center

Free-agent Celtic veteran will play 19th NBA season as Hornet . . . Signed two-year deal with optional third year and reported $5.5-million guarantee . . . Playing time under 2,000 minutes for first time since 1977-78 . . . Remarkably, he remained effective . . . Still among the top 10 centers in the league . . . NBA's 12th all-time scorer with 22,494 points. Passed Larry Bird Nov. 26 . . . Is just 27 rebounds shy of 14,000. Only seven players have attained that mark. Moved ahead of Wes Unseld (13,769) into eighth place on all-time boarding list Feb. 22 . . . Only Kareem Abdul-Jabbar (1,560) played more games than "Chief" (1,443) . . . Fifth all-time in blocks (2,252) . . . Last active member of greatest frontline ever with Larry Bird and Kevin

McHale . . . Made $4 million . . . Born Aug. 30, 1953, in Shreveport, La. . . . Warriors picked him No. 8 out of Centenary in '76 . . . Came to Celts with '80 first-rounder June 9, 1980, for two first-rounders. When Celts took McHale, deal became one of greatest sports heists ever.

Year	Team	G	FG	FG Pct.	FT	FT Pct.	Reb.	Ast.	TP	Avg.
1976-77	Golden State	77	288	.503	121	.708	543	74	697	9.1
1977-78	Golden State	82	430	.472	165	.625	680	95	1025	12.5
1978-79	Golden State	76	554	.499	196	.698	916	115	1304	17.2
1979-80	Golden State	72	510	.507	203	.715	783	122	1223	17.0
1980-81	Boston	82	635	.545	282	.710	777	144	1552	18.9
1981-82	Boston	80	669	.542	252	.710	866	140	1590	19.9
1982-83	Boston	78	619	.550	271	.698	827	141	1509	19.3
1983-84	Boston	80	623	.546	274	.745	857	139	1520	19.0
1984-85	Boston	79	551	.542	292	.743	840	125	1394	17.6
1985-86	Boston	81	530	.549	245	.731	770	145	1305	16.1
1986-87	Boston	80	588	.566	227	.735	851	173	1403	17.5
1987-88	Boston	74	442	.589	177	.734	628	115	1061	14.3
1988-89	Boston	80	596	.570	294	.719	996	175	1486	18.6
1989-90	Boston	79	505	.580	233	.747	796	103	1243	15.7
1990-91	Boston	81	485	.598	237	.767	856	66	1207	14.9
1991-92	Boston	79	468	.535	179	.772	705	70	1115	14.1
1992-93	Boston	79	416	.535	162	.689	740	61	994	12.6
1993-94	Boston	74	356	.491	154	.740	542	82	866	11.7
	Totals	1413	9265	.540	3964	.722	13973	2085	22494	15.9

SCOTT BURRELL 23 6-7 218   Forward

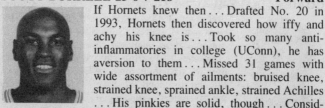

If Hornets knew then . . . Drafted No. 20 in 1993, Hornets then discovered how iffy and achy his knee is . . . Took so many anti-inflammatories in college (UConn), he has aversion to them . . . Missed 31 games with wide assortment of ailments: bruised knee, strained knee, sprained ankle, strained Achilles . . . His pinkies are solid, though . . . Considered a tough small-forward defender. Led team with 2.33 steals per game . . . Shot doesn't do much for anybody . . . Born Jan. 12, 1971, in Hamden, Conn. . . . Baseball stud, too. Twice drafted, by Mariners and Blue Jays . . . Made $850,000.

Year	Team	G	FG	FG Pct.	FT	FT Pct.	Reb.	Ast.	TP	Avg.
1993-94	Charlotte	51	98	.419	46	.657	132	62	244	4.8

TONY BENNETT 25 6-0 175 Guard

Left his game at Wisconsin-Green Bay . . . Two years, and has shown very little development . . . Could save a lot of time by simply handing over the ball when pressured, rather than giving up the dribble too soon . . . Still, he had a 4.08-to-1 assist-to-turnover ratio . . . Can shoot in practice . . . And has three-point range . . . Can't create, though . . . 35th pick on second round in '92 . . . Played for his dad in college . . . Born June 1, 1969, in Green Bay . . . Wisconsin's ''Mr. Basketball'' as high-school senior . . . Made $182,000.

Year	Team	G	FG	FG Pct.	FT	FT Pct.	Reb.	Ast.	TP	Avg.
1992-93	Charlotte	75	110	.423	30	.732	63	136	276	3.7
1993-94	Charlotte	74	105	.399	11	.733	90	163	248	3.4
	Totals	149	215	.411	41	.732	153	299	524	3.5

THE ROOKIE

DARRIN HANCOCK 22 6-5 205 Guard-Forward

Turned pro and signed to play in France last season after one year at Kansas and two at Garden City (Kan.) CC . . . No. 38 pick . . . Former National Junior College Player of the Year . . . Shot 52 percent and averaged 17.2 points in France's B League for Maurienne . . . Born Nov. 3, 1971, in Birmingham, Ala.

COACH ALLAN BRISTOW: This is going to be an interesting year. Bristow has added defensive whiz Johnny Bach, late of the Bulls, to his staff . . . One of biggest raps on Bristow has been defensive schemes and now he has one of very best alongside him . . . No one ever questioned his eye for talent . . . Look at the team he has helped assemble. Larry Johnson was his call. Ditto Alonzo Mourning . . . One tough SOB . . . His scouting and preparation approach have come under fire . . . But they love him in Charlotte . . . A little thin-skinned . . . Has strong rapport with players. And continually gets better . . . Is, shall we say, intense? . . . Goes with what's best for his team, and opponents be damned . . . Make them adjust, don't adjust to them . . . Adopted passing-game philosophy from Doug Moe in Denver,

where he spent seven years... Second-round pick of Sixers in 1973 after career at Virginia Tech... 10-year NBA career with four teams... Spent one season as Hornet exec before becoming coach in July 1992... Born Aug. 23, 1951, in Richmond, Va.

GREATEST PLAYER

This could change within a year, given Alonzo Mourning's presence. When you've only been around as a franchise for six seasons, there is not a whole lot to choose from. But if you have to choose, there is nothing wrong with choosing Larry Johnson.

Now if L.J.'s back goes on the blink again, then Mourning, entering his third season, could step right in and claim the handle of Greatest Hornet Ever. A case could be made for waterbug Muggsy Bogues, one of two remaining Hornets from the expansion draft. But it wasn't until L.J. arrived as the No. 1 overall pick in the 1991 draft that the Hornets began making some serious noise.

In his second year, Johnson was the All-Star Game starter and a second-team All-NBA choice. Now, after an injury-plagued third year, he is Charlotte's second all-time scorer and No. 1 all-time rebounder.

ALL-TIME HORNET LEADERS

SEASON

Points: Larry Johnson, 1,810, 1992-93
Assists: Tyrone Bogues, 867, 1989-90
Rebounds: Larry Johnson, 899, 1991-92

GAME

Points: Johnny Newman, 41 vs. Indiana, 1/25/92
Hersey Hawkins, 41 vs. Golden State, 2/9/94
Assists: Tyrone Bogues, 19 vs. Boston, 4/23/89
Rebounds: Larry Johnson, 23 vs. Minnesota, 3/10/92

CAREER

Points: Dell Curry, 6,214, 1988-94
Assists: Tyrone Bogues, 4,390, 1988-94
Rebounds: Larry Johnson, 3,211, 1991-94

CHICAGO BULLS

TEAM DIRECTORY: Chairman: Jerry Reinsdorf; VP-Operations: Jerry Krause; Dir. Media Services: Tim Hallam; Coach: Phil Jackson; Asst. Coaches: Jim Rodgers, Tex Winter, Jim Cleamons. Arena: United Center (21,500). Colors: Red, white and black.

Need a winner at the buzzer? Introducing Toni Kukoc.

SCOUTING REPORT

SHOOTING: The Bulls were third in the East, but no one executes their offense better, even without Michael Jordan. Will they do so again? Depends. Will Scottie Pippen be wearing a Bulls' uniform?

Their premier offensive force was on the trading block in the offseason and the legal entanglements of the collective bargaining agreement threw the league into a holding pattern. But if Pippen is back, the Bulls will retain one of the league's most unique players, a forward with point-guard skills, through whom much of the offense is funneled.

The Bulls took a hit through retirements (Bill Cartwright, John Paxson) and then were rocked to their foundation by the free-agent losses of Horace Grant to Orlando and Scott Williams to Philadelphia. Grant was unhappy in Chicago. The Bulls' brass said they were unhappy with Grant. But now the front office could learn what unhappiness is. After all, how can you lose the greatest offensive player ever (Jordan) and then the key defensive man (Grant) in successive years and keep smiling?

Now they have to hope there will be enough talent to keep matters respectable, with shooters B.J. Armstrong and Toni Kukoc, but if Pippen were dealt, it could be a long, lonely winter in the new United Center.

PLAYMAKING: Armstrong finally adapted to looking to create for others first. He had to, with Michael Jordan shagging fly balls and Pippen concentrating more on the duties of a small forward. The Bulls, regardless of who remains, will still execute in the Phil Jackson-Tex Winter precision mold, but the problem will be the executors. If Pippen is not around, the Bulls will have to get either two quality players or a marquee superstar.

REBOUNDING: Without Grant, the Bulls will be without their best rebounder for four years running. Williams was one of their best bench rebounders. Pippen also helped on the boards. So the Bulls could be a big group of plodding bangers (Luc Longley, Bill Wennington, etc.) and be devoid of so much of the athleticism which was the biggest factor in their three-year title run. Yeah, Jordan was THE factor, but when was the last time anyone called him non-athletic?

BULL ROSTER

No. Veterans	Pos.	Ht.	Wt.	Age	Yrs. Pro	College
10 B.J. Armstrong	G	6-2	185	25	5	Iowa
44 Corie Blount	F	6-10	242	25	1	Cincinnati
U-3 Jo Jo English	G	6-4	195	24	2	South Carolina
U-25 Steve Kerr	G	6-3	180	29	6	Arizona
R-7 Toni Kukoc	F	6-10	230	26	1	Croatia
13 Luc Longley	C	7-2	265	25	3	New Mexico
U-20 Pete Myers	G	6-6	180	31	6	Ark.-Little Rock
32 Will Perdue	C	7-0	240	29	6	Vanderbilt
33 Scottie Pippen	F	6-7	210	29	7	Central Arkansas
U-34 Bill Wennington	C	7-0	260	31	7	St. John's

R-restricted free agent
U-unrestricted free agent

Rd. Rookies	Sel. No.	Pos.	Ht.	Wt.	College
1 Dickey Simpkins	21	F	6-9	248	Providence
2 Kris Bruton	49	F	6-5	210	Benedict

DEFENSE: The Bulls already took a severe hit when assistant coach John Bach moved to Charlotte. Of course, Jackson can cover that hole.

But what would the Bulls possibly use to cover a gaping void left by Grant, the single most important element in their pressure defense? Or Pippen, who plays the passing lanes so well? Human spackle will only get you so far.

OUTLOOK: No one took the Bulls seriously at the start of last year when Jordan stunned the world by retiring. They were wrong as the Bulls won 55 games and extended the Knicks to seven games and, but for a foul call at the end of Game 5, could have wrapped up the Knicks in six.

In view of what has happened so far in the preseason and whatever is to come, there may be less expectations this year. Stay tuned for late developments.

BULL PROFILES

SCOTTIE PIPPEN 29 6-7 210   Forward-Guard

Time was, guys yanked themselves in crucial playoff games because of a headache . . . Now it's because somebody else gets called for a game-winning shot . . . Refused to go in for final seconds of Eastern semis Game 3 against Knicks when play was designed for Toni Kukoc . . . Looks upon Kukoc like a brother, the same way Cain viewed Abel . . . All-Star, All-Defense, All-NBA season, but went on trading block before draft . . . Graceful, elegant athlete who stepped up on court when Michael Jordan stepped up in batter's box . . . Shot poorly in playoffs (.435) . . . Missed 10 games early with bad ankle, Bulls went 4-6 . . . His 72 games were fewest of seven-year career . . . Personal-best scoring (22.0), double-figures in every game . . . Led Bulls in scoring, assists and steals, ranked second in rebounds . . . Bulls were 34-16 when he led them in scoring . . . Had 12th and 13th triple-doubles of his career . . . Great at playing passing lanes. Quickness allows him to rotate, making him so effective on double-teams . . . Born Sept. 25, 1965, in Hamburg, Ark. . . . Central Arkansas, '87 . . . Sonics' No. 5 pick. Went to Bulls for Olden Polynice and a No. 1 . . . Made $3.075 million.

Year	Team	G	FG	FG Pct.	FT	FT Pct.	Reb.	Ast.	TP	Avg.
1987-88	Chicago	79	261	.463	99	.576	298	169	625	7.9
1988-89	Chicago	73	413	.476	201	.668	445	256	1048	14.4
1989-90	Chicago	82	562	.489	199	.675	547	444	1351	16.5
1990-91	Chicago	82	600	.520	240	.706	595	511	1461	17.8
1991-92	Chicago	82	687	.506	330	.760	630	572	1720	21.0
1992-93	Chicago	81	628	.473	232	.663	621	507	1510	18.6
1993-94	Chicago	72	627	.491	270	.660	629	403	1587	22.0
	Totals	551	3778	.491	1571	.683	3765	2862	9302	16.9

TONI KUKOC 26 6-10 230   Forward

Ees grit kontree, no? . . . Will never be Scottie Pippen's pen pal . . . Bulls finally brought Euroflash in, ending courtship that seemingly started when Lindbergh took off for Paris . . . Megabucks deal started with $1.075 million last season . . . Outstanding range and uncanny ability to hit game-winning shot . . . Won three games at the buzzer in regular season . . . Drained 20-footer at buzzer to beat Knicks in Game 3 of Eastern semis, the same game Scottie sat and sulked . . . Still learning the NBA game . . . While he moves well without the ball, at times he can clog sets . . . Good passer . . . Scored 24 points at Dallas Nov. 26, took 11 rebounds at New Jersey Dec. 29 . . . Say it "KOO-coach" . . . Olympic silver medalist with '92 Croatians, '88 Yugoslavians . . . Bulls drafted him on second round in 1990 . . . Born Sept. 18, 1968, in Split, Croatia.

Year	Team	G	FG	FG Pct.	FT	FT Pct.	Reb.	Ast.	TP	Avg.
1993-94	Chicago	75	313	.431	156	.743	297	252	814	10.9

B.J. Armstrong played in 363rd straight game.

B.J. ARMSTRONG 27 6-2 185   Guard

With whatzisname gone, Armstrong had to step up everywhere. And did. Career-high scoring (14.8)... Shooting down a bit. With no Michael Jordan, his shots were just open at times, instead of WIDE open... All-Star Game starter... Good, productive playoffs. Improved statistically in all areas—except games played, of course... Only Bull to start all 82 games... His missed one game (rookie year) in five-year career ... Has played in current team-high 363 straight games... Committed just nine turnovers in 360 playoff minutes... Terrific spot-up shooter. Lived off Jordan, living off Scottie Pippen. But he can find his own shot... Thing is, when you had those two, why look?... Born Sept. 9, 1967, in Detroit... Left Iowa as school's all-time assists king. Taken No. 18 in 1989... Made $620,000.

Year	Team	G	FG	FG Pct.	FT	FT Pct.	Reb.	Ast.	TP	Avg.
1989-90	Chicago	81	190	.485	69	.885	102	199	452	5.6
1990-91	Chicago	82	304	.481	97	.874	149	301	720	8.8
1991-92	Chicago	82	335	.481	104	.806	145	266	809	9.9
1992-93	Chicago	82	408	.499	130	.861	149	330	1009	12.3
1993-94	Chicago	82	479	.476	194	.855	170	323	1212	14.8
	Totals	409	1716	.484	594	.853	715	1419	4202	10.3

STEVE KERR 29 6-3 180   Guard

Couldn't make it in Phoenix. Couldn't make it in Cleveland. Couldn't make it in Orlando. So he was one of three guys to play in all 82 games for 55-victory Bulls... A specialist: long-range and three-point spot-up guy... His .419 was NBA's fourth-best three-point mark... Is NBA's all-time three-point percentage leader at .445... Fifth on the team in scoring. And everything came off the bench... Never was considered a strong ball-handler... Did nothing to change assessment... Career-best 8.6 points in sixth year... Born Sept. 27, 1965, in Beirut, Lebanon... Knee problems at Arizona. He was a second-round pick of Suns in 1988... Went to Cavaliers for a second-rounder. Did three nondescript seasons with Cavs, who shipped him to Orlando on Feb. 3, 1992, for a second-rounder . . . Signed as free agent with Bulls Sept. 29, 1993 . . . Made $150,000 minimum.

Year	Team	G	FG	FG Pct.	FT	FT Pct.	Reb.	Ast.	TP	Avg.
1988-89	Phoenix	26	20	.435	6	.667	17	24	54	2.1
1989-90	Cleveland	78	192	.444	63	.863	98	248	520	6.7
1990-91	Cleveland	57	99	.444	45	.849	37	131	271	4.8
1991-92	Cleveland	48	121	.511	45	.833	78	110	319	6.6
1992-93	Clev.-Orl.	52	53	.434	22	.917	45	70	134	2.6
1993-94	Chicago	82	287	.497	83	.856	131	210	709	8.6
	Totals	343	772	.472	264	.852	406	793	2007	5.9

LUC LONGLEY 25 7-2 265   Center

It was a g'day when Bulls got him from Timberwolves for the ever-disappointing Stacey King, Feb. 23, 1994 . . . First Australian ever to play in NBA . . . Once in Chicago, he showed some strong post moves and evidence of a game that were nonexistent in Minnesota . . . Must be the tall buildings . . . Shot .483 and averaged 7.6 points for Bulls . . . Real obstacle-type. Big body who clogs lanes on defense . . . No Jesse Owens, but he can move defensively . . . Member of '88 and '92 Aussie Olympic teams . . . Drafted out of New Mexico in 1991 as the seventh pick in the lottery . . . Born Jan. 19, 1969, in Melbourne, Australia . . . Dad played Australian Rules Football . . . Made $1.59 million.

Year	Team	G	FG	FG Pct.	FT	FT Pct.	Reb.	Ast.	TP	Avg.
1991-92	Minnesota	66	114	.458	53	.663	257	53	281	4.3
1992-93	Minnesota	55	133	.455	53	.716	240	51	319	5.8
1993-94	Minn.-Chi.	76	219	.471	90	.720	433	109	528	6.9
	Totals	197	466	.463	196	.703	930	213	1128	5.7

PETE MYERS 31 6-6 180   Guard

Was only about 23 points, four assists, one steal and four rebounds a night away from replacing Michael Jordan . . . Talk about following a tough act . . . Did commendable job, though . . . He's a defensive type whom Bulls once kept just to defend Jordan in practice . . . He played in all 82 games, starting all but one . . . Shot career-best .455 in Bulls' offensive system. But he's hardly what you'd consider a shooter . . . Shows some strong moves to the basket . . . Scored career-best 7.9 points . . . Has been around since leaving Arkansas-Little Rock in '86 . . . Bulls drafted him on sixth round and he made the Opening Night roster . . . Waived following year and played with Spurs, Sixers, Knicks, Nets and Spurs again before signing as free agent on Oct. 7, 1993 . . . Born Sept. 15, 1963, in Mobile, Ala. . . . Made $150,000 minimum.

Year	Team	G	FG	FG Pct.	FT	FT Pct.	Reb.	Ast.	TP	Avg.
1986-87	Chicago	29	19	.365	28	.651	17	21	66	2.3
1987-88	San Antonio	22	43	.453	26	.667	37	48	112	5.1
1988-89	Phil.-N.Y.	33	31	.425	33	.688	33	48	95	2.9
1989-90	N.Y.-N.J.	52	89	.396	66	.660	96	135	244	4.7
1990-91	San Antonio	8	10	.435	9	.818	18	14	29	3.6
1993-94	Chicago	82	253	.455	136	.701	181	245	650	7.9
	Totals	226	445	.435	298	.685	382	511	1196	5.3

BILL WENNINGTON 31 7-0 260   Center

Chicago held a sale for minimum-wage free-agent contracts and this guy showed up, too . . . And once again they got something out of him . . . Scored a career-high 7.1 points . . . Began year strictly as insurance. But injuries struck and Bulls turned in their policies. As a result, the St. John's product played in last 72 games . . . If you've seen Will Perdue play, you've seen this guy's game . . . But add a mid-range jumper to the mix . . . Did two years in Italy before signing with Bulls on Sept. 29, 1993 . . . Dallas picked him No. 16 in 1985 draft . . . Traded in June 1990 to Kings for Rodney McCray and a pair of second-rounders . . . One unfulfilling year in Sacramento led him to Italy . . . Born April 26, 1963, in Montreal . . . Member of '84 Canadian Olympic team.

Year	Team	G	FG	FG Pct.	FT	FT Pct.	Reb.	Ast.	TP	Avg.
1985-86	Dallas	56	72	.471	45	.726	132	21	189	3.4
1986-87	Dallas	58	56	.424	45	.750	129	24	157	2.7
1987-88	Dallas	30	25	.510	12	.632	39	4	63	2.1
1988-89	Dallas	65	119	.433	61	.744	286	46	300	4.6
1989-90	Dallas	60	105	.449	60	.800	198	41	270	4.5
1990-91	Sacramento	77	181	.436	74	.787	340	69	437	5.7
1993-94	Chicago	76	235	.488	72	.818	353	70	542	7.1
	Totals	422	793	.456	369	.769	1477	275	1958	4.6

WILL PERDUE 29 7-0 240   Center

Began season on end of bench. Ended season pretty much in the stands . . . Left off playoff roster . . . So don't blame him for failure to get fourth straight ring . . . As elegant as low tide . . . Banger, physical type . . . He's 7-feet and white, so there'll always be a job somewhere ("And now, starting at center for YOUR Toronto Raptors . . . ") . . . Missed 29 games with broken finger, missed lots of others with broken game . . . Fan favorite . . . Coach's desperation . . . Was basically the No. 5 center . . . No team needs that much depth . . . Can get some offensive rebounds. At least when he gets time. But saw Bill Cartwright, Luc Longley, Bill Wennington and Scott Williams ahead of him on depth chart . . . Born Aug. 29, 1965, in Melbourne, Fla. . . . Vanderbilt, '88. Was picked No. 11 by Bulls . . . Made $1.2 million.

Year	Team	G	FG	FG Pct.	FT	FT Pct.	Reb.	Ast.	TP	Avg.
1988-89	Chicago	30	29	.403	8	.571	45	11	66	2.2
1989-90	Chicago	77	111	.414	72	.692	214	46	294	3.8
1990-91	Chicago	74	116	.494	75	.670	336	47	307	4.1
1991-92	Chicago	77	152	.547	45	.495	312	80	350	4.5
1992-93	Chicago	72	137	.557	67	.604	287	74	341	4.7
1993-94	Chicago	43	47	.420	23	.719	126	34	117	2.7
	Totals	373	592	.489	290	.625	1320	292	1475	4.0

JO JO ENGLISH 24 6-4 195   Guard

Involved in one of Bulls' greatest trades ever. Fought with Knicks' Derek Harper in Game 3 of Eastern semis. He was banned for one game, Harper for two . . . Started season with Minnesota and was picked up for second-rounder Nov. 4. Waived, brought back . . . Saw strictly spot duty but is a pretty decent defender with active hands . . . Had 10 blocked shots in 419 minutes. That was two more blocks than 7-foot Bill Cartwright had in 780 minutes . . . Undrafted out of South Carolina in 1992 . . . Did six games as free agent with Bulls while shuttling back and forth to CBA in '92–93 . . . Minimum wage of $150,000 . . . Born Feb. 4, 1970, in Frankfurt, West Germany.

Year	Team	G	FG	FG Pct.	FT	FT Pct.	Reb.	Ast.	TP	Avg.
1992-93	Chicago	6	3	.300	0	.000	6	1	6	1.0
1993-94	Chicago	36	56	.434	10	.476	45	38	130	3.6
	Totals	42	59	.424	10	.435	51	39	136	3.2

THE ROOKIES

DICKEY SIMPKINS 22 6-9 248   Forward
Real name is LuBara Dixon . . . Came on strong in pre-draft camps
and tournaments . . . Was second-leading rebounder at Providence
College behind Michael Smith and where he played school-record
125 games . . . Strong, inside player, Bulls grabbed him at No. 21
. . . Born April 6, 1972, in Washington, D.C.

KRIS BRUTON 21 6-5 210   Forward
A mystery to everyone except GM Jerry Krause, who calls him
a "big leaper who can jump out of the building." . . . Played at
little-known Benedict College (S.C.), where he averaged 20.4 ppg
and 9.9 rebounds as senior . . . Was 49th pick.

COACH PHIL JACKSON: Any chance of a fourth straight
title flamed out in controversial end-game call
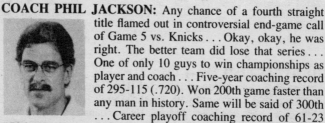
of Game 5 vs. Knicks . . . Okay, okay, he was
right. The better team did lose that series . . .
One of only 10 guys to win championships as
player and coach . . . Five-year coaching record
of 295-115 (.720). Won 200th game faster than
any man in history. Same will be said of 300th
. . . Career playoff coaching record of 61-23
(.726), the best percentage ever . . . Showed last season (if there
was any doubt) that he is truly a magnificent coach . . . When
Michael Jordan retired, many picked Bulls to be barely .500. They
won 55 . . . Played for '73 champ Knicks . . . Coached Albany
('84) to CBA crown . . . Only man to coach both NBA and CBA
champs . . . A thinker . . . Makes adjustments that drive peers to
new careers . . . Big on psyche jobs. And good at it . . . He and
Pat Riley are sort of like Scottie Pippen and Toni Kukoc . . . Chose
basketball over ministry and was second-round pick of Knicks in
'67 from North Dakota, where he was two-time All-American for
Bill Fitch . . . A 13-year NBA career was plagued by back problems. That injury kept him from playing with 1969-70 champion
Knicks . . . Former assistant with Nets and Bulls . . . Born Sept.
17, 1945, in Deer Lodge, Mont.

His Airness: The one and only Michael Jordan.

GREATEST PLAYER

Don't you love it when subjective choices leave no room for debate? The only question surrounding Michael Jordan here, is not whether he was the greatest Bull ever. Rather, was he the greatest player ever?

Before stunning the world with his retirement last year, Jordan left a legacy and a flair that may never be equalled. After claiming his third straight championship ring—averaging a record 41.0 in the Finals—there was little left for His Airness to conquer. Except sliders.

He was the playoff MVP for three straight years. He tied Wilt Chamberlain's record of leading the league in scoring seven straight seasons. He was the 18th player to score 20,000 points. He won Olympic gold. He won an NCAA title with North Carolina. His image is emblazoned on millions of sneakers and 10 times that many posters. He was, probably still is, the single most recognizable athlete in the world. "Be Like Mike" was a national catchphrase.

And, quite simply, no one can be like Mike.

ALL-TIME BULL LEADERS

SEASON

Points: Michael Jordan, 3,041, 1986-87
Assists: Guy Rodgers, 908, 1966-67
Rebounds: Tom Boerwinkle, 1,133, 1970-71

GAME

Points: Michael Jordan, 69 vs. Cleveland, 3/28/90
Assists: Ennis Whatley, 22 vs. New York, 1/14/84
　　　　　Ennis Whatley, 22 vs. Atlanta, 3/3/84
Rebounds: Tom Boerwinkle, 37 vs. Phoenix, 1/8/70

CAREER

Points: Michael Jordan, 21,541, 1984-93
Assists: Michael Jordan, 3,935, 1984-93
Rebounds: Tom Boerwinkle, 5,745, 1968-78

CLEVELAND CAVALIERS

TEAM DIRECTORY: Chairman: Gordon Gund; Pres./Team Division: Wayne Embry; Dir. Player Personnel: Gary Fitzsimmons; Dir. Pub. Rel.: Bob Price; Coach: Mike Fratello; Asst. Coaches: Richie Adubato, Ron Rothstein, Jim Boylan. Arena: Gateway Arena (20,750). Colors: Red, white and black.

Explosive Gerald Wilkins was Cavs' leading scorer.

SCOUTING REPORT

SHOOTING: When they're healthy, they can be almost precision-like. When they're not, they can be like, well, last year when they were a decidedly middle-of-the-road 13th.

Form the line, the Cavs will always excel with Mark Price, one of the best ever. And from three-point range, they'll excel with Price, one of the best ever. Now, can they ever come up with a way to relieve what has become a huge burden on their stud point guard? They have the means. Now, do they have a way to keep them healthy?

PLAYMAKING: No problems here. Not with Price. And not with his backup, Terrell Brandon.

In Price, the Cavs have a classic point. Drive and dish inside or kick outside. Overplay the pass and he'll nail you. And he's smart and poised against any pressure: the Cavs led the league in fewest turnovers, were second in assist-turnover ratio.

With Brandon, the only problem is getting him enough playing time, which may be easier to come by as Price, having hit the big Three-0 in February, will get a reduction in minutes.

REBOUNDING: Tyrone Hill made a big, big difference. But not enough to lift the Cavs past the 19th ranking in the league.

Once again, the Cavs were skulking near the bottom of the heap—21st—in offensive rebounding. The rap, of course, always has been they lacked toughness. And Hill brought some of that. Now they will get more from newly-signed Michael Cage, who was a Sonic free agent.

And another Cavs' rebounding problem stems from one of their strengths—shot-blocking. The Cavs go for the rejects and wind up out of position. They usually, though, hold their own on the defensive glass, although down the stretch last season they were going with a frontline held together with airplane glue and paper clips.

DEFENSE: As long as Mike Fratello breathes a competitive breath, his teams will defend. Cleveland always boasted a ferocious shot-blocking brigade, led by the likes of Larry Nance and John (Hot Rod) Williams. And last season behind Fratello's blueprint, they assembled the finest defensive effort in team history.

Cleveland opponents stayed under 100 points 49 times and the Cavs kept foes under 80 five times, nearly one-third (16) the number of sub-80 efforts they had recorded in 23 years. And never

CAVALIER ROSTER

No. Veterans	Pos.	Ht.	Wt.	Age	Yrs. Pro	College
R-16 Gary Alexander	F	6-7	240	25	1	South Florida
10 John Battle	G	6-2	190	31	9	Rutgers
11 Terrell Brandon	G	5-11	180	24	2	Oregon
— Michael Cage	F-C	6-9	240	32	10	San Diego State
43 Brad Daugherty	C	7-0	263	29	8	North Carolina
35 Danny Ferry	F	6-10	236	28	4	Duke
23 Rod Higgins	F	6-7	217	34	12	Fresno State
32 Tyrone Hill	F	6-9	245	26	4	Xavier
8 Tim Kempton	C-F	6-10	255	30	5	Notre Dame
R-12 Gerald Madkins	G	6-4	200	25	1	UCLA
24 Chris Mills	F	6-6	216	24	1	Arizona
R-22 Larry Nance	F	6-10	235	35	13	Clemson
14 Bobby Phills	G	6-5	217	24	3	Southern
25 Mark Price	G	6-0	178	30	8	Georgia Tech
21 Gerald Wilkins	G-F	6-6	210	31	9	Tenn.-Chattanooga
18 John Williams	F-C	6-11	245	32	8	Tulane

R-restricted free agent

Rd. Rookies	Sel. No.	Pos.	Ht.	Wt.	College
2 Gary Collier	42	G	6-4	195	Tulsa

had they allowed less than last season's 97.1 points per game.

But in the defense-oriented NBA world of the '90s, everyone is racking up impressive numbers. The Cavs lack the lateral quickness to contest among the truly elite defensive teams in the league.

OUTLOOK: They'll be in a new arena downtown. They'll have a new logo. But the Cavs will face some of their same old problems.

The health of Brad Daugherty remains a prime concern. He'll go into a season hoping rest, not surgery, will cure the back woes that wiped out one-third of his last campaign. How will Nance respond to another year and more health concerns? Movement along the trade front is near-impossible with the strangulating contracts of Danny Ferry and Williams.

Some of the familiar pluses will still be around. Like Price, but he can't do it alone. Fratello performed a near-miracle last year, guiding this battered and somewhat aging bunch to 47 victories. But for years, the Cavs, with a nice array of quality talent, have tried to get over the hump and failed. This year looms no different.

CAVALIER PROFILES

MARK PRICE 30 6-0 178   Guard

Couldn't do it all. No Daugherty. No Nance. No Williams. Gee, wonder who defenses keyed on?... Third-team All-NBA... Had a good season despite all the pressure. Defenses jumped out at him and there wasn't much to pass to... Minutes need shortening. Unless Cavs want an exhausted lump of bandaged jelly starting at point... Dream Team II member...
A dream shooter: .485 lifetime, including .409 from three-point range (which is fourth-best all-time in NBA)... Won second straight three-point shootout at All-Star Weekend. Hit 20 of 25 shots... Led Cavs in scoring (17.3) for second time... Shot .888 from line. And that was one of his worst seasons... 31 games of 20 or more points... His team-best 7.8 assists per were ninth best in NBA... Bad playoffs: .349 shooting. Bulls wore him down... In past four seasons, Cavs are 199-113 with Price in lineup, 34-64 without him... Career-high-tying six steals vs. Nuggets Feb. 15... Born Feb. 15, 1964, in Bartlesville, Okla.... Dad Denny coaches Phillips U. in Enid, Okla.... Brother Brent a Bullet... Mavs' second-round pick from Georgia Tech in '86. Stolen by Cavs for a second-rounder... Made $2.85 million.

Year	Team	G	FG	FG Pct.	FT	FT Pct.	Reb.	Ast.	TP	Avg.
1986-87	Cleveland	67	173	.408	95	.833	117	202	464	6.9
1987-88	Cleveland	80	493	.506	221	.877	180	480	1279	16.0
1988-89	Cleveland	75	529	.526	263	.901	226	631	1414	18.9
1989-90	Cleveland	73	489	.459	300	.888	251	666	1430	19.6
1990-91	Cleveland	16	97	.497	59	.952	45	166	271	16.9
1991-92	Cleveland	72	438	.488	270	.947	173	535	1247	17.3
1992-93	Cleveland	75	477	.484	289	.948	201	602	1365	18.2
1993-94	Cleveland	76	480	.478	238	.888	228	589	1316	17.3
	Totals	534	3176	.485	1735	.906	1421	3871	8786	16.5

BRAD DAUGHERTY 29 7-0 263   Center

Season could have been worse—only if he were involved with Whitewater... Ended season on injured list with herniated lumbar disc... Also suffered with on-going bouts of vertigo and later a viral infection... Looked like he was headed for back surgery but docs prescribed rest ...Drop in scoring due to Mike Fratello's share-the-wealth offense... Still was doing well (17.0) when back went out . . . Game's best passing center. Went over the 2,000-assist mark vs. Miami Jan. 29 . . . Got 10,000th career point vs. Bucks Dec. 20 . . . And got his 5,000th rebound (he's Cavs' all-time boarder) at Indiana Jan. 4 . . . Has not had an 82-game season in eight years . . . Not the defensive monster size would suggest; has never had 100 blocks in a season. Of course, with Larry Nance and John Williams alongside, doesn't need to . . . Born Oct. 19, 1965, in Black Mountain, N.C. . . . Made $3.541 million . . . No. 1 pick of the '86 draft out of North Carolina after Cavs shipped Roy Hinson to Philly for the top pick.

Year	Team	G	FG	FG Pct.	FT	FT Pct.	Reb.	Ast.	TP	Avg.
1986-87	Cleveland	80	487	.538	279	.696	647	304	1253	15.7
1987-88	Cleveland	79	551	.510	378	.716	665	333	1480	18.7
1988-89	Cleveland	78	544	.538	386	.737	718	285	1475	18.9
1989-90	Cleveland	41	244	.479	202	.704	373	130	690	16.8
1990-91	Cleveland	76	605	.524	435	.751	830	253	1645	21.6
1991-92	Cleveland	73	576	.570	414	.777	760	262	1566	21.5
1992-93	Cleveland	71	520	.571	391	.795	726	312	1432	20.2
1993-94	Cleveland	50	296	.488	256	.785	508	149	848	17.0
	Totals	548	3823	.532	2741	.747	5227	2028	10389	19.0

TERRELL BRANDON 24 5-11 180   Guard

Nice to be wanted . . . One of league's most sought-after commodities . . . Best backup point guard in East. Maybe the whole league . . . He wants to start. And a lot of teams want him starting for them . . . Had an awful start to his third season as he was floored by mononucleosis and missed first nine games. Took a long time for strength to return . . . Got better as season progressed. Tied career-high 22 points April 12 vs. Bucks . . . Very, very quick. Pushes the ball up, sees the court. Can break down a defense with penetration . . . Led Cavs in assists 14 times . . . Cavs chalk .420 shooting up to the mono thing. Shot .478 his second season . . . Eleventh pick in '92 draft out of Oregon . . . Became restricted free agent after season . . . Born May 20, 1970, in Portland, Ore. . . . Made $840,000.

Year	Team	G	FG	FG Pct.	FT	FT Pct.	Reb.	Ast.	TP	Avg.
1991-92	Cleveland	82	252	.419	100	.806	162	316	605	7.4
1992-93	Cleveland	82	297	.478	118	.825	179	302	725	8.8
1993-94	Cleveland	73	230	.420	139	.858	159	277	606	8.3
	Totals	237	779	.440	357	.832	500	895	1936	8.2

LARRY NANCE 35 6-10 235   Forward

You want to talk about terrible timing? Perennially underrated guy suffered through wide assortment of knee injuries in his contract year ... Probably waits until the "To be or not to be" soliloquy in Hamlet to tell a knock-knock joke ... Played just 33 games. Fewest in brilliant 13-year career ... On injured list three different times. Two arthroscopic surgeries on right knee ... Also strained a tendon in left foot ... After first 'scope, came back too soon and problems snowballed ... Missed last 20 games ... Oldest starting forward in league ... Other than knee, keeps himself in great shape ... NBA's eighth and Cavs' No. 1 all-time shot-blocker (2,027). 2,000th block at Detroit Jan. 31 ... Good jumper, strong moves to the basket ... Long, gangly arms. Perfect for rebounding and shot-blocking ... Stock-car enthusiast ... Born Feb. 29, 1959, in Anderson, S.C. ... Suns picked him No. 20 in '81 out of Clemson ... Sent to Cavs Feb. 25, 1988. Cavs got Nance, Mike Sanders, first-rounder for Kevin Johnson, Mark West, Ty Corbin, a first and two seconds ... Made $2.84 million.

Year	Team	G	FG	FG Pct.	FT	FT Pct.	Reb.	Ast.	TP	Avg.
1981-82	Phoenix	80	227	.521	75	.641	256	82	529	6.6
1982-83	Phoenix	82	588	.550	193	.672	710	197	1370	16.7
1983-84	Phoenix	82	601	.576	249	.707	678	214	1451	17.7
1984-85	Phoenix	61	515	.587	180	.709	536	159	1211	19.9
1985-86	Phoenix	73	582	.581	310	.698	618	240	1474	20.2
1986-87	Phoenix	69	585	.551	381	.773	599	233	1552	22.5
1987-88	Phoe.-Clev.	67	487	.529	304	.779	607	207	1280	19.1
1988-89	Cleveland	73	496	.539	267	.799	581	159	1259	17.2
1989-90	Cleveland	62	412	.511	186	.778	516	161	1011	16.3
1990-91	Cleveland	80	635	.524	265	.803	686	237	1537	19.2
1991-92	Cleveland	81	556	.539	263	.822	670	232	1375	17.0
1992-93	Cleveland	77	533	.549	202	.818	668	223	1268	16.5
1993-94	Cleveland	33	153	.487	64	.753	227	49	370	11.2
	Totals	920	6370	.546	2939	.755	7352	2393	15687	17.1

JOHN WILLIAMS 32 6-11 245   Forward-Center

Anybody want to play center? Raise your hand. Er, not the broken one, Hot Rod ... Had a real productive year. Then broke hand and missed all of playoffs ... Cavs' all-time offensive rebound leader. Has led the team in that category in six of his eight seasons since leaving Tulane in '85 ... Cleared of collegiate point-shaving allegations ... Cavs gambled and scooped him up at No. 45 on second round in '85 . . . Made $4.57 million, part of the $26.5-mil, seven-year free-agent offer sheet from Heat that Cavs matched June 16, 1986 . . . Scored season-high 23 points four times . . . Started last 29 games at center. Averaged 16.8 points, 8.4 rebounds in those games . . . Led Cavs in rebounds and blocked shots . . . Seven of his eight years with 100-plus blocks . . . Tied career-high with 18 boards vs. Dallas April 2 . . . Born Aug. 9, 1962, in Sorrento, La.

Year	Team	G	FG	FG Pct.	FT	FT Pct.	Reb.	Ast.	TP	Avg.
1986-87	Cleveland	80	435	.485	298	.745	629	154	1168	14.6
1987-88	Cleveland	77	316	.477	211	.756	506	103	843	10.9
1988-89	Cleveland	82	356	.509	235	.748	477	108	948	11.6
1989-90	Cleveland	82	528	.493	325	.739	663	168	1381	16.8
1990-91	Cleveland	43	199	.463	107	.652	290	100	505	11.7
1991-92	Cleveland	80	341	.503	270	.752	607	196	952	11.9
1992-93	Cleveland	67	263	.470	212	.716	415	152	738	11.0
1993-94	Cleveland	76	394	.478	252	.728	575	193	1040	13.7
	Totals	587	2832	.486	1910	.735	4162	1174	7575	12.9

TYRONE HILL 26 6-9 245   Forward

Nice guy. Until he takes the court. Then he turns into Attila the Hun . . . But it was something the Cavs needed for eons. For years, they were so genteel on the court . . . So he brought a real nastiness . . . Led Cavs in rebounds per minute (16.6 per 48 minutes), second only to Dennis Rodman among all NBA forwards . . . Averaged 8.8 boards . . . In keeping with team policy, suffered assorted ails: left thumb (twice), right knee. Missed 25 games . . . In 19 starts, averaged 16.1 points, 10.2 rebounds . . . Career-high 25 points vs. Clips March 29 . . . Shooting disintegrated in playoffs (.407 after .543 regular season), but he got 10.3 rebounds per . . . Good post game . . . Cavs gave up their 1994 first-rounder to Warriors to get him July 15, 1993 . . . Could have used three more just like him . . . Warriors picked him No. 11, out of Xavier, in 1990 . . . Made $1.075 million . . . Born March 17, 1968, in Cincinnati.

Year	Team	G	FG	FG Pct.	FT	FT Pct.	Reb.	Ast.	TP	Avg.
1990-91	Golden State	74	147	.492	96	.632	383	19	390	5.3
1991-92	Golden State	82	254	.522	163	.694	593	47	671	8.2
1992-93	Golden State	74	251	.508	138	.624	754	68	640	8.6
1993-94	Cleveland	57	216	.543	171	.668	499	46	603	10.6
	Totals	287	868	.517	568	.657	2229	180	2304	8.0

GERALD WILKINS 31 6-6 210 Guard-Forward

Might have had his best overall season . . . Was only Cav to play all 82 games . . . Team season-high 38 points at Orlando Jan. 12 . . . Hit six three-pointers in that game, tying Cavs' all-time mark . . . Leading Cav playoff scorer . . . Hired a "shot doctor" before season . . . Had career-best .395 on treys . . . But one of league's truly good guys can still be as erratic as the tides . . . No one ever questioned his explosiveness, however . . . Can break down a defense with super-quick step and nuclear leaping ability . . . A good, active defender who never got the credit he deserved on that end . . . Very tough one-on-one . . . Plays three when the need is for speed . . . Led team with 105 steals . . . Passed 10,000 points. Ironically, against his former Knick team, in New York March 12 . . . Dominique's his brother . . . Was second-round find by Knicks (No. 47 overall) in 1985 out of Tennessee-Chattanooga . . . Cavs got him as a free agent Oct. 8, 1992, for a $500,000 free-agent steal when Knicks renounced him after seven years . . . Cavs re-did him and he made $2.278 million last season . . . Born Sept. 11, 1963, in Atlanta.

Year	Team	G	FG	FG Pct.	FT	FT Pct.	Reb.	Ast.	TP	Avg.
1985-86	New York	81	437	.468	132	.557	208	161	1013	12.5
1986-87	New York	80	633	.486	235	.701	294	354	1527	19.1
1987-88	New York	81	591	.446	191	.786	270	326	1412	17.4
1988-89	New York	81	462	.451	186	.756	244	274	1161	14.3
1989-90	New York	82	472	.457	208	.803	371	330	1191	14.5
1990-91	New York	68	380	.473	169	.820	207	275	938	13.8
1991-92	New York	82	431	.447	116	.730	206	219	1016	12.4
1992-93	Cleveland	80	361	.453	152	.840	214	183	890	11.1
1993-94	Cleveland	82	446	.457	194	.776	303	255	1170	14.3
	Totals	717	4213	.460	1583	.748	2317	2377	10318	14.4

DANNY FERRY 28 6-10 236 Forward

It is beyond the joke stage . . . Object of the single worst trade in Cav history. And there had been some real duds . . . Got him and Reggie Williams for Ron Harper, two first-round picks and second-rounder . . . Gave him astronomical contract. Have gotten nothing . . . Contract makes him untradeable. Almost as much as his game . . . Confidence is shot. Coaching confidence in him is beyond that . . . Even with Nance, Daugherty and Williams hurt, he couldn't get playoff time. Played four minutes. Got lit up by Toni Kukoc for nine points. Nailed to the bench after that . . . Cavs cringe over six remaining years for $33.2 million . . . Can't create a shot. Can't defend. Can't handle the ball. Can't rebound . . . Can hum a mean "Star Spangled Banner" . . . Too slow for three, too weak for four . . . So he sits and wallows . . . Plays well against the Knicks for some reason: tied career high with 21 points against them Nov. 7 . . . Son of former pro and Bullet GM Bob Ferry . . . No. 2 pick of Clips in '89 after All-American, Naismith Award career at Duke . . . Wouldn't go to L.A., did a year in Italy . . . Born Oct. 17, 1966, in Hyattsville, Md. . . . Made $3.543 million for 965 minutes.

Year	Team	G	FG	FG Pct.	FT	FT Pct.	Reb.	Ast.	TP	Avg.
1990-91	Cleveland	81	275	.428	124	.816	286	142	697	8.6
1991-92	Cleveland	68	134	.409	61	.836	213	75	346	5.1
1992-93	Cleveland	76	220	.479	99	.876	279	137	573	7.5
1993-94	Cleveland	70	149	.446	38	.884	141	74	350	5.0
	Totals	295	778	.441	322	.845	919	428	1966	6.7

CHRIS MILLS 24 6-6 216   Forward

Folks got suspicious when he lasted until No. 22 in '93 draft . . . Nothing wrong. Some teams just goofed apparently . . . Came in with a shooter's rep but proved to be more effective inside . . . Utterly fearless type . . . But at 6-6, needs to improve outside shot, which is just decent . . . Stepped up in playoffs; was Cavs' second-best scorer (17.0) after 9.4 regular season . . . Spot starter. But then, who wasn't with all the Cav injuries? . . . Double-figure points in 39 games . . . Good, solid defender. And strong, smart passer . . . Cavs would like a little more rebounding, but he gave them 5.1 per, with a high of 14 . . . Made $850,000 . . . Pac-10 Player of the Year at Arizona as a senior. Played frosh year at Kentucky . . . Born Jan. 25, 1970, in Los Angeles.

Year	Team	G	FG	FG Pct.	FT	FT Pct.	Reb.	Ast.	TP	Avg.
1993-94	Cleveland	79	284	.419	137	.778	401	128	743	9.4

BOBBY PHILLS 24 6-5 217   Guard

Took up bench space for two years. Got a chance last year and showed some skills . . . Runs floor on the break, provides a feisty brand of defense and can shoot with some range (.471) . . . We're not talking Scottie Pippen here, but he was a nice surprise after collecting dust since signing as a free agent with Cavs in March 1992 out of the CBA . . . Was drafted on the second round by Bucks out of Southern U. in 1991 . . . He's Bobby Phills II. Bobby Phills I is Dr. Phills, his dad, the Dean of Agriculture and Home Economics at Southern in Baton Rouge, La. . . . Born in Baton Rouge, Dec. 20, 1969 . . . Made $312,000 . . . Has degree in pre-veterinary medicine.

Year	Team	G	FG	FG Pct.	FT	FT Pct.	Reb.	Ast.	TP	Avg.
1991-92	Cleveland	10	12	.429	7	.636	8	4	31	3.1
1992-93	Cleveland	31	38	.463	15	.600	17	10	93	3.0
1993-94	Cleveland	72	242	.471	113	.720	212	133	598	8.3
	Totals	113	292	.468	135	.699	237	147	722	6.4

GERALD MADKINS 25 6-4 200   Guard

Wasn't exactly what the Cavs expected . . . Of course, they didn't expect him to fracture his hand in the second game and sit the next 46 . . . Signed as free-agent point guard June 14, 1993, after selection as CBA Rookie of the Year . . . But Cavs soon ran into the age-old question: is he a one or a two? . . . Had trouble getting the team into the offense. Bad sign for a one. Had trouble with his range and his shot (.355). Bad sign for a two . . . Hard to assess because of injury, though . . . Undrafted out of UCLA in 1992 . . . Born April 18, 1969, in Merced, Cal. . . . Made $475,000.

Year	Team	G	FG	FG Pct.	FT	FT Pct.	Reb.	Ast.	TP	Avg.
1993-94	Cleveland	22	11	.355	8	.800	11	19	35	1.6

MICHAEL CAGE 32 6-9 240   Forward-Center

Sonics' unrestricted free agent signed with Cavs in August . . . His minutes continued to disappear but his impact did not . . . Is second on SuperSonics' all-time rebounding list . . . Offensive boards a specialty . . . Got 30 rebounds on the final night of 1987-88 season to edge Charles Oakley for NBA crown . . . Has played in 411 straight regular-season games, the fourth-best streak in the league among active players . . . In six years since Seattle got him from Clippers as part of a three-team draft day deal that also included Hersey Hawkins and Charles

Smith, he has missed just two games ... Left San Diego State in 1984 as school's all-time leader in scoring, rebounding and games played, before L.A. Clippers took him with the 14th pick ... Born Jan. 28, 1962, in West Memphis, Ark.... Made $1.502 million.

Year	Team	G	FG	FG Pct.	FT	FT Pct.	Reb.	Ast.	TP	Avg.
1984-85	L.A. Clippers	75	216	.543	101	.737	392	51	533	7.1
1985-86	L.A. Clippers	78	204	.479	113	.649	417	81	521	6.7
1986-87	L.A. Clippers	80	457	.521	341	.730	922	131	1255	15.7
1987-88	L.A. Clippers	72	360	.470	326	.688	938	110	1046	14.5
1988-89	Seattle	80	314	.498	197	.743	765	126	825	10.3
1989-90	Seattle	82	325	.504	148	.698	821	70	798	9.7
1990-91	Seattle	82	226	.508	70	.625	558	89	522	6.4
1991-92	Seattle	82	307	.566	106	.620	728	92	720	8.8
1992-93	Seattle	82	219	.526	61	.469	659	69	499	6.1
1993-94	Seattle	82	171	.545	36	.486	444	45	378	4.6
	Totals	795	2799	.513	1499	.676	6644	864	7097	8.9

JOHN BATTLE 31 6-2 190   Guard

You have the dodo bird, Tyrannosaurus Rex. And 6-2 shooting guards ... Spot player who's very limited in time and contributions ... Can't handle the ball well enough to play point ... At his size, has trouble creating shots ... Had a few decent games. Like tying his career-high 22 points twice. And setting new personal best with 14 assists vs. Utah Dec. 21 ... Around only because of contract. Signed six-year unrestricted free agent pact in July 1991. But even then, off-guards weren't so big ... Did six seasons with Hawks, who took him on fourth round in '85 out of Rutgers ... Born Nov. 9, 1962, in Washington, D.C. ... Made $1.12 million.

Year	Team	G	FG	FG Pct.	FT	FT Pct.	Reb.	Ast.	TP	Avg.
1985-86	Atlanta	64	101	.455	75	.728	62	74	277	4.3
1986-87	Atlanta	64	144	.457	93	.738	60	124	381	6.0
1987-88	Atlanta	67	278	.454	141	.750	113	158	713	10.6
1988-89	Atlanta	82	287	.457	194	.815	140	197	779	9.5
1989-90	Atlanta	60	275	.506	102	.756	99	154	654	10.9
1990-91	Atlanta	79	397	.461	270	.854	159	217	1078	13.6
1991-92	Cleveland	76	316	.480	145	.848	112	159	779	10.3
1992-93	Cleveland	41	83	.415	56	.778	29	54	223	5.4
1993-94	Cleveland	51	130	.476	73	.753	39	83	338	6.6
	Totals	584	2011	.466	1149	.795	813	1220	5222	8.9

Mark Price again led Cavs in scoring, was third-team NBA.

ROD HIGGINS 34 6-7 217   **Forward**

Never throw out the sneakers . . . Thought his career was over after 11 seasons when he was released by Suns in preseason . . . Cavs called. So he signed on as pro-rated minimum-wage free agent Dec. 23, 1993 . . . First player ever in NBA to play with four teams in same season: 1985-86, Sonics, Spurs, Nets and Bulls . . . Spent three years with Bulls prior, did six fairly productive years in Golden State after his pinball year . . . Played 69 games with Kings in 1992-93 . . . Had a CBA tour thrown in . . . Started 11 games for Cavs. Didn't hurt . . . Still has something of a shot . . . Born Jan. 31, 1960, in Monroe, La. . . . Second-rounder to Bulls out of Fresno State in 1982.

Year	Team	G	FG	FG Pct.	FT	FT Pct.	Reb.	Ast.	TP	Avg.
1982-83	Chicago	82	313	.448	209	.792	366	175	848	10.3
1983-84	Chicago	78	193	.447	113	.724	206	116	500	6.4
1984-85	Chicago	68	119	.441	60	.667	147	73	308	4.5
1985-86	Sea.-S.A.-N.J.-Chi	30	39	.368	19	.704	51	24	98	3.3
1986-87	Golden State	73	214	.519	200	.833	237	96	631	8.6
1987-88	Golden State	68	381	.526	273	.848	293	188	1054	15.5
1988-89	Golden State	81	301	.476	188	.821	376	160	856	10.6
1989-90	Golden State	82	304	.481	234	.821	422	129	909	11.1
1990-91	Golden State	82	259	.463	185	.819	354	113	776	9.5
1991-92	Golden State	25	87	.412	48	.814	85	22	255	10.2
1992-93	Sacramento	69	199	.412	130	.861	193	119	571	8.3
1993-94	Cleveland	36	71	.436	31	.738	82	36	195	5.4
	Totals	774	2480	.466	1690	.808	2812	1251	7001	9.0

THE ROOKIE

GARY COLLIER 23 6-4 195 **Guard**
Played some forward in college, but strictly off-guard for pros . . .
Four-year .509 shooter at Tulsa . . . Was 42nd player selected . . .
First player in Tulsa history with 1,500 points and 500 rebounds
. . . Work ethic is a major plus . . . Missouri Valley Conference
Player of the Year . . . Led Tulsa to Sweet 16 . . . Born Oct. 8,
1971, in Fort Worth, Tex.

COACH MIKE FRATELLO: Too bad the Tele-strator could

not suit up . . . Magnificent coaching job with
a team decimated by injuries . . . In his first year
back in the business from three-year NBC-TV
color job, he may have done the NBA's best
coaching job no one seemed to notice . . . His
47 victories made him Cavs' winningest first-
year coach . . . 371-285 (.566) for eight head-
coaching seasons, seven in Atlanta . . . Seemed
to back off a bit from his ultra-intense mode and everyone benefitted . . . Explosions at players few and far between . . . Super job
keeping team morale high. Team played hard every night . . . Always was and remains good defensive strategist. Cavs had best
defensive season in their history, allowing 97.1 ppg . . . Sound X-
and-O guy . . . Seven years with Hawks produced four 50-victory
seasons, 324-250 (.564) record . . . 1986-87 NBA Coach of the
Year . . . Did assistant tours under Hubie Brown with Knicks and
Hawks, plus under Kevin Loughery with Hawks . . . College assistant at James Madison, Rhode Island, Villanova . . . Montclair

State (N.J.) College grad . . . Born Feb. 24, 1947, in Hackensack, N.J. . . . Named Cavs' coach June 17, 1993.

GREATEST PLAYER

There were so many down times in Cleveland in the franchise's early years that some great players, such as Austin Carr, were often overlooked. And there were so many injuries in recent seasons that landmark moves—such as Brad Daugherty becoming the team's all-time scoring and rebounding leader—were often overlooked. But in those recent years, one guy could never be overlooked, in good times and bad, as the Greatest Player in Franchise history, point guard Mark Price.

Sure, Daugherty has a strong case. No. 1 in points, No. 1 in rebounding. But Daugherty never has been considered No. 1 at his position in the league, or the conference for that matter, even for one year. Price has.

His shooting is legendary; witness his three-point accuracy in those All-Star Weekend shootout competitions. He's the greatest free-throw shooter in NBA history (.906 in eight years). And on a team level, he's the all-time assist king (3,871), second in steals (699, will become No. 1 this season barring trade or injury) and the best three-point shooter.

ALL-TIME CAVALIER LEADERS

SEASON

Points: Mike Mitchell, 2,012, 1980-81
Assists: John Bagley, 735, 1985-86
Rebounds: Jim Brewer, 891, 1975-76

GAME

Points: Walt Wesley, 50 vs. Cincinnati, 2/19/71
Assists: Geoff Huston, 27 vs. Golden State, 1/27/82
Rebounds: Rick Roberson, 25 vs. Houston, 3/4/72

CAREER

Points: Brad Daugherty, 10,389, 1986-94
Assists: Mark Price, 3,871, 1986-94
Rebounds: Brad Daugherty, 5,227, 1986-94

DETROIT PISTONS

TEAM DIRECTORY: Managing Partner: Bill Davidson; Pres.: Tom Wilson; Dir Player Personnel: Billy McKinney; Dir. Scouting: John Hammord; Dir. Pub. Rel.: Matt Dobek; Coach: Don Chaney; Asst. Coaches: Brendan Malone, Walt Perrin. Arena: The Palace, Auburn Hills (21,454). Colors: Red, white and blue.

Joe Dumars remains the one Piston constant.

SCOUTING REPORT

SHOOTING: They could be average. Maybe even above average. And that's reason to rejoice in Detroit this season. Mediocrity in virtually anything would represent a huge step forward.

Only two teams (Dallas and Minnesota) scored less than Don Chaney's Pistons last season, so their dead-end ranking in the East didn't come from all those fabulous nothing-but-net jumpers or those dashing drives to the hole with great finishes. The Pistons could provide a decent perimeter game with Joe Dumars, Allan Houston and Terry Mills, the center-turned-jump shooter. After that, it's been pretty much pray to hit the farm, let alone the barn.

But now they've added a proven center, Mark West, from the Suns. He shot .566 last year.

PLAYMAKING: The lord of Detroit playmaking, Isiah Thomas, is gone. Lindsey Hunter now has the job. If only he had Isiah's instincts. Or even half of Isiah's instincts.

The Pistons are betting he does. There was a late-season stretch last season where Hunter displayed sound judgment and sounder passes. Of course, when he plays alongside Dumars all should be well. But the Pistons are trying to rebuild and pull themselves out of a hole that reaches halfway to the Orient. So Houston has to get time.

It's not like the Pistons can pull out last season's videotape to see how it's done. Detroit, as was the case in many stat categories, ranked dead last in the East in assists. Grant Hill (the 6-8 prize from Duke, third overall in the draft), who figures to swing, could provide relief. He's smart. He's polished. But he is a rookie.

REBOUNDING: West, with ex-76er Eric Leckner as backup, should help somewhat in improving last year's 24th ranking in league rebounding. (That was with Olden Polynice for half a season.) First-rounder Bill Curley of Boston College and second-rounder Jevon Crudup of Missouri could add board strength as well.

DEFENSE: Remember the "Bad Boys?" That's about all Pistons fans will have this season on defense: memories.

Mark Macon is a superlative defensive guard. But he is so incredibly dismal offensively, minutes are hard to come by. Dumars, of course, always has been in a class virtually by himself, but he can't stop the opposing frontlines. And neither can anybody in Detroit. With Hunter and Dumars, there'll be adequate ball-

PISTON ROSTER

No. Veterans	Pos.	Ht.	Wt.	Age	Yrs. Pro	College
33 Greg Anderson	F-C	6-10	230	30	7	Houston
34 Pete Chilcutt	F-C	6-10	232	26	3	North Carolina
4 Joe Dumars	G	6-3	195	31	9	McNeese State
20 Allan Houston	G	6-6	200	23	1	Tennessee
1 Lindsey Hunter	G	6-2	170	24	1	Jackson State
23 Charles Jones	C-F	6-9	235	37	11	Albany State
– Eric Leckner	C-F	6-11	265	28	5	Wyoming
30 Marcus Liberty	F	6-8	205	26	4	Illinois
2 Mark Macon	G	6-5	185	25	3	Temple
6 Terry Mills	F	6-10	250	27	4	Michigan
– Mark West	C	6-10	246	33	11	Old Dominion
12 David Wood	F	6-9	230	29	4	Nevada-Reno

Rd. Rookies	Sel. No.	Pos.	Ht.	Wt.	College
1 Grant Hill	3	G-F	6-8	225	Duke
1 Bill Curley	22	F	6-9	220	Boston College
2 Jevon Crudup	48	F	6-8	222	Missouri

pressure at times. But the Pistons ranked 25th in turnovers forced, easily the worst in the East.

And there was one more telling stat: nine Pistons fouled out all year. Nine. Now, either they play the smartest defense on earth. Or the laziest, most non-aggressive. You decide.

On the plus side, the addition of West gives the Pistons a veteran shot-blocker who got more swats last season than full-time starting centers like Robert Parish, Benoit Benjamin, Rik Smits and Felton Spencer.

OUTLOOK: If you REALLY like what looms for the Pistons, you're a masochist. Or sadist.

It will be Dumars' team now, with Thomas assembling a franchise unit up in Toronto. But Dumars has only a shell of what was a two-time championship group. And his overall health is in question, as the consummate team player has begun showing signs of meltdown and breakdown. Somehow, Dumars, with support from West, will find a way to keep the Pistons semi-competitive, but if he breaks down, you're looking at Dallas-East.

PISTON PROFILES

JOE DUMARS 31 6-3 195   Guard

Consummate team player. Too bad he was on consummate bad team . . . All the minutes are starting to take effect. May be breaking down. His 69 games were lowest in five years and tied career low . . . Troubles with knee, hamstring, rotten teammates . . . When healthy, he's lethal scorer (20.4, 13th in league), excellent defender . . . Started very slowly but finished strong, despite bad atmosphere around team . . . If he stays healthy, he could have strong resurgence with Isiah Thomas now among brass in Toronto. Pistons will be his team—unless youth movement pushes him out the door . . . Dream Team II member . . . MVP of 1989 Finals . . . Born May 5, 1963, in Natchitoches, La. . . . One of biggest draft steals in recent memory: No. 18 pick in '85, out of McNeese State . . . Made $1.28 million.

Year	Team	G	FG	FG Pct.	FT	FT Pct.	Reb.	Ast.	TP	Avg.
1985-86	Detroit	82	287	.481	190	.798	119	390	769	9.4
1986-87	Detroit	79	369	.493	184	.748	167	352	931	11.8
1987-88	Detroit	82	453	.472	251	.815	200	387	1161	14.2
1988-89	Detroit	69	456	.505	260	.850	172	390	1186	17.2
1989-90	Detroit	75	508	.480	297	.900	212	368	1335	17.8
1990-91	Detroit	80	622	.481	371	.890	187	443	1629	20.4
1991-92	Detroit	82	587	.448	412	.867	188	375	1635	19.9
1992-93	Detroit	77	677	.466	343	.864	148	308	1809	23.5
1993-94	Detroit	69	505	.452	276	.836	151	261	1410	20.4
	Totals	695	4464	.473	2584	.848	1544	3274	11865	17.1

LINDSEY HUNTER 24 6-2 170   Guard

You don't mind a point guard shooting—unless he shoots .375, as this guy did as a rookie. And he's not, shall we say, a drive-and-dish guy . . . Drive and shoot. Or shoot and forget the drive . . . But after Piston brass pulled hair from scalps most of the year, he came up with strong end-of-season streak in which he led Pistons to six wins in eight games . . . Whatta choice at No. 10, out of Jackson State . . . He showed he can distribute, can find the wings. May have halted brass from conducting new point-guard search . . . Could use a real player in the middle to work off . . . No complaints on his defense. And he loves playing it . . .

SWAC Player of the Year as senior ... Born Oct. 3, 1970, in
Utica, Miss.... Made $902,000.

Year	Team	G	FG	FG Pct.	FT	FT Pct.	Reb.	Ast.	TP	Avg.
1993-94	Detroit	82	335	.375	104	.732	189	390	843	10.3

TERRY MILLS 27 6-10 250   Forward

Keep him away from the Dunkin' Donuts Diet
and you have something ... Down to 250
pounds after reporting at 262. He was a rather
unsightly 284 the previous year ... Emerged as
a team leader. Now as long as he doesn't lead
himself to the fridge between meals, he'll help
... A Patrick Ewing wannabe, although he
does have three-point range (24-of-73) ... Sec-
ond in league (to Shawn Kemp) in fouls committed ... So it's not
that great, but Pistons wanted someone near the top in *something*
... Fair, at best, post-up game. Probably because he doesn't use
it enough ... Signed away from Nets as a restricted free agent,
Sept. 30, 1992 ... Second leg of five-year, $9.5-million deal that
paid $1.617 million last season ... Born Dec. 21, 1967, in Detroit
... Bucks took him 16th out of Michigan in 1990 ... Held out,
pigged out and was sent out to Denver for Danny Schayes (Aug.
1, 1990), then sent to Nets Jan. 23, 1991.

Year	Team	G	FG	FG Pct.	FT	FT Pct.	Reb.	Ast.	TP	Avg.
1990-91	Den.-N.J.	55	134	.465	47	.712	229	33	315	5.7
1991-92	New Jersey	82	310	.463	114	.750	453	84	742	9.0
1992-93	Detroit	81	494	.461	201	.791	472	111	1199	14.8
1993-94	Detroit	80	588	.511	181	.797	672	177	1381	17.3
	Totals	298	1526	.480	543	.777	1826	405	3637	12.2

ALLAN HOUSTON 23 6-6 200   Guard

He can shoot. Thankfully, because watching
him play defense, the first reaction is he should
be shot ... But most rookies are bad defenders
... And don't judge the shooting on his .405
debut. He just needs to recognize what's a good
shot ... Tremendous range, almost Reggie
Miller-like ... Can get his shot off, too, so Pistons are encouraged. Except when they think
of the shots he got off ... It's called needing experience ... Good

finisher, though... Needs to bulk up, which was his offseason project... Played for his dad, Wade, at Tennessee. So maybe some of his shots were excused... Born April 4, 1971, in Louisville... Left Vols with 2,801 points. Only Pete Maravich scored more in SEC... No. 11 pick in 1993... Made $735,000.

Year	Team	G	FG	FG Pct.	FT	FT Pct.	Reb.	Ast.	TP	Avg.
1993-94	Detroit	79	272	.405	89	.824	120	100	668	8.5

GREG (CADILLAC) ANDERSON 30 6-10 230 · F-C

Awful early. Looked like National Pasta Poster Child after doing a year in Italy... Rebounding, and overall game, picked up after departure of Olden Polynice... Well-traveled. And not just overseas... Started career with Spurs as No. 23 pick out of Houston in 1987 (he majored in ''Recreation'')... Did time in Milwaukee, New Jersey, Denver and Detroit before sunny Italy... Pistons got him back as an unrestricted free agent on Oct. 8, 1993... Whole game is inside... Range of a yardstick... Defense is adequate, and he does block some shots (68 in 77 games)... Born June 22, 1964, in Houston... Made $650,000 ... Really, a bargain... Brother, Mike, was a Grambling QB.

Year	Team	G	FG	FG Pct.	FT	FT Pct.	Reb.	Ast.	TP	Avg.
1987-88	San Antonio	82	379	.501	198	.604	513	79	957	11.7
1988-89	San Antonio	82	460	.503	207	.514	676	61	1127	13.7
1989-90	Milwaukee	60	219	.507	91	.535	373	24	529	8.8
1990-91	Mil.-N.J.-Den.	68	116	.430	60	.522	318	16	292	4.3
1991-92	Denver	82	389	.456	167	.623	941	78	945	11.5
1993-94	Detroit	77	201	.543	88	.571	571	51	491	6.4
	Totals	451	1764	.491	811	.564	3392	309	4341	9.6

MARK WEST 33 6-10 246 Center

Traded by Suns to Pistons in August for second-round draft picks in 1996 and 1999... Low profile, but was one of the most dependable Suns in his consistency... No. 1 among all active players in career shooting (.592) because he knows his range and never tries to be an offensive star... Trails only Artis Gilmore (.599) on the all-time list... Played every game for the sixth straight season, running his ironman streak to

501 in a row, second only to A.C. Green for current players . . . Suns got him from Cleveland in the 1988 deal that also included Kevin Johnson in exchange for Larry Nance and Mike Sanders . . . Born Nov. 5, 1960, in Ft. Campbell, Ky . . . .Made $1 million.

Year	Team	G	FG	FG Pct.	FT	FT Pct.	Reb.	Ast.	TP	Avg.
1983-84	Dallas	34	15	.357	7	.318	46	13	37	1.1
1984-85	Mil.-Clev.	66	106	.546	43	.494	251	15	255	3.9
1985-86	Cleveland	67	113	.541	54	.524	322	20	280	4.2
1986-87	Cleveland	78	209	.543	89	.514	339	41	507	6.5
1987-88	Clev.-Phoe.	83	316	.551	170	.596	523	74	802	9.7
1988-89	Phoenix	82	243	.653	108	.535	551	39	594	7.2
1989-90	Phoenix	82	331	.625	199	.691	728	45	861	10.5
1990-91	Phoenix	82	247	.647	135	.655	564	37	629	7.7
1991-92	Phoenix	82	196	.632	109	.637	372	22	501	6.1
1992-93	Phoenix	82	175	.614	86	.518	458	29	436	5.3
1993-94	Phoenix	82	162	.566	58	.500	295	33	382	4.7
	Totals	820	2113	.592	1058	.582	4449	368	5284	6.4

MARK MACON 25 6-5 185 Guard

What will come first, a new species of mammal, the discovery of a new solar system or this guy's next made shot? . . . Bet on the mammal . . . Cannot shoot and has no clue what a good shot is. Otherwise, he's offensively potent . . . Now on the defensive end: Eureka! . . . He must become the reincarnation of T.R. Dunn . . . Super guy, so you kind of pull for him to make it with one-dimensional game. But it's the dimension coaches usually beg for . . . Got little time after he came with Marcus Liberty in trade-deadline deal that landed a hurting Alvin Robertson in Denver . . . Made $1.498 million (ouch) . . . No. 8 in 1991 draft, out of Temple . . . All-Atlantic-10 four straight years. Must be a defensive league . . . Born April 14, 1969, in Saginaw, Mich.

Year	Team	G	FG	FG Pct.	FT	FT Pct.	Reb.	Ast.	TP	Avg.
1991-92	Denver	76	333	.375	135	.730	220	168	805	10.6
1992-93	Denver	48	158	.415	42	.700	103	126	358	7.5
1993-94	Den.-Det.	42	69	.375	23	.676	41	51	163	3.9
	Totals	166	560	.385	200	.717	364	345	1326	8.0

DAVID WOOD 29 6-9 230   Forward

Poor man's Bill Laimbeer, except in the Hated-by-Foes Dept. . . . Then he's an equal for chippy play . . . How can anybody get Rolando Blackman to take a swing at him? This guy did . . . Is, however, extraordinarily devout off court . . . Tweener. Too slow for small forward, too small to muscle bigger power forwards . . . Has nice range and can hit an occasional three . . . Serviceable bench player . . . Gets a lot through hustle and diving after loose balls . . . Arrived with Sean Elliott in the pre-season Dennis Rodman trade . . . Undrafted out of Nevada after two years at collegiate power Skagit Valley (Wash.) . . . Cup of coffee (no time for cream or sugar) with Bulls in 1988-89 . . . Played all 82 games with Rockets in '90-91. Traded to Spurs for 1995 second-rounder . . . Born Nov. 30, 1964, in Spokane, Wash. . . . Made $488,000.

Year	Team	G	FG	FG Pct.	FT	FT Pct.	Reb.	Ast.	TP	Avg.
1988-89	Chicago	2	0	.000	0	.000	0	0	0	0.0
1990-91	Houston	82	148	.424	108	.812	246	94	432	5.3
1992-93	San Antonio	64	52	.444	46	.836	97	34	155	2.4
1993-94	Detroit	78	119	.459	62	.756	239	51	322	4.1
	Totals	226	319	.440	216	.800	582	179	909	4.0

CHARLES JONES 37 6-9 235   Center-Forward

Yep, THE Charles Jones. Betcha thought he retired a decade ago . . . But he actually helped, and Pistons wanted him back . . . Blew out right anterior cruciate ligament April 1, 1993. Bullets didn't ask him back but he made remarkable comeback . . . Signed as Piston free agent during season and played in 42 games . . . Great team guy. Still a quality shot-blocker who gives everything against monsters. Gets pushed around, comes back for more . . . The last of the four pro Jones brothers (Caldwell, Major and Wil) . . . Always a defensive player first. A field-goal game is a good game . . . Despite signing more free-agent contracts than any GM, he had only played with Sixers, Bulls and Bullets since Suns drafted him out of Albany (Ga.) State on eighth round in

1979 . . . Four CBA seasons . . . Born April 3, 1957, in McGehee, Ark.

Year	Team	G	FG	FG Pct.	FT	FT Pct.	Reb.	Ast.	TP	Avg.
1983-84	Philadelphia	1	0	.000	1	.250	0	0	1	1.0
1984-85	Chi.-Wash.	31	67	.528	40	.690	184	26	174	5.6
1985-86	Washington	81	129	.508	54	.628	321	76	312	3.9
1986-87	Washington	79	118	.474	48	.632	356	80	284	3.6
1987-88	Washington	69	72	.407	53	.707	325	59	197	2.9
1988-89	Washington	53	60	.480	16	.640	257	42	136	2.6
1989-90	Washington	81	94	.508	68	.648	504	139	256	3.2
1990-91	Washington	62	67	.540	29	.580	359	48	163	2.6
1991-92	Washington	75	33	.367	20	.500	317	62	86	1.1
1992-93	Washington	67	33	.524	22	.579	277	42	88	1.3
1993-94	Detroit	42	36	.462	19	.559	235	29	91	2.2
	Totals	641	709	.481	370	.626	3135	603	1788	2.8

ERIC LECKNER 28 6-11 265   Center-Forward

Summer acquisition from 76ers for second-round draft pick in 1996 or 1997 . . . Born to be a backup . . . Big and strong type with nice work ethic . . . Sixers also played him a little at four . . . Got 31 starts after Shawn Bradley went down. Averaged 6.1 points, 5.2 rebounds as a starter . . . Career-high 17 rebounds vs. Minnesota March 15 . . . Signed for $300,000 as free agent in preseason after spending one year in Italy . . . First round, No. 17, pick of Jazz in 1988, out of Wyoming . . . WAC Tourney MVP three straight years . . . Traded by Jazz with Bobby Hansen to Kings in three-team deal that involved Washington and Sixer Jeff Malone (who went to Utah) June 25, 1990 . . . Sent by Kings to Charlotte Jan. 29, 1991, for '95 second-rounder . . . To Italy after Hornets didn't re-sign him . . . Born May 27, 1966, in Inglewood, Cal.

Year	Team	G	FG	FG Pct.	FT	FT Pct.	Reb.	Ast.	TP	Avg.
1988-89	Utah	75	120	.545	79	.699	199	16	319	4.3
1989-90	Utah	77	125	.563	81	.743	192	19	331	4.3
1990-91	Sac.-Char.	72	131	.446	62	.559	295	39	324	4.5
1991-92	Charlotte	59	79	.513	38	.745	206	31	196	3.3
1993-94	Philadelphia	71	139	.486	84	.646	282	86	362	5.1
	Totals	354	594	.505	344	.669	1174	191	1532	4.3

THE ROOKIES

GRANT HILL 22 6-8 225   Guard-Forward

Calvin's kid . . . Pistons grabbed him with the third pick in the draft but many feel he was the second-best, behind Glenn Robinson

. . . Unanimous All-American . . . ACC Player of Year at Duke, where he played on two title teams ('91 and '92) and led Blue Devils to runner-up spot in '94 . . . Complete package: size, speed, ball-handling, defense, scorer . . . Held Robinson to 13 points in NCAAs . . . Born Oct. 5, 1972, in Dallas.

BILL CURLEY 22 6-9 220   **Forward**
Funny, he doesn't look like a point guard . . . Spurs passed on need for ball-handler to take big man from Boston College at No. 22 and later dealt him to Pistons in trade that brought back Sean Elliott .·. Led Eagles in scoring and rebounding each of four seasons . . . Set school record with 126 games played . . . Born May 29, 1972, in Boston.

JEVON CRUDUP 22 6-8 222   **Forward**
Could help Pistons renew their image as terrorizing defenders . . . Magnificent post defense from this somewhat offensively-limited specimen . . . Honorable mention All-American . . . Sixth all-time rebounder, third all-time shot-blocker at Missouri . . . Taken No. 48 on second round . . . Born April 27, 1972, in Kansas City, Mo.

COACH DON CHANEY: Had problems running Pistons last year . . . Red Auerbach, Pat Riley and Knute Rockne would have had problems running Pistons last year . . . Curious game moves—maybe he was just looking to future . . . In second leg of three-year, $1.8-million deal. And Pistons are still paying Ron Rothstein (remainder of $1.65 million) . . . Two times was Detroit assistant, the second time under Rothstein before succeeding him after '92-93 . . . 1991 Coach of the Year with Houston. Sacked, replaced by Rudy Tomjanovich . . . 138-108 in 3½ years with Rockets. Made playoffs each of his three full years. His .561 winning percentage is second only to Rudy T. in Houston history . . . Coached Clippers for two-plus seasons that he'd rather forget (53-232) . . . Assistant to Mike Fratello in Atlanta . . . U. of Houston. Played on '68 team that beat UCLA in Astrodome . . . Drafted No. 12 by Celtics in 1968. Only guy to play with both Larry Bird and Bill Russell . . . 11 NBA seasons produced 8.4 ppg and two title rings. Was second-team All-Defense five times . . . Born March 22, 1946, in Baton Rouge, La.

GREATEST PLAYER

If the franchise were moving any slower toward respectability, it would have been going backwards. Oh, there were some great players, but it wasn't until the Pistons in 1981 announced their draft choice, the No. 2 overall pick in the draft, that they found their greatest performer ever, the man who would lead them to a pair of World Championships as the gangleader of ''The Bad Boys,'' Isiah Thomas.

Thomas called it quits after last season, his 13th, and took an ownership/basketball operations role with expansionist Toronto. Before leaving he rewrote the Pistons' record book. He finished as Detroit's all-time leader in points (18,822), games played (979), assists (9,061) and steals (1,861). And he was the Finals MVP in 1990, the year Detroit won the second of back-to-back titles.

He will be remembered as the greatest little man to ever play among the redwood centers and forwards. Thomas, who left Indiana after his sophomore season—and an NCAA title—had numerous legendary performances, but perhaps none greater than in the 1984 playoffs against the Knicks when he scored 16 points in 94 seconds.

ALL-TIME PISTON LEADERS

SEASON

Points: Dave Bing, 2,213, 1970-71
Assists: Isiah Thomas, 1,123, 1984-85
Rebounds: Bob Lanier, 1,205, 1972-73

GAME

Points: Kelly Tripucka, 56 vs. Chicago, 1/29/83
Assists: Kevin Porter, 25 vs. Phoenix, 4/1/79
　　　　　Kevin Porter, 25 vs. Boston, 3/9/79
　　　　　Isiah Thomas, 25 vs. Dallas, 2/13/85
Rebounds: Dennis Rodman, 34 vs. Indiana, 3/4/92

CAREER

Points: Isiah Thomas, 18,822, 1981-94
Assists: Isiah Thomas, 9,061, 1981-94
Rebounds: Bill Laimbeer, 9,330, 1982-94

INDIANA PACERS

TEAM DIRECTORY: Owners: Herb Simon, Melvin Simon; Pres.: Donnie Walsh; VP-Basketball: George Irvine; Media Rel. Dir.: David Benner; Coach: Larry Brown; Asst. Coaches: Bill Blair, Gar Heard, Billy King. Arena: Market Square Arena (16,530). Colors: Blue and yellow.

SCOUTING REPORT

SHOOTING: Yes, the Pacers desperately need a forward who can score. But know what? Even with their abundance of big guys and lack of a perimeter game beyond Reggie Miller, the Pacers were the best-shooting team in the East last season at .486. Only the .492 supplied by the racehorse Warriors was better.

Of course, it all starts with Miller, perhaps the purest shooter in the game today. When he's on from the outside, it doesn't matter what the other guys do. Larry Brown also focused a lot more of the offense around Rik Smits inside, making the Pacers pretty much a carbon of their Knicks with a post-two-guard-anchored offense (although the Pacers are far superior at the two with Miller). For the rest of the high percentage, the Pacers relied on put-backs, layups and high-percentage shots around a forward corps with a collective range measured in inches.

PLAYMAKING: Playing point guard for Brown is usually a thankless task. No one does it well enough to suit him. So when he goes after someone who has performed the duty in the past, there must be something special about the guy.

And there is something special about Mark Jackson.

Forget the Pacers' assist numbers from last year. None of them matter because there's a new sheriff in town, Jackson, whom the Pacers got from the Clippers for a swap of unproved first-round picks, plus two guys who were not even on the playoff roster, Malik Sealy and Pooh Richardson (one of the latest to discover how tough it is playing point for Brown).

REBOUNDING: Only Chicago, New Jersey and New York were better last year. And with one more year of experience, the Davis bookends, Dale and Antonio, should help keep the Pacers in the upper echelon. Now if they ever get Smits to board like a 7-4 guy, they could be downright frightening.

The Pacers quickly became the darlings of the lunchpail set.

In a banner season, Rik Smits scored 40 in one game.

Blue-collar workers like the Davises helped them captivate their city, a city that always had been more concerned with whom Bobby Knight might recruit than what the Pacers actually did. Derrick McKey is legit off the boards at small forward and Miller can get his share at off guard. Now add Jackson, one of the league's best rebounding points, and there's no reason to suggest they won't be near the top again.

PACER ROSTER

No.	Veterans	Pos.	Ht.	Wt.	Age	Yrs. Pro	College
12	Lester Conner	G	6-4	180	35	11	Oregon State
33	Antonio Davis	F-C	6-9	230	26	1	Texas-El Paso
32	Dale Davis	F	6-11	230	25	3	Clemson
10	Vern Fleming	G	6-5	185	32	10	Georgia
43	Scott Haskin	F-C	6-11	250	24	1	Oregon State
13	Mark Jackson	G	6-3	185	29	7	St. John's
9	Derrick McKey	F	6-10	225	28	7	Alabama
31	Reggie Miller	G	6-7	185	29	7	UCLA
5	Sam Mitchell	F	6-7	210	31	5	Mercer
4	Byron Scott	G	6-4	200	33	11	Arizona State
45	Rik Smits	C	7-4	255	28	6	Marist
41	LaSalle Thompson	F-C	6-10	260	33	12	Texas
44	Kenny Williams	F	6-9	200	25	4	Elizabeth City State
3	Haywoode Workman	G	6-3	180	28	3	Oral Roberts

Rd.	Rookies	Sel. No.	Pos.	Ht.	Wt.	College
1	Greg Minor	25	G-F	6-6	210	Louisville
2	William Njoku	41	F	6-9	215	Ghana
2	Damon Bailey	44	G	6-2	171	Indiana

DEFENSE: It's what Borwn preaches most. And obviously the Pacers listened. Ready? Indiana held opponents to 97.5 points and .450 field-goal percentyage, both team-record lows. Yeah, the Indiana Pacers. You know those guys who for years couldn't guard closed doors with automatic weapons.

They pressed. They trapped. They were relentless. Say whatever you want about Brown, but the guy wins wherever he goes. And wherever he goes, the first thing he usually starts talking about is defense.

OUTLOOK: The steal of Jackson may have upset the balance of power in the East. In Jackson, the Pacers now possess one of the two elements that was sorely lacking last year: a solid drive-and-dish guy who also possesses scoring ability. Jackson was miserable with the Clippers. And wouldn't he love to gain a little payback on the Knicks in, say, the conference finals?

In Brown, the Pacers may very well have the best game-coach around. He took the point-less Pacers to the Eastern finals last year. And although the East will be stronger, there's no one overly anxious to bet that he won't do that again.

PACER PROFILES

REGGIE MILLER 29 6-7 185   Guard

Wait a minute! This guy can be on Dream Team II, can score 25 points in a single playoff quarter, can frighten any defense. But he can't make the All-Star team? . . . Put on one of the greatest playoff shooting displays ever when he sank Knicks in Game 5 of the Eastern Finals with 25-point, fourth-quarter fury that included five three-pointers . . . Game's purest shooter . . . Superb at using picks or simple catch-and-shoot . . . Phenomenal release . . . Yeah, he's Cheryl's brother . . . Actually, she's Reggie's sister . . . Still talks trash, but not as much . . . Bought into Larry Brown's team concept. Hence, points, free throws, shots and three-point tries were all at five-year low . . . Guess what? He will play defense. And can . . . In 16 playoff games, his man shot 41 percent. And he outscored him every time . . . Became the franchise's all-time leading scorer when he passed Billy Knight April 17. Has 10,879 points . . . Fourth player in history to hit 800 three-pointers . . . Has 100 steals five straight seasons . . . Club-record 57 points at Charlotte, Nov. 28, 1992 . . . Born Aug. 24, 1965, in Riverside, Cal. . . . Made $3.21 million . . . Drafted No. 11 in 1987, out of UCLA.

Year	Team	G	FG	FG Pct.	FT	FT Pct.	Reb.	Ast.	TP	Avg.
1987-88	Indiana	82	306	.488	149	.801	190	132	822	10.0
1988-89	Indiana	74	398	.479	287	.844	292	227	1181	16.0
1989-90	Indiana	82	661	.514	544	.868	295	311	2016	24.6
1990-91	Indiana	82	596	.512	551	.918	281	314	1855	22.6
1991-92	Indiana	82	562	.501	442	.858	318	314	1695	20.7
1992-93	Indiana	82	571	.479	427	.880	258	262	1736	21.2
1993-94	Indiana	79	524	.503	403	.908	212	248	1574	19.9
	Totals	563	3618	.498	2803	.877	1846	1825	10879	19.3

RIK SMITS 28 7-4 255   Center

Every year, it was the same thing: Smits needs to bulk up, Smits needs to bulk up . . . So Larry Brown came aboard and said Smits needs to slim down . . . By gum, he had something there . . . The Dunking Dutchman dropped some weight, it took pressure off his knees, he stayed healthy and produced . . . Now why didn't other coaches think of that? . . . Career-high 40-point game April 22, en route to career-best scoring year (15.7) . . . But not everything changed . . . He still commits some of the dumbest fouls this side of Patrick Ewing's rookie year . . . Six years in league and he still can't average 30 minutes . . . Strong post-up game and a good face-up jumper . . . Finished strong: had three 30-point games, all in last eight games . . . Born Aug. 23, 1966, in Eindhoven, Holland . . . Made $2.5 million . . . No. 2 pick in 1988 draft, out of Marist.

Year	Team	G	FG	FG Pct.	FT	FT Pct.	Reb.	Ast.	TP	Avg.
1988-89	Indiana.	82	386	.517	184	.722	500	70	956	11.7
1989-90	Indiana.	82	515	.533	241	.811	512	142	1271	15.5
1990-91	Indiana.	76	342	.485	144	.762	357	84	828	10.9
1991-92	Indiana.	74	436	.510	152	.788	417	116	1024	13.8
1992-93	Indiana.	81	494	.486	167	.732	432	121	1155	14.3
1993-94	Indiana.	78	493	.534	238	.793	483	156	1224	15.7
	Totals	473	2666	.511	1126	.770	2701	689	6458	13.7

MARK JACKSON 29 6-3 185   Guard

Team player has had more frustrations than assists in two seasons as a Clipper and wound up a Pacer in deal that sent Malik Sealy and Pooh Richardson to Clippers . . . Was to have begun the second installment on a five-year contract . . . Finished eighth in the league in assists . . . Three-team deal involving Clippers, Knicks and Magic that also included Charles Smith and Stanley Roberts had sent lifetime New Yorker to the West Coast in September 1992 . . . Born April 1, 1965, in Brooklyn, N.Y., and starred at St. John's . . . Knicks picked him No. 18 in '87 . . . Made $2,000,000.

Year	Team	G	FG	FG Pct.	FT	FT Pct.	Reb.	Ast.	TP	Avg.
1987-88	New York	82	438	.432	206	.774	396	868	1114	13.6
1988-89	New York	72	479	.467	180	.698	341	619	1219	16.9
1989-90	New York	82	327	.437	120	.727	318	604	809	9.9
1990-91	New York	72	250	.492	117	.731	197	452	630	8.8
1991-92	New York	81	367	.491	171	.770	305	694	916	11.3
1992-93	L.A. Clippers	82	459	.486	241	.803	388	724	1181	14.4
1993-94	L.A. Clippers	79	331	.452	167	.791	348	678	865	10.9
	Totals	550	2651	.464	1202	.760	2293	4639	6734	12.2

DALE DAVIS 25 6-11 230   Forward

If he ever had a shot, he'd be illegal in 49 states ... No range at all. His repertoire is one-handed dunks, two-handed dunks. When he's feeling zany or particularly versatile, he might go the layup route ... But every team would love him on their side ... His 10.9 rebounds per game established a club record ... First player in Pacers' NBA history to have three 20-rebound games in same season. Which could make him the first Pacer with 60 rebounds in same season ... Shot .529, and that was his three-year low ... Had 280 offensive rebounds. That was 11 shy of his team record. And it was fifth-most of any forward in NBA. Plus, he missed 16 games with broken wrist ... He was No. 13 pick out of Clemson in 1991 ... Led ACC in rebounding three straight seasons ... Born March 25, 1969, in Toccoa, Ga. ... Made $688,000.

Year	Team	G	FG	FG Pct.	FT	FT Pct.	Reb.	Ast.	TP	Avg.
1991-92	Indiana	64	154	.552	87	.572	410	30	395	6.2
1992-93	Indiana	82	304	.568	119	.529	723	69	727	8.9
1993-94	Indiana	66	308	.529	155	.527	718	100	771	11.7
	Totals	212	766	.549	361	.538	1851	199	1893	8.9

ANTONIO DAVIS 26 6-9 230   Forward-Center

Gee, they must be getting tough over in Europe ... Either that or nobody else is left standing after this guy's three-year tour ... Pacers drafted him on second round in 1990 out of UTEP and sent him to Europe for three years ... How he plays isn't taught overseas ... Devastatingly strong inside player. Uses strength to play backup center, too ... No relation to Dale Davis, other than being his bookend ... And, in rookie year, he showed more diverse offensive game ... Has a jumper to 15 feet ... But post-up game needs work ... So does free-throw shooting. In fact, the way he shoots free throws (.642), he might want to try that with his back to basket ... Team's second-best rebounder behind Dale, but ahead of the 7-4 starting center ... Sixth-leading rebounder among rookies ... Born Oct. 31, 1968, in Oakland ... Made $565,000.

Year	Team	G	FG	FG Pct.	FT	FT Pct.	Reb.	Ast.	TP	Avg.
1993-94	Indiana	81	216	.508	194	.642	505	55	626	7.7

DERRICK McKEY 28 6-10 225   Forward

He has an offensive game... Yeah, and the Pope's married... Came from Seattle with the immortal Gerald Paddio for Detlef Schrempf, Nov. 1, 1993... But he was sort of like a missionary among the heathens, bringing defense to Indiana... One of league's premier defensive small forwards... Registered 111 steals, third-best mark among Eastern forwards... Scoring average dropped for fifth straight year: 12.0 was lowest since rookie year... Good passer. Second on team in assists... May have a reluctance to shoot... Tried to add a three-point shot to his game. Made 9-of-31. Should have tried adding another floor to his house instead... Shot 41 percent in playoffs after 50-percent regular season... Born Oct. 10, 1966, in Meridian, Miss.... No. 9 pick in 1987 draft, out of Alabama, by Seattle... Made $1.262 million.

Year	Team	G	FG	FG Pct.	FT	FT Pct.	Reb.	Ast.	TP	Avg.
1987-88	Seattle	82	255	.491	173	.772	328	107	694	8.5
1988-89	Seattle	82	487	.502	301	.803	464	219	1305	15.9
1989-90	Seattle	80	468	.493	315	.782	489	187	1254	15.7
1990-91	Seattle	73	438	.517	235	.845	423	169	1115	15.3
1991-92	Seattle	52	285	.472	188	.847	268	120	777	14.9
1992-93	Seattle	77	387	.496	220	.741	327	197	1034	13.4
1993-94	Indiana	76	355	.500	192	.756	402	327	911	12.0
	Totals	522	2675	.497	1624	.791	2701	1326	7090	13.9

HAYWOODE WORKMAN 28 6-3 180   Guard

Well, he doesn't really screw up... Unless he shoots... Dependable, non-flashy, meat-and-potatoes point guard... Had 2.7 assists for every turnover... Began season as third point guard... Finished as starter... Averaged 9.8 assists in last month... Shooting? Oh, did we mention he doesn't screw up much?... Ironically, he came into the league in 1989 as a shooter out of Oral Roberts... Good team guy. Never causes any problems... Poor man's Terry Porter. Does the job without true point-guard skills... Tough defensively, applied good ball pressure... Second-round pick of Hawks in 1989. Did one year with Bullets, two in Italy... Signed as free agent with Pacers, Aug.

31, 1993 . . . Born Jan. 23, 1966, in Charlotte . . . Earned $320,000.

Year	Team	G	FG	FG Pct.	FT	FT Pct.	Reb.	Ast.	TP	Avg.
1989-90	Atlanta	6	2	.667	2	1.000	3	2	6	1.0
1990-91	Washington	73	234	.454	101	.759	242	353	581	8.0
1993-94	Indiana	65	195	.424	93	.802	204	404	501	7.7
	Totals	144	431	.441	196	.781	449	759	1088	7.6

KENNY WILLIAMS 25 6-9 200   Forward

The clock is ticking away on his chances . . . This supremely athletic type will dazzle with some special performances, then basically disappear. When Pacer patience is at lowest ebb, he dazzles again, starting cycle all over . . . He can do it. Example: March 16, he started in win over Suns and got 18 points, 11 rebounds, seven assists and zero turnovers in 38 minutes . . . Hasn't exactly mastered the playbook . . . Came to NBA with one year of community-college ball . . . Prop 48 victim, he transferred to Barton County (Kan.) CC after signing letter of intent with North Carolina . . . Played one year, transferred to Elizabeth City State (N.C.). Didn't play . . . Pacers took him in second round in 1990 . . . Born June 9, 1969, in Elizabeth City, N.C. . . . Made $375,000.

Year	Team	G	FG	FG Pct.	FT	FT Pct.	Reb.	Ast.	TP	Avg.
1990-91	Indiana	75	93	.520	34	.680	131	31	220	2.9
1991-92	Indiana	60	113	.518	26	.605	129	40	252	4.2
1992-93	Indiana	57	150	.532	48	.706	228	38	348	6.1
1993-94	Indiana	68	191	.488	45	.703	205	52	427	6.0
	Totals	260	547	.511	153	.680	693	161	1247	4.8

BYRON SCOTT 33 6-4 200   Guard

Lakers pulled the plug. But Pacers discovered life remained . . . So did Orlando, burned by Scott three-pointer at buzzer in Game 1 of opening round . . . Signed as a free agent Dec. 7. Promptly went out and scored eight points that night . . . Member of Lakers' glory teams, won title rings in '85, '87 and '88 . . . His 2,897 career playoff points was highest of any player involved in last year's playoffs . . . Did exactly what Pacers hoped: supplied offense and some veteran cool off bench . . . No. 4 overall pick of Clippers, then in San Diego, in 1983, out of Arizona State

... Draft rights were sent to Lakers with Swen Nater for Norm Nixon, Eddie Jordan and two second-rounders, Oct. 10, 1983 ... Made about $600,000 ... Born March 28, 1961, in Ogden, Utah.

Year	Team	G	FG	FG Pct.	FT	FT Pct.	Reb.	Ast.	TP	Avg.
1983-84	Los Angeles	74	334	.484	112	.806	164	177	788	10.6
1984-85	L.A. Lakers	81	541	.539	187	.820	210	244	1295	16.0
1985-86	L.A. Lakers	76	507	.513	138	.784	189	164	1174	15.4
1986-87	L.A. Lakers	82	554	.489	224	.892	286	281	1397	17.0
1987-88	L.A. Lakers	81	710	.527	272	.858	333	335	1754	21.7
1988-89	L.A. Lakers	74	588	.491	195	.863	302	231	1448	19.6
1989-90	L.A. Lakers	77	472	.470	160	.766	242	274	1197	15.5
1990-91	L.A. Lakers	82	501	.477	118	.797	246	177	1191	14.5
1991-92	L.A. Lakers	82	460	.458	244	.838	310	226	1218	14.9
1992-93	L.A. Lakers	58	296	.449	156	.848	134	157	792	13.7
1993-94	Indiana	67	256	.467	157	.805	110	133	696	10.4
	Totals	834	5219	.491	1963	.830	2526	2399	12950	15.5

VERN FLEMING 32 6-5 185 Guard

Still going ... He just didn't go very far in injury-plagued season that was limited to 55 games ... Was squashed by Shaquille O'Neal, who drove dental plate through his lips ... Also took 25 stitches in knee in that same April 2 incident ... Became second Pacer to score 9,000 NBA points ... Nice guy. Has never had a technical in his 761 career games, an NBA record ... Had his first ever DNP-coach's decision. And he had four of them ... Like we said, Larry Brown is tough to please at the point ... More of a two-guard, despite awkward shot rotation ... Neither a creator nor penetrater ... Pacers' all-time leader in seasons, games, minutes, steals and assists ... Born Feb. 4, 1962, in Long Island City, N.Y. ... Made $1.56 million ... First-round pick, No. 18, out of Georgia in '84.

Year	Team	G	FG	FG Pct.	FT	FT Pct.	Reb.	Ast.	TP	Avg.
1984-85	Indiana	80	433	.470	260	.767	323	247	1126	14.1
1985-86	Indiana	80	436	.506	263	.745	386	505	1136	14.2
1986-87	Indiana	82	370	.509	238	.788	334	473	980	12.0
1987-88	Indiana	80	442	.523	227	.802	364	568	1111	13.9
1988-89	Indiana	76	419	.515	243	.799	310	494	1084	14.3
1989-90	Indiana	82	467	.508	230	.782	322	610	1176	14.3
1990-91	Indiana	69	356	.531	161	.729	214	369	877	12.7
1991-92	Indiana	82	294	.482	132	.737	209	266	726	8.9
1992-93	Indiana	75	280	.505	143	.726	169	224	710	9.5
1993-94	Indiana	55	147	.462	64	.736	123	173	358	6.5
	Totals	761	3644	.503	1961	.766	2754	3929	9284	12.2

SAM MITCHELL 31 6-7 210   Forward

Every team needs one like him...Locker-room leader, a conduit from coaching staff, but still a team guy...Too slow, too small, too unskilled. Yet he does the job...Stepped in as an emergency starter for Dale Davis early in season when things were going south, and team won 11 of 18 games...And that was turning point of season...Shot .547, averaged 9.6 points and 4.8 rebounds as a starter...Didn't miss a game with injury or illness...Playoff non-factor, though...Came to Pacers from T-Wolves in the Chuck Person-Pooh Richardson swap Sept. 8, 1992...Led league in fouls in 1990-91...Drafted by Houston in third round, out of Mercer, in 1985...Played in CBA and France for four years before Minnesota signed him as a free agent in July 1989...Born Sept. 2, 1963, in Columbus, Ga....Made $715,000.

Year	Team	G	FG	FG Pct.	FT	FT Pct.	Reb.	Ast.	TP	Avg.
1989-90	Minnesota.......	80	372	.446	268	.768	462	89	1012	12.7
1990-91	Minnesota.......	82	445	.441	307	.775	520	133	1197	14.6
1991-92	Minnesota.......	82	307	.423	209	.786	473	94	825	10.1
1992-93	Indiana.........	81	215	.445	150	.811	248	76	584	7.2
1993-94	Indiana.........	75	140	.458	82	.745	190	65	362	4.8
	Totals	400	1479	.440	1016	.778	1893	457	3980	10.0

SCOTT HASKIN 24 6-11 250   Forward-Center

Didn't exactly impact, you know?...27 games, 186 minutes. Usually when janitors were sweeping up...Good practice player...Tended to freeze up in games. Subject of famous Larry Brown line: "It's a good thing he was wearing a mouthpiece so he wouldn't swallow his tongue."...Yet Brown loves him for practice work ethic...Ruptured Achilles tendon and won't be back until February...Has some skills: shot-blocker, nice hook...Could be a serviceable backup center. If he doesn't freeze...Born Sept. 19, 1970, in Riverside, Cal....Pacers took him No. 14 in 1993, out of Oregon State...Made $833,000 as a rookie.

Year	Team	G	FG	FG Pct.	FT	FT Pct.	Reb.	Ast.	TP	Avg.
1993-94	Indiana.........	27	21	.467	13	.684	55	6	55	2.0

LaSALLE THOMPSON 33 6-10 260   Forward-Center

There's still some games left . . . Sets devastating picks . . . And when you've got Reggie Miller on your side, pick- and screen-setters are sort of nice . . . Was a decent shooter back when trolley cars were in vogue . . . Can still drop in a hook every now and then . . . Fewest games (30) of 12-year career. In fact, the 52 games he missed were just three shy of the number (55) he missed in 11 previous seasons . . . Age and injuries are setting in. Two bouts with knee tendinitis . . . Pacers acquired him and Randy Wittman from Kings for Wayman Tisdale and a second-rounder Feb. 20, 1989 . . . Born June 23, 1961, in Cincinnati . . . Picked No. 5 overall out of Texas in 1982 by Kings . . . Made $2.0 million.

Year	Team	G	FG	FG Pct.	FT	FT Pct.	Reb.	Ast.	TP	Avg.
1982-83	Kansas City	71	147	.512	89	.650	375	33	383	5.4
1983-84	Kansas City	80	333	.523	160	.717	709	86	826	10.3
1984-85	Kansas City	82	369	.531	227	.721	854	130	965	11.8
1985-86	Sacramento	80	411	.518	202	.732	770	168	1024	12.8
1986-87	Sacramento	82	362	.481	188	.737	687	122	912	11.1
1987-88	Sacramento	69	215	.471	118	.720	427	68	550	8.0
1988-89	Sac.-Indiana	76	416	.489	227	.808	718	81	1059	13.9
1989-90	Indiana	82	223	.473	107	.799	630	106	554	6.8
1990-91	Indiana	82	276	.488	72	.692	563	147	625	7.6
1991-92	Indiana	80	168	.468	58	.817	381	102	394	4.9
1992-93	Indiana	63	104	.488	29	.744	178	34	237	3.8
1993-94	Indiana	30	27	.351	16	.533	75	16	70	2.3
	Totals	877	3051	.496	1493	.736	6367	1093	7599	8.7

LESTER CONNER 35 6-4 180   Guard

One Pacer observer summed up this veteran with: "Well, he can't shoot but he is dating a soap-opera star." . . . Sixth NBA stop in 12 seasons, first five years with Warriors . . . Signed 10-day contract April 5 for prorated minimum. Wound up on playoff roster . . . Solid-citizen type. Cheerleader on bench . . . Always tough defensively . . . Never was much of a shooter, but never had dated a soap-opera star before, either . . . Did time with Rockets, Nets, Bucks and Clippers . . . Born

Sept. 17, 1959, in Memphis, Tenn. . . . No. 14 pick in 1982 by Warriors, out of Oregon State, his third college.

Year	Team	G	FG	FG Pct.	FT	FT Pct.	Reb.	Ast.	TP	Avg.
1982-83	Golden State	75	145	.479	79	.699	221	253	369	4.9
1983-84	Golden State	82	360	.493	186	.718	305	401	907	11.1
1984-85	Golden State	79	246	.451	144	.750	246	369	640	8.1
1985-86	Golden State	36	51	.375	40	.741	62	43	144	4.0
1987-88	Houston	52	50	.463	32	.780	38	59	132	2.5
1988-89	New Jersey	82	309	.457	212	.788	355	604	843	10.3
1989-90	New Jersey	82	237	.414	172	.804	265	385	648	7.9
1990-91	N.J.-Mil.	74	96	.464	68	.723	112	165	260	3.5
1991-92	Milwaukee	81	103	.431	81	.704	184	294	287	3.5
1992-93	L.A. Clippers	31	28	.452	18	.947	49	65	74	2.4
1993-94	Indiana	11	14	.368	3	.500	24	31	31	2.8
	Totals	685	1639	.453	1035	.752	1861	2669	4335	6.3

THE ROOKIES

GREG MINOR 23 6-6 210   Guard-Forward

No truth to the rumor Clippers decided to include him in the Mark Jackson-Pooh Richardson deal when someone told owner Donald T. Sterling he did not just draft Harold Miner . . . L.A. picked him 25th, then shipped him to Pacers . . . Helped his cause by being named to the all-tournament teams at Portsmouth and Phoenix predraft camps . . . Swingman at Louisville . . . Born Sept. 18, 1971, in Sandersville, Ga.

WILLIAM NJOKU 22 6-9 215   Forward

Can you say potential? . . . Ghana-born, Canadian-schooled . . . Out of St. Mary's, Nova Scotia . . . Very impressive four-year stats: 21.0 scoring, .525 shooting, 9.4 rebounds and .395 shooting on three-pointers . . . Named to Canadian Interuniversity Athletic Union first team . . . Was the 41st player selected . . . Born March 5, 1972, in Ghana.

DAMON BAILEY 23 6-2 171   Guard

And wasn't this a popular selection with the draft held in Hoosier Dome? . . . Hometown favorite after surviving four years with Bobby Knight . . . All-Big Ten choice was Indiana's fifth all-time scorer, tied for second in assists . . . Selected No. 44 . . . Averaged 19.6 points last year . . . Born Oct. 21, 1971, in Bedford, Ind.

COACH LARRY BROWN: Get it out of your system: Wow,  one full year without a job change... There. Feel better?... The guy can flat-out coach... Preparation and work are Brown team trademarks... All those who thought Pacers would be in the Eastern Conference finals last November, raise your hands... Liars... Led Pacers to a 47-35 record, their best ever in the NBA ... And he took them to conference finals. Pacers had never won a playoff round... Coach of the Month for an 11-2 February... Reunited with ABA buddy Donnie Walsh, Pacer GM, when he replaced Bob Hill after 1992-93 season... Was with Clippers for a year and a half before Pacers. Posted 64-53 record... All-time NBA coaching record of 481-377 (.561) ... Wins wherever he goes. And that includes New Jersey, San Antonio in NBA, Carolina and Denver in ABA, UCLA and Kansas in college... In 22 seasons as a head coach, he has had just one losing campaign... Pro record, including ABA, is 710-484... Also was 177-61 in college, winning NCAA title with Kansas in 1988... Five-year ABA playing career after leaving North Carolina... 1964 Olympic gold medalist... Born Sept. 14, 1940, in Brooklyn, N.Y.

GREATEST PLAYER

If you go back to the Pacers' ABA days, you'll come up with the likes of George McGinnis and Billy Knight when discussing the franchise's finest talent. But why go back that far? There's no need to, not when the greatest scorer and best shooter in the franchise's history, Reggie Miller, resides in the present.

When he scored 14 points at Detroit on April 17, Miller slipped past Knight as the Pacers' all-time scorer and finished his seventh season with 10,879 points. For years, the book on Miller has been, basically, mug him. He has taken the poundings and came back for more. And he's more than a shooter. His 1,825 assists rank second in the team's NBA days.

Miller has had some huge games and big moments, but none compared to the scintillating fourth quarter against the Knicks in Game 5 of the Eastern Conference finals in a Pacer victory that put the Knicks on the brink of elimination. Miller, perhaps urged on by Spike Lee's courtside taunts, riddled the best defensive team in the NBA for 25 points in the fourth quarter.

ALL-TIME PACER LEADERS

SEASON

Points: George McGinnis, 2,353, 1974-75 (ABA)
  Billy Knight, 2,075, 1976-77
Assists: Don Buse, 689, 1975-76 (ABA)
  Don Buse, 685, 1976-77
Rebounds: Mel Daniels, 1,475, 1970-71 (ABA)
  Clark Kellogg, 860, 1982-83

GAME

Points: George McGinnis, 58 vs. Dallas, 11/28/72 (ABA)
  Reggie Miller, 57 vs. Charlotte, 11/28/92
Assists: Don Buse, 20 vs. Denver, 3/26/76 (ABA)
  Vern Fleming, 18 vs. Houston, 11/23/90
  Micheal Williams, 18 vs. New York 11/13/91
Rebounds: George McGinnis, 37 vs. Carolina, 1/12/71 (ABA)
  Herb Williams, 29 vs. Denver, 1/23/89

CAREER

Points: Billy Knight, 10,780, 1974-83 (ABA and NBA)
  Reggie Miller, 10,879, 1987-94
Assists: Vern Fleming, 3,929, 1984-94
  Don Buse, 2,747, 1972-77, 1980-82 (ABA)
Rebounds: Mel Daniels, 7,622, 1968-74 (ABA)
  Herb Williams, 4,494, 1981-89

MIAMI HEAT

TEAM DIRECTORY: Partners: Ted Arison, Zev Bufman, Billy Cunningham, Lewis Schaffel (Managing Partner); Dir. Scouting: Chris Wallace; Scouting Coordinator: Tony Fiorentino; Dir. Pub. Rel.: Mark Pray; Coach: Kevin Loughery; Asst. Coaches: Alvin Gentry, Bob Staak. Arena: Miami Arena (15,200). Colors: Orange, red, yellow, black and white.

SCOUTING REPORT

SHOOTING: Rony Seikaly will always be in the 50 percent neighborhood with his quality post-up game. But after that, the Heat are as consistent as the weather.

They'll be awesome one night, awful the next. That's what happens when there is such a reliance on a perimeter game. And that's what the Heat use. Steve Smith and Glen Rice can blow any team away from long range—including Miami, if their shots are off. But generally, the perimeter game is quality while the inside game, after Seikaly, is not. Thus the Heat will suffer wild fluctuations in shooting percentages from night to night. Sometimes, from quarter to quarter. From the line, they shot .785 last year, the finest mark in the league. The problem is getting to the line—they were 13th in free-throws attempted.

PLAYMAKING: Now they're not quite pining for Sherman Douglas again. But ever since they traded him away for Brian Shaw, the Heat have been unable to find a genuine penetrating point guard. So what if Douglas penetrated usually for himself? At least he penetrated.

The lack of dribble penetration remains a constant thorn in the Heat's collective side. Although Miami rang up over 103 points a game, the seventh-best mark in the NBA, they were sixth from the bottom in assists last season.

Smith has proven, and the Heat now apparently are convinced, that he is not a point guard. He ended last season at the two. So when the Heat's number came up in the draft, they summoned Khalid Reeves, who has the definite body of a point guard at 6-1. But he has the reputation of a shooter. "They took a shooter on a team of shooters," one scout assessed.

REBOUNDING: One of the better strengths with Seikaly. Write his name in the starting lineup, figure he's good for 10 at least

Glen Rice, Heat's leading scorer, made 132 three-pointers.

with a lot more possible (he had a 34-board game two seasons ago).

But virtually since their inception, the Heat have sought the Charles Oakley-like horse: a night-in, night-out moose who has the body to wear down opponents, the strength to clear out opponents and the will and desire to outlast opponents. Always, they come back to Grant Long, the undersized ball of heart who has sacrificed any range to try to exert muscle he really doesn't have.

The Heat have tried John Salley, a shot-blocker and leaper and positional type lacking the brute force. They've tried Alec Kessler. They've tried Matt Geiger. The search goes on.

DEFENSE: Overall, it's adequate, especially when Salley brings some shot-blocking characteristics to the front line. Seikaly isn't going to make any All-Defense teams, but he can clog the lane and get in some people's way. Perhaps more importantly, Seikaly's offense will make opposing centers work, thus providing a possible fatigue factor. There's nothing great at small forward but again, the Heat are reasonably adequate, if undeniably soft. But up front, although Salley will swat away a shot or two, there simply is nothing resembling an intimidator.

Then there's the backcourt. This is trouble. And it will be even worse if Shaw goes elsewhere. C'mon, Smith and Harold Miner

HEAT ROSTER

No.	Veterans	Pos.	Ht.	Wt.	Age	Yrs. Pro	College
U-2	Keith Askins	G-F	6-8	223	26	4	Alabama
34	Willie Burton	G-F	6-8	219	26	4	Minnesota
12	Vernell Coles	G	6-2	185	26	4	Virginia Tech
52	Matt Geiger	C	7-0	245	25	2	Georgia Tech
33	Alec Kessler	F-C	6-11	240	27	4	Georgia
43	Grant Long	F	6-9	248	28	6	Eastern Michigan
32	Harold Miner	G	6-5	215	23	2	USC
41	Glen Rice	G-F	6-8	220	27	5	Michigan
22	John Salley	F-C	6-11	250	30	8	Georgia Tech
4	Rony Seikaly	C	6-11	252	29	6	Syracuse
U-20	Brian Shaw	G	6-6	194	28	5	Cal-Santa Barbara
3	Steve Smith	G	6-8	213	25	3	Michigan State

R-restricted free agent
U-unrestricted free agent

Rd.	Rookies	Sel. No.	Pos.	Ht.	Wt.	College
1	Khalid Reeves	12	G	6-1	206	Arizona
2	Jeff Webster	40	F	6-6	232	Oklahoma

in the game at the same time? Opposing backcourt gentlemen, start your engines. Smith and Miner could represent the worst defensive backcourt in the NBA. When the Heat need backcourt stops, they've gone to Shaw and Bimbo Coles. But Shaw's free agency could leave an even bigger gap in an area already populated by a huge void.

OUTLOOK: Virtually the same people. Thus, same strengths, same problems. And probably the same outlook.

After the Heat qualified for the playoff in 1991-92, there was real excitement in Miami and in NBA circles. They were a team on the rise, a team of the future, a team to be reckoned with. Then they flopped badly. Last year saw a resurgence and 42 victories, the most in franchise history. But that excitement just isn't there.

Kevin Loughery is back with a new contract and the Heat could go either way when they hand out the playoff invites. They might be walking back to the lottery in the vastly improved East. Or they might squeeze in again with one of the lower first-round seeds. Either way, realistic NBA championship thoughts are as far removed from Miami as icebergs.

HEAT PROFILES

RONY SEIKALY 29 6-11 252   Center

Even his statistical consistency began to slip . . . Lowest scoring (15.1) since rookie year . . . Dropped to 17th (10.3 per) in rebounding . . . Bad playoffs. Failed to average double figures either in scoring or rebounding . . . Still no real consistency night to night . . . Remains one of better low-post scorers . . . In six seasons, has missed 97 starts with injury and ails . . . Missed 22 last season . . . Runs floor well but must be prodded at times . . . With the Shaqs and Zos and Patricks in East, now an under-sized defender . . . And it's not like he gets tons of bulky help . . . Worked extensively on short-range jumper. Pretty much got it down. Pretty much ignored it . . . Holds single-game franchise record for rebounds with 34, including 26 defensive, vs. Bullets, March 3, 1993 . . . Third straight year with better than 70 percent from foul line . . . They're probably dancing in the streets at Syracuse, where he left in '88 to become Heat's No. 9 pick, their first-ever lottery choice . . . Born May 10, 1965, in Beirut, Lebanon . . . High school in Greece . . . Made $3.057 million.

Year	Team	G	FG	FG Pct.	FT	FT Pct.	Reb.	Ast.	TP	Avg.
1988-89	Miami	78	333	.448	181	.511	549	55	848	10.9
1989-90	Miami	74	486	.502	256	.594	766	78	1228	16.6
1990-91	Miami	64	395	.481	258	.619	709	95	1050	16.4
1991-92	Miami	79	463	.489	370	.733	934	109	1296	16.4
1992-93	Miami	72	417	.480	397	.735	846	100	1232	17.1
1993-94	Miami	72	392	.488	304	.720	740	136	1088	15.1
	Totals	439	2486	.483	1766	.662	4544	573	6742	15.4

STEVE SMITH 25 6-8 213   Guard

Helps to have friends in high places . . . Member of Dream Team II . . . More a testament to Heat partner Billy Cunningham's influence on selection committee than his game . . . Had a nice scoring year: 17.3 points. But after three years of teasing, the great point-guard theory has pretty much been put to rest and he played more as the two . . . Not like Heat overstocked at point, either. They were third-worst team in the East in both assists-to-turnovers and steals-to-turnovers . . . Stepped up in playoffs and led team in scoring . . . Terrific range on shot: 184 three-

pointers...Drives, but not in penetrate-and-dish mode...
Wretched defensively...So bad, that when he teamed with Harold Miner, no defensive whiz himself, Miner drew the tougher
assignment...78 games gave Heat their first full season out of
him since drafting him No. 5 out of Michigan State in '91...
Knee woes knocked him out of 55 games his first two years...
Born March 31, 1969, in Highland Park, Mich....Made $2.252
million.

Year	Team	G	FG	FG Pct.	FT	FT Pct.	Reb.	Ast.	TP	Avg.
1991-92	Miami	61	297	.454	95	.748	188	278	729	12.0
1992-93	Miami	48	279	.451	155	.787	197	267	766	16.0
1993-94	Miami	78	491	.456	273	.835	352	394	1346	17.3
	Totals	187	1067	.454	523	.803	737	939	2841	15.2

GLEN RICE 27 6-8 220   Guard-Forward

Score 20 one night, score 20 the next, you
average 20. Score 30 one night, 10 the next,
you still average 20...Yup, he took the frustrating way...Team's top scorer three straight
years. Even if he does it the hard way...Good
pack-type rebounder. Six or seven go up, he
finds a way to come away with the ball. One-
on-one, not so hot...Can blow away any team
with his shot, including Heat...And where exactly were you,
Mr. Rice, during the playoffs? Any witnesses to support your
claim you were playing?...Shot .382 vs. Hawks in first round
...Remains one of league's deadliest long-range types (.381 on
threes)...Has made at least 130 treys three straight years...
Found a little more consistency on his jumper. But Heat would
like more...Ball-handling? Still working on it. Sometimes, it
takes years and years to get these things down...Made $2.002
million...Member of Michigan's '89 NCAA champs...Born
May 28, 1967, in Flint, Mich....No. 4 pick in '89.

Year	Team	G	FG	FG Pct.	FT	FT Pct.	Reb.	Ast.	TP	Avg.
1989-90	Miami	77	470	.439	91	.734	352	138	1048	13.6
1990-91	Miami	77	550	.461	171	.818	381	189	1342	17.4
1991-92	Miami	79	672	.469	266	.836	394	184	1765	22.3
1992-93	Miami	82	582	.440	242	.820	424	180	1554	19.0
1993-94	Miami	81	663	.467	250	.880	434	184	1708	21.1
	Totals	396	2937	.456	1020	.829	1985	875	7417	18.7

GRANT LONG 28 6-9 248 Forward

Wow. Here's a real news bulletin. Heat are still undersized at power forward . . . They've tried for years to bulk up and they keep coming back to this undersized guy . . . One of the few guys who really plays with grit and heart every night in south Florida . . . One of two starters (Steve Smith the other) whose scoring increased in playoffs vs. Hawks . . . Of course, he missed a playoff game through suspension for his involvement in the ugly Game 2 brawl . . . Tries to compensate for lack of bulk with quickness. Averaged 1.29 steals in season nagged by injuries . . . Good off-ball defender . . . Season-high 24 points vs. Celts March 7 . . . Has 15-foot range, but to use it takes him away from basket . . . He and Rony Seikaly only two remaining original Heat . . . Cousin of Pistons' Terry Mills . . . Born March 12, 1966, in Wayne, Mich. . . . Second-round pick out of Eastern Michigan in '88 . . . Earned $1.41 million.

Year	Team	G	FG	FG Pct.	FT	FT Pct.	Reb.	Ast.	TP	Avg.
1988-89	Miami	82	336	.486	304	.749	546	149	976	11.9
1989-90	Miami	81	257	.483	172	.714	402	96	686	8.5
1990-91	Miami	80	276	.492	181	.787	568	176	734	9.2
1991-92	Miami	82	440	.494	326	.807	691	225	1212	14.8
1992-93	Miami	76	397	.469	261	.765	568	182	1061	14.0
1993-94	Miami	69	300	.446	187	.786	495	170	788	11.4
	Totals	470	2006	.478	1431	.769	3270	998	5457	11.6

VERNELL (BIMBO) COLES 26 6-2 185 Guard

Hard to find a better backup point in the East . . . Unless you take three-point shooting into consideration . . . Took an oh-fer in the second half on treys . . . Overall, missed 53 of his last 59 three-point attempts, finishing at 20-of-99 . . . Real solid defender with scoring ability. Averaged an assist every 6.5 minutes . . . Not bad at all off the bench . . . Good driving scorer, too . . . Tough off the dribble. Without the ball, well, he's tough off the dribble . . . Emerged as Heat's second-best scorer (13.8) in playoffs. Shot .532 vs. Hawks . . . Right, he only took a few threes (1-of-4) . . . Also topped team in playoff assists. But Heat hardly scored, so his 3.4 apg didn't sent team brass into mad rush to re-do contract . . . Born April 22, 1968, in Covington, Va. . . . After career at Virginia Tech, was drafted by Kings on second round in '90 and traded to Heat for Rory Sparrow June 27, 1990.

Year	Team	G	FG	FG Pct.	FT	FT Pct.	Reb.	Ast.	TP	Avg.
1990-91	Miami	82	162	.412	71	.747	153	232	401	4.9
1991-92	Miami	81	295	.455	216	.824	189	366	816	10.1
1992-93	Miami	81	318	.464	177	.805	166	373	855	10.6
1993-94	Miami	76	233	.449	102	.779	159	263	588	7.7
	Totals	320	1008	.449	566	.799	667	1234	2660	8.3

HAROLD MINER 23 6-5 215   Guard

Sometimes, "Baby Jordan" was less effective than Baby Huey . . . Yes, he can be an offensive power. Given the right circumstances. Like someone of his defensive ability guarding him . . . Has to finish as strong as his moves . . . Makes the first step. Makes the move. Sees the basket. Puts up a sissy shot . . . But give him time. It was only his second year and he shot .477, averaged in double figures . . . Playoff non-entity. Only got 57 minutes. And they play pack-it-in-halfcourt stuff . . . Great quickness, but overall defensively, well, you wouldn't want to put him on Reggie Miller. Or Roger Miller . . . Won Slam Dunk contest as a rookie . . . Made 31 starts after being the only Heat player without a start his first season . . . Born May 5, 1971, in Inglewood, Cal. . . . Made $1.186 million . . . No. 12 pick out of USC in '92 . . . Only second player in Pac-10 history to score 2,000 points. Some chap known as Lew Alcindor at UCLA was first.

Year	Team	G	FG	FG Pct.	FT	FT Pct.	Reb.	Ast.	TP	Avg.
1992-93	Miami	73	292	.475	163	.762	147	73	750	10.3
1993-94	Miami	63	254	.477	149	.828	156	95	661	10.5
	Totals	136	546	.476	312	.792	303	168	1411	10.4

JOHN SALLEY 30 6-11 250   Forward-Center

Call off the APB. The guy the Heat traded for Sept. 8, 1992, might finally have shown up . . . Strong last month, stronger playoffs (11.0 points, eight rebounds) . . . Heat flirting with idea of starting him again. Last time they tried, it worked about as well as sugar in a gas tank . . . His first year in Miami was a wash with a left foot stress fracture . . . Could be the regular shot-blocker and interior defender the Heat crave . . . If they're looking to him for versatile offense, they're in big trouble . . . Key element of Detroit's two championship teams came to Miami for a first-rounder (turned out to be No. 10 pick in '93, Lindsey Hunter) . . . Drafted No. 11 out of Georgia Tech by Pistons in '86 . . . Born May 16, 1964, in Brooklyn, N.Y. . . . Paid $2.452 million.

Year	Team	G	FG	FG Pct.	FT	FT Pct.	Reb.	Ast.	TP	Avg.
1986-87	Detroit	82	163	.562	105	.614	296	54	431	5.3
1987-88	Detroit	82	258	.566	185	.709	402	113	701	8.5
1988-89	Detroit	67	166	.498	135	.692	335	75	467	7.0
1989-90	Detroit	82	209	.512	174	.713	439	67	593	7.2
1990-91	Detroit	74	179	.475	186	.727	327	70	544	7.4
1991-92	Detroit	72	249	.512	186	.715	296	116	684	9.5
1992-93	Miami	51	154	.502	115	.799	313	83	423	8.3
1993-94	Miami	76	208	.477	164	.729	407	135	582	7.7
	Totals	586	1586	.513	1250	.712	2815	713	4425	7.6

BRIAN SHAW 28 6-6 194   Guard

A stop-gap . . . Heat found he was their best solution to the point-guard mess (they hope draftee Khalid Reeves is the answer) . . . Shaw always has been hounded by the "point guard in shooting guard body/mentality" thing . . . Has bounced back and forth between one and two . . . Good leadership, if not classic point physical skills . . . Sound defensively . . . Maybe we should just forget the whole shooting thing (.407, .393, .417 the last three years) . . . NINE assists in five playoff starts? . . . Hurry up, Khalid . . . On April 8, 1993, at Milwaukee, he hit NBA record 10 three-point shots on 15 attempts . . . Drafted No. 24 in 1988 out of Cal-Santa Barbara by Celtics, who traded him for Sherman Douglas Jan. 10, 1992 . . . Spent 1989-90 in Italy before return to Celts . . . Born March 22, 1966, in Oakland . . . Made $1.512 million.

Year	Team	G	FG	FG Pct.	FT	FT Pct.	Reb.	Ast.	TP	Avg.
1988-89	Boston	82	297	.433	109	.826	376	472	703	8.6
1990-91	Boston	79	442	.469	204	.819	370	602	1091	13.8
1991-92	Bos.-Mia.	63	209	.407	72	.791	204	250	495	7.9
1992-93	Miami	68	197	.393	61	.782	257	235	498	7.3
1993-94	Miami	77	278	.417	64	.719	350	385	693	9.0
	Totals	369	1423	.430	510	.798	1557	1944	3480	9.4

WILLIE BURTON 26 6-8 219   Guard-Forward

Tremendous offensive skills... Tremendous inconsistency to make those tremendous offensive skills tremendously disappointing... Another tweener type... Why doesn't the league just start playing 6-on-6 with a new tweener position?... Another disappointing season: .438 shooting, 7.0 points... Another playoff non-entity... Career plagued by injury and bout with depression since being the No. 9 selection out of Minnesota in 1990... 79 combined games the last two seasons... Made $1.002 million... Not much return on the investment... Born May 26, 1968, in Detroit.

Year	Team	G	FG	FG Pct.	FT	FT Pct.	Reb.	Ast.	TP	Avg.
1990-91	Miami	76	341	.441	229	.782	262	107	915	12.0
1991-92	Miami	68	280	.450	196	.800	244	123	762	11.2
1992-93	Miami	26	54	.383	91	.717	70	16	204	7.8
1993-94	Miami	53	124	.438	120	.759	136	39	371	7.0
	Totals	223	799	.439	636	.773	712	285	2252	10.1

KEITH ASKINS 26 6-8 223   Guard-Forward

Coming to a post-office bulletin board near you... Most Wanted... Well, maybe not... May be the chippiest player in the league... Sucker punch of Atlanta's Doug Edwards in playoffs a classic cheap shot... Fined $15,000 and suspended for three games by NBA... Probably was too light... Was the first player ever to draw two flagrant fouls in same game. Did it against Knicks April 2, 1993... As a player, has shown some limited improvement. Shooting barely scratching 41 percent in four years, though... Not much range... Defensively adequate, but usual Heat problem: plays bigger, bulkier types... Made $312,000... Born Dec. 15, 1967, in Athens, Ala.... Scholarathlete at Alabama, Class of '90... Signed with Heat as undrafted free agent Sept. 7, 1990.

Year	Team	G	FG	FG Pct.	FT	FT Pct.	Reb.	Ast.	TP	Avg.
1990-91	Miami	39	34	.420	12	.480	68	19	86	2.2
1991-92	Miami	59	84	.410	26	.703	142	38	219	3.7
1992-93	Miami	69	88	.413	29	.725	198	31	227	3.3
1993-94	Miami	37	36	.409	9	.900	82	13	85	2.3
	Totals	204	242	.412	76	.679	490	101	617	3.0

MATT GEIGER 25 7-0 245   Center

Shaved his head in preseason as part of team unity thing... Really shouldn't have... A competent backup center who brings bulk and pretty good defensive position, a real rarity around these guys... Decent back-to-basket game. Turnarounds to 10 feet that led to .574 shooting... Good offensive rebounder... Now you are allowed to rebound at the other end, too... Nearly 40 percent of his boards were offensive. Got just 11 non-productive playoff minutes... Hey, it was more than any Hornet got... Second-year pay of $250,000... Second-round pick out of Georgia Tech in 1992... Born Sept. 10, 1969, in Salem, Mass.... Did two years at Auburn before Georgia Tech.

Year	Team	G	FG	FG Pct.	FT	FT Pct.	Reb.	Ast.	TP	Avg.
1992-93	Miami	48	76	.524	62	.674	120	14	214	4.5
1993-94	Miami	72	202	.574	116	.779	303	32	521	7.2
	Totals	120	278	.559	178	.739	423	46	735	6.1

ALEC KESSLER 27 6-11 240   Forward-Center

His best bet for NBA future may be as a trainer ... Medical school student... Extremely smart. Except he hasn't been able to figure out that 6-11 guys are more valuable with their head under the rim... Never saw a playoff minute ... Rarely saw regular-season minutes for that matter... Used 15 times for 66 minutes... Yeah, they kind of look at 1990's first-rounder as a bust... Ponderously slow... Other than a perimter shot, not much... Academic All-American at Georgia. Left as Bulldogs' all-time scorer. Since eclipsed... Made $922,000 in final year of deal. Maybe final year with Heat... Was picked 12th by Rockets and traded for the rights to Dave Jamerson and Carl Herrera... Born Jan. 13, 1967, in Minneapolis.

Year	Team	G	FG	FG Pct.	FT	FT Pct.	Reb.	Ast.	TP	Avg.
1990-91	Miami	78	199	.425	88	.672	336	31	486	6.2
1991-92	Miami	77	158	.413	94	.817	314	34	410	5.3
1992-93	Miami	40	57	.467	36	.766	91	14	155	3.9
1993-94	Miami	15	11	.440	6	.750	10	2	33	2.2
	Totals	210	425	.426	224	.744	751	81	1084	5.2

THE ROOKIES

KHALID REEVES 22 6-1 206   Guard

Led Arizona to Final Four as a senior when he averaged 24.2 points . . . First Arizona player ever with over 800 points in one season . . . Listed height took a hit, from 6-3, in pre-draft camps . . . Second-team All-American and MVP of West Regional . . . The No. 12 selection . . . Born July 12, 1972, in the Bronx, N.Y.

JEFF WEBSTER 23 6-6 232   Forward

Heat hope this Oklahoma bruiser can turn out to be the power forward they've sought . . . Was the 40th player taken . . . Third-leading scorer in Sooner history . . . Averaged 23.7 points as a senior . . . All-Big Eight his final season . . . Averaged 7.8 rebounds . . . Inside player who scorers on dunk, putbacks, post-ups . . . Born Feb. 19, 1971, in Pine Bluff, Ark.

COACH KEVIN LOUGHERY: So what if he was No. 2? He  still has a job . . . Signed on for two more years and an option ($750,000 per) when Heat's apparent first choice, Duke's Mike Krzyzewski, said no . . . Media said thanks. Loughery a huckuva lot easier to spell than Krzyzewski . . . Guided Heat to best record ever following major dud of 1992-93 . . . Three-year record with Heat: 116-130 (.472) . . . In all or parts of 16 seasons with six NBA teams, he has a record of 457-633 (.419) . . . Head coach in Philadelphia (1972-73), New Jersey (1976-81), Atlanta (1981-83), Chicago (1983-85) and Washington (1985-88) . . . Was 168-84 in three ABA seasons, including two championships, with Nets . . . NBA's all-time technical-foul leader . . . But has been more laid back with Miami. Each year, though, sees more of the old volatile ways returning . . . 11-year pro with three NBA teams . . . Detroit picked him 13th in 1962 out of St. John's . . . Career produced 15.3 scoring average, mostly with Bullets . . . Born March 28, 1940, in Brooklyn, N.Y.

GREATEST PLAYER

When a team has only been in existence for six years, the nominees for greatest player quickly get whittled to a precious few. Glen Rice is the team's all-time leading scorer. But for the one player who has had the great impact on the Heat, the choice for Greatest Player has to go to Rony Seikaly.

The Lebanon-born center is the greatest rebounder, by far, in Heat history, averaging better than 10 a game. And he is one of a rare breed of active players to be able to say they had a 30-rebound game. Seikaly established the all-time single-game Miami record—as well as the best individual game of the 1992-93 season—when he collected 34 rebounds against Washington on March 3, 1993. His collection included a team-record 26 defensive boards.

Seikaly also is Miami's second all-time scorer with 6,742 points, trailing only Rice.

ALL-TIME HEAT LEADERS

SEASON

Points: Glen Rice, 1,765, 1991-92
Assists: Sherman Douglas, 624, 1990-91
Rebounds: Rony Seikaly, 934, 1991-92

GAME

Points: Glen Rice, 46 vs. Orlando, 4/11/92
Assists: Sherman Douglas, 17 vs. Atlanta, 2/26/90
Rebounds: Rony Seikaly, 34 vs. Washington, 3/3/93

CAREER

Points: Glen Rice, 7,417, 1989-94
Assists: Sherman Douglas, 1,243, 1988-91
Rebounds: Rony Seikaly, 4,544, 1988-94

MILWAUKEE BUCKS

TEAM DIRECTORY: Pres.: Herb Kohl; VP-Bus. Oper.: John Steinmiller; VP-Basketball Oper./Head Coach: Mike Dunleavy; VP-Player Personnel: Lee Rose; Dir. Pub. Rel.: Bill King II; Coach: Mike Dunleavy; Asst. Coaches: Frank Hamblen, Jim Eyen, Butch Carter. Arena: Bradley Center (18,633). Colors: Hunter green, purple and silver.

SCOUTING REPORT

SHOOTING: Want to just pass the airsickness bag and call it even in this category?

The Bucks had the absolute worse offense in the East, although they outshot the Nets, .447-.445, to make that all-important escape from the cellar field-goal percentage spot. They averaged 96.9 points, which you might get away with if you're the Knicks. But the Bucks most assuredly are nothing like the Knicks.

They didn't hit three-pointers, they couldn't hit free throws and their transition game was a horror because it's hard to run when you don't rebound. Now if the prayers of the Bucks and their fans carry any weight, then maybe the solution is coming neatly wrapped in a 6-7, 225-pound package marked "Glenn Robinson." Adding him to last year's first-rounder, Vin Baker, who exceeded expectations, gives Milwaukee a foundation—and a solid one—on which to continue rebuilding.

PLAYMAKING: See? They weren't as bad as Dallas. At least they did one thing right.

The one-two point-guard combination of Eric Murdock and Lee Mayberry provided the Bucks with their one real bright spot last season. Murdock, by the end of the campaign (his second in Milwaukee) was exuding the confidence of a court leader and was 13th in the NBA in assists—and remember, Mayberry was getting a goodly chunk of the playing time. Now these guys might be able to set up plays. But then the Bucks have to make their shots.

On second thought, it was amazing Murdock was able to finish 13th.

REBOUNDING: They took the fewest rebounds of any team in the NBA last season and yet they ranked ahead of 10 teams in the statistical breakdowns. Why? Well, when you play defense the way the Bucks did, the other guys don't miss too often and

Eric Murdock has emerged as a bonafide court leader.

so defensive rebounds drops. Baker, as a rookie, led the team in boarding but simply wasn't enough. After the Bucks unloaded Frank Brickowski, there simply was nobody with the bulk necessary to crash the board on an effective, nightly basis.

DEFENSE: Terrible. Lousy. Putrid. Pathetic.

And that's on the good nights.

Individually, the Bucks are bad defenders. And it doesn't get much better when you lump them together. Oh, there's a bright

BUCK ROSTER

No.	Veterans	Pos.	Ht.	Wt.	Age	Yrs. Pro	College
42	Vin Baker	F	6-11	234	22	1	Hartford
17	Jon Barry	G	6-5	195	25	2	Georgia Tech
–	Marty Conlon	F	6-11	245	26	3	Providence
U-00	Anthony Cook	F-C	6-9	240	27	4	Arizona
U-40	Joe Courtney	F	6-9	235	25	2	Southern Mississippi
10	Todd Day	G-F	6-6	200	24	2	Arkansas
99	Roy Hinson	F-C	6-9	215	33	12	Rutgers
U-54	Brad Lohaus	F-C	6-11	238	30	7	Iowa
11	Lee Mayberry	G	6-1	175	24	2	Arkansas
5	Eric Murdock	G	6-1	190	26	3	Providence
–	Ed Pinckney	F	6-9	215	31	9	Villanova

U-unrestricted free agent

Rd.	Rookies	Sel. No.	Pos.	Ht.	Wt.	College
1	Glenn Robison	1	F	6-7	225	Purdue
1	Eric Mobley	18	C	6-10	250	Pittsburgh
2	Andrei Fetisov	36	C	6-10	215	Russia
C-2	Voshon Lenard	46	G	6-3	205	Minnesota

C-returned to college

spot here and there, specifically with the play of the point guards. But beyond that, there is no shot-blocker, no banger, no one guy to shut down the opposition's horse. The Bucks had hoped the since-departed Ken Norman would fill that role last year. But then the Bucks had hoped they wouldn't lose 62 games last year, either.

Baker showed some definite defensive promise with a good feel for rotations and some blocked shots. But there was next to nothing up front to help him. He'll get some this season in Robinson. How much? Well, the rest of the NBA is curious about that, too.

OUTLOOK: Go to every category and you keep coming up with the same solution: Glenn Robinson. The rookie who would be the NBA's first $100-million man may have to earn every penny.

This is rebuilding, pure and simple. The Bucks have no illusions. Even with a cast of three hopefully solid rookies, led by the grand prize of all rookies, the Bucks know there is more losing in store. They just hope to keep the pain to a minimum.

Overall, the outlook is considerably brighter through Robinson, and Mike Dunleavy has the patience. Of course, being his own boss, he can afford it.

BUCK PROFILES

VIN BAKER 22 6-11 234   Forward

Skinny and gangly, he looks like his last decent meal was back in the '80s . . . Looks can be deceiving . . . After it became obvious Bucks were headed to oblivion, he got playing time. And did he play! . . . Exploded onto the All-Rookie team, shooting .501 and averaging 13.5 points . . . Made 62 starts . . . Exceeded expectations . . . Also played at center and showed he can run the court and blend that with an explosive inside game . . . Rebounder (7.6) and shot-blocker (1.39), too . . . His 277 offensive rebounds were sixth-best in the East. Warriors' Chris Webber, the No. 1 pick, was the only rookie with more . . . No. 8 pick in 1993 out of Hartford, the school's first-ever draft pick . . . Sings in his dad's church choir . . . Born Nov. 23, 1971, in Lake Wales, Fla. . . . Made $866,000.

Year	Team	G	FG	FG Pct.	FT	FT Pct.	Reb.	Ast.	TP	Avg.
1993-94	Milwaukee	82	435	.501	234	.569	621	163	1105	13.5

TODD DAY 24 6-6 200   Guard-Forward

Shut up and play . . . And play better . . . Considered a major disappointment in second year . . . The 1992 lottery pick, No. 8, came with rep as a big-time Arkansas scorer and shooter . . . Shot .415 from the floor (.223 on threes) and .698 from the line . . . Hardly big time . . . Very cocky, but perhaps it's a front . . . Trash-talks everyone . . . Tried it on Scottie Pippen and Chris Mullin. Promptly got toasted . . . Talks better than he plays, which is sort of irksome to Bucks, who paid him $1.722 million last season . . . Trade rumors went beyond whispers . . . Teams defy him to hit outside . . . Can't defend a tree stump . . . Left as Razorbacks' all-time scorer (2,395 points), passing former Bucks' great Sidney Moncrief . . . Born Jan. 7, 1970, in Memphis, Tenn.

Year	Team	G	FG	FG Pct.	FT	FT Pct.	Reb.	Ast.	TP	Avg.
1992-93	Milwaukee	71	358	.432	213	.717	291	117	983	13.8
1993-94	Milwaukee	76	351	.415	231	.698	310	138	966	12.7
	Totals	147	709	.424	444	.707	601	255	1949	13.3

ERIC MURDOCK 26 6-1 190 Guard

Here's one reason why Milwaukee's lone strength was at point guard last year... Firmly established himself as a pro in his second year in Milwaukee after trade from Utah with Blue Edwards for Jay Humphries and Larry Krystkowiak, June 24, 1992... Was headed for oblivion in Utah behind John Stockton... Fifth in NBA in steals with 2.40. That was the most by anybody in the East not named Scottie Pippen... Finished 13th in assists at 6.7... Turnovers were down: 2.5 per game, not bad for a starting point guard... Led team with 15.3 points—that was lowest team-leading total in East... One rap is he doesn't penetrate enough... And despite the steals, he became more of an offensive player in his third year... Good leader, scored better as season progressed... No. 21 pick by Jazz in 1991 out of Providence College, where he finished as NCAA's all-time steals leader (376)... Second team All-American as a senior... Born June 14, 1968, in Somerville, N.J.... Made $800,000.

Year	Team	G	FG	FG Pct.	FT	FT Pct.	Reb.	Ast.	TP	Avg.
1991-92	Utah	50	76	.415	46	.754	54	92	203	4.1
1992-93	Milwaukee	79	438	.468	231	.780	284	603	1138	14.4
1993-94	Milwaukee	82	477	.468	234	.813	261	546	1257	15.3
	Totals	211	991	.464	511	.792	599	1241	2598	12.3

LEE MAYBERRY 24 6-1 175 Guard

And here's the other reason for Milwaukee's point-guard strength... More defensive-oriented than Eric Murdock, minus the quick hands for steals... Quick feet make him tenacious on-ball defender... Often came in during the fourth quarter and simply stayed as his play warranted it... Shooting needs work. Lots of work (.415 floor, .690 line)... Low turnovers... Has never had a 20-point game... Good, heady player. Quiet, mild-mannered sort... Low (No. 23) first-round pick in 1992 out of Arkansas, where he was a teammate of Todd Day... Left Arkansas as school's all-time assists king... Born June 12, 1970, in Tulsa, Okla.... Made $670,000.

Year	Team	G	FG	FG Pct.	FT	FT Pct.	Reb.	Ast.	TP	Avg.
1992-93	Milwaukee	82	171	.456	39	.574	118	273	424	5.2
1993-94	Milwaukee	82	167	.415	58	.690	101	215	433	5.3
	Totals	164	338	.435	97	.638	219	488	857	5.2

ED PINCKNEY 31 6-9 215   Forward

Showed Celtics the right knee was sound after injury-wrecked seven-game season in 1992-93 ... So they traded him ... Went June 30 to Bucks along with a second-round pick for Derek Strong and Blue Edwards ... Bucks had to clear some money for Glenn Robinson ... A complementary player who never lived up to the billing he received as collegiate Player of the Year in 1985, when he led Villanova to stunning NCAA Finals upset of Georgetown ... Still shows awful inconsistency ... Double-digits across the board one night, zeroes the next ... Shot .522 and averaged 6.3 boards, though ... Was 10th pick, by Suns, in 1985 ... Went to Sacramento for Eddie Johnson, June 21, 1987 ... Then on to Boston with Joe Kleine for Danny Ainge and Brad Lohaus, Feb. 23, 1989 ... Born Mar. 27, 1963, in the Bronx, N.Y. ... Made $1.47 million.

Year	Team	G	FG	FG Pct.	FT	FT Pct.	Reb.	Ast.	TP	Avg.
1985-86	Phoenix	80	255	.558	171	.673	308	90	681	8.5
1986-87	Phoenix	80	290	.584	257	.739	580	116	837	10.5
1987-88	Sacramento	79	179	.522	133	.747	230	66	491	6.2
1988-89	Sac.-Bos.	80	319	.513	280	.800	449	118	918	11.5
1989-90	Boston	77	135	.542	92	.773	225	68	362	4.7
1990-91	Boston	70	131	.539	104	.897	341	45	366	5.2
1991-92	Boston	81	203	.537	207	.812	564	62	613	7.6
1992-93	Boston	7	10	.417	12	.923	43	1	32	4.6
1993-94	Boston	76	151	.522	92	.736	478	62	394	5.2
	Totals	630	1673	.539	1348	.767	3218	628	4694	7.5

JON BARRY 25 6-5 195   Guard

It's tough being a fifth guard in a four-guard rotation ... Fans love him. Plays recklessly, dives for loose ball, gets more floor burns than points ... Problem is, he probably would contribute if given consistent minutes. Without consistent time, consistent play (.414 shooting, for example) is near-impossible ... Father, Rick, is a Hall of Famer ... Three brothers play, or have played, Division I ball ... Can score in streaks ... Simply never had a chance to establish himself ... Made $650,000 ... Once rebounded for Mike Dunleavy during practice sessions in Houston ... Obviously, didn't win himself any brownie points ... Born July 25, 1969, in Oakland ... Celtics picked him at No. 21 in 1992 after his career at Georgia Tech. Held out and was traded with second-rounder to Bucks for Alaa Abdelnaby, Dec. 4, 1992.

Year	Team	G	FG	FG Pct.	FT	FT Pct.	Reb.	Ast.	TP	Avg.
1992-93	Milwaukee	47	76	.369	33	.673	43	68	206	4.4
1993-94	Milwaukee	72	158	.414	97	.795	146	168	445	6.2
	Totals	119	234	.398	130	.760	189	236	651	5.5

MARTY CONLON 26 6-11 245   Forward

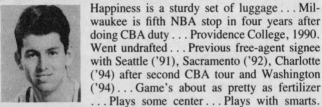

Happiness is a sturdy set of luggage ... Milwaukee is fifth NBA stop in four years after doing CBA duty ... Providence College, 1990. Went undrafted ... Previous free-agent signee with Seattle ('91), Sacramento ('92), Charlotte ('94) after second CBA tour and Washington ('94) ... Game's about as pretty as fertilizer ... Plays some center ... Plays with smarts. Might not win it for you, but won't lose it, either ... Born Jan. 19, 1968, in the Bronx, N.Y.

Year	Team	G	FG	FG Pct.	FT	FT Pct.	Reb.	Ast.	TP	Avg.
1991-92	Seattle	45	48	.475	24	.750	69	12	120	2.7
1992-93	Sacramento	46	81	.474	57	.704	123	37	219	4.8
1993-94	Char.-Wash.	30	95	.576	43	.811	139	34	233	7.8
	Totals	121	224	.513	124	.747	331	83	572	4.7

BRAD LOHAUS 30 6-11 238   Forward-Center

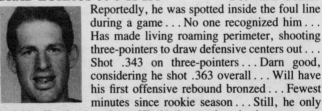

Reportedly, he was spotted inside the foul line during a game ... No one recognized him ... Has made living roaming perimeter, shooting three-pointers to draw defensive centers out ... Shot .343 on three-pointers ... Darn good, considering he shot .363 overall ... Will have his first offensive rebound bronzed ... Fewest minutes since rookie season ... Still, he only had 33 offensive boards ... His 11 three-point tries in a game set team record on Mar. 27, 1993 ... Finished up two-year deal with Bucks that paid him $967,000 last season ... Iowa, Class of 1987 ... Second on team in blocks (55, behind Vin Baker). Had led team four years running ... Born Sept. 29, 1964, in New Ulm, Minn. ... Celtics picked him on second round in 1987 ... Traded to Sacramento with Danny Ainge for Ed Pinckney and Joe Kleine

(Feb. 23, 1989)... Minnesota took him in 1989 expansion draft,
● then sent him to Bucks Jan. 4, 1990 for Randy Breuer.

Year	Team	G	FG	FG Pct.	FT	FT Pct.	Reb.	Ast.	TP	Avg.
1987-88	Boston.........	70	122	.496	50	.806	138	49	297	4.2
1988-89	Bos.-Sac........	77	210	.432	81	.786	256	66	502	6.5
1989-90	Minn.-Mil.	80	305	.460	75	.728	398	168	732	9.2
1990-91	Milwaukee	81	179	.431	37	.685	217	75	428	5.3
1991-92	Milwaukee	70	162	.450	27	.659	249	74	408	5.8
1992-93	Milwaukee	80	283	.461	73	.723	276	127	724	9.1
1993-94	Milwaukee	67	102	.363	20	.690	150	62	270	4.0
	Totals	525	1363	.445	363	.736	1684	621	3361	6.4

THE ROOKIES

GLENN ROBINSON 21 6-7 225   Forward
The prize... "Big Dog" was the No. 1 pick, Milwaukee's prize
for such a lousy season... Immediately gave owners coronaries
by announcing hopes for $100-million deal... No telling how
much he'll ask for his second month... Consensus Player of the
Year at Purdue... Left following junior year after becoming only
15th player in NCAA history to score 1,000 points in a single
season... Led nation in scoring (30.3)... Born Jan. 10, 1973,
in Gary, Ind.

ERIC MOBLEY 24 6-10 250   Center
Out of Pittsburgh, he was Bucks' second first-round selection,
taken at No. 18... Plays a physical inside game... No range...
Shots are mainly dunks... He is a shot-blocker with long wing-
span... Had 73 rejects as senior, when he was third-team All-
Big East... Born Feb. 1, 1970, in the Bronx, N.Y.

ANDREI FETISOV 22 6-10 215   Center
Russian who played one year in Spanish League... The 36th pick,
by Boston. Celtics didn't wait to see if they'd struck gold again,
ala Dino Radja. Dealt his rights and Ed Pinckney to Bucks for
Derek Strong and Blue Edwards on June 30, one day after draft
... Will likely play in Europe.

VOSHON LENARD 21 6-3 205   Forward
He's listed because they drafted him. But he's not here. Had been
an early entry after three years at Minnesota, but changed his

mind, deciding to go back to school ... Bucks retain rights for next year ... Set Minnesota record for three-pointers in a career (195) ... Averaged 21.6 in Big Ten play ... Size is a definite drawback. Will eventually play guard in NBA, but can he handle the ball well enough? ... No. 46, selected in second round ... Born May 14, 1973, in Detroit.

COACH MIKE DUNLEAVY: He can coach; you'd just never know it from two-year record with Bucks: 48-116 (.293) ... Hasn't had a lot to work with, especially last year, when it was next to impossible to assign roles due to too many tweeners ... There was some player griping. But what do you expect? They rocked NBA for 20 victories ... But Bucks are rebuilding, and with three straight lottery picks, the future is on decided upswing ... Good X's and O's guy ... Huge contract (eight years) and has owner's blessing ... Plus, he's VP of Basketball Operations ... Won 58 as Laker coach, taking them to Finals in 1990-91 ... Then, in injury-riddled, Magic Johnson-retirement season, led L.A. to 43 triumphs ... Sixth-round pick of Philly in 1976 after career at South Carolina ... Nine NBA seasons, plus two later years where he came off bench as player/coach in emergencies, brought 8.0-ppg average ... Led NBA in three-point shooting in '83 ... Three-year Buck assistant ... Born March 21, 1954, in Brooklyn, N.Y.

GREATEST PLAYER

Rarely does one guy come in and made a monumental difference in a team. And rarer still does it happen with a rookie. But then again, rarely does anyone like Kareem Abdul-Jabbar come along.

The Bucks came into existence at precisely the right time: the 1968-69 season. And with a cast of expansionist rejects, they were lousy enough to qualify for the first pick, which they won in a coin toss with Phoenix. And the timing was perfect because the plum of the draft was Abdul-Jabbar, still known then as Lew Alcindor.

A 29-game improvement occured the following year and Abdul-Jabbar brought Milwaukee its only NBA title in his second season. In Kareem's five full seasons in Milwaukee (he played an injury-riddled sixth), the Bucks averaged 60.8 victories. As a Buck, he averaged 30.4 points and 15.3 rebounds. So while arguments can be made for the superb all-around play and longevity of perennial all-star Sidney Moncrief, it's hard to debate one of the greatest ever, Abdul-Jabbar, as being the best ever in a Milwaukee uniform.

ALL-TIME BUCK LEADERS

SEASON

Points: Kareem Abdul-Jabbar, 2,822, 1971-72
Assists: Oscar Robertson, 668, 1970-71
Rebounds: Kareem Abdul-Jabbar, 1,346, 1971-72

GAME

Points: Kareem Abdul-Jabbar, 55 vs. Boston, 12/10/71
Assists: Guy Rodgers, 22 vs. Detroit, 10/31/68
Rebounds: Swen Nater, 33 vs. Atlanta, 12/19/76

CAREER

Points: Kareem Abdul-Jabbar, 14,211, 1969-75
Assists: Paul Pressey, 3,272, 1982-90
Rebounds: Kareem Abdul-Jabbar, 7,161, 1969-75

NEW JERSEY NETS

TEAM DIRECTORY: Chairman: Alan Aufzien; Vice Chairman: Jerry Cohen; Pres.-COO: Jon Spoelstra; Exec. VP/GM-Basketball Oper.: Willis Reed; Dir. Pub. Rel.: John Mertz; Coach: Butch Beard; Asst. Coaches: Paul Silas, Johnny Davis. Arena: Brendan Byrne Meadowlands Arena (20,049). Colors: Red, white and blue.

SCOUTING REPORT

SHOOTING: When the shots make sense, the Nets go beyond formidable. But when they take Net shots, they wind up shooting .445 as a team, like they did last season when they surpassed only Dallas in the entire league. And surpassing Dallas in anything isn't worth bragging about.

The Nets, though, made up for their dismal shooting with a relentless effort on the boards that leads to numerous putbacks. Or at least they did under Chuck Daly. On three-pointers, they have a stockpile of capable shooters, including the 6-10 do-it-all power forward All-Star, Derrick Coleman. And through Kenny Anderson's penetrations, they get to the line a staggering number of times. Nobody went to the foul line more than the Nets last season. And it's not like they draw that many illegal-defense technicals. So although they were last in the East in shooting, they can still put up points, one, two or three at a time.

PLAYMAKING: Anderson. That's all you need to know about the Nets in this category.

But what the Nets need to know about Anderson, who was fourth in the league last season with 9.6 assists per, is how will he respond to offseason wrist surgery. And who is going to be his backup? They're hoping first-round pick of two drafts past, Rex Walters, can fill the void. He has the instincts. Speed is another matter for the two-guard by college trade, point by high-school experience. If Walters can handle the post, then the Nets, with Anderson shouldering the bulk of the duty, should again finish in the top 10 for assist-to-turnovers.

REBOUNDING: Nobody grabbed more rebounds than the Nets last season. Nobody.

Problem was, lots of their boards came off their own misses as they led the East in offensive boards and trailed only Portland— by two crummy boards—for the league lead.

Kenny Anderson: One of best point guards in game.

In Coleman, the Nets will find double-figure rebounds every night. Chris Morris, for all his dreadful shots and bad passes, can hit the glass with authority. When the spirit moves him, that is. Then there is the ever-enigmatic Benoit Benjamin in the middle. He can rebound. He can do a lot of things. Problem is, he doesn't most of the time.

DEFENSE: This could be interesting. The Nets are coming off their Chuck Daly plan. And Chuck Daly spells D-E-F-E-N-S-E in any city. Now they're coming under the ways of Butch Beard.

Surprisingly, however, the Nets were mediocre in most defensive stats last year, including points allowed (101.0), turnovers forced (15.2) and opponent field-goal percentage (.458). None were bad, none were great. And in the '90s, you need great defense to win.

The Nets have everything in place to be of the ilk of their cross-river rival Knicks. They have the size. They have the quickness. Now it will be up to Beard to give them the motivation.

NET ROSTER

No.	Veterans	Pos.	Ht.	Wt.	Age	Yrs. Pro	College
7	Kenny Anderson	G	6-1	170	24	3	Georgia Tech
00	Benoit Benjamin	C	7-0	260	29	9	Creighton
42	P.J. Brown	F	6-10	225	26	1	Louisiana Tech
44	Derrick Coleman	F	6-10	235	27	4	Syracuse
21	Kevin Edwards	G	6-3	202	29	6	DePaul
43	Armon Gilliam	F	6-9	245	30	7	UNLV
22	Sean Higgins	F	6-9	215	25	3	Michigan
4	Rick Mahorn	F-C	6-10	260	36	13	Hampton
34	Chris Morris	F	6-8	220	28	6	Auburn
U-22	Johnny Newman	F-G	6-7	205	30	8	Richmond
U-33	Dwayne Schintzius	C	7-2	285	26	4	Florida
2	Rex Walters	G	6-4	190	24	1	Kansas
55	Jayson Williams	F-C	6-10	245	26	4	St. John's

U-unrestricted free agent

Rd.	Rookies	Sel. No.	Pos.	Ht.	Wt.	College
1	Yinka Dare	14	C	6-10	271	George Washington

OUTLOOK: A general rule of thumb for New Jersey is that whenever something is going good, a counter balance will come along and screw it up. Two years ago, Anderson broke his wrist. Last season, Jayson Williams opened his mouth about the Knicks. So the playoffs were short, sweet affairs.

Daly helped bring respectability and credibility on a nightly basis. And now Beard, a veteran NBA type but one who has been away from the pro game for four years and who has not been a head coach before, is taking over for a franchise that has petitioned the league to change its name to "Swamp Dragons" (honest). Beard began by pointing to the second round of the playoffs as a goal and claiming Coleman's negative ways loom as one of the chief elements to reverse. Coleman responded with a basic "what negative ways?" inquiry.

Then came the draft and the Nets went out and, despite proclaiming the need for a shooter, scooped up Yinka Dare, a certified project whose college coach said wasn't ready. Dare promptly came in and said he is going to be one of the greats soon. No problem.

Things might have been going too good for too long in the swamp.

NET PROFILES

DERRICK COLEMAN 27 6-10 235   Forward

Imagine if he practiced! . . . Best season . . . Clearly emerged as team leader with more sustained efforts than ever . . . Averaged 20-10 points and rebounds for second straight season . . . Only other forwards to do same last season were Karl Malone and Charles Barkley . . . All-Star starter . . . Name it, he does it . . . Shoots. And with range. Rebounds. Puts ball on floor. Passes . . . Needs to improve passing against double-teams, though. Especially as he's always double-teamed . . . 47 double-doubles, two triple-doubles . . . Season highs: 36 points, 19 rebounds, nine blocks . . . Led Nets in scoring, boarding and blocks . . . Career-high 77 games . . . As physically gifted as any player in the game . . . Knicks stumped him in playoffs after he owned them in regular season . . . Wore him down with tag-team style, constantly running fresh bodies. Yet he averaged 24.5 . . . But shot .392 . . . Left Syracuse as NCAA's all-time rebounder (1.537). First collegian with 2,000 points, 1,500 boards, 300 blocks . . . No. 1 pick in '90 . . . Rookie of the Year . . . Born June 21, 1967, in Mobile, Ala. . . . Detroit-bred . . . Made $3.44 million.

Year	Team	G	FG	FG Pct.	FT	FT Pct.	Reb.	Ast.	TP	Avg.
1990-91	New Jersey	74	514	.467	323	.731	759	163	1364	18.4
1991-92	New Jersey	65	483	.504	300	.763	618	205	1289	19.8
1992-93	New Jersey	76	564	.460	421	.808	852	276	1572	20.7
1993-94	New Jersey	77	541	.447	439	.774	870	262	1559	20.2
	Totals	292	2102	.468	1483	.771	3099	906	5784	19.8

KENNY ANDERSON 24 6-1 170   Guard

Remember the fractured wrist suffered last season that everyone said didn't need surgery? . . . Everyone was wrong . . . Underwent summer surgery on left wrist injured Feb. 28, 1993, on flagrant foul by Knick John Starks . . . "I don't want to use the wrist as an excuse . . ." . . . That was quicksilver point guard's most oft-repeated phrase in his third year out of Georgia Tech . . . Grimaced on every bump . . . Still, became one of the NBA's premier points . . . All-Star starter . . . Career highs across the boards . . . Career-high 45 points, second-most ever by a Net, vs. Pistons April 15 . . . Three triple-doubles . . . Already second on all-time Nets' assist list . . . 9.6 assists per fourth-best in NBA, second-best in East . . . 18.8 scoring average the best of any NBA point guard . . . Three triple-doubles, five in career . . . Shot okay most of season, had dreadful 32 percent March. Overall plunged to .417 . . . Great ball-handler, better penetrator . . . Never got untracked vs. Knick team defense in playoffs . . . No. 2 pick in '91 behind Larry Johnson . . . Born Oct. 9, 1970, in Queens, N.Y. . . . Made $2.925 million.

Year	Team	G	FG	FG Pct.	FT	FT Pct.	Reb.	Ast.	TP	Avg.
1991-92	New Jersey	64	187	.390	73	.745	127	203	450	7.0
1992-93	New Jersey	55	370	.435	180	.776	226	449	927	16.9
1993-94	New Jersey	82	576	.417	346	.818	322	784	1538	18.8
	Totals	201	1133	.418	599	.795	675	1436	2915	14.5

KEVIN EDWARDS 29 6-3 202   Guard

Finally felt wanted, finally produced . . . Chuck Daly simply termed him "a professional." . . . Doesn't overwhelm in any one area but is solid across the board . . . One of the few Nets who didn't look terrified of Knicks in playoffs . . . Shot better as season progressed . . . Finished at .458. His best for a full season . . . Started every game, along with Kenny Anderson . . . Virtually pushed out the door in Miami, so Nets, desperate to replace the late Drazen Petrovic, signed him as a free agent July 8 . . . Career highs in minutes, points, rebounds and three-pointers . . . Good, heady defender. Went back up over 100 steals . . . Season-high 28 points extra sweet; came against Heat Dec. 13 . . . College backcourt teammate of Rod Strickland at DePaul . . . Picked 20th by Heat in 1988 . . . Made $1.2 million the free-agent way . . . Born Oct. 30, 1965, in Cleveland Heights, Ohio.

Year	Team	G	FG	FG Pct.	FT	FT Pct.	Reb.	Ast.	TP	Avg.
1988-89	Miami	79	470	.425	144	.746	262	349	1094	13.8
1989-90	Miami	78	395	.412	139	.760	282	252	938	12.0
1990-91	Miami	79	380	.410	171	.803	205	240	955	12.1
1991-92	Miami	81	325	.454	162	.848	211	170	819	10.1
1992-93	Miami	40	216	.468	119	.844	121	120	556	13.9
1993-94	New Jersey	82	471	.458	167	.770	281	232	1144	14.0
	Totals	439	2257	.434	902	.793	1362	1363	5506	12.5

BENOIT BENJAMIN 29 7-0 260   Center

How to put this delicately? . . . Woof, arf, bark . . . If you can't play for Chuck Daly and your college coach, Willis Reed, who took a monster gamble to get you, who in blazes can you play for? . . . Said media was too harsh out West. It would change in the East when they saw what he can do . . . What exactly does he do? . . . To say he has stone hands would insult rocks. Probably cost Kenny Anderson and Derrick Coleman 1,000 assists . . . Once seen getting back on defense . . . Mistaken identity . . . Came to camp overweight, never got untracked . . . Took offense to media reports of pudginess . . . Maddening element: he has talent . . . Soft touch among good offensive skills . . . Shot .480 . . . And he blocks shots . . . Just doesn't hustle . . . If he gets off to bad start, goes in the tank . . . Gets off to lots of bad starts . . . Challenged home crowd over boos . . . No. 3 pick of Clippers in '85 from Creighton . . . Went to Sonics for Olden Polynice and two No. 1s, Feb. 21, 1991 . . . To L.A. with Doug Christie for Sam Perkins, Feb. 22, 1993 . . . To Nets for Sam Bowie, June 21, 1993 . . . Born Nov. 22, 1964, in Monroe, La. . . . Made $3.575 million.

Year	Team	G	FG	FG Pct.	FT	FT Pct.	Reb.	Ast.	TP	Avg.
1985-86	L.A. Clippers	79	324	.490	229	.746	600	79	878	11.1
1986-87	L.A. Clippers	72	320	.449	188	.715	586	135	828	11.5
1987-88	L.A. Clippers	66	340	.491	180	.706	530	172	860	13.0
1988-89	L.A. Clippers	79	491	.541	317	.744	696	157	1299	16.4
1989-90	L.A. Clippers	71	362	.526	235	.732	657	159	959	13.5
1990-91	LAC-Sea.	70	386	.496	210	.712	723	119	982	14.0
1991-92	Seattle	63	354	.478	171	.687	513	76	879	14.0
1992-93	Sea.-LAL	59	133	.491	69	.663	209	22	335	5.7
1993-94	New Jersey	77	283	.480	152	.710	499	44	718	9.3
	Totals	636	2993	.496	1751	.719	5013	963	7738	12.2

ARMON GILLIAM 30 6-9 245   Forward

He'll put up numbers . . . One of only three Nets in all 82 games but under 2,000 minutes for second straight season . . . Versatile guy and with Nets' problems at center was often undersized man in the middle . . . Abysmal passer . . . Overall defense may be one notch above his passing . . . Double-figure points every season in the league, but his seventh campaign produced career-low 11.8 points . . . Good mid-range touch, turnarounds and hook led to .510 shooting . . . Shooting dipped, as did virtually everyone's, in playoffs vs. Knicks but was still productive (10.5 ppg)... Born May 28, 1964, in Pittsburgh... No. 2 pick in '87, to Suns after consensus All-American and Final Four year at UNLV... Traded to Charlotte for Kurt Rambis Dec. 13, 1989... Went to Sixers with Dave Hoppen for Mike Gminski Jan. 14, 1991... Signed with Nets as free agent Aug. 11, 1993 ... Made $1.2 million.

Year	Team	G	FG	FG Pct.	FT	FT Pct.	Reb.	Ast.	TP	Avg.
1987-88	Phoenix	55	342	.475	131	.679	434	72	815	14.8
1988-89	Phoenix	74	468	.503	240	.743	541	52	1176	15.9
1989-90	Phoe.-Char.	76	484	.515	303	.723	599	99	1271	16.7
1990-91	Char.-Phil.	75	487	.487	268	.815	598	105	1242	16.6
1991-92	Philadelphia	81	512	.511	343	.807	660	118	1367	16.9
1992-93	Philadelphia	80	359	.464	274	.843	472	116	992	12.4
1993-94	New Jersey	82	348	.510	274	.759	500	69	970	11.8
	Totals	523	3000	.496	1833	.772	3804	631	7833	15.0

CHRIS MORRIS 28 6-8 220   Forward

If Chuck Daly had stayed, this guy was gone ...Missed 32 games with injury. Thus, 50 games his lowest since Nets made him the No. 4 pick in '88 draft out of Auburn...But it wasn't the injuries that gave Daly that burning sensation...More like bad passes, worse decisions and even worse shots...Averaged nearly three three-point-shot tries a game... Made 53, including team-record six vs. Detroit March 1... Awful in transition defense, but great on offensive end... So he can run the floor. Just doesn't always do it... Was on a 23-of-39 shooting streak when he broke his thumb in early March... Gave Nets their only playoff-game win, hitting two clutch overtime free throws with :01.5 left for one-point victory over Knicks in Game 3 of first round... But he shot .273 in the series... Born Jan. 20, 1966, in Atlanta... Made $1.96 million.

Year	Team	G	FG	FG Pct.	FT	FT Pct.	Reb.	Ast.	TP	Avg.
1988-89	New Jersey	76	414	.457	182	.717	397	119	1074	14.1
1989-90	New Jersey	80	449	.422	228	.722	422	143	1187	14.8
1990-91	New Jersey	79	409	.425	179	.734	521	220	1042	13.2
1991-92	New Jersey	77	346	.477	165	.714	494	197	879	11.4
1992-93	New Jersey	77	436	.481	197	.794	454	106	1086	14.1
1993-94	New Jersey	50	203	.447	85	.720	228	83	544	10.9
	Totals	439	2257	.450	1036	.734	2516	868	5812	13.2

RICK MAHORN 36 6-10 260   Forward-Center

Coach in training . . . Final year of contract. Final year in league . . . Coming soon to an injury-list transaction notice . . . Spends time on injured list, comes off when Nets need him . . . But never, ever devalue his presence in a lockerroom . . . Studies game, passes observations . . . Great wit. Laugh or he'll kill you . . . One of the Piston "Bad Boys" ringleaders . . . Came back from Italy to play for Chuck Daly . . . Will stay around for intangibles and occasional jarring pick or interior bang . . . Signed as free agent with Nets Nov. 9, 1992 . . . Born Sept. 21, 1958, in Hartford, Conn. . . . Second-round pick by Bullets in 1980 out of Hampton (Va.) Institute . . . Three-time NAIA All-American . . . From Washington to Detroit (June 17, 1985) for Dan Roundfield. Picked by T-Wolves in expansion draft. Refused to go. Traded to Sixers for a first-rounder and two seconds, Oct. 27, 1989 . . . Made $650,000.

Year	Team	G	FG	FG Pct.	FT	FT Pct.	Reb.	Ast.	TP	Avg.
1980-81	Washington	52	111	.507	27	.675	215	25	249	4.8
1981-82	Washington	80	414	.507	148	.632	704	150	976	12.2
1982-83	Washington	82	376	.490	146	.575	779	115	898	11.0
1983-84	Washington	82	307	.507	125	.651	738	131	739	9.0
1984-85	Washington	77	206	.499	71	.683	608	121	483	6.3
1985-86	Detroit	80	157	.455	81	.681	412	64	395	4.9
1986-87	Detroit	63	144	.447	96	.821	375	38	384	6.1
1987-88	Detroit	67	276	.574	164	.756	565	60	717	10.7
1988-89	Detroit	72	203	.517	116	.748	496	59	522	7.3
1989-90	Philadelphia	75	313	.497	183	.715	568	98	811	10.8
1990-91	Philadelphia	80	261	.467	189	.788	621	118	711	8.9
1992-93	New Jersey	74	101	.472	88	.800	279	33	291	3.9
1993-94	New Jersey	28	23	.489	13	.650	54	5	59	2.1
	Totals	912	2892	.498	1447	.703	6414	1017	7235	7.9

P.J. BROWN 26 6-10 225   Forward

This guy's good . . . And he's going to get better . . . Expected to have a small role. Wound up being the starting small forward . . . Long arms with never-quit rebounding, defending mentality . . . A small forward who defends? By gum, it's crazy but it might work . . . Offseason bulk-up program. That was one drawback . . . Great knack for the ball . . . But best skills are defensive . . . Lacks confidence in his shot (.415) . . . Among rookie leaders in rebounds (6.2 per) and blocks (1.18)... Second on team in blocks... Had 53 more offensive rebounds than the 7-foot Benoit Benjamin... Personal-best 17 boards vs. Golden State Jan. 29... Was second-round draft pick out of Louisiana Tech in '92... Did a year in Greece... Little playoff time... A really nice guy, too... Born Oct. 14, 1968, in Detroit... A $600,000 rookie.

Year	Team	G	FG	FG Pct.	FT	FT Pct.	Reb.	Ast.	TP	Avg.
1993-94	New Jersey	79	167	.415	115	.757	493	93	450	5.7

REX WALTERS 24 6-4 190   Guard

Yeah, we know you were a shooting guard in college. Fine. Swell. Go play point... Conversion goes into effect full time this season ... Why not? He has great passing instincts and simply a good feel for getting the ball to the right place at the right time... Good leaper, dunking type a la Rex Chapman... Played typical rookie defense after being No. 16 pick overall out of Kansas... But has good nose for passing lanes... Rarely used in first year: 48 games, 386 minutes... Can tell the grandkids he was in the playoffs. For one full minute... Made half his three-pointers (14-of-28). Has range and definitely can shoot... Lefty... Born Feb. 12, 1970, in Omaha, Neb.... Made $650,000.

Year	Team	G	FG	FG Pct.	FT	FT Pct.	Reb.	Ast.	TP	Avg.
1993-94	New Jersey	48	60	.522	28	.824	38	71	162	3.4

JOHNNY NEWMAN 30 6-7 205   Forward-Guard

Only so much room on the Nets' roster for small forwards... Signed Higgins and already had Morris, Brown. And J. New... Expected to start the season elsewhere after reaching unrestricted free agency... Was stolen from Hornets for Rumeal Robinson Dec. 10, 1993... Solid scorer but slight build always a drawback ... Good shot with range, nice moves to basket with explosive dunks off leaping ability... Underrated, active defender... Just a solid swingman... Averaged 9.5 ppg with Nets in 63 games... Born Nov. 28, 1963, in Danville, Va.... Second-round pick of Cavs out of Richmond in '86... Signed as free agent by Knicks Nov. 12, 1987... After three solid years, went to Charlotte when Knicks did not match free-agent offer sheet July 28, 1990 . . . Made $1.435 million.

Year	Team	G	FG	FG Pct.	FT	FT Pct.	Reb.	Ast.	TP	Avg.
1986-87	Cleveland	59	113	.411	66	.868	70	27	293	5.0
1987-88	New York	77	270	.435	207	.841	159	62	773	10.0
1988-89	New York	81	455	.475	286	.815	206	162	1293	16.0
1989-90	New York	80	374	.476	239	.799	191	180	1032	12.9
1990-91	Charlotte	81	478	.470	385	.809	254	188	1371	16.9
1991-92	Charlotte	55	295	.477	236	.766	179	146	839	15.3
1992-93	Charlotte	64	279	.522	194	.808	143	117	764	11.9
1993-94	Char.-N.J.	81	313	.471	182	.809	180	72	832	10.3
	Totals	578	2577	.471	1795	.808	1382	954	7197	12.5

SEAN HIGGINS 25 6-9 215 Forward

If Yinka Dare is a bust and Nets get hammered for drafting project center, blame this guy . . . Team brass claimed knowing they had him set for a two-year free-agent contract made it easier to draft Dare and bypass a shooter . . . Signed June 30 after doing a year in Greece, where supposedly he rediscovered his shot . . . Did three years in the NBA, averaging 6.5 points in 117 games in stops in San Antonio, Orlando and Golden State . . . Wowed Nets with shooting in workouts . . . Member of Michigan's '89 NCAA championship team . . . Second-round pick of Magic . . . Born Dec. 30, 1968, in Los Angeles.

Year	Team	G	FG	FG Pct.	FT	FT Pct.	Reb.	Ast.	TP	Avg.
1990-91	San Antonio	50	97	.458	28	.848	63	35	225	4.5
1991-92	S.A.-Orl.	38	127	.458	31	.861	102	41	291	7.7
1992-93	Golden State	29	96	.447	35	.745	68	66	240	8.3
	Totals	117	320	.455	94	.810	233	142	756	6.5

JAYSON WILLIAMS 26 6-10 245 Forward-Center

Yeah, he ticked off Net coaches . . . Brazenly predicted Nets would have no problem with Knicks in playoffs . . . Knicks breathed fire. Nets had problem . . . Body by Fisher, brain by Tonka Toy . . . Exceptional offensive rebounder: 109 in 877 minutes. That's one every eight minutes, six over 48 minutes . . . Overall averaged nearly one board per three minutes . . .

And one foot in mouth per six . . . Chuck Daly leaving saved his job in New Jersey . . . Has good backup skills. Quick enough to drive past centers from key . . . Works hard . . . Has to be a backup because he'd foul out in about five minutes . . . Born Feb. 22, 1968, in Ritter, S.C. . . . Made $950,000 . . . Was No. 21 pick by Suns in '90 out of St. John's. Suns couldn't sign him. Sent to 76ers Oct. 28, 1990, for a first-rounder . . . To Nets for conditional draft picks Oct. 8, 1992.

Year	Team	G	FG	FG Pct.	FT	FT Pct.	Reb.	Ast.	TP	Avg.
1990-91	Philadelphia	52	72	.447	37	.661	111	16	182	3.5
1991-92	Philadelphia	50	75	.364	56	.636	145	12	206	4.1
1992-93	New Jersey......	12	21	.457	7	.389	41	0	49	4.1
1993-94	New Jersey......	70	125	.427	72	.605	263	26	322	4.6
	Totals	184	293	.415	172	.612	560	54	759	4.1

DWAYNE SCHINTZIUS 26 7-2 285   Center

Very skilled offensive player . . . Good offense . . . Can do things offensively . . . You REALLY don't want to talk about his defense . . . Lost to molasses in a foot race . . . No. 24 pick of Spurs out of Florida in 1990 is still a project . . . Spent most of season on injured list after back surgery . . . 30 games, 319 minutes, nothing noteworthy . . . Cannot move on the court . . . But has hands, shot and passing ability . . . Born Oct. 14, 1968, in Brandon, Fla. . . . From Spurs to Kings for Antoine Carr Sept. 23, 1991 . . . Waived, signed by Nets as free agent Oct. 1, 1992 . . . Made $921,000 through preseason offer sheet from Bucks that Nets matched.

Year	Team	G	FG	FG Pct.	FT	FT Pct.	Reb.	Ast.	TP	Avg.
1990-91	San Antonio	42	68	.439	22	.550	121	17	158	3.8
1991-92	Sacramento.......	33	50	.427	10	.833	118	20	110	3.3
1992-93	New Jersey......	5	2	.286	3	1.000	8	2	7	1.4
1993-94	New Jersey......	30	29	.345	10	.588	89	13	68	2.3
	Totals	110	149	.410	45	.625	336	52	343	3.1

THE ROOKIE

YINKA DARE 22 6-10 271   Center

Total project . . . Nets surprised many with this choice at No. 14. But Nets do a lot of surprising things, not all good . . . Everybody cautioned him about leaving George Washington early, including his coach Mike Jarvis, who once coached a high-school kid named Patrick Ewing... Claims he will be great... GWU's all-time shot-blocker in just two seasons (140, 2.33 per game)... Born Oct. 10, 1972, in Kabba, Nigeria.

COACH BUTCH BEARD: First-time NBA head coach...

Didn't promise any miracles when he was appointed to succeed the retired Chuck Daly on June 28... Set a simple goal: get to the second round of the playoffs... With talent on hand, is do-able... Hall of Fame coach Red Holzman claimed he hired Beard as an assistant because he was the first player picked up off waivers who came in and learned his system in one day ... Considered a superb communicator and good motivator... Talks and listens to players... Six years as an NBA assistant; four with Knicks, two with Nets... Head coach at Howard University past four seasons, where he compiled 45-69 record... Good friend of Net GM Willis Reed, which sort of helped him get the job... Was one of Reed's assistants in New Jersey... Nine-year pro career included stops in Atlanta, Cleveland, Seattle, Golden State and New York... Louisville, Class of '69... Born May 4, 1947, in Hardinburg, Ky.... Got three-year deal for reported $1 million... First name: Alfred.

GREATEST PLAYER

It should be an easy choice. Greatest Net? Julius Erving. Case closed. But Dr. J. played during the Nets' ABA days and he remains sort of a sore point to New Jersey executives, who constantly hear the "What if the Nets never sold Erving?" comment. Well, they did. And because they did—and because Dr. J. ruled the ABA—the choice is the Nets' all-time leading scorer and rebounder, plus a guy who rivals Erving in the class act department: Buck Williams.

Before he was traded to Portland in June 1989, Williams, out of Maryland, soared to the top of the Nets' all-time charts for points (10,440), rebounds (7,576, both offensive and defensive), games (635), free-throws made (2,476) and minutes (23,100). In addition, he's third in steals (599) and second in blocked shots (696).

Williams was the Nets' chief claim to legitimacy during some of the leanest and most troubled years of a troubled franchise. But the Nets should have figured they had something special after they drafted him because he went on to win the Rookie of the Year Award in 1981-82.

ALL-TIME NET LEADERS

SEASON

Points: Rick Barry, 2,518, 1971-72 (ABA)
Assists: Kevin Porter, 801, 1977-78
Rebounds: Billy Paultz, 1,035, 1971-72 (ABA)

GAME

Points: Julius Erving, 63 vs. San Diego (4 OT), 2/14/75 (ABA)
Assists: Kevin Porter, 29 vs. Houston, 2/24/78
Rebounds: Billy Paultz, 33 vs. Pittsburgh, 2/17/71 (ABA)

CAREER

Points: Buck Williams, 10,440, 1981-89
Assists: Billy Melchionni, 2,251, 1969-75 (ABA)
Rebounds: Buck Williams, 7,576, 1981-89

NEW YORK KNICKS

TEAM DIRECTORY: Pres.: David Checketts; VP-GM: Ernie Grunfeld; VP-Pub. Rel.: John Cirillo; Mgr. Media Rel.: Tim Donovan; Mgr. Publications and Inf.: Dennis D'Agostino; Dir. Scouting Services: Dick McGuire: Coach: Pat Riley; Asst. Coaches: Jeff Van Gundy, Bob Salmi, Jeff Nix. Arena: Madison Square Garden (19,763). Colors: Orange, white and blue.

SCOUTING REPORT

SHOOTING: Pat Riley, during the NBA Finals, summed up the Knick offense most succinctly: "Occasionally, we hit a shot."

Here it is. The weak link. The Achilles' Heel. The Sore Spot. Call it what you want. It has been the Knicks' bane and probably

Patrick Ewing: Still in quest of championship ring.

will continue to be so. They were 18th in shooting (.460), 21st in scoring (98.5).

In Patrick Ewing, the Knicks have the greatest jump-shooting center ever. But after him (and at .496 he was under .500 for the first time since his 50-game rookie season), the Knicks' most reliable jump-shooter is probably Charles Oakley, the power forward who couldn't finish on a bet but is deadly from 15 feet.

John Starks is one of the game's ultimate streak shooters. Witness his powerful 27-point Game 6. Pity his pathetic 2-of-18 Game 7. The Knicks pray Derek Harper shoots with the aplomb he showed down the stretch and that perimeter threat Hubert Davis, now the only backup two, shakes off a dismal playoffs to display his sweet jumper again. Also off the bench, Anthony Mason must continue to find a way to score with his funky little jumpers and hooks and Greg Anthony (.394) must think pass over shot first, second, third and fourth.

PLAYMAKING: The most intriguing storyline early in 1994-95 about the Knicks will be at point guard. It was expected to be a Grand Central Station rush hour in training camp with Harper, Doc Rivers, Anthony, draftee Charlie Ward and the coaching staff favorite with little realistic chance, Corey Gaines.

The Knicks were very middle of the road (17th) in the NBA in assists to turnovers. Their offensive problems were well documented in the Finals. The first choice is Harper, with at least two years left in his 33-year-old legs. He can run the break at least, something the Knicks have been waiting for Anthony to show during three years. Ward, the Heisman quarterback, isn't ready yet. And Rivers is coming back from months of inactivity and reconstructive knee surgery.

REBOUNDING: Ah, a strong point. But what would you expect with Oakley, Ewing, Mason and a coach who coined the phrase, "No rebounds, no rings!"

Say anything you want about the Knicks, but never deny their maniacal fervor on the boards. This is rebounding by committee, with Oakley the incumbent chairman. Few players in the league go after EVERY rebound the way he does. Both he and Ewing were double-digit boarders and no other Eastern team had two. Bet that scenario again.

And the Knicks can come in waves. Charles Smith, at 6-11, is capable and then Anthony Bonner and Mason come off the bench. The Knicks were the NBA's best defensive rebounders, second best overall last year.

KNICK ROSTER

No.	Veterans	Pos.	Ht.	Wt.	Age	Yrs. Pro	College
50	Greg Anthony	G	6-2	185	26	3	UNLV
4	Anthony Bonner	F	6-8	225	26	4	St. Louis
44	Hubert Davis	G	6-5	183	24	1	North Carolina
33	Patrick Ewing	C	7-0	240	32	9	Georgetown
U-7	Corey Gaines	G	6-3	185	29	4	Loyola Marymount
11	Derek Harper	G	6-4	206	33	11	Illinois
14	Anthony Mason	F	6-7	250	28	5	Tennessee State
34	Charles Oakley	F	6-9	245	30	9	Virginia Union
25	Doc Rivers	G	6-4	185	33	11	Marquette
54	Charles Smith	F	6-10	244	29	6	Pittsburgh
3	John Starks	G	6-5	185	29	5	Oklahoma State
U-32	Herb Williams	C-F	6-11	260	36	13	Ohio State

U-unrestricted free agent

Rd.	Rookies	Sel. No.	Pos.	Ht.	Wt.	College
1	Monty Williams	24	F	6-7	225	Notre Dame
1	Charlie Ward	26	G	6-1	190	Florida State

DEFENSE: And here's why so many hated the Finals. Scoring 100 points against the Knicks is Halley's Comet and Papal weddings in frequency. Sixty-two times foes failed to hit 100 as the Knicks surrendered an average of 91.5 points, the fourth-best mark ever. They also led the league in opponent field-goal shooting at .431.

Theirs is a help, rotate defense. Nothing tricky, no gimmicks. Very little double-teaming (unless Shaquille O'Neal's in town). They simply play one-on-one gut checks. And no one in the NBA does it better.

OUTLOOK: They went to the Finals last time. This time, they'll be lucky to get to the conference finals.

The East just will be better. The Knicks will again bang and bump and board and outwork the planet. But unless some offense is found, they will have a harder time surviving in the playoffs. Remember, both Chicago and Indiana extended them to seven games. Orlando will be better. Charlotte will be healthier. Indiana is improved. Sing no sad songs for the Knicks. But don't book the Finals' hotel just yet.

KNICK PROFILES

PATRICK EWING 32 7-0 240   Center

May never get that close again . . . Has dreamed of a title ring every moment of nine-year career . . . Got to the Finals—and shot .363 against Rockets . . . Yeah, yeah, yeah, he shoots too many jumpers . . . But that ability is part of what makes him special . . . Set all-time playoff series record for blocked shots with 30 in seven-game Finals vs. Rockets . . . Took over all-time team lead in points, blocked shots, free throws, field goals and interviews cut short . . . Got Knicks to Finals with 22-rebound, Game 7 effort against Pacers that included utterly frightening follow-up dunk to win . . . Eighth All-Star Game selection, seventh straight . . . Despite public perception, a heckuva nice guy . . . Born Aug. 5, 1962, in Kingston, Jamaica . . . Immigrated at 12 to Cambridge, Mass., where he was high school All-Everything at Rindge-Latin . . . Was All-Everything and more at Georgetown, leading Hoyas to three NCAA championship games, winning in '84 over Houston . . . Knicks made him No. 1 pick in first-ever lottery in '85 . . . Team co-captain . . . Scraped out a living on $3.625 million.

Year	Team	G	FG	FG Pct.	FT	FT Pct.	Reb.	Ast.	TP	Avg.
1985-86	New York	50	386	.474	226	.739	451	102	998	20.0
1986-87	New York	63	530	.503	296	.713	555	104	1356	21.5
1987-88	New York	82	656	.555	341	.716	676	125	1653	20.2
1988-89	New York	80	727	.567	361	.746	740	188	1815	22.7
1989-90	New York	82	922	.551	502	.775	893	182	2347	28.6
1990-91	New York	81	845	.514	464	.745	905	244	2154	26.6
1991-92	New York	82	796	.522	377	.738	921	156	1970	24.0
1992-93	New York	81	779	.503	400	.719	980	151	1959	24.2
1993-94	New York	79	745	.496	445	.765	885	179	1939	24.5
	Totals	680	6386	.522	3412	.742	7006	1431	16191	23.8

JOHN STARKS 29 6-5 185   Guard

The sky is falling! The sky is falling! The sky is—Oops! Sorry, it's just this guy hanging out on the perimeter again . . . In the time it took to read this sentence, he put up four three-pointers in Game 7 vs. Rockets . . . Knicks' lifeblood got drained when it mattered most: he shot 2-of-18, missing all of a record 11 three-point attempts, in seventh game . . . Wonder why they called the 19.0 scorer "Feast or Famine" . . . All-Star selection . . . Has guts by the ton, won't back down . . . Was leading the team in assists when he tore cartilage in left knee March 9, causing him to miss last 23 games of regular season . . . Incredibly, he returned for playoffs . . . Undrafted out of Oklahoma State. Had stint with Warriors . . . Signed as Knick free agent Oct. 1, 1990 . . . Born Aug. 10, 1965, in Tulsa, Okla. . . . Made $1.12 million.

Year	Team	G	FG	FG Pct.	FT	FT Pct.	Reb.	Ast.	TP	Avg.
1988-89	Golden State	36	51	.408	34	.654	41	27	146	4.1
1990-91	New York	61	180	.439	79	.752	131	204	466	7.6
1991-92	New York	82	405	.449	235	.778	191	276	1139	13.9
1992-93	New York	80	513	.428	263	.795	204	404	1397	17.5
1993-94	New York	59	410	.420	187	.754	185	348	1120	19.0
	Totals	318	1559	.431	798	.769	752	1259	4268	13.4

CHARLES OAKLEY 30 6-9 245   Forward

If everybody worked the way this guy does, they'd be no unemployment problem . . . Relentless bruiser finally got some recognition with his first All-Star selection plus initial pick as first team All-Defense . . . Fourth all-time Knick rebounder . . . Terrific mid-range face-up jumper . . . But bulk of scoring comes on second shots and putbacks . . . Dives into strands nightly in pursuit of loose balls . . . Only Knick to play in every game, despite litany of aches and pains . . . Played throughout playoffs with badly bruised right foot, sprained left ankle . . . A rebound every 3.04 minutes . . . Turnover-prone . . . Born Dec. 18, 1963, in Cleveland . . . Cavs took him No. 9 out of Virginia Union in '85 and immediately sent him to Bulls for Keith Lee . . . Came to Knicks from Bulls for Bill Cartwright, June 27, 1988 . . . Made $2.0 million.

Year	Team	G	FG	FG Pct.	FT	FT Pct.	Reb.	Ast.	TP	Avg.
1985-86	Chicago	77	281	.519	178	.662	664	133	740	9.6
1986-87	Chicago	82	468	.445	245	.686	1074	296	1192	14.5
1987-88	Chicago	82	375	.483	261	.727	1066	248	1014	12.4
1988-89	New York	82	426	.510	197	.773	861	187	1061	12.9
1989-90	New York	61	336	.524	217	.761	727	146	889	14.6
1990-91	New York	76	307	.516	239	.784	920	204	853	11.2
1991-92	New York	82	210	.522	86	.735	700	133	506	6.2
1992-93	New York	82	219	.508	127	.722	708	126	565	6.9
1993-94	New York	82	363	.478	243	.776	965	218	969	11.8
	Totals	706	2985	.495	1793	.736	7685	1691	7789	11.0

CHARLES SMITH 29 6-10 244   Forward

Underwent arthroscopic surgery on both knees in summer of '93 . . . Felt fine. Looked good. Was strong . . . So he bashed left knee in freak preseason collision with Charles Oakley . . . Season was a wash . . . Missed 39 games, had career-low points . . . Starts games strong, then fades. Or finds foul trouble . . . Showed some range on shot: eight three-pointers. Had one in first five seasons . . . Pittsburgh, Class of '88 . . . Came to Knicks from Clippers Sept. 22, 1992, as part of three-team trade involving Orlando. Knicks gave up Mark Jackson and a first-rounder, also got Doc Rivers and the unlamented Bo Kimble . . . No. 3 pick by Philly in '88, went to Clippers on draft night for rights to Hersey Hawkins . . . Born July 16, 1965, in Bridgeport, Conn. . . . Made $2.557 million in first year of seven-year, $26.6-million deal.

Year	Team	G	FG	FG Pct.	FT	FT Pct.	Reb.	Ast.	TP	Avg.
1988-89	L.A. Clippers	71	435	.495	285	.725	465	103	1155	16.3
1989-90	L.A. Clippers	78	595	.520	454	.794	524	114	1645	21.1
1990-91	L.A. Clippers	74	548	.469	384	.793	608	134	1480	20.0
1991-92	L.A. Clippers	49	251	.466	212	.785	301	56	714	14.6
1992-93	New York	81	358	.469	287	.782	432	142	1003	12.4
1993-94	New York	43	176	.443	87	.719	165	50	447	10.4
	Totals	396	2363	.483	1709	.774	2495	599	6444	16.3

DOC RIVERS 33 6-4 185   Guard

Could be most intriguing story around Knicks in '94-95 . . . Then again, could be most intriguing story away from Knicks in '94-95 . . . Tore left anterior cruciate ligament Dec. 16 . . . Enters training camp after 10 months away from game . . . So Knicks will have two 33-year-old point guards . . . Rehabbed phenomenally fast, however. There was some thought about activating him for late playoff rounds . . . Clutch-type player: big rebound, pass, steal or basket guy . . . Not a classic drive-and-dish point . . . Born in Maywood, Ill., Oct. 13, 1961 . . . Marquette, Class of '83. Hawks grabbed him on second round and kept him for eight years before sending him to Clippers in June 1991 for draft picks . . . Clippers eventually shipped him to Knicks along with Charles Smith and Bo Kimble in three-team deal that cost Knicks Mark Jackson and draft picks . . . Perennial All-Interview team. Was more interesting on crutches than most guys in sneakers ... Made $1.1 million.

Year	Team	G	FG	FG Pct.	FT	FT Pct.	Reb.	Ast.	TP	Avg.
1983-84	Atlanta	81	250	.462	255	.785	220	314	757	9.3
1984-85	Atlanta	69	334	.476	291	.770	214	410	974	14.1
1985-86	Atlanta	53	220	.474	172	.608	162	443	612	11.5
1986-87	Atlanta	82	342	.451	365	.828	299	823	1053	12.8
1987-88	Atlanta	80	403	.453	319	.758	366	747	1134	14.2
1988-89	Atlanta	76	371	.455	247	.861	286	525	1032	13.6
1989-90	Atlanta	48	218	.454	138	.812	200	264	598	12.5
1990-91	Atlanta	79	444	.435	221	.844	253	340	1197	15.2
1991-92	L.A. Clippers	59	226	.424	163	.832	147	233	641	10.9
1992-93	New York	77	216	.437	133	.821	192	405	604	7.8
1993-94	New York	19	55	.433	14	.636	39	100	143	7.5
	Totals	723	3079	.451	2318	.787	2378	4604	8745	12.1

DEREK HARPER 33 6-4 206   Guard

Yes, Virginia, there is an Almighty ... Paroled from Dallas on Jan. 6 when Knicks sent disgruntled Tony Campbell and a conditional '97 first-round pick for Mavs' all-time assist leader ... Was first player ever to improve scoring average in each of first eight seasons ... Had rousing playoff run. Was in position to claim MVP of Finals if Knicks won ... Upon arrival in New York, he struggled learning new system. Played tentatively. Fans wanted Campbell back ... But he got it together and, after moving into starting lineup, led Knicks to 21-6 record ... Great positional defender, with pickpocket hands that usually embarrass one opponent per night with strip ... Born in Elberton, Ga., Oct. 13, 1961 ... No. 11 overall pick by Dallas out of Illinois as undergrad in '83 ... Made $2.234 million.

Year	Team	G	FG	FG Pct.	FT	FT Pct.	Reb.	Ast.	TP	Avg.
1983-84	Dallas	82	200	.443	66	.673	172	239	469	5.7
1984-85	Dallas	82	329	.520	111	.721	199	360	790	9.6
1985-86	Dallas	79	390	.534	171	.747	226	416	963	12.2
1986-87	Dallas	77	497	.501	160	.684	199	609	1230	16.0
1987-88	Dallas	82	536	.459	261	.759	246	634	1393	17.0
1988-89	Dallas	81	538	.477	229	.806	228	570	1404	17.3
1989-90	Dallas	82	567	.488	250	.794	244	609	1473	18.0
1990-91	Dallas	77	572	.467	286	.731	233	548	1519	19.7
1991-92	Dallas	65	448	.443	198	.759	170	373	1152	17.7
1992-93	Dallas	62	393	.419	239	.756	123	334	1126	18.2
1993-94	Dal.-N.Y.	82	303	.407	112	.687	141	334	791	9.6
	Totals	851	4773	.469	2083	.747	2181	5026	12310	14.5

GREG ANTHONY 26 6-2 185   Guard

Knicks' patience on the brink with his shot . . . Third year out of UNLV saw regression is shooting (.394). And he shot .415 in second year out of UNLV. That's not swell, you know? . . . Often suffers from confidence factor. When Knicks obtained Derek Harper in January, he went into a virtual shell . . . Great ball-pressuring point guard, but has troubles leading break, which is a problem for a point guard . . . Is the guy left open when defenses double on Patrick Ewing . . . Nailed 48 three-point shots after getting 12 in first two seasons . . . Still, he's left open for a reason . . . Was the No. 12 pick in '91 . . . Born Nov. 15, 1967, in Las Vegas . . . Made $1.269 million.

Year	Team	G	FG	FG Pct.	FT	FT Pct.	Reb.	Ast.	TP	Avg.
1991-92	New York	82	161	.370	117	.741	136	314	447	5.5
1992-93	New York	70	174	.415	107	.673	170	398	459	6.6
1993-94	New York	80	225	.394	130	.774	189	365	628	7.9
	Totals	232	560	.393	354	.730	495	1077	1534	6.6

ANTHONY MASON 28 6-7 250   Forward

Mace will get in your face, but Pat Riley got on his case . . . Was suspended for last three regular-season games for "conduct detrimental to the team." . . . Spoke out about playing time and questioned Riley's views on offense. That made his future in New York iffy . . . May have achieved redemption through monster playoffs, which included defense on Hakeem Olajuwon in Finals that gave The Dream fits . . . Very active. Ball-handling skills better than some guards . . . Good mid-range shot, nice hooks . . . Another success story, with stops in Turkey, CBA, USBL and, even worse at the time, New Jersey and Denver . . . A New York favorite from Springfield Gardens, Queens . . . Born Dec. 14, 1966, in Miami . . . Tennessee State, '88 . . . Third-round pick of Blazers . . . Signed as Knick free agent July 30, 1991 . . . Made $1.1 million.

Year	Team	G	FG	FG Pct.	FT	FT Pct.	Reb.	Ast.	TP	Avg.
1989-90	New Jersey	21	14	.350	9	.600	34	7	37	1.8
1990-91	Denver	3	2	.500	6	.750	5	0	10	3.3
1991-92	New York	82	203	.509	167	.642	573	106	573	7.0
1992-93	New York	81	316	.502	199	.682	640	170	831	10.3
1993-94	New York	73	206	.476	116	.720	427	151	528	7.2
	Totals	260	741	.492	497	.675	1679	434	1979	7.6

HUBERT DAVIS 24 6-5 183   Guard

It's okay, Hubert. You can come out now. The playoffs are over and you're back home . . . A pure shooter, Davis had massive troubles on road in playoffs . . . Played tentatively. May have started with Game 6 end-game turnover vs. Pacers in conference finals. Pass slipped through his hands. In essence, so did any remaining contributions . . . But he became a New York hero when he coolly sank two free throws at :02.1 to beat Bulls in Game 5 that enabled Knicks to continue advance that brought them to Finals . . . Free throws came at home, of course . . . Really, he only needs more experience . . . Made the fifth four-point play in Knick history on Opening Night vs. Boston . . . One of the league's truly nice guys . . . Uncle is fellow North Carolina product Walter Davis . . . No. 20 pick in '92 . . . Born May 17, 1970, in Winston-Salem, N.C. . . . Made $764,000.

Year	Team	G	FG	FG Pct.	FT	FT Pct.	Reb.	Ast.	TP	Avg.
1992-93	New York	50	110	.438	43	.796	56	83	269	5.4
1993-94	New York	56	238	.471	85	.825	67	165	614	11.0
	Totals	106	348	.460	128	.815	123	248	883	8.3

COREY GAINES 29 6-3 185   Guard

Insurance policy after Doc Rivers went down and before Derek Harper came aboard . . . Was leading CBA in assists when Knicks called. Signed as free agent for minimum prorated wage Dec. 19 . . . Fourth NBA stop since leaving Loyola Marymount in '88 . . . Saw time with Nets, 76ers and Nuggets . . . Originally drafted on third round by Seattle, who waived him in '88 preseason . . . Helped Knicks defeat Pistons Jan. 15, directing 13-point turnaround in six minutes . . . Coaching staff loves his demeanor and attitude. If there's any room, they'll keep him . . . Born June 1, 1965, in Los Angeles.

Year	Team	G	FG	FG Pct.	FT	FT Pct.	Reb.	Ast.	TP	Avg.
1988-89	New Jersey	32	27	.422	12	.750	19	67	67	2.1
1989-90	Philadelphia	9	4	.333	1	.250	5	26	10	1.1
1990-91	Denver	10	28	.400	22	.846	14	91	83	8.3
1993-94	New York	18	9	.450	13	.867	13	30	33	1.8
	Totals	69	68	.410	48	.787	51	214	193	2.8

HERB WILLIAMS 36 6-11 260   Center-Forward

Great locker-room influence. And you could do far worse for a backup . . . Realizes his situation and accepts it . . . Plays when Patrick Ewing needs a rest or gets in foul trouble . . . Made $1.6 million on one-year, free-agent deal . . . Still plays effective defense, can rebound and score . . . Despite age that makes him seem like a holdover from Harding Administration, he stays in great shape . . . Many forget this guy had some super years for truly nondescript Pacer teams . . . The 14th pick by Indiana, out of Ohio State in '81 . . . Traded to Mavs for Detlef Schrempf and a second-rounder Feb. 21, 1989 . . . First Ohio State player ever to crack 2,000 points . . . Born Feb. 16, 1958, in Columbus, Ohio . . . Signed as free agent by Knicks in November 1992.

Year	Team	G	FG	FG Pct.	FT	FT Pct.	Reb.	Ast.	TP	Avg.
1981-82	Indiana.	82	407	.477	126	.670	605	139	942	11.5
1982-83	Indiana.	78	580	.499	155	.705	583	262	1315	16.9
1983-84	Indiana.	69	411	.478	207	.702	554	215	1029	14.9
1984-85	Indiana.	75	575	.475	224	.657	634	252	1375	18.3
1985-86	Indiana.	78	627	.492	294	.730	710	174	1549	19.9
1986-87	Indiana.	74	451	.480	199	.740	543	174	1101	14.9
1987-88	Indiana.	75	311	.425	126	.737	469	98	748	10.0
1988-89	Ind.-Dal.	76	322	.436	133	.686	593	124	777	10.2
1989-90	Dallas	81	295	.444	108	.679	391	119	700	8.6
1990-91	Dallas	60	332	.507	83	.638	357	95	747	12.5
1991-92	Dallas	75	367	.431	124	.725	454	94	859	11.5
1992-93	New York	55	72	.411	14	.667	146	19	158	2.9
1993-94	New York	70	103	.442	27	.643	182	28	233	3.3
	Totals	948	4853	.469	1820	.699	6221	1793	11533	12.2

ANTHONY BONNER 26 6-8 225   Forward

Christmas came in October when Knicks signed this unrestricted free agent for $650,000 . . . Supremely active type. Solid defender and a terrific finisher . . . Range, however, goes up to about an arm's length . . . Shot better from the floor (.563) than he did from the line (.476) . . . Got to .476 only because he got hot at the end . . . Locker room wit . . . Springs in his shoes. Leaps out of the building . . . And he couldn't play in Sacramento? . . . Made 38 starts and Knicks won 29 of those games . . . Pat Riley called him a "gift" . . . Non-factor in later playoff rounds as Knicks sought offense . . . Born June 8, 1968, in St. Louis . . .

Stayed home for college: St. Louis, Class of '90 . . . Went to NIT finals two straight years . . . Kings picked him 23rd in '90.

Year	Team	G	FG	FG Pct.	FT	FT Pct.	Reb.	Ast.	TP	Avg.
1990-91	Sacramento......	34	103	.448	44	.579	161	49	250	7.4
1991-92	Sacramento......	79	294	.447	151	.627	485	125	740	9.4
1992-93	Sacramento......	70	229	.461	143	.593	455	96	601	8.6
1993-94	New York.......	73	162	.563	50	.476	344	88	374	5.1
	Totals	256	788	.471	388	.585	1445	358	1965	7.7

THE ROOKIES

MONTY WILLIAMS 23 6-7 225   Forward
Many saw him as a risk because of hypertrophic cardiomyopathy, a condition that causes thickening of muscle between chambers of the heart . . . Sat out two years, given clean bill of health by National Institute of Health . . . Good inside-outside player who can handle the ball . . . Played for ex-Knick coach John MacLeod at Notre Dame . . . First-rounder with versatile skills lasted until No. 24, due likely to the heart problem . . . Born Oct. 8, 1971, in Fredericksburg, Va.

CHARLIE WARD 24 6-1 190   Guard
Best football player in draft . . . Won Heisman Trophy and Sullivan Award as nation's top amateur athlete after guiding Florida State to its first-ever NCAA national football title . . . Point guard who sees the court . . . Very quick, great leadership skills . . . Needs to improve ball-handling and shooting . . . But he only played two months a year and Knicks adore the improvement and potential . . . No. 26 choice on first round . . . Born Oct. 12, 1970, in Tallahassee, Fla.

COACH PAT RILEY: Still not happy in New York. By his own words, "I won't be happy in New York until we win a championship." . . . Came within six points of getting that real mushy feeling . . . Master motivator. Prepares for every conceivable scenario, including situations that have yet to arise since man began walking erect . . . NBA Coach of the Year in 1992-93. Voted Coach of the Decade for the '80s . . . Has recorded at least 50 wins in each of his 12 seasons as a head coach

Charles Oakley: All-Defense and first All-Star Game.

. . . All-time regular-season record of 701-272 (.720) . . . All-time playoff record of 131-70 (.652) . . . Made it to Finals eight times in 12 years, winning four, all with Lakers . . . Also has title rings as a player and an assistant . . . Running out of fingers . . . Has coached six 60-victory seasons, including Knick franchise-tying run in '92-93 . . . Incredibly hard-working, driven type . . . Born March 20, 1945, in Rome, N.Y. . . . Drafted by Dallas Cowboys but chose basketball after San Diego Rockets took him No. 7 out of Kentucky in '67 . . . Nine-year NBA career . . . His book, *The Winner Within*, hit best-seller list.

Willis Reed inspired Knicks to first title in 1970.

GREATEST PLAYER

The greatest moment in Knick history came not during a game or in a champagne-drenched locker room but moments before an opening tap. And it was supplied by the greatest Knick ever, Willis Reed.

As players from both sides warmed up for the seventh game of the 1970 Finals, one was conspicuously absent. Reed, his tattered leg in a brace, filled the void when he limped through the walkway from the locker room at Madison Square Garden. The Captain sent the Garden in to a frenzy and the Lakers into a catatonic state.

"We lost the game right there," Jerry West later recalled. Reed scored only four points, but his mere presence was worth dozens. Others had better career stats, although Reed, now the Nets' VP-GM, wasn't too shabby. He's still the leading rebounder and third all-time scorer for the Knicks. In 1981, the 10-year Knick was inducted into the Basketball Hall of Fame.

ALL-TIME KNICK LEADERS

SEASON

Points: Patrick Ewing, 2,347, 1989-90
Assists: Mark Jackson, 868, 1987-88
Rebounds: Willis Reed, 1,191, 1968-69

GAME

Points: Bernard King, 60 vs. New Jersey, 12/25/85
Assists: Richie Guerin, 21 vs. St. Louis, 12/12/58
Rebounds: Harry Gallatin, 33 vs. Ft. Wayne, 3/15/53
              Willis Reed, 33 vs. Cincinnati, 2/2/71

CAREER

Points: Patrick Ewing, 16,191, 1985-94
Assists: Walt Frazier, 4,791, 1967-77
Rebounds: Willis Reed, 8,414, 1964-74

ORLANDO MAGIC

TEAM DIRECTORY: Chairman/Pres./CEO: Rich DeVos; Vice Chairmen: Cheri Vander Weide, Doug DeVos, Dan De Vos; GM/COO: Pat Williams; Exec. VP: Jack Swope; VP-Basketball Oper.: John Gabriel; Dir. Publicity/Media Rel.: Alex Martins; Coach: Brian Hill; Asst. Coaches: Bob Hill, Tree Rollins. Arena: Orlando Arena (15,151). Colors: Electric blue, quick silver, magic black.

(Note: At press time Horace Grant's contested contract awaited resolution.)

SCOUTING REPORT

SHOOTING: Only Golden State (.492) and Indiana (.486) shot better than Orlando (.485). The Magic will always be up there in shooting because of Shaquille O'Neal's monstrously high percentage (.599 to lead the league). He dunks, he spins, he lays it in. So where's the problem? Well, the foul line for starters. O'Neal

Shaq O'Neal's .599 shooting topped the NBA.

is a throwback to Wilt Chamberlain. It's tough to dunk from 15 feet. At .678, with Shaq's .554 playing a huge part, the Magic were the worst in the East from the line. No room for debate. Shaq simply must improve.

Orlando boasts a potentially quality perimeter game forged around Nick Anderson and Dennis Scott (his 394 treys were second in the NBA). But the key remains Shaq. And the Pacers in the playoffs showed how vulnerable he can be with a tag-team approach. Run body after body at him, make him a passer (he's not the best) and the Magic can be had. Especially when Scott shoots .405, as he did in the regular season.

In Penny Hardaway, Orlando came up with a penetrating gem who is only going to get better and better. But there's no real threat off the bench. The Magic can shoot you to death with their first five, shoot themselves in the foot with their second. And now they've gone for the gold with the addition of ex-Bull Horace Grant to their arsenal.

PLAYMAKING: Orlando established a team record and placed eighth in the league with assists (2,070). And much of that was due to the insertion of Hardaway at point guard for the final 50 games. Hardaway lacks only experience. Each game brought more confidence in the position. He began the season as the off-guard but was moved to point and the Magic never quit until they were in the playoffs for the first time, boasting 42 victories. Hardaway has terrific peripheral vision and pushes the ball. There are aspects he's still learning—like anticipating passing-lane thefts and he can be rattled under pressure, but what rookie can't be? With his slashing ability and last-second dishes, the Magic seem solid at this spot.

REBOUNDING: Shaq will get his. And so will Grant, who was the Bulls' best rebounder. He should alleviate some of the board pressure on Shaq.

Until now the Magic hadn't come up with a forward rebounding mule. They thought they had found the answer a few drafts back in Brian Williams, but their patience ran out and now Williams is turning into that mule. Only he's doing so in Denver. Last year, the in-season trade for Anthony Avent was seen as the cure.

DEFENSE: With Hardaway's quick hands, the Magic can apply some nightmare pressure of the ball. With Shaq patrolling the lane, the Magic can be intimidating inside. So why are they just average defensively?

MAGIC ROSTER

No.	Veterans	Pos.	Ht.	Wt.	Age	Yrs. Pro	College
25	Nick Anderson	F-G	6-6	205	25	5	Illinois
00	Anthony Avent	F	6-9	235	25	2	Seton Hall
14	Anthony Bowie	G	6-6	190	31	5	Oklahoma
11	Litterial Green	G	6-1	185	24	2	Georgia
–	Horace Grant	F	6-10	235	29	7	Clemson
R-43	Geert Hammink	C	7-0	262	25	1	Louisiana State
R-1	Anfernee Hardaway	G	6-7	195	23	1	Memphis State
34	Greg Kite	C	6-11	260	33	11	Brigham Young
42	Larry Krystkowiak	F	6-9	240	30	7	Montana
32	Shaquille O'Neal	C	7-1	303	22	2	Louisiana State
U-30	Tree Rollins	C	7-1	255	39	17	Clemson
5	Donald Royal	F	6-8	210	28	4	Notre Dame
3	Dennis Scott	G-F	6-8	229	26	4	Georgia Tech
R-55	Keith Tower	F-C	6-11	250	24	1	Notre Dame
31	Jeff Turner	F	6-9	240	32	8	Vanderbilt

R-restricted free agent
U-unrestricted free agent

Rd.	Rookies	Sel. No.	Pos.	Ht.	Wt.	College
1	Brooks Thompson	27	G	6-4	200	Oklahoma State
2	Rodney Dent	31	F	6-9	240	Kentucky

A lot lies upstairs. They need maturity. The Magic are a young team enjoying their ride to fame and prosperity. In Orlando, there's Mickey Mouse and there's Shaq plus other assorted Magic persons. They are adored. They are idolized. But they have made absolutely no committment individually or collectively to be a great defensive team.

Yeah, scoring points is kind of important. But until the players adopt an attitude that trying to outscore the opposition is not the way to go, Orlando will remain what they are—a very good team, a playoff team, but a team without real championship fiber.

OUTLOOK: It's bright. Unless you consider the city of Orlando's expectations. ''Like we're gonna go undefeated, win the title and Shaq'll score a bazillion points. Wow, let's go to Space Mountain.'' The expectations of the city are a touch unreal. Especially when you realize the Magic have been to the playoffs once and got clocked in three straight games.

Now it will be Shaq, Penny and Horace who will give fits to most opponents. But Brian Hill's Magic can't live with Scott shooting .405. He and Anderson must lose the one-dimensional approach. But there's no question that the addition of Grant alters the Magic kingdom. Maybe this won't be another season of saying wait 'til next year.

MAGIC PROFILES

SHAQUILLE O'NEAL 22 7-1 303   Center

Already a national institution... Film star, commercial regular, media icon, sneaker endorser, rap singer... And a pretty good basketball player... Lost scoring title on final day when David Robinson scored a mere 71 points... Third-team All-NBA center... Had franchise-record 53 points vs. T-Wolves Apr. 20 ... Face it, if you don't know about him, you've been living in a cave for two years... Eight games of 40 or more points... Dream Team II member... Scored 42 points Opening Night at Miami... Franchise's first triple-double at New Jersey Nov. 20 (24 points, team-record 28 rebounds, team-record 15 blocks)... The 15 blocks were two shy of Elmore Smith's all-time NBA record... A foul-line disaster (.554)... Caught a lot of heat for his off-court activities... Didn't handle criticism well. Grew sullen toward media... Got more sullen when Pacers snuffed him in playoffs, exposing a limited offensive game... Pacers showed he can be stopped with lots of bodies playing tagteam. And sending him to line (.471)... Averaged 20.7 points in playoffs... Rookie of the Year in 1992-93 after leaving LSU following junior season... No. 1 pick in draft... First rookie in NBA history to be Player of the Week his first week... Eastern All-Star starting center first two years... Born March 6, 1972, in Newark, N.J.... Made $3.9 million.

Year	Team	G	FG	FG Pct.	FT	FT Pct.	Reb.	Ast.	TP	Avg.
1992-93	Orlando	81	733	.562	427	.592	1122	152	1893	23.4
1993-94	Orlando	81	953	.599	471	.554	1072	195	2377	29.3
	Totals	162	1686	.582	898	.572	2194	347	4270	26.4

ANFERNEE HARDAWAY 23 6-7 195   Guard

A Penny for your franchise... See, it's not all just Shaq down in Mickey Mouse's backyard ... May have been the one Orlando player to truly step it up in the playoffs (18.7 ppg, 16.0 regular season)... Became the team's real leader by season's end... Tremendous penetrator and passer... Magic Johnson-like passes. But, like Earvin, a sound, fundamental player... All-Rookie team, just missed Rookie to the Year...

Good, quick hands on defense, plays passing lanes and anticipates well... Troubled by the Muggsy Bogues-type scatback guards ... But there aren't many of them... Led all rookies in steals and assists... Began season as shooting guard. Inevitable switch came after New Year's... Magic will be his team this season... Born July 18, 1971, in Memphis, Tenn.... Drafted No. 3 by Warriors and his rights were immediately sent to Magic, along with three future first-rounders, for Chris Webber, whom Magic took No. 1 ... Made $1.244 million.

Year	Team	G	FG	FG Pct.	FT	FT Pct.	Reb.	Ast.	TP	Avg.
1993-94	Orlando	82	509	.466	245	.742	439	544	1313	16.0

DENNIS SCOTT 26 6-8 229   Guard-Forward

Probably would have been traded to Clippers if he didn't have tendency to resemble the Pillsbury Dough Boy... One-dimensional player ... Can shoot with exceptional range (155-for-388 on three-pointers)... Team record for three-pointers made... Had string of 12 straight games with a trey... It's two-pointers he has trouble with. Overall, shot .405...

Can't defend a corpse... Entering last year of contract that paid him $2.82 million... Career bests in steals and assists... He was healthy. Made it to all 82 games after playing only 72 in two previous years combined... Born Sept. 8, 1968, in Hagerstown, Md.... Fourth player picked in 1990, out of Georgia Tech, where he was College Player of the Year in '90.

Year	Team	G	FG	FG Pct.	FT	FT Pct.	Reb.	Ast.	TP	Avg.
1990-91	Orlando	82	503	.425	153	.750	235	134	1284	15.7
1991-92	Orlando	18	133	.402	64	.901	66	35	359	19.9
1992-93	Orlando	54	329	.431	92	.786	186	136	858	15.9
1993-94	Orlando	82	384	.405	123	.774	218	216	1046	12.8
	Totals	236	1349	.418	432	.784	705	521	3547	15.0

NICK ANDERSON 25 6-6 205   Forward-Guard

Just how long are the Magic supposed to wait? ... Another year, another model of inconsistency... He can make a case this time, though ... Started the year at guard, ended at small forward... Didn't wow 'em at either spot... Doesn't handle well enough at two, can't defend well enough for three... One huge positive, though: His strength overwhelms most guards on post-ups. Very solid, strong inside game...And he can step out for threes (101-of-314)...Can shoot a team into a game but play the same team right out of same game...Season-high 36 points vs. Knicks, who had NBA's No. 1 defense...Not a great ball-handler. Defense remains suspect...First lap in four-year, $12 million pact paid him $2.67 million...Out of Illinois ...No. 11 pick in 1989. First selection in team history...Born Jan. 20, 1968, in Chicago.

Year	Team	G	FG	FG Pct.	FT	FT Pct.	Reb.	Ast.	TP	Avg.
1989-90	Orlando	81	372	.494	186	.705	316	124	931	11.5
1990-91	Orlando	70	400	.467	173	.668	386	106	990	14.1
1991-92	Orlando	60	482	.463	202	.667	384	163	1196	19.9
1992-93	Orlando	79	594	.449	298	.741	477	265	1574	19.9
1993-94	Orlando	81	504	.478	168	.672	476	294	1277	15.8
	Totals	371	2352	.468	1027	.695	2039	952	5968	16.1

HORACE GRANT 29 6-10 235   Forward

Bulls accused new Magic signee of backing out of handshake deal that would have kept him in Chicago for five years at a reported $20 million ...Bulls' best rebounder for fifth straight year, despite missing 12 games with assorted ailments...Led team in blocks. Again... Strong, solid offensive playoffs (16.2 points, .542 shooting) although rebounds were down (7.4)...Superb offensive rebounder. Scores off putbacks and dunks but also is equipped with solid mid-range jumper...Has never shot under 50 percent in seven seasons...His quickness allows him to trap and still get back and rebound...Identical twin brother of Blazers' Harvey...Always felt overlooked behind Michael Jordan and Scottie Pippen. And he was...Played in his first All-Star Game...Born July 4, 1965, in Augusta, Ga., a few minutes before Harvey...ACC Player of the Year at Clemson in '87 when he led conference in scoring, rebounding and shooting ...No. 10 pick by Bulls in '87...Made $1.965 million.

Year	Team	G	FG	FG Pct.	FT	FT Pct.	Reb.	Ast.	TP	Avg.
1987-88	Chicago	81	254	.501	114	.626	447	89	622	7.7
1988-89	Chicago	79	405	.519	140	.704	681	168	950	12.0
1989-90	Chicago	80	446	.523	179	.699	629	227	1071	13.4
1990-91	Chicago	78	401	.547	197	.711	659	178	1000	12.8
1991-92	Chicago	81	457	.578	235	.741	807	217	1149	14.2
1992-93	Chicago	77	421	.508	174	.619	729	201	1017	13.2
1993-94	Chicago	70	460	.524	137	.596	769	236	1057	15.1
	Totals	546	2844	.530	1176	.675	4721	1316	6866	12.6

JEFF TURNER 32 6-9 240 Forward

Maybe if players would listen to him. Complained to team about work ethic. They laughed, turned portable CD players louder—and promptly got swept in playoffs... You don't last this long with his talent level without heart and desire the size of Mt. Everest... Good perimeter shooter and that's about it... Gets a rebound every lunar eclipse or so... Offseason knee surgery makes contributions questionable for 1994-95... Power forward by default... Every power forward the Magic brings in fails miserably... Gets bullied by bigger forwards, can't guard small forwards' quickness... No. 17 pick by Nets in 1984... Did Europe for two years, then signed free-agent deal with Magic July 12, 1989... Vanderbilt product... Born April 9, 1962, in Bangor, Me.... Made $900,000.

Year	Team	G	FG	FG Pct.	FT	FT Pct.	Reb.	Ast.	TP	Avg.
1984-85	New Jersey	72	171	.454	79	.859	218	108	421	5.8
1985-86	New Jersey	53	84	.491	58	.744	137	14	226	4.3
1986-87	New Jersey	76	151	.465	76	.731	197	60	378	5.0
1989-90	Orlando	60	132	.429	42	.778	227	53	308	5.1
1990-91	Orlando	71	259	.487	85	.759	363	97	609	8.6
1991-92	Orlando	75	225	.451	79	.693	246	92	530	7.1
1992-93	Orlando	75	231	.529	56	.800	252	107	528	7.0
1993-94	Orlando	68	199	.467	35	.778	271	60	451	6.6
	Totals	550	1452	.472	510	.762	1911	591	3451	6.3

ANTHONY BOWIE 31 6-6 190 Guard

Open-court player who got as much time as Jim Bowie by season's end... A backup guard on a team with a half-dozen guards... Never found a niche once talent level rose on team... Minutes were down over 40 percent... A decent, if sometimes erratic, shot... And a pretty good defender against most backups... A playoff non-entity... Born Nov. 9, 1963, in Tulsa, Okla.... Has seen the world. Third-round pick of Houston in '86 out of Oklahoma. Waived, re-signed. Waived. Played in CBA. Signed by Nets. Waived, signed by Spurs (March 20, 1989). Traded back to Houston for cash (Aug. 15, 1989). Waived. Played

in Italy. Signed by Bulls. Waived. Signed as free agent by Magic
(Dec. 31, 1991)... Made $900,000... CBA's MVP in 1988-89.

Year	Team	G	FG	FG Pct.	FT	FT Pct.	Reb.	Ast.	TP	Avg.
1988-89	San Antonio	18	72	.500	10	.667	56	29	15	8.6
1989-90	Houston	66	119	.406	40	.741	118	96	284	4.3
1991-92	Orlando	52	312	.493	117	.860	245	163	758	14.6
1992-93	Orlando	77	268	.471	67	.798	194	175	618	8.0
1993-94	Orlando	70	139	.481	41	.837	120	102	320	4.6
	Totals	283	910	.472	275	.814	733	565	2135	7.5

DONALD ROYAL 28 6-8 210   Forward

Effective role player. Now pinning down exactly what is his role is another matter... Plays shooting guard and both forward spots... Fearless type who sacrifices his body. And he gets to the line: 269 free throws in 1,357 minutes. Roughly one every five minutes... Active defensively, long arms, good reach... Shot .501, but don't confuse that with range. Is a drive-and-draw-foul guy... Former CBAer... Born May 2, 1966, in New Orleans... Out of Notre Dame in 1987, he was drafted on third round but waived by Cavs... Hit Israel, too... Signed as free agent and released by T-Wolves, Spurs and Magic before return trip to Orlando (Aug. 24, 1992)... Made $890,000, big jump from previous year's minimum wage.

Year	Team	G	FG	FG Pct.	FT	FT Pct.	Reb.	Ast.	TP	Avg.
1989-90	Minnesota.......	66	117	.459	153	.777	137	43	387	5.9
1991-92	San Antonio	60	80	.449	92	.692	124	34	252	4.2
1992-93	Orlando	77	194	.496	318	.815	295	80	706	9.2
1993-94	Orlando	74	174	.501	199	.740	248	61	547	7.4
	Totals	277	565	.482	762	.770	804	218	1892	6.8

GREG KITE 33 6-11 260   Center

Under that gruff exterior lies the heart of a graceful, offensively gifted gazelle... And under the Rocky Mountains lies a leprechaun's pot of gold... Suffered calf muscle tear Jan. 4 and waved bye-bye to season... Never could score. Last year did nothing to change that notion... A physical, bulky banger who annoys opponents with hatchetman mode... But guess what? He is effective... Uses position for a couple of rebounds a game... Won championship rings with Celtics in '84 and '86 ... Signed as free agent Aug. 14, 1990... No. 21 pick of Celts out of Brigham Young in '83... Stints with Clippers, Hornets and Kings... An utter horror at the foul line... Born Aug. 5, 1961, in Houston... Made $985,000.

Year	Team	G	FG	FG Pct.	FT	FT Pct.	Reb.	Ast.	TP	Avg.
1983-84	Boston	35	30	.455	5	.313	62	7	65	1.9
1984-85	Boston	55	33	.375	22	.688	89	17	88	1.6
1985-86	Boston	64	34	.374	15	.385	128	17	83	1.3
1986-87	Boston	74	47	.427	29	.382	169	27	123	1.7
1987-88	Bos.-LAC	53	92	.449	40	.506	264	47	224	4.2
1988-89	LAC-Char.	70	65	.430	20	.488	243	36	150	2.1
1989-90	Sacramento	71	101	.432	27	.500	377	76	230	3.2
1990-91	Orlando	82	166	.491	63	.512	588	59	395	4.8
1991-92	Orlando	72	94	.437	40	.588	402	44	228	3.2
1992-93	Orlando	64	38	.452	13	.542	193	10	89	1.4
1993-94	Orlando	29	13	.371	8	.364	70	4	34	1.2
	Totals	669	713	.441	282	.491	2585	344	1709	2.6

GEERT HAMMINK 25 7-0 262   Center

See, it wasn't so bad backing up Shaq at LSU. It landed him an NBA job backing up Shaq in Orlando... Or at least a chance ... Real banger type, good practice player... Has some range on shot... Born July 12, 1969, in Didam, Holland... No. 26 pick on first round by Magic in 1993... Played in Italy and Spain in 1993-94... Signed with Magic April 21. Played one game, three minutes... Got $150,000 minimum and became restricted free agent.

Year	Team	G	FG	FG Pct.	FT	FT Pct.	Reb.	Ast.	TP	Avg.
1993-94	Orlando	1	1	.333	0	0	1	1	2	2.0

KEITH TOWER 24 6-11 250   Forward-Center

Somebody has to be Shaq's sacrificial practice lamb... Might as well be a guy who doesn't play... On injured list most of season with stuff that sounds really medically official (acute medial sesamoiditis of left foot, non-healing skin lesion, mid-foot sprain) but there are other ways of saying "13th man disease."... Little defense, no offense, less speed... Born May 15, 1970, in Pittsburgh... Notre Dame, Class of 1992... Signed as free agent with Magic for minimum $150,000 wage on Sept. 23, 1993.

Year	Team	G	FG	FG Pct.	FT	FT Pct.	Reb.	Ast.	TP	Avg.
1993-94	Orlando	11	4	.444	0	.000	6	1	8	0.7

WAYNE (TREE) ROLLINS 39 7-1 255   Center

Once a player, always a player. Even after you become an assistant coach . . . On Jan. 10, two days after Greg Kite went down, Magic activated this assistant, making him NBA's lone player-coach . . . After series of 10-day contracts, they signed him for the remainder of the season . . . His 17th playing season, fifth team . . . Always a good defender since coming out of Clemson in 1977 as the No. 14 pick, by Atlanta . . . NBA's fourth all-time shot-blocker with 2,506, an average of 2.27 . . . Led NBA with 343 blocks in 1982-83 and was on All-Defense first team in 1983-84 . . . Signed with Cavs as unrestricted free agent in '88 . . . Did time also with Pistons and Rockets . . . Named Magic assistant coach July 10, 1993, basically, to work with Shaquille O'Neal . . . Born June 16, 1955, in Winter Haven, Fla. . . . Made $150,000 minimum.

Year	Team	G	FG	FG Pct.	FT	FT Pct.	Reb.	Ast.	TP	Avg.
1977-78	Atlanta	80	253	.487	104	.703	552	79	610	7.6
1978-79	Atlanta	81	297	.535	89	.631	588	49	683	8.4
1979-80	Atlanta	82	287	.558	157	.714	774	76	731	8.9
1980-81	Atlanta	40	116	.552	46	.807	286	35	278	7.0
1981-82	Atlanta	79	202	.584	79	.612	611	59	483	6.1
1982-83	Atlanta	80	261	.510	98	.726	743	75	620	7.8
1983-84	Atlanta	77	274	.518	118	.621	593	62	666	8.6
1984-85	Atlanta	70	186	.549	67	.720	442	52	439	6.3
1985-86	Atlanta	74	173	.499	69	.767	458	41	415	5.6
1986-87	Atlanta	75	171	.546	63	.724	488	22	405	5.4
1987-88	Atlanta	76	133	.512	70	.875	459	20	336	4.4
1988-89	Cleveland	60	62	.449	12	.632	139	19	136	2.3
1989-90	Cleveland	48	57	.456	11	.688	153	24	125	2.6
1990-91	Detroit	37	14	.424	8	.571	42	4	36	1.0
1991-92	Houston	59	46	.535	26	.867	171	15	118	2.0
1992-93	Houston	42	11	.268	9	.750	60	10	31	0.7
1993-94	Orlando	45	29	.547	18	.600	96	9	76	1.7
	Totals	1105	2572	.523	1044	.700	6655	651	6188	5.6

ANTHONY AVENT 25 6-9 235 Forward

He was going to be the answer to the ever-present power-forward problem . . . The Edsel was going to be the car of the future . . . How do you spell disappointment? . . . A dolphin has better hands . . . Can't catch or finish, doesn't care to bang. Lacks the meanness inherent to a power forward . . . Other than those points, a perfect power forward . . . May have blown a golden opportunity . . . Problem is, he does have talent: 26 points Nov. 26, 17 rebounds Nov. 6 . . . Obtained from Milwaukee on Jan. 15 for Anthony Cook and a 1994 first-rounder . . . Born Oct. 18, 1969, in Rocky Mount, N.C. Grew up in Newark, N.J. . . . Made $650,000 . . . Drafted out of Seton Hall, the 15th pick, by Hawks in 1991 . . . Went to Bucks in three-way deal that also included Denver, July 1, 1991 . . . Played 1991-92 season in Italy.

Year	Team	G	FG	FG Pct.	FT	FT Pct.	Reb.	Ast.	TP	Avg.
1992-93	Milwaukee	82	347	.433	112	.651	512	91	806	9.8
1993-94	Mil.-Orl.	74	150	.377	89	.724	338	65	389	5.3
	Totals	156	497	.414	201	.681	850	156	1195	7.7

THE ROOKIES

BROOKS THOMPSON 24 6-4 200 Guard

White men can jump . . . Sounds like a lefty Rex Chapman . . . Great range . . . The final selection of the first round, No. 27 overall, out of Oklahoma State . . . Played first two years at Texas A&M . . . All-Big Eight pick. Averaged 16.9 as a senior . . . Set five OSU three-point records . . . Born July 19, 1970, in Dallas.

RODNEY DENT 23 6-9 240 Forward

Headed for monster season—maybe monster career—when he blew out knee as senior . . . Torn anterior cruciate ligament in his left knee . . . Only played 11 games as senior at Kentucky and was the 31st player selected . . . Had 16 blocks in 11 games and was shooting .676 before injury . . . Christmas baby. Born Dec. 24, 1970, in Edison, Ga.

Nick Anderson had season-high 36 points vs. Knicks.

COACH BRIAN HILL: Relax, Brian, the job is yours . . . Meticulous in preparation, does a lot, maybe too much, himself . . . That indicates a touch of insecurity . . . But that's normal for guy who was in his first year on the job and was swamped by community's expectations, which bordered on absurd . . . Basic Mike Fratello system with lots of defense emphasized. And intensity . . . Assisted Fratello in Atlanta for four seasons . . .

Head coach at Lehigh for eight seasons and spent six collegiate years as assistant . . . Joined Magic staff in 1990-91 and did the assistant's route before replacing Matt Guokas, June 30, 1993 . . . More aggressive approach led Magic to best record in team history, 50-32, a 24-percent improvement . . . Born Sept. 19, 1947, in East Orange, N.J. . . . Brother, Fred Hill, is the baseball coach at Rutgers . . . Attended Kennedy (Neb.) College, where he was track and baseball standout.

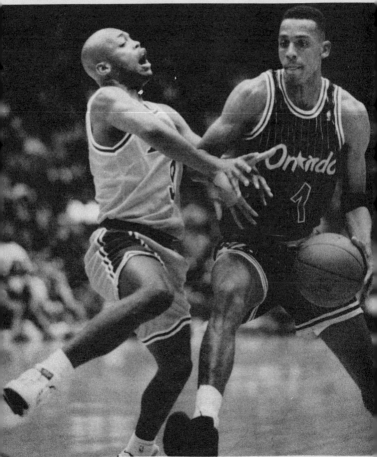

Anfernee Hardaway was obvious pick for All-Rookie team.

GREATEST PLAYER

Gee, wonder who it could be? Greg Kite or Shaq?

Sorry, Greg.

Few players in recent memory have had the impact on a franchise Shaquille O'Neal has had on the Magic. In his very first season, he carried them to a .500 record. In his second, the Magic became a playoff entry.

Already, he is as much a part of America as Wonder Bread. His second season placed him first in the NBA in field-goal percentage, second in scoring and rebounding. Already, he has been an All-Star Game starter twice. Barring injury, that status will continue probably for as long as he continues playing, based on his enormous popularity.

And that popularity only increased this past summer when O'Neal, who spent his previous offseason filming the successful movie *Blue Chips*, was a member of Dream Team II at the World Championships.

ALL-TIME MAGIC LEADERS

SEASON

Points: Shaquille O'Neal, 2,377, 1993-94
Assists: Scott Skiles, 735, 1992-93
Rebounds: Shaquille O'Neal, 1,122, 1992-93

GAME

Points: Shaquille O'Neal, 53 vs. Minnesota, 4/20/94
Assists: Scott Skiles, 30 vs. Denver, 12/30/90
Rebounds: Terry Catledge, 22 vs. Philadelphia, 11/13/91

CAREER

Points: Nick Anderson, 5,968, 1989-94
Assists: Scott Skiles, 3,176, 1989-94
Rebounds: Nick Anderson, 2,039, 1989-94

PHILADELPHIA 76ERS

TEAM DIRECTORY: Owner: Harold Katz; GM/Coach: John Lucas; Dir. Player Personnel: Gene Shue; Dir. Scouting: Tony DiLeo; Dir. Pub. Rel.: Joe Favorito; Asst. Coaches: Ron Adams, Maurice Cheeks, Tom Thibodeau. Arena: The Spectrum (18,168). Colors: Red, white and blue.

SCOUTING REPORT

SHOOTING: They couldn't score. Therefore, it's a good assumption that the Sixers couldn't shoot.

Philly can't wait for the blooming of Shawn Bradley.

Tim Perry may symbolize the Sixer offensive frustration. One night, he couldn't be stopped with a bulldozer. The next night, he couldn't hit the bulldozer. From two feet away.

Inside, Clarence Weatherspoon is the force. Undersized, but still a force. Shawn Bradley is a patience, patience, patience project as he enters his second year which the Sixers fervently hope will be a healthy one. For mid-range, Jeff Malone still should have enough left to present problems, while beyond the three-point line Dana Barros is one of the best—as is Perry at forward. At least on those nights when he can hit the bulldozer.

PLAYMAKING: It may all come down to a rookie, B.J. Tyler. He has had his problems, but none that new coach John Lucas is not aware of. Tyler did some time in Lucas' Texas substance abuse rehab. Lucas has faith in the U. of Texas lightning bolt and if that faith translates into production, the Sixers may have come up with a steal at No. 20. His assists-to-turnover ratio is terrific. And that's an area where the Sixers weren't last season.

But assume the logical, that Tyler cannot just step in, and the 76ers have the same cast: Johnny Dawkins, who has never regained top form from his devastating 1990 knee injury, and Barros, who is to classic point-guard play what cheese steaks are to haute cuisine. Only Washington, Detroit and Dallas had fewer assists than the Sixers last season. Chalk that up to poor shooting, but also to the lack of a true point guard. Maybe the most significant addition to the staff will be Maurice Cheeks, a basketball game-situation encyclopedia and the best point guard in Sixer history.

REBOUNDING: Nothing special here, even with Bradley healthy. It could be, though, if Bradley tones up and bulks up and gains the muscle necessary. But that will take some time. Meanwhile, the Sixers will try to do it again with an undersized power forward in Weatherspoon after having tried it for years with an undersized power forward named Barkley. The Sixers last season ranked 24th in overall rebounds. When they won, the Sixers outrebounded their opponents by an average of four a game. When they lost, which was lots—57 times to be precise—the Sixers were outrebounded by an average of 10 a game. They have added a proven rebounder with the signing of free agent Scott Williams from the Bulls.

DEFENSE: It all depends on Bradley. Just like the season. Because of his enormous size and even more enormous wingspan, even the gutsiest of players must think twice about driving it inside

76ER ROSTER

No. Veterans	Pos.	Ht.	Wt.	Age	Yrs. Pro	College
R-3 Dana Barros	G	5-10	165	27	5	Boston College
76 Shawn Bradley	C	7-6	245	22	1	Brigham Young
12 Johnny Dawkins	G	6-2	170	31	8	Duke
20 Greg Graham	G	6-4	183	23	1	Indiana
25 Jeff Malone	G	6-4	205	33	11	Mississippi State
23 Tim Perry	F	6-9	220	29	6	Temple
R-35 C. Weatherspoon	F	6-6	245	24	2	Southern Miss.
– Scott Williams	C-F	6-10	230	26	4	North Carolina

R-restricted free agent
U-unrestricted free agent

Rd.Rookies	Sel. No.	Pos.	Ht.	Wt.	College
1 Sharone Wright	6	F-C	6-10	260	Clemson
1 B.J. Tyler	20	G	6-1	175	Texas
2 Derrick Alston	33	C	6-9	225	Duquesne

against the Sixers. Bradley can alter shots by sneezing. And the defense was coming along nicely with Bradley plugging the middle and the Sixers funneling everything into him, or at least trying to. In the first 31 games, the Sixers allowed just 98.6 points a game. In the last 51, of which Bradley missed 33, they surrendered 108 points per. As a result, the Sixers staggered out of 1993-94 as one of the worst defensive units: their .484 opponent field-goal percentage was the fourth worst in the league. And their 105.6-point yield was fifth from the bottom.

OUTLOOK: It has to be brighter. For one, Lucas will bring a never-say-die spirit. And if there is anyone in the league who knows about battling back from adversity, it's him. He helped transform the Spurs into a power. True, he had the Admiral and some talent to work with but probably not as much as generally assumed.

The Sixers aren't looking for powerhouse stature this season. Respectability and competitiveness will do fine. And that's just what they may get, assuming that Bradley can stay around for most of 82 games. There are some playoff whispers in Philly—not too loud, mind you. And while the playoffs seem a touch unrealistic, the Sixers could pull it off if one of the Central Division preseason playoff choices disappoints.

76ER PROFILES

SHAWN BRADLEY 22 7-6 245   Center

Yes, he had the grace and elegance of a telephone pole on ice skates. But when he went down with injury, the Sixers were 20-29. They were 5-28 without him . . . The rookie must have done something right . . . Sixers admitted he was huge project when they made him the No. 2 overall pick in the draft, right after Chris Webber, right before Anfernee Hardaway . . . Made strides every game . . . But season ended in collision with Portland's Harvey Grant Feb. 18. Dislocated left kneecap and chipped a bone in joint . . . Before leaving, he blocked 147 shots, ninth-best total by a Sixer . . . Blocked six or more seven times, high of nine . . . As raw as steak tartare. But, ho, the potential . . . Highs of 24 points and 14 rebounds . . . Played just one year at Brigham Young, where he set frosh NCAA records for blocks . . . Then spent two years completing Church Mission in Australia . . . Born March 22, 1972, in Landstuhl, Germany . . . Monster contract paid him $2.7 million last year.

Year	Team	G	FG	FG Pct.	FT	FT Pct.	Reb.	Ast.	TP	Avg.
1993-94	Philadelphia	49	201	.409	102	.607	306	98	504	10.3

CLARENCE WEATHERSPOON 24 6-6 245   Forward

If only he were a few inches taller . . . All-Star in the making anyway . . . Fearless performer, supplies toughness and work ethic on a nightly basis . . . Dramatic improvement from rookie season . . . And he was pretty darn good as a rookie . . . Has more points, 2,768, in first two seasons than any Sixer ever . . . 10.1 rebounds per game ranked ninth among all NBA forwards . . . Has played every game in his two years . . . Had Sixers' only triple-double (15 points, 15 rebounds, 13 assists) vs. Charlotte Feb. 7 . . . 45 double-doubles, eighth-highest ever by a Sixer . . . Career-high 23 rebounds vs. Magic March 9 . . . Career-high 31 points vs. Cavs Feb. 2 . . . Set team rookie scoring record in 1992-93 . . . But as rookie, saw his shot blocked more than any player ever in same season . . . Youngest of 13 children . . . Born Sept. 8, 1970, in Crawford, Miss. . . . Sixers took him No. 9 in 1992

. . . Three straight Metro Conference Player-of-Year Awards at Southern Mississippi . . . Made $1.04 million.

Year	Team	G	FG	FG Pct.	FT	FT Pct.	Reb.	Ast.	TP	Avg.
1992-93	Philadelphia	82	494	.469	291	.713	589	147	1280	15.6
1993-94	Philadelphia	82	602	.483	298	.693	832	192	1506	18.4
	Totals	164	1096	.477	589	.703	1421	339	2786	17.0

TIM PERRY 29 6-9 220   Forward

Inconsistency, thy name is Perry . . . Looks All-World one night . . . Looks not of this world the next . . . Example: tied for NBA-best 9-of-9 single-game shooting Dec. 20. It came after a 1-of-7 game. And before a 2-of-6 . . . Career-high 31 points, including team-record 7-of-15 three-pointers Feb. 7 vs. Hornets. So he was 2-of-7 with four points the next game . . . Can run, jump, block shots . . . Just can't do it in consecutive games . . . For the second straight year, he had just three 20-point games. And he's the starting small forward . . . Part of the Charles Barkley trade. Came from Suns with Andrew Lang and Jeff Hornacek for Sir Charles June 17, 1992 . . . Suns drafted him No. 7 in 1988 out of Temple . . . Atlantic-10 Player of the Year in '88 . . . Born June 4, 1965, in Freehold, N.J. . . . Made $1.65 million.

Year	Team	G	FG	FG Pct.	FT	FT Pct.	Reb.	Ast.	TP	Avg.
1988-89	Phoenix	62	108	.537	40	.615	132	18	257	4.1
1989-90	Phoenix	60	100	.513	53	.589	152	17	254	4.2
1990-91	Phoenix	46	75	.521	43	.614	126	27	193	4.2
1991-92	Phoenix	80	413	.523	153	.712	551	134	982	12.3
1992-93	Philadelphia	81	287	.468	147	.710	409	126	731	9.0
1993-94	Philadelphia	80	272	.435	102	.580	404	94	719	9.0
	Totals	409	1255	.489	538	.654	1774	416	3136	7.7

JOHNNY DAWKINS 31 6-2 170   Guard

There's something left. Will he use it? . . . Extraordinarily mediocre season sent Sixers hunting for point-guard help in draft . . . Never was a classic point guard. But he was closer than Dana Barros last season . . . Career lows, by far, in shooting (.418) and scoring (6.6) . . . Finished strong, but by then the season was a wash . . . Has suffered since the departure of Charles Barkley as Sixers looked to backcourt for more offense, cutting his time . . . Doesn't finish . . . Never an exceptional penetrator . . . Game lost a lot when he tore anterior cruciate ligament in right knee Nov. 8, 1990 . . . Has never been the same since . . . No. 10 pick, to San Antonio, out of Duke in 1986 . . . Came to Sixers with Jay Vincent for Maurice Cheeks, Christian Welp and David Wingate Aug. 28, 1989 . . . Left Duke as school's all-time leading scorer and as No. 2 all-time in the ACC . . . First ACC player with 2,000 points, 500 assists, 500 rebounds . . . Born Sept. 28, 1963, in Washington, D.C. . . . Made $2.1 million.

Year	Team	G	FG	FG Pct.	FT	FT Pct.	Reb.	Ast.	TP	Avg.
1986-87	San Antonio	81	334	.437	153	.801	169	290	835	10.3
1987-88	San Antonio	65	405	.485	198	.896	204	480	1027	15.8
1988-89	San Antonio	32	177	.443	100	.893	101	224	454	14.2
1989-90	Philadelphia	81	465	.489	210	.861	247	601	1162	14.3
1990-91	Philadelphia	4	26	.634	10	.909	16	28	63	15.8
1991-92	Philadelphia	82	394	.437	164	.882	227	567	988	12.0
1992-93	Philadelphia	74	258	.437	113	.796	136	339	655	8.9
1993-94	Philadelphia	72	177	.418	84	.840	123	263	475	6.6
	Totals	491	2236	.456	1032	.855	1223	2792	5659	11.5

DANA BARROS 27 5-10 165   Guard

A guy could get a complex . . . Traded twice in four days. Went from Sonics with Eddie Johnson and draft considerations to Hornets for Kendall Gill Aug. 31, 1993 . . . Picked up the luggage at baggage claim and went to Philly along with Greg Graham, Sidney Green and a '94 first-rounder for Hersey Hawkins Sept. 3, 1993 . . . Had perhaps best stretch of career in midseason. In 48 starts, averaged 15.4 points, shot 49 percent . . . Faded badly: 10 points, 40 percent shooting in last 22 games . . . Superior three-point shooter. That's his trademark . . . Set Sixer season records for treys tried (354) and made (135—which also put him fifth all-time on team list) . . . Single-game career highs in assists (13) and rebounds (13) . . . Twice won games at buzzer . . . Defensive matchup problems . . . By no means an instinctive point . . . Gets to the hole and finishes . . . Born April 13, 1967, in Boston. Sonics took him No. 16 in '89 out of Boston College . . . Earned $750,000.

Year	Team	G	FG	FG Pct.	FT	FT Pct.	Reb.	Ast.	TP	Avg.
1989-90	Seattle	81	299	.405	89	.809	132	205	782	9.7
1990-91	Seattle	66	154	.495	78	.918	71	111	418	6.3
1991-92	Seattle	75	238	.483	60	.759	81	125	619	8.3
1992-93	Seattle	69	214	.451	49	.831	107	151	541	7.8
1993-94	Philadelphia	81	412	.469	116	.800	196	424	1075	13.3
	Totals	372	1317	.455	392	.820	587	1016	3435	9.2

JEFF MALONE 33 6-4 205   Guard

In one of Sixers' blockbuster trades last year. But not exactly a guy you want to rebuild around . . . Once a model shooting guard. Now the range is getting closer and closer to the basket . . . Came from Jazz with a '94 first-round pick for Jeff Hornacek, Sean Green and a future second-rounder Feb. 24 . . . Shot 50 percent in 16 of 27 games for 76ers . . . Still runs curl patterns to precision . . . Season-high 32 points vs. Bucks April 6 . . . Lowest scoring since rookie season . . . Wasn't real chummy with Utah namesake Karl last season . . . Always a better one-on-one defender than given credit for . . . Born June 28, 1961, in Mobile, Ala. . . . No. 10 pick out of Mississippi State by Bullets in 1983 . . . Went to Jazz as part of three-team trade involving Sacramento and Pervis Ellison, June 25, 1990 . . . Made $2.38 million.

Year	Team	G	FG	FG Pct.	FT	FT Pct.	Reb.	Ast.	TP	Avg.
1983-84	Washington	81	408	.444	142	.826	155	151	982	12.1
1984-85	Washington	76	605	.499	211	.844	206	184	1436	18.9
1985-86	Washington	80	735	.483	322	.868	288	191	1795	22.4
1986-87	Washington	80	689	.457	376	.885	218	298	1758	22.0
1987-88	Washington	80	648	.476	335	.882	206	237	1641	20.5
1988-89	Washington	76	677	.480	296	.871	179	219	1651	21.7
1989-90	Washington	75	781	.491	257	.877	206	243	1820	24.3
1990-91	Utah	69	525	.508	231	.917	206	143	1282	18.6
1991-92	Utah	81	691	.511	256	.898	233	180	1639	20.2
1992-93	Utah	79	595	.494	236	.852	173	128	1429	18.1
1993-94	Utah-Phil.	77	525	.486	205	.830	199	125	1262	16.4
	Totals	854	6879	.485	2867	.871	2269	2099	16695	19.5

GREG GRAHAM 23 6-4 183   Guard

Green as a dollar bill . . . Good athleticism. Strong defensive skills and instincts . . . Shooting? Well, he was a rookie, don't forget . . . Big Ten Defensive Player of the Year for Indiana as senior. Also was first player ever to lead conference in both field-goal percentage and three-point percentage . . . Must have left his shooting eye somewhere between Bloomington and Philadelphia . . . Had a 16-point game . . . Changed uniform number from 11 to 20, number he wore in college, at midseason . . . Didn't help shooting (.400) . . . Hornets drafted him

No. 17 . . . Sixers got his rights Sept. 3, 1993, from Charlotte along with Dana Barros, Sidney Green and a '94 first-rounder for Hersey Hawkins . . . Born Nov. 26, 1970, in Indianapolis . . . Made $700,000.

Year	Team	G	FG	FG Pct.	FT	FT Pct.	Reb.	Ast.	TP	Avg.
1993-94	Philadelphia	70	122	.400	92	.836	86	66	338	4.8

SCOTT WILLIAMS 26 6-10 230   Center-Forward

Unrestricted Bulls' free agent signed long-term contract in July with 76ers . . . Last season was a wash through injury. Strained right-knee tendon knocked him out of first 41 games . . . Very active rebounder when healthy . . . Good strong-defender type . . . Plays backup at both power forward and center . . . Versatile guy who knows his limitations . . . Got stronger as season progressed. Best month was April, when he averaged 9.7 points, 7.1 rebounds . . . Why some teams succeed: he was un-drafted out of North Carolina and signed as a free agent in July 1990 . . . Born March 21, 1968, in Hacienda Heights, Cal. . . . Made $613,000 and was worth it.

Year	Team	G	FG	FG Pct.	FT	FT Pct.	Reb.	Ast.	TP	Avg.
1990-91	Chicago	51	53	.510	20	.714	98	16	127	2.5
1991-92	Chicago	63	83	.483	48	.649	247	50	214	3.4
1992-93	Chicago	71	166	.466	90	.714	451	68	422	5.9
1993-94	Chicago	38	114	.483	60	.612	181	39	289	7.6
	Totals	223	416	.479	218	.669	977	173	1052	4.7

THE ROOKIES

SHARONE WRIGHT 21 6-10 260   Forward-Center

If he pans out, Clarence Weatherspoon can move to small forward and abuse opponents there while the No. 6 pick in the draft can give Sixers their first legit-sized power forward since before Charles Barkley . . . Clemson product will also be backup center . . . Early entry. Honorable-mention All-American . . . Fourth-leading rebounder in school's history. But he trails some good ones: Tree Rollins, Dale Davis and Horace Grant . . . Born Jan. 30, 1973, in Macon, Ga.

Clarence Weatherspoon made great strides in second year.

B.J. TYLER 23 6-1 175   **Guard**
When John Lucas coached San Antonio, he got to know B.J., the Texas point guard . . . So when Lucas moved to Philly—in need of a true point guard—Tyler became a perfect pick in the 20th slot . . . Great pressure defender, with frightening quickness . . . In just 76 games, he finished in Texas' all-time top 10 in points, assists, steals and three-pointers . . . Born April 30, 1971, in Galveston, Tex.

DERRICK ALSTON 22 6-9 225   Center

Duquesne product went in second round, at No. 33 . . . Dukes' all-time leader in blocked shots (229) and field-goal percentage (.561) . . . Led Atlantic-10 in scoring . . . A .561 career field-goal shooter. But he's had troubles at the line (.576) . . . Born Aug. 20, 1972, in the Bronx, N.Y. . . . Raised in Hoboken, N.J.

COACH JOHN LUCAS: He proved he had the right stuff in San Antonio and now he takes on a new challenge as VP-Basketball Operations, GM and coach of the troubled 76ers . . . Followed up a 40-22 finish to 1992-93 with the Spurs (after replacing Jerry Tarkanian without any NBA or college coaching experience) by going 55-27 last season . . . That matched the second-best mark in San Antonio history . . . Season ended in disappointing fashion when the Spurs were eliminated in the first round of the playoffs . . . Lifetime 95-49 (.660) . . . Every coach agrees it is a players' league now, but he takes that theory all the way . . . Spurs decided on everything from what time to practice, fines and, sometimes, even what plays to run . . . Former point guard now knows all about running a team on and off the court . . . Houston made former Maryland star No. 1 pick in 1976 draft . . . That was the start to 14-year career that included moments like being named to the all-rookie team and setting an NBA record with 14 assists in one quarter and finishing second in the league in assists twice . . . Spent time with Rockets, Warriors, Bullets, Spurs, Bucks and SuperSonics . . . The same career also included being suspended twice after testing positive for drugs . . . Some of the darkest moments became the impetus for some of the brightest—serving as a role model for other recovering addicts while starting prominent drug-treatment programs in Houston . . . Sober since March 14, 1986 . . . While breaking Pete Maravich's high-school scoring record in North Carolina, he also won three straight tennis single's titles and played on the Junior Davis Cup Team. Later became an All-American in tennis at Maryland and played World Team Tennis in the late 1970s . . . Born Oct. 31, 1953, in Durham, N.C.

Dynamic Dr. J led Sixers to 1983 NBA championship.

GREATEST PLAYER

Wait a minute. How can a team list Wilt Chamberlain among its alumni and then have somebody else selected as its Greatest Player?

Simple. Have Julius Erving also included among the alumni.

Sure, Wilt needs no case presented for him. But the all-time great spent only four years with the 76ers. He was a Philly and Golden State Warrior, a Laker, etc. Dr. J. spent 11 years in a Sixer uniform. And in addition to scoring over 18,000 points, all he really did was revolutionize the game.

Erving brought playground moves into the league for good. There were others who tried, but none ever did it with the flair of The Doctor. His 18,364 points stand as the third-best all-time Sixer high. He's also third in minutes, second in offensive and defensive rebounds, fourth in free throws. The Hall of Famer was an all-star in each of his 11 Philly seasons and helped the Sixers to the 1983 NBA championship.

ALL-TIME 76ER LEADERS

SEASON

Points: Wilt Chamberlain, 2,649, 1965-66
Assists: Maurice Cheeks, 753, 1985-86
Rebounds: Wilt Chamberlain, 1,957, 1966-67

GAME

Points: Wilt Chamberlain, 68 vs. Chicago, 12/16/67
Assists: Wilt Chamberlain, 21 vs. Detroit, 2/2/68
      Maurice Cheeks, 21 vs. New Jersey, 10/30/82
Rebounds: Wilt Chamberlain, 43 vs. Boston, 3/6/65

CAREER

Points: Hal Greer, 21,586, 1958-73
Assists: Maurice Cheeks, 6,212, 1978-89
Rebounds: Dolph Schayes, 11,256, 1948-64

WASHINGTON BULLETS

TEAM DIRECTORY: Chairman: Abe Pollin; Pres.: Susan O'Malley; Vice Chairman: Jerry Sachs; GM: John Nash; Dir. Communications: Matt Williams; Coach: Jim Lynam; Asst. Coaches: Bob Stark, Derek Smith. Arena: USAir Arena (18,756). Colors: Red, white and blue.

SCOUTING REPORT

SHOOTING: Here's the team strength. Unfortunately for the Bullets, their chief weapon is ranked 12th among the other teams in the league. And, far more unfortunately, is that the other teams get to shoot, too.

Ironman Tom Gugliotta topped Bullets in rebounds, steals.

The two key scoring positions, the two and three positions, both produced superior shooting numbers. Off-guard Rex Chapman, now that he apparently can identify a good shot from a bad one, came in at .498 while small forward Don MacLean, the NBA's Most Improved Player, was .502. Barring injury, those two should continue to progress, along with swingman Calbert Cheaney, who flashed enough during his rookie season to provide even more hope.

In Tom Gugliotta (.466), the Bullets have something of a hybrid four. He steps outside with range and puts the ball on the floor. But the Bullets are going to need more inside from him. But if rookie Juwan Howard develops as hoped, Gugliotta can move over to small forward and the Bullets potentially could be huge up front. They look for ex-Magic Scott Skiles to fill a point-guard gap. At center, Pervis Ellison, now gone to the Celtics, was always hurt and Kevin Duckworth is always Kevin Duckworth. The Bullets pray they can get something out of draftee Jim McIlvaine, Marquette's defensive specialist.

PLAYMAKING: Creativity was as an ancient custom. The Bullets were a maddeningly plodding team last year: dribble, pass, shoot. Only the Pistons in the East managed fewer assists.

The Bullets spent a good chunk of two seasons searching for a solution, but they always came back to Michael Adams, whose 480 assists were among the fewest put up by regularly starting point guards. Adams could shoot a mean three, but he didn't pass well enough to help carry this team through offensive adversity. And the Bullets traded him to Charlotte. The feisty Skiles is a good drive-and-dish guy.

REBOUNDING: THE worst. Period. Nobody had fewer rebounds last season. With so many players intent on perimeter shooting, the Bullets simply don't crash the boards, although you'd think that was the case with the way they routinely get punched out in transition. They established a franchise low in offensive rebounds, so there was no surprise that they drafted for size with Howard and 7-1 McIlvaine. Well, if the Bullets want to make any noise at all, the rookies better be good. Real good.

DEFENSE: Want to know why Wes Unseld would rather have had teeth pulled than return? Look at Washington's defensive numbers: surrendered 107.7 points and .508 shooting. Only the Clippers gave up more points. And nobody allowed better shooting.

BULLET ROSTER

No.	Veterans	Pos.	Ht.	Wt.	Age	Yrs. Pro	College
32	Mitchell Butler	G	6-5	210	23	1	UCLA
3	Rex Chapman	G	6-4	205	27	6	Kentucky
40	Calbert Cheaney	G-F	6-7	209	23	1	Indiana
00	Kevin Duckworth	C	7-0	275	30	8	Eastern Illinois
24	Tom Gugliotta	F	6-10	240	26	2	North Carolina State
34	Don MacLean	F	6-10	225	24	2	UCLA
77	Gheorghe Muresan	C	7-7	315	23	1	Romania
14	Doug Overton	G	6-3	190	25	2	LaSalle
20	Brent Price	G	6-1	175	25	2	Oklahoma
–	Scott Skiles	G	6-1	180	30	8	Michigan State
33	Larry Stewart	F	6-8	220	26	3	Coppin State
15	Kenny Walker	F	6-8	220	30	6	Kentucky

Rd.	Rookies	Sel. No.	Pos.	Ht.	Wt.	College
1	Juwan Howard	5	F	6-8	250	Michigan
2	Jim McIlvaine	32	C	7-1	240	Marquette

In transition, the Bullets are simply an awful team and this must be the first area incoming head coach Jim Lynam addresses. Layups were surrendered with alarming frequency because there's no real shot-blocker around. And those are the strengths.

The backcourt of Chapman and the departed Adams was an opposing team's dream, the Bullets' nightmare. Cheaney may provide some relief defensively at two. Skiles is no Dennis Johnson, but he's better than Adams. Overall, the Bullets will be a bit better here.

OUTLOOK: For six straight years, the Bullets have found themselves studying the dynamics of lottery ping-pong balls while others head off to the postseason. Odds are better than not it will be seven straight years.

Oh, they'll be improved and behind team president Susan O'Malley they'll have ingenious promotions and they'll draw remarkably well for a team going nowhere. But in the end, even with Lynam on the sidelines, the Bullets will go nowhere.

The improvement will continue but until Washington can come up with a legitimate center and something resembling cohesive defense, they'll be among the bottom-rung teams. There is talent here and there will be improvement.

But not enough to avoid the seven-year playoff itch.

BULLET PROFILES

TOM GUGLIOTTA 26 6-10 240   Forward

The cornerstone... Ironman type, he has missed only five games in two seasons... Led team in minutes, rebounds and steals... Eighth in NBA in steals (2.2 per). ''Googs'' and Scottie Pippen were only forwards among top 10 in thefts... Eight steals vs. Denver March 1 was one off all-time Bullet mark... His team-best 172 were six shy of Bullet record... Attitude and work ethic are the stuff of coach's dreams... Shooting percentage went up from .426 to .466... Can shoot the three-pointer well for a 6-10 guy... Decent defender... Problem is foot speed. He's not quick enough for speedy small forwards. And at power forward he can be overwhelmed by brute muscular types... All-Rookie team two years ago when he led all rookies in assists (3.8) and steals (1.6) and was third in rebounds (9.6)... Was the No. 6 pick out of North Carolina State... College saw steady improvement each year. Looks like he's on same course in pros... Born Dec. 19, 1969, in Huntington Station, N.Y.... Made $1.65 million in second year of seven-year pact.

Year	Team	G	FG	FG Pct.	FT	FT Pct.	Reb.	Ast.	TP	Avg.
1992-93	Washington......	81	484	.426	181	.644	781	306	1187	14.7
1993-94	Washington......	78	540	.466	213	.685	728	276	1333	17.1
	Totals	159	1024	.446	394	.666	1509	582	2520	15.8

REX CHAPMAN 27 6-4 205   Guard

Check the weather. Hell may have frozen over. This guy finally arrived... Was having an all-star year when injuries stepped in... Missed 22 games with knee and ankle woes... Tied for team lead in scoring at 18.2 ppg, shot .498, both career bests... Question never was one of athleticism. Has superior vertical leap... Never could identify a good shot—until last year... Averaged 19 points, shot .553 in January before ankle injury struck... His .378 percentage on three-pointers is Bullet career best... Got 5,000th point March 9... Defense is another matter... Just doesn't do it... Left Kentucky after two years and was first-ever draft pick of Charlotte Hornets in 1988... Came to

Bullets Feb. 19, 1992 in exchange for Tom Hammonds . . . Born
Oct. 5, 1967, in Bowling Green, Ky. . . . Made $2.004 million.

Year	Team	G	FG	FG Pct.	FT	FT Pct.	Reb.	Ast.	TP	Avg.
1988-89	Charlotte	75	526	.414	155	.795	187	176	1267	16.9
1989-90	Charlotte	54	377	.408	144	.750	179	132	945	17.5
1990-91	Charlotte	70	410	.445	234	.830	191	250	1102	15.7
1991-92	Char.-Wash.	22	113	.448	36	.679	58	89	270	12.3
1992-93	Washington.	60	287	.477	132	.810	88	116	749	12.5
1993-94	Washington.	60	431	.498	168	.816	146	185	1094	18.2
	Totals	341	2144	.443	869	.797	849	948	5427	15.9

DON MacLEAN 24 6-10 225   Forward

Game is as simple as American pie. As effective as pie laced with strychnine . . . Voted
league's Most Improved Player . . . Bullets felt
he was good when they got him from Clippers
with William Bedford for John "Hot Plate"
Williams Oct. 8, 1992. But they never thought
he was this good . . . Tied Rex Chapman for
team scoring lead . . . Double figures in 63 of
75 games . . . Uncanny knack for three-point plays . . . Was wearing down a bit toward end. Might have been fatigue (minutes went
from 674 to 2,487) . . . Shot .502 from floor, .824 from line . . .
Not much as a passer . . . Led NCAA Division I with .921 free-
throw pct. in 1992 at UCLA . . . Drafted No. 19 by Pistons, who
traded him to Clips for Olden Polynice and two second-rounders.
Then came move to Bullets . . . Born Jan. 16, 1970, in Palo Alto,
Cal. . . . Made $601,000.

Year	Team	G	FG	FG Pct.	FT	FT Pct.	Reb.	Ast.	TP	Avg.
1992-93	Washington.	62	157	.435	90	.811	122	39	407	6.6
1993-94	Washington.	75	517	.502	328	.824	467	160	1365	18.2
	Totals	137	674	.485	418	.821	589	199	1772	12.9

SCOTT SKILES 30 6-1 180   Guard

In exchange of future draft picks, he was traded
to Bullets by Magic in July . . . Fell off the
planet once Anfernee Hardaway assumed point
guard full-time . . . Just not effective as a
backup in limited minutes . . . But took it
professionally. Didn't complain, led cheerlead-
ing section from bench. In fact, even suggested
a move to coaching staff . . . Wants to coach
some day and front-office executives in league voted him most

likely player to be successful with suit and clipboard . . . Ranked fourth in NBA three-point percentage (.412) . . . Sees floor well. Had 20 assists vs. Blazers Dec. 1 . . . Born March 5, 1964, in LaPorte, Ind. . . . No. 22 pick by Bucks in 1986, out of Michigan State . . . Traded by Bucks to Pacers in '89 for a second-rounder . . . Went to Magic in expansion draft, June 15, 1989 . . . Made $1.722 million.

Year	Team	G	FG	FG Pct.	FT	FT Pct.	Reb.	Ast.	TP	Avg.
1986-87	Milwaukee	13	18	.290	10	.833	26	45	49	3.8
1987-88	Indiana	51	86	.411	45	.833	66	180	223	4.4
1988-89	Indiana	80	198	.448	130	.903	149	390	546	6.8
1989-90	Orlando	70	190	.409	104	.874	159	334	536	7.7
1990-91	Orlando	79	462	.445	340	.902	270	660	1357	17.2
1991-92	Orlando	75	359	.414	248	.895	202	544	1057	14.1
1992-93	Orlando	78	416	.467	289	.892	290	735	1201	15.4
1993-94	Orlando	82	276	.429	195	.878	189	503	815	9.9
	Totals	528	2005	.434	1361	.890	1351	3391	5784	11.0

KEVIN DUCKWORTH 30 7-0 275   Center

In the real world, he'd be indicted for fraud. Or grand larceny, for taking $2.312 million . . . He rewarded Bullets with 6.6 ppg, 4.7 rpg . . . Did absolutely nothing. But he sulks when criticized . . . Played 69 games, started 52. Shot a nifty .417 . . . His 325 rebounds were the fewest by any center in the league with at least 50 starts . . . Once had a post-up game with effective one-hander . . . Gas once cost 25 cents, too . . . May be league's worst regular interior defender . . . Listed at 275. Try 330 . . . Bullets got him from Portland for Harvey Grant, June 24, 1993 . . . Born April 11, 1964, in Harvey, Ill. . . . Second-rounder went to Spurs out of Eastern Illinois in 1986 . . . Went from Spurs to Blazers for Walter Berry, Dec. 18, 1986.

Year	Team	G	FG	FG Pct.	FT	FT Pct.	Reb.	Ast.	TP	Avg.
1986-87	S.A.-Port.	65	130	.476	92	.687	223	29	352	5.4
1987-88	Portland	78	450	.496	331	.770	576	66	1231	15.8
1988-89	Portland	79	554	.477	324	.757	635	60	1432	18.1
1989-90	Portland	82	548	.478	231	.740	509	91	1327	16.2
1990-91	Portland	81	521	.481	240	.772	531	89	1282	15.8
1991-92	Portland	82	362	.461	156	.690	497	99	880	10.7
1992-93	Portland	74	301	.438	127	.730	387	70	729	9.9
1993-94	Washington	69	184	.417	88	.667	325	56	456	6.6
	Totals	610	3050	.470	1589	.740	3683	560	7689	12.6

Don MacLean was voted NBA's "Most Improved Player."

CALBERT CHEANEY 23 6-7 209   Guard-Forward

Big part of the future . . . Typical rookie season for the No. 6 pick in '93 lottery . . . Had hard time adjusting under vet-oriented Wes Unseld . . . All the usual raps at forward: tweener size, not big or strong enough as a forward . . . Emergence of Rex Chapman made minutes at guard tough . . . But showed what could be in store: had two 30-point games . . . Flu and foot problems limited him to 65 games . . . 21 starts. Averaged 15.8 points as starter . . . Double-figures in 13 of last 15 games . . . Born July 17, 1971, in Evansville, Ind. . . . Indy state high-school champ hurdler... College Player of the Year as a senior for Indiana... All-time scoring champ in Big Ten... Earned $2 million.

Year	Team	G	FG	FG Pct.	FT	FT Pct.	Reb.	Ast.	TP	Avg.
1993-94	Washington......	65	327	.470	124	.770	190	126	779	12.0

DOUG OVERTON 25 6-3 190   Guard

When they give you a job, you're supposed to accept it. Not give it back... Bullets hoped to make him the starting point guard in preseason... That idea went up in flames... Real disappointing year after signs of promise in 1992-93 rookie debut... Points plunged from 8.1 to 3.6, assists from 3.5 to 1.5, shooting from .471 to .403. You get the idea... Couldn't grasp the big picture. Or, essentially, the basketball... Confidence seemed to fall to sub-basement... Just not a classic point type the Bullets sought... Had 18 assists in one game as rookie... Born Aug. 3, 1969 in Philadelphia... Drafted on second round by Pistons out of LaSalle in 1991... Signed as Bullet free agent Oct. 19, 1992 ... Made $500,000.

Year	Team	G	FG	FG Pct.	FT	FT Pct.	Reb.	Ast.	TP	Avg.
1992-93	Washington......	45	152	.471	59	.728	106	157	366	8.1
1993-94	Washington......	61	87	.403	43	.827	69	92	218	3.6
	Totals	106	239	.443	102	.767	175	249	584	5.5

BRENT PRICE 25 6-1 175   Guard

Good genes. Bad game... Kid brother of Cavs' all-star Mark Price... Comparison ends there... Tough to find a role. Point guard by trade... But not a point guard. Can't shoot (.433). So he's not a shooting guard... Not too many options left for a 6-1 guy... Virtually faints against any kind of pressure... Can't create a shot... Decent standstill shooter. But needs time to set up... Averaged 10.5 points in 13 starts, though ... Knows the game. Just doesn't play it very well... His dad, Denny, is coach at Phillips U. (Okla.)... 1992 second-rounder out of Oklahoma was born in Enid, Okla. Dec. 9, 1968... Made $283,000.

Year	Team	G	FG	FG Pct.	FT	FT Pct.	Reb.	Ast.	TP	Avg.
1992-93	Washington......	68	100	.358	54	.794	103	154	262	3.9
1993-94	Washington......	65	141	.433	68	.782	90	213	400	6.2
	Totals	133	241	.398	122	.787	193	367	662	5.0

LARRY STEWART 26 6-8 220   Forward

A TV movie waiting to happen . . . Utterly bizarre year, included his being shot in an apparent robbery in his suburban home . . . Shot twice, through neck and thigh . . . Started year on injury list with broken right foot . . . Returned. Broke foot again . . . Played just three games . . . Had been considered a super find out of Coppin State in 1991 . . . Undrafted, signed as free agent Sept. 23, 1991 . . . Two solid role-playing years . . . Not really athletically gifted, but got the job done with determination, smarts . . . Shot team-high .543, ninth-best mark in NBA in '92-93 . . . Had 32-point game vs. Heat April 23, 1993 . . . Used at both forward spots . . . Received four-year free-agent offer from Spurs that Bullets matched after rookie season . . . Made $600,000 . . . Born Sept. 21, 1968, in Philadelphia.

Year	Team	G	FG	FG Pct.	FT	FT Pct.	Reb.	Ast.	TP	Avg.
1991-92	Washington......	76	303	.514	188	.807	449	120	794	10.4
1992-93	Washington......	81	306	.543	184	.727	383	146	796	9.8
1993-94	Washington......	3	3	.375	7	.700	7	2	13	4.3
	Totals	160	612	.527	379	.764	839	268	1603	10.0

GHEORGHE MURESAN 23 7-7 333   Center

"Me squash Americans little with foots big." . . . Romania-born project spoke through translator . . . Size 19 shoe . . . Mammoth presence. At his size, he is as mobile as Louisiana . . . A huge project, he was definitely worth a 30th-pick gamble in 1993 . . . Despite rawness, he was still more productive than Kevin Duckworth: 5.6 ppg, 3.6 rpg in 12.0 minutes . . . Showed progress as season wore on . . . Soft hands . . . Rotten at foul line . . . But there's something here . . . Alonzo Mourning shot 6-of-18 against him. Patrick Ewing moved out beyond 20 feet . . . Four steals vs. Pacers April 19 . . . Born Feb. 14, 1971, in Triteni, Transylvania, Romania . . . Cluj University (The Fightin' Vampires?) . . . Played in France . . . Tallest Bullet ever . . . Parents are both under 6-feet . . . Made $500,000.

Year	Team	G	FG	FG Pct.	FT	FT Pct.	Reb.	Ast.	TP	Avg.
1993-94	Washington......	54	128	.545	48	.676	192	18	304	5.6

KENNY WALKER 30 6-8 220 Forward

The Sky has fallen . . . Brought to training camp as free agent purely out of desperation as one Bullet after another limped away . . . And he stuck. Played 73 games . . . Pretty much the same player he was with Knicks for five seasons . . . Still has no shot, but is extremely active at both ends . . . Bangs his head on clouds when leaping for rebounds . . . A slasher offensively, good active defender and shot-blocker . . . But gets pushed around by bulkier guys . . . Tremendous attitude and heart . . . Played in Europe after 1991 release by Knicks, who had drafted him No. 5 out of Kentucky in 1986 . . . Came up with career-high 14 rebounds against former team Nov. 10 . . . Came back from Achilles tear suffered in Europe in 1992 . . . Former slam-dunk champ . . . One of nicest guys in NBA . . . Born Aug. 18, 1964, in Roberta, Ga. . . . Nicknamed ''Sky'' in college for leaping ability . . . Earned $400,000.

Year	Team	G	FG	FG Pct.	FT	FT Pct.	Reb.	Ast.	TP	Avg.
1986-87	New York	68	285	.491	140	.757	338	75	710	10.4
1987-88	New York	82	344	.473	138	.775	389	86	826	10.1
1988-89	New York	79	174	.489	66	.776	230	36	419	5.3
1989-90	New York	68	204	.531	125	.723	343	49	535	7.9
1990-91	New York	54	83	.435	64	.780	157	13	230	4.3
1993-94	Washington	73	132	.482	87	.696	289	33	351	4.8
	Totals	424	1222	.486	620	.749	1746	292	3071	7.2

MITCHELL BUTLER 23 6-5 210 Guard

Someone please tell him he's not 6-10 . . . Uncanny ability to get shot blocked . . . But not bad for an undrafted rookie . . . Good strength . . . Had 12 rebounds vs. Mavs . . . Spot starter . . . Showed steady progression. Averaged nearly 10 points and 4.2 rebounds in April . . . Out of UCLA, he made team with strong summer-league showing . . . Signed Oct. 5, 1993, to make-good contract . . . Outside game needs work, especially at his size . . . California High School Player of the Year as a senior . . . Minimum wage of $150,000 . . . Born Dec. 15, 1970, in Los Angeles.

Year	Team	G	FG	FG Pct.	FT	FT Pct.	Reb.	Ast.	TP	Avg.
1993-94	Washington	75	207	.495	104	.578	225	77	518	6.9

Rex Chapman blossomed into his best season.

THE ROOKIES

JUWAN HOWARD 21 6-8 250   **Forward**
Early entry. Everybody else did at Michigan, so he emerged as
the fifth overall selection... Third-team All-American was one
of only five players ever to finish with over 1,500 points at Michigan. And he did it in three years... In final college game, he
scored 30 points and took 13 rebounds against eventual national-
champ Arkansas... Born Feb. 7, 1973, in Chicago.

JIM McILVAINE 22 7-1 240   **Center**
Projected by most as a first-rounder, Marquette's all-time leading
shot-blocker lasted until No. 32... Solid choice by Bullets, who
are bankrupt in the middle... His 399 career rejections rank fifth
in NCAA Division I history... Holds top four Marquette single
season shot-block marks... Scored 13.6 points last season...
Born July 30, 1972, in Racine, Wis.

COACH JIM LYNAM: He's got friends in high places. Like  Bullet GM John Nash, who was his GM during coaching days in Philadelphia... So Nash lured him from Sixer front office and back onto sidelines after Wes Unseld packed it in at season's end... Yes, he can coach... Great motivator. Extreme patience with young guys. That's exactly what Bullets need... His predecessor, Unseld, tended to go with vets...
Very intense... Exceptional game coach... Issued standard new coach promise to run more... Also likes low-post offense... The only guy Bullets courted... Had 194-173 head-coaching mark with 76ers in 4½ seasons before taking GM job... Was 52-91 in one-plus years with Clippers... Assistant under Jack Ramsay in Portland in 1981-82... Spent 10 college years at Fairfield, American and his alma mater, St. Joseph's (Pa.), where he is a member of school's Hall of Fame... Born Sept. 15, 1941, in Philadelphia.

GREATEST PLAYER

He was an undersized center coming out of Louisville and joining a team that never knew a winning season. But they couldn't stop the measurement of 6-7 Wes Unseld with a vertical ruler. They had to measure his heart and desire. And mankind owns no tool big enough.

Starting with 56 victories in his rookie season when Unseld joined Wilt Chamberlain as the only players ever to win both the Rookie of the Year and MVP Awards in the same year, the Bullets posted 10 winning campaigns, including an NBA title in '78 when he was the playoffs MVP. His 13 years earned him a spot in the Hall of Fame.

The numbers speak for themselves: he's the NBA's seventh all-time rebounder. He passed 10,000 points and 10,000 rebounds. He's the Bullets' all-time leader in games played, rebounds, minutes and, yes, assists. Forget the numbers. If ever there was a player who did "the little things," it was Unseld. His picks devastated opponents. And no one ever threw better outlet passes.

The lone blemish on Unseld's remarkable Bullet career came as head coach. In six seasons, he managed just a 202-345 record. His teams often were berift of talent but they always played hard for Unseld, the greatest name in Bullets' history.

ALL-TIME BULLET LEADERS

SEASON

Points: Walt Bellamy, 2,495, 1961-62
Assists: Kevin Porter, 734, 1980-81
Rebounds: Walt Bellamy, 1,500, 1961-62

GAME

Points: Earl Monroe, 56 vs. Los Angeles, 2/3/68
Assists: Kevin Porter, 24 vs. Detroit, 3/23/80
Rebounds: Walt Bellamy, 37 vs. St. Louis, 12/4/64

CAREER

Points: Elvin Hayes, 15,551, 1972-81
Assists: Wes Unseld, 3,822, 1968-81
Rebounds: Wes Unseld, 13,769, 1968-81

1994 NBA COLLEGE DRAFT

Sel. No.	Team	Name	College	Ht.
1.	Milwaukee	Glenn Robinson	Purdue	6-7
2.	Dallas	Jason Kidd	California	6-3
3.	Detroit	Grant Hill	Duke	6-8
4.	Minnesota	Donyell Marshall	Connecticut	6-8
5.	Washington	Juwan Howard	Michigan	6-8
6.	Philadelphia	Sharone Wright	Clemson	6-10
7.	L.A. Clippers	Lamond Murray	California	6-6
8.	Sacramento	Brian Grant	Xavier	6-8
9.	Boston	Eric Montross	North Carolina	7-0
10.	L.A. Lakers	Eddie Jones	Temple	6-6
11.	a-Seattle	Carlos Rogers	Tennessee State	6-10
12.	Miami	Khalid Reeves	Arizona	6-1
13.	Denver	Jalen Rose	Michigan	6-6

No. 3: Pistons' Grant Hill from Duke.

No. 4: Donyell Marshall, a T-Wolf from Connecticut.

Sel. No.	Team	Name	College	Ht.
14.	New Jersey	Yinka Dare	George Washington	6-10
15.	b-Indiana	Eric Plakowski	Nebraska	6-6
16.	Golden State	Cliff Rozier	Louisville	6-10
17.	Portland	Aaron McKie	Temple	6-4
18.	Milwaukee	Eric Mobley	Pittsburgh	6-10
19.	Dallas	Tony Dumas	Missouri-KC	6-4
20.	Philadelphia	B.J. Tyler	Texas	6-1
21.	Chicago	Dickey Simpkins	Providence	6-9
22.	c-San Antonio	Bill Curley	Boston College	6-9
23.	Phoenix	Wesley Person	Auburn	6-5

a-Traded to Golden State
b-Traded to L.A. Clippers
c-Traded to Detroit

No. 6 overall: Clemson's Sharone Wright, a new Sixer.

Sel. No.	Team	Name	College	Ht.
24.	New York	Monty Williams	Notre Dame	6-7
25.	d-L.A. Clippers	Greg Minor	Louisville	6-6
26.	New York	Charlie Ward	Florida State	6-1
27.	Orlando	Brooks Thompson	Oklahoma State	6-4
28.	Dallas	Deon Thomas	Illinois	6-7
29.	Phoenix	Antonio Lang	Duke	6-8
30.	Minnesota	Howard Eisley	Boston College	6-2
31.	Orlando	Rodney Dent	Kentucky	6-9

d-Traded to Indiana

North Carolina's Eric Montross (9) joins Celtics.

Lakers landed Temple's Eddie Jones as No. 10.

Nets' lone pick was George Washington's Yinka Dare (14).

Golden State made Louisville's Cliff Rozier 16th pick.

Temple's Aaron McKie is a Trailblazer (17).

Bucks tagged Pittsburgh's Eric Mobley as No. 18.

Missouri-KC's Tony Dumas (19) was Mavs' second pick.

Sel. No.	Team	Name	College	Ht.
32.	Washington	Jim McIlvaine	Marquette	7-1
33.	Philadelphia	Derrick Alston	Duquesne	6-9
34.	Atlanta	Gaylon Nickerson	NW Oklahoma State	6-3
35.	Sacramento	Michael Smith	Providence	6-7
36.	e-Boston	Andrei Fetisov	Forum Valladolid	6-10
37.	Seattle	Dontonio Wingfield	Cincinnati	6-7
38.	Charlotte	Darrin Hancock	Kansas	6-5
39.	f-Golden State	Anthony Miller	Michigan State	6-8
40.	Miami	Jeff Webster	Oklahoma	6-6
41.	Indiana	William Njoku	St. Mary's (Canada)	6-9
42.	Cleveland	Gary Collier	Tulsa	6-4

e-Traded to Milwaukee
f-Traded to L.A. Lakers

Bulls opted for Providence's Dickey Simpkins (21).

BC's Bill Curley (22, Spurs) was traded to Pistons.

Florida State Heisman QB Charlie Ward is Knick (26).

Sel. No.	Team	Name	College	Ht.
43.	Portland	Shawnelle Scott	St. John's	6-10
44.	Indiana	Damon Bailey	Indiana	6-2
45.	Golden State	Dwayne Morton	Louisville	6-6
46.	Milwaukee	Voshon Lenard	Minnesota	6-3
47.	Utah	Jamie Watson	South Carolina	6-6
48.	Detroit	Jevon Crudup	Missouri	6-8
49.	Chicago	Kris Bruton	Benedict College	6-5
50.	Phoenix	Charles Claxton	Georgia	6-11
51.	Sacramento	Lawrence Funderburke	Ohio State	6-8
52.	Phoenix	Anthony Goldwire	Houston	6-1
53.	Houston	Albert Burditt	Texas	6-7
54.	g-Seattle	Zeljko Rebraca	Partizan	6-11

g-Traded to Minnesota

Notre Dame's Monty Williams went to Knicks as 24.

LAC trade made Louisville's Greg Minor a Pacer (25).

1993-94
NATIONAL BASKETBALL ASSOCIATION

FINAL STANDINGS

EASTERN CONFERENCE

Atlantic Division	Won	Lost	Pct.
New York	57	25	.695
Orlando	50	32	.610
New Jersey	45	37	.549
Miami	42	40	.512
Boston	32	50	.390
Philadelphia	25	57	.305
Washington	24	58	.293

Central Division	Won	Lost	Pct.
Atlanta	57	25	.695
Chicago	55	27	.671
Cleveland	47	35	.573
Indiana	47	35	.533
Charlotte	41	41	.500
Detroit	20	62	.244
Milwaukee	20	62	.244

WESTERN CONFERENCE

Midwest Division	Won	Lost	Pct.
Houston	58	24	.707
San Antonio	55	27	.671
Utah	53	29	.646
Denver	42	40	.512
Minnesota	40	62	.244
Dallas	13	69	.159

Pacific Division	Won	Lost	Pct.
Seattle	63	19	.768
Phoenix	56	26	.683
Golden State	50	32	.610
Portland	47	35	.573
L.A. Lakers	33	49	.402
Sacramento	28	54	.341
L.A. Clippers	27	55	.329

PLAYOFFS

EASTERN CONFERENCE
First Round
Atlanta defeated Miami (3-2)
Indiana defeated Orlando (3-0)
New York defeated New Jersey (3-1)
Chicago defeated Cleveland (3-0)
Semifinals
Indiana defeated Atlanta (4-2)
New York defeated Chicago (4-3)
Finals
New York defeated Indiana (4-3)

WESTERN CONFERENCE
First Round
Denver defeated Seattle (3-2)
Utah defeated San Antonio (3-1)
Houston defeated Portland (3-1)
Phoenix defeated Golden State (3-0)
Semifinals
Utah defeated Denver (4-3)
Houston defeated Phoenix (4-3)
Finals
Houston defeated Utah (4-1)

CHAMPIONSHIP
Houston defeated New York (4-3)

1993-94 NBA INDIVIDUAL HIGHS

Most Minutes Played, Season: 3,533, Sprewell, Golden State
Most Minutes Played, Game: 56, K. Malone, Utah vs. San Antonio, 2/23 (2 OT); Rodman, San Antonio at Utah, 2/23 (2 OT) 48, 57 times, most recently by Brown, Boston vs. Charlotte, 4/21
Most Points, Game: 71, Robinson, San Antonio at L.A. Clippers, 4/24
Most Field Goals Made, Game: 26, Robinson, San Antonio at L.A. Clippers, 4/24
Most Field Goal Attempts, Game: 41, Robinson, San Antonio at L.A. Clippers, 4/24
Most 3-Pt. Field Goals Made, Game: 8, Majerle, Phoenix at L.A. Clippers, 11/9; Richmond, Sacramento at L.A. Clippers, 2/25
Most 3-Pt. Field Goal Attempts, Game: 16, Van Exel, L.A. Lakers vs. Utah, 4/24
Most Free Throws Made, Game: 20, Anderson, New Jersey vs. Detroit, 4/15 (2 OT) 18, Robinson, San Antonio at L. A. Clippers, 4/24
Most Free Throw Attempts, Game: 25, Robinson, San Antonio at L.A. Clippers, 4/24
Most Rebounds, Game: 32, Rodman, San Antonio at LAC, 4/24
Most Offensive Rebounds, Game: 14, O'Neal, Orlando vs. Boston, 2/15; Polynice, Sacramento at Milwaukee, 3/11
Most Defensive Rebounds, Game: 23, Rodman, San Antonio vs. Dallas, 1/22
Most Offensive Rebounds, Season: 435, Rodman, San Antonio
Most Defensive Rebounds, Season: 914, Rodman, San Antonio
Most Assists, Game: 25, K. Johnson, Phoenix vs. San Antonio, 4/6
Most Blocked Shots, Game: 15, O'Neal, Orlando at New Jersey, 11/20
Most Steals, Game: 10, K. Johnson, Phoenix vs. Washington, 12/9
Most Personal Fouls, Season: 312, Kemp, Seattle
Most Games Disqualified, Season: 11, Kemp, Seattle; Smits, Indiana

INDIVIDUAL SCORING LEADERS
Minimum 70 games or 1,400 points

	G	FG	FT	Pts.	Avg.
Robinson, San Antonio	80	840	693	2383	29.8
O'Neal, Orlando	81	953	471	2377	29.3
Olajuwon, Houston	80	894	388	2184	27.3
Wilkins, Atl.-L.A. Clippers	74	698	442	1923	26.0
K. Malone, Utah	82	772	511	2063	25.2
Ewing, New York	79	745	445	1939	24.5
Richmond, Sacramento	78	635	426	1823	23.4
Pippen, Chicago	72	627	270	1587	22.0
Barkley, Phoenix	65	518	318	1402	21.6
Rice, Miami	81	663	250	1708	21.1
Sprewell, Golden State	82	613	353	1720	21.0
Manning, LAC-Atlanta	68	586	228	1403	20.6
Dumars, Detroit	69	505	276	1410	20.4
Coleman, New Jersey	77	541	439	1559	20.2
Harper, L.A. Clippers	75	569	299	1508	20.1
C. Robinson, Portland	82	641	352	1647	20.1
Miller, Indiana	79	524	403	1574	19.9
Jackson, Dallas	82	637	285	1576	19.2
Mashburn, Dallas	79	561	306	1513	19.2
Willis, Atlanta	80	627	268	1531	19.1

REBOUND LEADERS
Minimum 70 games or 800 rebounds

	G	Off.	Def.	Tot.	Avg.
Rodman, San Antonio	79	453	914	1367	17.3
O'Neal, Orlando	81	384	688	1072	13.2
Willis, Atlanta	80	335	628	963	12.0
Olajuwon, Houston	80	229	726	955	11.9
Polynice, Det.-Sac.	68	299	510	809	11.9
Mutombo, Denver	82	286	685	971	11.8
Oakley, New York	82	349	616	965	11.8
K. Malone, Utah	82	235	705	940	11.5
Coleman, New Jersey	77	262	608	870	11.3
Ewing, New York	79	219	666	885	11.2
Grant, Chicago	70	306	463	769	11.0
Divac, L.A. Clippers	79	282	569	851	10.8
Kemp, Seattle	79	312	539	851	10.8
Robinson, San Antonio	80	241	614	855	10.7
Thorpe, Houston	82	271	599	870	10.6
Williams, Portland	81	315	528	843	10.4
Seikaly, Miami	72	244	496	740	10.3
Weatherspoon, Philadelphia	82	254	578	832	10.1
Gugliotta, Washington	78	189	539	728	9.3
Green, Phoenix	82	275	478	753	9.2

FIELD-GOAL LEADERS
Minimum 300 FG Made

	FG	FGA	Pct.
O'Neal, Orlando	953	1591	.599
Mutombo, Denver	365	642	.569
Thorpe, Houston	449	801	.561
Webber, Golden State . . .	572	1037	.552
Kemp, Seattle	533	990	.538
Vaught, L.A. Clippers . . .	373	695	.537
Ceballos, Phoenix	425	795	.535
Smits, Indiana	493	923	.534
D. Davis, Indiana	308	582	.529
Olajuwon, Houston	894	1694	.528
Stockton, Utah	458	868	.528
Grant, Chicago	460	878	.524
Polynice, Det.-Sac.	346	662	.523
Radja, Boston	491	942	.521
L. Johnson, Charlotte . . .	346	672	.515
Mills, Detroit	588	1151	.511
Gilliam, New Jersey	348	682	.510
Augmon, Atlanta	439	861	.510
Owens, Golden State	492	971	.507
Robinson, San Antonio . .	840	1658	.507

3-POINT FIELD-GOAL LEADERS
Minimum 50 Made

	FG	FGA	Pct.
Murray, Portland	50	109	.459
Armstrong, Chicago	60	135	.444
Miller, Indiana	123	292	.421
Kerr, Chicago	52	124	.419
Skiles, Orlando	68	165	.412
Murdock, Milwaukee	69	168	.411
Richmond, Sacramento	127	312	.407
Smith, Houston	89	220	.405
Curry, Charlotte	152	378	.402
Davis, New York	53	132	.402
Scott, Orlando	155	388	.399
Price, Cleveland	118	297	.397
Wilkins, Cleveland	84	212	.396
Ellis, San Antonio	131	332	.395
E. Johnson, Charlotte . . .	59	150	.393
McMillan, Seattle	52	133	.391
Porter, Portland	110	282	.390
Chapman, Washington . .	64	165	.388
Dumars, Detroit	124	320	.388
Majerle, Phoenix	192	503	.382

FREE-THROW LEADERS
Minimum 125 FT Made

	FT	FTA	Pct.
Abdul-Rauf, Denver	219	229	.956
Miller, Indiana	403	444	.908
Pierce, Seattle	189	211	.896
Threatt, L.A. Lakers	138	155	.890
Price, Cleveland	238	268	.888
Rice, Miami	250	284	.880
Hornacek, Phi.-Utah	260	296	.878
Skiles, Orlando	195	222	.878
Porter, Portland	204	234	.872
Smith, Houston	135	155	.871
Hawkins, Charlotte	312	362	.862
Elie, Houston	154	179	.860
Brandon, Cleveland	139	162	.858
Armstrong, Chicago	194	227	.855
Anderson, San Antonio . .	145	171	.848
Wilkins, Atlanta-LAC	442	522	.847
Legler, Dallas	142	169	.840
M. Williams, Minnesota	333	397	.839
Dumars, Detroit	276	330	.836
Smith, Miami	273	327	.835

ASSISTS LEADERS
Minimum 70 games or 400 assists

	G	A	Avg.
Stockton, Utah	82	1031	12.6
Bogues, Charlotte	77	780	10.1
Blaylock, Atlanta	81	789	9.7
K. Anderson, New Jersey	82	784	9.6
K. Johnson, Phoenix	67	637	9.5
Strickland, Portland	82	740	9.0
Douglas, Boston	78	683	8.8
Jackson, L.A. Clippers . .	79	678	8.6
Price, Cleveland	76	589	7.8
M. Williams, Minnesota	71	512	7.2
Adams, Washington	70	480	6.9
Webb, Sacramento	79	528	6.7
Murdock, Milwaukee	82	546	6.7
Hardaway, Orlando	82	544	6.6
Workman, Indiana	65	404	6.2
Skiles, Orlando	82	503	6.1
Payton, Seattle	82	494	6.0
Van Exel, L.A. Lakers . . .	81	466	5.8
Pippen, Chicago	72	403	5.6
McMillan, Seattle	73	387	5.3

STEALS LEADERS				BLOCKED-SHOTS LEADERS			
Minimum 70 games or 125 steals				Minimum 70 games or 100 blocked shots			
	G	St.	Avg.		G	Blk.	Avg.
McMillan, Seattle	73	216	2.96	Mutombo, Denver	82	336	4.10
Pippen, Chicago	72	211	2.93	Olajuwon, Houston	80	297	3.71
Blaylock, Atlanta	81	212	2.62	Robinson, San Antonio . .	80	265	3.31
Stockton, Utah	82	199	2.43	Mourning, Charlotte	60	188	3.13
Murdock, Milwaukee	82	197	2.40	Bradley, Philadelphia	49	147	3.00
Hardaway, Orlando	82	190	2.32	O'Neal, Orlando	81	231	2.85
Payton, Seattle	82	188	2.29	Ewing, New York	79	217	2.75
Gugliotta, Washington . . .	78	172	2.21	Miller, Phoenix	69	156	2.26
Sprewell, Golden State . .	82	180	2.20	Webber, Golden State . . .	76	164	2.16
Brown, Boston	77	156	2.03	Kemp, Seattle	79	166	2.10
Lever, Dallas	81	159	1.96	Campbell, L.A. Lakers . . .	76	146	1.92
K. Anderson, New Jersey	82	158	1.93	Coleman, New Jersey . . .	77	142	1.84
Harper, L.A. Clippers . . .	75	144	1.92	Williams, Cleveland	76	130	1.71
Gill, Seattle	79	151	1.91	Spencer, L.A. Clippers . .	76	127	1.67
K. Johnson, Phoenix	67	125	1.87	D. Davis, Indiana	66	106	1.61
Augmon, Atlanta	82	149	1.82	K. Malone, Utah	82	126	1.54
Kemp, Seattle	79	142	1.80	Koncak, Atlanta	82	125	1.52
Strickland, Portland	82	147	1.79	Divac, L.A. Lakers	79	112	1.42
Robinson, San Antonio . .	80	139	1.74	Weatherspoon, Phi.	82	116	1.41
Bogues, Charlotte	77	133	1.73	Baker, Milwaukee	82	114	1.39

Vin Baker's rebounds and shot-making made him All-Rookie.

1993-94 ALL-NBA TEAM

FIRST			SECOND		
Pos.	Player, Team		Pos.	Player, Team	
F	Scottie Pippen, Chicago		F	Shawn Kemp, Seattle	
F	Karl Malone, Utah		F	Charles Barkley, Phoenix	
C	Hakeem Olajuwon, Houston		C	David Robinson, San Antonio	
G	John Stockton, Utah		G	Mitch Richmond, Sacramento	
G	Latrell Sprewell, Golden State		G	Kevin Johnson, Phoenix	

THIRD	
Pos.	Player, Team
F	Derrick Coleman, New Jersey
F	Dominique Wilkins, LAC
C	Shaquille O'Neal, Orlando
G	Mark Price, Cleveland
G	Gary Payton, Seattle

*1993-94 NBA ALL-ROOKIE TEAM

FIRST	SECOND
Player, Team	Player, Team
Chris Webber, Golden State	Dino Radja, Boston
Anfernee Hardaway, Orlando	Nick Van Exel, L.A. Lakers
Vin Baker, Milwaukee	Shawn Bradley, Philadelphia
Jamal Washburn, Dallas	Toni Kukoc, Chicago
Isaiah Rider, Minnesota	Lindsey Hunter, Detroit

*Chosen without regard to position

1993-94 NBA ALL-DEFENSIVE TEAM

FIRST		SECOND	
Pos.	Player, Team	Pos.	Player, Team
F	Scottie Pippen, Chicago	F	Dennis Rodman, San Antonio
F	Charles Oakley, New York	F	Horace Grant, Chicago
C	Hakeem Olajuwon, Houston	C	David Robinson, San Antonio
G	Gary Payton, Seattle	G	Nate McMillan, Seattle
G	Mookie Blaylock, Atlanta	G	Latrell Sprewell, Golden State

MOST VALUABLE PLAYER

1955-56	Bob Pettit, St. Louis	1975-76	Kareem Abdul-Jabbar, L.A.
1956-57	Bob Cousy, Boston	1976-77	Kareem Abdul-Jabbar, L.A.
1957-58	Bill Russell, Boston	1977-78	Bill Walton, Portland
1958-59	Bob Pettit, St. Louis	1978-79	Moses Malone, Houston
1959-60	Wilt Chamberlain, Philadelphia	1979-80	Kareem Abdul-Jabbar, L.A.
1960-61	Bill Russell, Boston	1980-81	Julius Erving, Philadelphia
1961-62	Bill Russell, Boston	1981-82	Moses Malone, Houston
1962-63	Bill Russell, Boston	1982-83	Moses Malone, Philadelphia
1963-64	Oscar Robertson, Cincinnati	1983-84	Larry Bird, Boston
1964-65	Bill Russell, Boston	1984-85	Larry Bird, Boston
1965-66	Wilt Chamberlain, Philadelphia	1985-86	Larry Bird, Boston
1966-67	Wilt Chamberlain, Philadelphia	1986-87	Magic Johnson, L.A. Lakers
1967-68	Wilt Chamberlain, Philadelphia	1987-88	Michael Jordan, Chicago
1968-69	Wes Unseld, Baltimore	1988-89	Magic Johnson, L.A. Lakers
1969-70	Willis Reed, New York	1989-90	Magic Johnson, L.A. Lakers
1970-71	Lew Alcindor, Milwaukee	1990-91	Michael Jordan, Chicago
1971-72	Kareem Adbul-Jabbar, Milwaukee	1991-92	Michael Jordan, Chicago
1972-73	Dave Cowens, Boston	1992-93	Charles Barkley, Phoenix
1973-74	Kareem Abdul-Jabbar, Milwaukee	1993-94	Hakeem Olajuwon, Houston
1974-75	Bob McAdoo, Buffalo		

ROOKIE OF THE YEAR

1952-53	Don Meineke, Fort Wayne	1973-74	Ernie DiGregorio, Buffalo
1953-54	Ray Felix, Baltimore	1974-75	Keith Wilkes, Golden State
1954-55	Bob Pettit, Milwaukee	1975-76	Alvan Adams, Phoenix
1955-56	Maurice Stokes, Rochester	1976-77	Adrian Dantley, Buffalo
1956-57	Tom Heinsohn, Boston	1977-78	Walter Davis, Phoenix
1957-58	Woody Sauldsberry, Philadelphia	1978-79	Phil Ford, Kansas City
1958-59	Elgin Baylor, Minneapolis	1979-80	Larry Bird, Boston
1959-60	Wilt Chamberlain, Philadelphia	1980-81	Darrell Griffith, Utah
1960-61	Oscar Robertson, Cincinnati	1981-82	Buck Williams, New Jersey
1961-62	Walt Bellamy, Chicago	1982-83	Terry Cummings, San Diego
1962-63	Terry Dischinger, Chicago	1983-84	Ralph Sampson, Houston
1963-64	Jerry Lucas, Cincinnati	1984-85	Michael Jordan, Chicago
1964-65	Willis Reed, New York	1985-86	Patrick Ewing, New York
1965-66	Rick Barry, San Francisco	1986-87	Chuck Person, Indiana
1966-67	Dave Bing, Detroit	1987-88	Mark Jackson, New York
1967-68	Earl Monroe, Baltimore	1988-89	Mitch Richmond, Golden State
1968-69	Wes Unseld, Baltimore	1989-90	David Robinson, San Antonio
1969-70	Lew Alcindor, Milwaukee	1990-91	Derrick Coleman, New Jersey
1970-71	Dave Cowens, Boston	1991-92	Larry Johnson, Charlotte
	Geoff Petrie, Portland	1992-93	Shaquille O'Neal, Orlando
1971-72	Sidney Wicks, Portland	1993-94	Chris Webber, Golden State
1972-73	Bob McAdoo, Buffalo		

FINALS MVP AWARD

1969	Jerry West, Los Angeles	1982	Magic Johnson, Los Angeles
1970	Willis Reed, New York	1983	Moses Malone, Philadelphia
1971	Kareem-Abdul-Jabbar, Milwaukee	1984	Larry Bird, Boston
1972	Wilt Chamberlain, Los Angeles	1985	K. Abdul-Jabbar, L.A. Lakers
1973	Willis Reed, New York	1986	Larry Bird, Boston
1974	John Havlicek, Boston	1987	Magic Johnson, L.A. Lakers
1975	Rick Barry, Golden State	1988	James Worthy, L.A. Lakers
1976	Jo Jo White, Boston	1989	Joe Dumars, Detroit
1977	Bill Walton, Portland	1990	Isiah Thomas, Detroit
1978	Wes Unseld, Washington	1991	Michael Jordan, Chicago
1979	Dennis Johnson, Seattle	1992	Michael Jordan, Chicago
1980	Magic Johnson, Los Angeles	1993	Michael Jordan, Chicago
1981	Cedric Maxwell, Boston	1994	Hakeem Olajuwon, Houston

DEFENSIVE PLAYER OF THE YEAR

1982-83	Sidney Moncrief, Milwaukee	1988-89	Mark Eaton, Utah
1983-84	Sidney Moncrief, Milwaukee	1989-90	Dennis Rodman, Detroit
1984-85	Mark Eaton, Utah	1990-91	Dennis Rodman, Detroit
1985-86	Alvin Robertson, San Antonio	1991-92	David Robinson, San Antonio
1986-87	Michael Cooper, L.A. Lakers	1992-93	Hakeem Olajuwon, Houston
1987-88	Michael Jordan, Chicago	1993-94	Hakeem Olajuwon, Houston

SIXTH MAN AWARD

1982-83	Bobby Jones, Philadelphia	1988-89	Eddie Johnson, Phoenix
1983-84	Kevin McHale, Boston	1989-90	Ricky Pierce, Milwaukee
1984-85	Kevin McHalc, Boston	1990-91	Detlef Schrempf, Indiana
1985-86	Bill Walton, Boston	1991-92	Detlef Schrempf, Indiana
1986-87	Ricky Pierce, Milwaukee	1992-93	Cliff Robinson, Portland
1987-88	Roy Tarpley, Dallas	1993-94	Dell Curry, Charlotte

MOST IMPROVED PLAYER

1985-86	Alvin Robertson, San Antonio	1990-91	Scott Skiles, Orlando
1986-87	Dale Ellis, Seattle	1991-92	Pervis Ellison, Washington
1987-88	Kevin Duckworth, Portland	1992-93	Chris Jackson, Denver
1988-89	Kevin Johnson, Phoenix	1993-94	Don MacLean, Washington
1989-90	Rony Seikaly, Miami		

IBM AWARD
Determined by Computer Formula

1983-84	Magic Johnson, Los Angeles	1989-90	David Robinson, San Antonio
1984-85	Michael Jordan, Chicago	1990-91	David Robinson, San Antonio
1985-86	Charles Barkley, Philadelphia	1991-92	Dennis Rodman, Detroit
1986-87	Charles Barkley, Philadelphia	1992-93	Hakeem Olajuwon, Houston
1987-88	Charles Barkley, Philadelphia	1993-94	David Robinson, San Antonio
1988-89	Michael Jordan, Chicago		

COACH OF THE YEAR

1962-63	Harry Gallatin, St. Louis	1978-79	Cotton Fitzsimmons, Kansas City
1963-64	Alex Hannum, San Francisco	1979-80	Bill Fitch, Boston
1964-65	Red Auerbach, Boston	1980-81	Jack McKinney, Indiana
1965-66	Dolph Schayes, Philadelphia	1981-82	Gene Shue, Washington
1966-67	Johnny Kerr, Chicago	1982-83	Don Nelson, Milwaukee
1967-68	Richie Guerin, St. Louis	1983-84	Frank Layden, Utah
1968-69	Gene Shue, Baltimore	1984-85	Don Nelson, Milwaukee
1969-70	Red Holzman, New York	1985-86	Mike Fratello, Atlanta
1970-71	Dick Motta, Chicago	1986-87	Mike Schuler, Portland
1971-72	Bill Sharman, Los Angeles	1987-88	Doug Moe, Denver
1972-73	Tom Heinsohn, Boston	1988-89	Cotton Fitzsimmons, Phoenix
1973-74	Ray Scott, Detroit	1989-90	Pat Riley, L.A. Lakers
1974-75	Phil Johnson, Kansas City-Omaha	1990-91	Don Chaney, Houston
1975-76	Bill Fitch, Cleveland	1991-92	Don Nelson, Golden State
1976-77	Tom Nissalke, Houston	1992-93	Pat Riley, New York
1977-78	Hubie Brown, Atlanta	1993-94	Lenny Wilkens, Atlanta

J. WALTER KENNEDY CITIZENSHIP AWARD

1974-75	Wes Unseld, Washington	1985-86	Michael Cooper, L.A. Lakers
1975-76	Slick Watts, Seattle		Rory Sparrow, New York
1976-77	Dave Bing, Washington	1986-87	Isiah Thomas, Detroit
1977-78	Bob Lanier, Detroit	1987-88	Alex English, Denver
1978-79	Calvin Murphy, Houston	1988-89	Thurl Bailey, Utah
1979-80	Austin Carr, Cleveland	1989-90	Glenn Rivers, Atlanta
1980-81	Mike Glenn, New York	1990-91	Kevin Johnson, Phoenix
1981-82	Kent Benson, Detroit	1991-92	Magic Johnson, L.A. Lakers
1982-83	Julius Erving, Philadelphia	1992-93	Terry Porter, Portland
1983-84	Frank Layden, Utah	1993-94	Joe Dumars, Detroit
1984-85	Dan Issel, Denver		

NBA CHAMPIONS

Season	Champion	Eastern Division			Western Division		
		W.	L.		W.	L.	
1946-47	Philadelphia	49	11	Washington	39	22	Chicago
1947-48	Baltimore	27	21	Philadelphia	29	19	St. Louis
1948-49	Minneapolis	38	22	Washington	45	15	Rochester
1949-50	Minneapolis	51	13	Syracuse	39	25	Indianap.*
1950-51	Rochester	36	30	New York	44	24	Minneapolis
1951-52	Minneapolis	37	29	New York	41	25	Rochester
1952-53	Minneapolis	47	23	New York	48	22	Minneapolis
1953-54	Minneapolis	42	30	Syracuse	46	26	Minneapolis
1954-55	Syracuse	43	29	Syracuse	43	29	Ft. Wayne
1955-56	Philadelphia	45	27	Philadelphia	37	35	Ft. Wayne
1956-57	Boston	44	28	Boston	34	38	StL-Mpl-FtW
1957-58	St. Louis	49	23	Boston	41	31	St. Louis
1958-59	Boston	52	20	Boston	49	23	St. Louis
1959-60	Boston	59	16	Boston	46	29	St. Louis
1960-61	Boston	57	22	Boston	51	28	St. Louis
1961-62	Boston	60	20	Boston	54	26	Los Angeles
1962-63	Boston	58	22	Boston	53	27	Los Angeles
1963-64	Boston	59	21	Boston	48	32	San Fran.
1964-65	Boston	62	18	Boston	49	31	Los Angeles
1965-66	Boston	54	26	Boston	45	35	Los Angeles
1966-67	Philadelphia	68	13	Philadelphia	44	37	San Fran.
1967-68	Boston	54	28	Boston	52	30	Los Angeles
1968-69	Boston	48	34	Boston	55	27	Los Angeles
1969-70	New York	60	22	New York	46	36	Los Angeles
1970-71	Milwaukee	42	40	Baltimore	66	16	Milwaukee
1971-72	Los Angeles	48	34	New York	69	13	Los Angeles
1972-73	New York	57	25	New York	60	22	Los Angeles
1973-74	Boston	56	26	Boston	59	23	Milwaukee
1974-75	Golden State	60	22	Washington	48	34	Golden State
1975-76	Boston	54	28	Boston	42	40	Phoenix
1976-77	Portland	50	32	Philadelphia	49	33	Portland
1977-78	Washington	44	38	Washington	47	35	Seattle
1978-79	Seattle	54	28	Washington	52	30	Seattle
1979-80	Los Angeles	59	23	Philadelphia	60	22	Los Angeles
1980-81	Boston	62	20	Boston	40	42	Houston
1981-82	Los Angeles	58	24	Philadelphia	57	25	Los Angeles
1982-83	Philadelphia	65	17	Philadelphia	58	24	Los Angeles
1983-84	Boston	62	20	Boston	54	28	Los Angeles

Season	Champion	Eastern Division W. L.			Western Division W. L.		
1984-85	L.A. Lakers	63	19	Boston	62	20	L.A. Lakers
1985-86	Boston	67	15	Boston	51	31	Houston
1986-87	L.A. Lakers	59	23	Boston	65	17	L.A. Lakers
1987-88	L.A. Lakers	54	28	Detroit	62	20	L.A. Lakers
1988-89	Detroit	63	19	Detroit	57	25	L.A. Lakers
1989-90	Detroit	59	23	Detroit	59	23	Portland
1990-91	Chicago	61	21	Chicago	58	24	L.A. Lakers
1991-92	Chicago	67	15	Chicago	57	25	Portland
1992-93	Chicago	57	25	Chicago	62	20	Phoenix
1993-94	New York	57	25	Houston	58	24	Houston

*1949-50 Central Division Champion: Minneapolis and Rochester tied 51-17.

NBA SCORING CHAMPIONS

Season	Pts./Avg.	Top Scorer	Team
1946-47	1389	Joe Fulks	Philadelphia
1947-48	1007	Max Zaslofsky	Chicago
1948-49	1698	George Mikan	Minneapolis
1949-50	1865	George Mikan	Minneapolis
1950-51	1932	George Mikan	Minneapolis
1951-52	1674	Paul Arizin	Philadelphia
1952-53	1564	Neil Johnston	Philadelphia
1953-54	1759	Neil Johnston	Philadelphia
1954-55	1631	Neil Johnston	Philadelphia
1955-56	1849	Bob Pettit	St. Louis
1956-57	1817	Paul Arizin	Philadelphia
1957-58	2001	George Yardley	Detroit
1958-59	2105	Bob Pettit	St. Louis
1959-60	2707	Wilt Chamberlain	Philadelphia
1960-61	3033	Wilt Chamberlain	Philadelphia
1961-62	4029	Wilt Chamberlain	Philadelphia
1962-63	3586	Wilt Chamberlain	San Francisco
1963-64	2948	Wilt Chamberlain	San Francisco
1964-65	2534	Wilt Chamberlain	San Fran.-Phila.
1965-66	2649	Wilt Chamberlain	Philadelphia
1966-67	2775	Rick Barry	San Francisco
1967-68	2142	Dave Bing	Detroit
1968-69	2327	Elvin Hayes	San Diego

Season	Pts./Avg.	Top Scorer	Team
1969-70	*31.2	Jerry West	Los Angeles
1970-71	*31.7	Lew Alcindor	Milwaukee
1971-72	*34.8	K. Abdul-Jabbar	Milwaukee
1972-73	*34.0	Nate Archibald	K.C.-Omaha
1973-74	*30.6	Bob McAdoo	Buffalo
1974-75	*34.5	Bob McAdoo	Buffalo
1975-76	*31.1	Bob McAdoo	Buffalo
1976-77	*31.1	Pete Maravich	New Orleans
1977-78	*27.2	George Gervin	San Antonio
1978-79	*29.6	George Gervin	San Antonio
1979-80	*33.1	George Gervin	San Antonio
1980-81	*30.7	Adrian Dantley	Utah
1981-82	*32.3	George Gervin	San Antonio
1982-83	*28.4	Alex English	Denver
1983-84	*30.6	Adrian Dantley	Utah
1984-85	*32.9	Bernard King	New York
1985-86	*30.3	Dominique Wilkins	Atlanta
1986-87	*37.1	Michael Jordan	Chicago
1987-88	*35.0	Michael Jordan	Chicago
1988-89	*32.5	Michael Jordan	Chicago
1989-90	*33.6	Michael Jordan	Chicago
1990-91	*31.2	Michael Jordan	Chicago
1991-92	*30.1	Michael Jordan	Chicago
1992-93	*32.6	Michael Jordan	Chicago
1993-94	*29.8	David Robinson	San Antonio

*Scoring title based on best average with at least 70 games played or 1,400 points

ALL-TIME NBA RECORDS

INDIVIDUAL
Single Game
Most Points: 100, Wilt Chamberlain, Philadelphia vs. New York, at Hershey, Pa., Mar. 2, 1962
Most FG Attempted: 63, Wilt Chamberlain, Philadelphia vs. New York, at Hershey, Pa., Mar. 2, 1962
Most FG Made: 36, Wilt Chamberlain, Philadelphia vs. New York, at Hershey, Pa., Mar. 2, 1962
Most Consecutive FG Made: 18, Wilt Chamberlain, San Francisco vs New York, at Boston, Nov. 27, 1963; Wilt Chamberlain, Philadelphia vs. Baltimore, at Pittsburgh, Feb. 24, 1967

Most 3-Pt FG Attempted: 19, Dennis Scott, Orlando vs Milwaukee, April 13, 1993

Most 3-Pt FG Made: 10, Brian Shaw, Miami at Milwaukee, April 8, 1993

Most FT Attempted: 34, Wilt Chamberlain, Philadelphia vs. St. Louis, at Philadelphia, Feb. 22, 1962

Most FT Made: 28, Wilt Chamberlain, Philadelphia vs New York, at Hershey, Pa., Mar. 2, 1962; Adrian Dantley, Utah vs Houston at Las Vegas, Nev., Jan. 4, 1984

Most Consecutive FT Made: 19, Bob Pettit, St. Louis vs Boston, at Boston, Nov. 22, 1961; Bill Cartwright, New York vs Kansas City, at N.Y., Nov. 17, 1981; Adrian Dantley, Detroit vs Chicago, at Chicago, Dec. 15, 1987 (OT)

Most FT Missed: 22, Wilt Chamberlain, Philadelphia vs Seattle, at Boston, Dec. 1, 1967

Most Assists: 30, Scott Skiles, Orlando vs Denver, at Orlando, Dec. 30, 1990

Most Personal Fouls: 8, Don Otten, Tri-Cities at Sheboygan, Nov. 24, 1949

Season

Most Points: 4,029, Wilt Chamberlain, Philadelphia, 1961-62

Highest Average: 50.4, Wilt Chamberlain, Philadelphia, 1961-62

Most FG Attempted: 3,159, Wilt Chamberlain, Philadelphia, 1961-62

Most FG Made: 1,597, Wilt Chamberlain, Philadelphia, 1961-62

Highest FG Percentage: .727, Wilt Chamberlain, Los Angeles, 1972-73

Most 3-Pt. FG Attempted: 529, Michael Adams, Denver, 1990-91

Most 3-Pt FG Made: 192, Dan Majerle, Phoenix, 1993-94

Most FT Attempted: 1,363, Wilt Chamberlain, Philadelphia, 1961-62

Most FT Made: 840, Jerry West, Los Angeles, 1965-66

Highest FT Percentage: .958, Calvin Murphy, Houston, 1980-81

Most Rebounds: 2,149, Wilt Chamberlain, Philadelphia, 1960-61

Most Assists: 1,164, John Stockton, Utah, 1990-91

Most Personal Fouls: 386, Darryl Dawkins, New Jersey, 1983-84

Most Disqualifications: 26, Don Meineke, Fort Wayne, 1952-53

Career

Most Points Scored: 38,387, Kareem Abdul-Jabbar, Milwaukee and Los Angeles Lakers, 1970-89

Highest Scoring Average: 32.3, Michael Jordan, Chicago, 1984-93

Most FG Attempted: 28,307, Kareem Abdul-Jabbar, Milwaukee and Los Angeles Lakers, 1970-89

Most FG Made: 15,837, Kareem Abdul-Jabbar, 1970-89

Highest FG Percentage: .599, Artis Gilmore, Chicago, San Antonio, Chicago, Boston, 1976-88

Most 3-Pt FG Attempted: 2,735, Michael Adams, Sacramento, Denver, Washington, 1985-94

Most 3-Pt FG Made: 1,013, Dale Ellis, Dallas, Seattle, Milwaukee, San Antonio, 1983-94

Most FT Attempted: 11,862, Wilt Chamberlain, 1960-73

Most FT Made: 8,509, Moses Malone, Buffalo, Houston, Philadelphia, Washington, Atlanta, Milwaukee, 1976-94

Highest FT Percentage: .906, Mark Price, Cleveland, 1986-94

Most Rebounds: 23,924, Wilt Chamberlain, 1960-73

Most Assists: 9,921, Magic Johnson, Los Angeles, 1979-91

Most Minutes: 57,446, Kareem Abdul-Jabbar, Milwaukee and Los Angeles Lakers, 1970-89

Most Games: 1,560, Kareem Abdul-Jabbar, Milwaukee and Los Angeles, 1970-89

Most Personal Fouls: 4,657, Kareem Abdul-Jabbar, Milwaukee and Los Angeles Lakers, 1970-89

Most Times Disqualified: 127, Vern Mikkelsen, Minneapolis, 1950-59

TEAM RECORDS
Single Game

Most Points, One Team: 173, Boston, vs Minneapolis at Boston, Feb. 27, 1959; Phoenix, vs Denver at Phoenix, Nov. 10, 1990; 186, Detroit, vs Denver at Denver, Dec. 13, 1983 (3 overtimes)

Most Points, Two Teams: 320, Golden State 162 vs Denver 158 at Denver, Nov. 2, 1990; 370, Detroit 186 vs Denver 184 at Denver, Dec. 13, 1983 (3 overtimes)

Most FG Attempted, One Team: 153, Philadelphia, vs Los Angeles at Philadelphia (3 overtimes), Dec. 8, 1961

Most FG Attempted, Two Teams: 291, Philadelphia 153 vs Los Angeles 138 at Philadelphia (3 overtimes), Dec. 8, 1961

Most FG Made, One Team: 72, Boston, vs Minneapolis at Boston, Feb. 27, 1959; 74, Denver, vs Detroit at Denver, Dec. 13, 1983 (3 overtimes)

Most FG Made, Two Teams: 142, Detroit 74 vs Denver 68 at Denver, Dec. 13, 1983 (3 overtimes)

Most FT Attempted, One Team: 86, Syracuse, vs Anderson at Syracuse (5 overtimes), Nov. 24, 1949

Most FT Attempted, Two Teams: 160, Syracuse 86 vs Anderson 74 at Syracuse (5 overtimes), Nov. 24, 1949

Most FT Made, One Team: 61, Phoenix, vs Utah, April 4, 1990 (1 overtime)

Most FT Made, Two Teams: 116, Syracuse 59 vs Anderson 57 at Syracuse (5 overtimes), Nov. 24, 1949

Most Rebounds, One Team: 109, Boston, vs Denver at Boston, Dec. 24, 1960

Most Rebounds, Two Teams: 188, Philadelphia 98 vs Los Angeles 90 at Philadelphia, Dec. 8, 1961 (3 overtimes)

Most Assists, One Team: 53, Milwaukee, vs Detroit at Detroit, Dec. 26, 1978

Most Assists, Two Teams: 88, Phoenix 47 vs San Diego 41 at Tucson, Ariz., Mar. 15, 1969; San Antonio 50 vs Denver 38 at San Antonio, April 15, 1984

Most Assists, Two Teams, OT: 93, Detroit 47 vs Denver 46 at Denver, Dec. 13, 1983 (3 overtimes)

Most Personal Fouls, One Team: 66, Anderson, at Syracuse (5 overtimes), Nov. 24, 1949

Most Personal Fouls, Two Teams: 122, Anderson 66 vs Syracuse 56 at Syracuse (5 overtimes), Nov. 24, 1949

Most Disqualifications, One Team: 8, Syracuse, vs Baltimore at Syracuse (1 overtime), Nov. 15, 1952

Most Disqualifications, Two Teams: 13, Syracuse 8 vs Baltimore 5 at Syracuse (1 overtime), Nov. 15, 1952

Most Points in a Losing Game: 184, Denver, vs Detroit at Denver Dec. 13, 1983 (3 overtimes)

Widest Point Spread: 68, Cleveland 148 vs Miami 80 at Miami, Dec. 17, 1991

Season

Most Games Won: 69, Los Angeles, 1971-72

Most Games Lost: 73, Philadelphia, 1972-73

Longest Winning Streak: 33, Los Angeles, Nov. 5, 1971 to Jan. 7, 1972

Longest Losing Streak: 20, Philadelphia, Jan. 9, 1973 to Feb. 11, 1973

Most Points Scored: 10,731, Denver, 1981-82

Most Points Allowed: 10,723, Denver, 1990-91

Highest Scoring Average: 126.5, Denver, 1981-82

Highest Average, Points Allowed: 130.8, Denver, 1990-91

Most FG Attempted: 9,295, Boston, 1960-61

Most FG Made: 3,980, Denver, 1981-82

Highest FG Percentage: .545, Los Angeles, 1984-85
Most FT Attempted: 3,411, Philadelphia, 1966-67
Most FT Made: 2,313, Golden State, 1989-90
Highest FT Percentage: .832, Boston, 1989-90

Scott Skiles set record for most assists in a game.

Official 1994-95 NBA Schedule

*Afternoon (EST)
**Morning (EST)

Fri Nov 4
NY at Bos
Mil at Phil
Orl at Wash
Ind at Atl
LAL at Det
Char at Chi
NJ at Hou
GS at SA
Minn at Den
Mia at Utah
**Port vs LAC
in Japan
Phoe at Sac

Sat Nov 5
Phil at Orl
Cle at Char
Det at Atl
Bos at Ind
Wash at Chi
LAL at Mil
Hou at Minn
NJ at Dal
GS at Den
**LAC vs Port
in Japan
Utah at Sea

Sun Nov 6
Mia at Phoe

Mon Nov 7
Phil at Chi
NJ at SA
Atl at Utah

Tue Nov 8
LAL at NY
Hou at Cle
Minn at Det
Den at Dal
Mia at GS

Wed Nov 9
Chi at NJ

Wash at Phil
Orl at Char
Hou at Ind
LAL at Minn
Utah at SA
Atl at Phoe
Sac at Sea

Thu Nov 10
Orl at NY
Mil at Cle
Ind at Det
Alt at LAC
Port at Sac

Fri Nov 11
Hou at Bos
Dal at Phil
NJ at Wash
Char at Mil
Chi at Minn
GS at Utah
Den at LAL
Phoe at Sea

Sat Nov 12
Hous at NJ
Orl at Phil
Wash at Mia
Det at Char
Ind at Cle
Dal at Chi
Bos at Minn
NY at SA
Utah at Den
Phoe vs LAC
at Anaheim
LAL at GS
Atl at Sac

Sun Nov 13
LAC at Sea

Mon Nov 14
NY at Utah

Tue Nov 15
Sea at NJ
Wash at Orl
Dal at Mia
Bos at Atl
Char at Cle
Phil at Det
Ind at Mil
Sac at Hou
SA at Den
LAL at LAC
Minn at GS
Phoe at Port

Wed Nov 16
Sea at Bos
Mia at Phil
Chi at SA
Minn at Phoe
NY at LAL

Thu Nov 17
Wash at NJ
LAC at Char
Sac at Dal
Chi at Hou
Det at Den
NY at GS
Cle at Port

Fri Nov 18
LAC at Phil
NJ at Orl
Bos at Mia
Mil at Atl
Sea at Ind
Det at Utah
Port at Phoe
Cle at LAL

Sat Nov 19
Atl at NY
Bos at Wash
Ind at Char
Sea at Mil
SA at Minn

Chi at Dal
Hou at Den
Utah at GS

Sun Nov 20
LAC at NJ
Cle at Sac
Det at Port

Mon Nov 21
SA at NY
Mia at Orl
Phoe at Utah

Tue Nov 22
Mil vs Bos
at Hart
GS at Char
Phil at Atl
Minn at Cle
Port at Hou
Chi at LAC
NJ at Sea

Wed Nov 23
Char at Bos
Hou at Orl
Cle at Mia
Mil at Det
Atl at Minn
Port at SA
Chi at Den
Sea at Utah
LAC at Phoe
Dal at LAL
NJ at Sac

Thu Nov 24
GS at Ind

Fri Nov 25
Orl at Bos
Cle vs Wash
at Balt
LAL at Atl
Mia at Det

Latrell Sprewell made first-team All-NBA in second year.

Playoffs were down, but Scottie Pippen had good numbers.

Mil at Ind
Phil at Minn
Port at Dal
Sea at SA
Chi at Utah
*NJ at LAC
Den at Sac

Sat Nov 26
*Char at NY
Bos at Phil
LAL at Wash
GS at Cle
Orl at Mil
Sea at Hous
Dal at Den
SA at Phoe

Sun Nov 27
GS at Det
NJ at Phoe
Utah at Sac
Ind at Port

Mon Nov 28
Minn at SA
Ind at Sea

Tue Nov 29
LAL at NJ
NY at Wash
Sac at Mia
Charl at Atl
Phoe at Mil
Minn at Dal
Den at Hou
LAC at GS
Utah at Port

Wed Nov 30
Det at Bos
Sac at Orl
Mia at Char
LAL at Cle
Phoe at Chi
SA at Sea

Thu Dec 1
Cle at Mil
Den at Dal
Minn at Utah
Ind at LAC
Hou at GS

Fri Dec 2
Phoe at Bos

Sac at Phil
Det at Wash
NY at Orl
NJ at Mia
Atl at Chi
Hou at LAL
SA at Port

Sat Dec 3
Wash at NY
Sac at NJ
Orl at Atl
Phil at Cle
Phoe at Det
Bos at Chi
Utah at Dal
Char at Den
Minn at LAC
Ind at GS
Mil at Sea

Sun Dec 4
Mil at Port

Mon Dec 5
NY at Phil
NJ at Chi
Char at LAC

Tue Dec 6
Bos at NY
Atl at NJ
Phoe at Wash
Orl at Cle
Det at Ind
Den at Minn
Dal at SA
Char at Utah
GS at LAL
Mil at Sac
Hou at Sea

Wed Dec 7
Atl at Bos
Cle at Orl
Phil at Mia
Mil at LAC

Thu Dec 8
Phoe at NJ
Wash at Dal
Char at Hou
Utah at SA
Sea at Sac

Fri Dec 9
Cle at Bos
Ind at Phil
Orl at Mia
NY at Atl
Chi at Det
LAC at LAL
GS at Port

Sat Dec 10
Phil at NY
Bos at NJ
Atl at Orl
Det at Cle
Mia at Ind
Chi at Mil
Phoe at Minn
Char at Dal
SA at Hou
Wash at Den
LAL at Utah
Sea at LAC
GS at Sac

Sun Dec 11
Sac at Port

Mon Dec 12
Den at Bos
Mia at NY
Orl at NJ
Wash at SA
Port at Utah
GS at Phoe

Tue Dec 13
Mia at Phil
Mil at Char
Minn at Atl
Ind at Cle
Det at Chi
LAL at Dal
Wash at Hou
Sac at GS

Wed Dec 14
Cle at NJ
Den at Orl
Char at Det
Atl at Ind
Phil at Mil
Utah at Minn
Bos at SA
Sea at Phoe
LAC at Port

Thu Dec 15
Utah at Wash
Den at Mia
Bos at Dal
LAL at Hou
GS vs LAC
  at Anaheim
NY at Sac
Port at Sea

Fri Dec 16
Cle at Phil
Chi at Atl
Char at Ind
NJ at Minn
NY at Phoe
Orl at GS

Sat Dec 17
Det at Phil
Minn at Wash
Atl at Mia
Den at Char
Utah at Chi
Bos at Hou
LAL at SA
Sac at Phoe
Dal vs LAC
  at Anaheim
Orl at Sea

Sun Dec 18
Mia at NJ
Utah at Mil
NY at Port

Mon Dec 19
Cle at Chi
Bos at Den
Wash at Phoe

Tue Dec 20
NJ at NY
Utah at Phil
Ind at Char
Mil at Atl
Minn at LAL
Dal at GS
Wash at Sac
Orl at Port
LAC at Sea

Wed Dec 21
Det at NJ
Mil at Mia

Chi at Ind
SA at Den
Orl at LAC

Thu Dec 22
Cle at NY
Phil at Char
Utah at Atl
Phoe at Hou
Wash at GS
Minn at Sac
Dal at Sea

Fri Dec 23
Phil at Bos
Mil at Orl
Char at Mia
NJ at Cle
Atl at Det
Ind at Chi
Hou a SA
Den at Phoe
Wash at LAC
Sac at LAL
Dal at Port

Sun Dec 25
*Sea at Den
*NY at Chi

Mon Dec 26
Orl at Wash
Hou at Mia
*Bos at Cle
NJ at Mil
LAC at Minn
Dal at Phoe
Phil at Port
Sac at Sea

Tue Dec 27
NY at NJ
Mia at Orl
Mil at Det
LAC at Chi
Phoe at Dal
Atl at Hou
Char at SA
Ind at Den
LAL at GS
Port at Sac

Wed Dec 28
Chi at Bos
Det at NY

Wash at Cle
Ind at Utah
Phil at Sea

Thu Dec 29
LAC at Mia
Orl at Char
SA at Atl
GS at Hou
Sea at LAL
Den at Port

Fri Dec 30
SA at Wash
LAC at Orl
Atl at Cle
Bos at Det
NJ at Ind
Mia at Chi
Char at Mil
NY at Minn
GS at Dal
Port at Den
Hou at Utah
LAL at Phoe
Phil at Sac

Tue Jan 3
Ind at NJ
Sea at Wash
Port at Atl
Den at Minn
Hou at Dal
Mil at Utah
Det at LAL
SA at GS
Phoe at Sac

Wed Jan 4
Mia at Bos
Atl at NY
NJ at Orl
Port at Char
Sea at Cle
Wash at Ind
Den at Chi
Phil at Phoe

Thu Jan 5
Minn at Mia
Dal at Hou
SA at Utah
Phil at LAC
Mil at GS
Det at Sac

Fri Jan 6
Port at Bos
Char at NJ
Minn at Orl
Wash at Atl
NY at Cle
Sea at Chi
Ind at Dal
Mil at LAL

Sat Jan 7
Port at Wash
Bos at Char
NJ at Atl
Chi at Cle
Ind at Hou
Phoe at Den
Phil at Utah
SA at LAC
Mia at Sac

Sun Jan 8
Minn at NY
Orl at Det
Mil at Den
Mia at LAL

Mon Jan 9
Wash at Bos
Dal at Utah
Mil at Phoe
LAL at Port

Tue Jan 10
Ind at NY
Atl at Wash
Char at Cle
NJ at Det
Orl at Chi
Sac at Minn
LAC at SA
Sea at GS

Wed Jan 11
Ind at Bos
Chi at Phil
Det at Orl
Minn at Char
Sac at Mil
LAC at Dal
Mia at Hou
Den at Utah
Phoe at LAL
GS at Port

Thu Jan 12
Mia at SA
Dal at Den
Cle at Phoe

Fri Jan 13
Utah at Bos
NJ at Phil
Ind at Wash
Orl at Atl
Sac at Chi
NY at Mil
Det at Minn
SA at Hou
GS at LAL
LAC at Sea

Sat Jan 14
Utah at NY
Minn at Nj
Phil at Orl
Chi at Char
Wash at Det
Mil at Ind
Mia at Dal
Hou at Den
Phoe at LAC
Cle at GS

Sun Jan 15
Sac at Bos
Dal at SA
Port at Sea

Mon Jan 16
*NJ at NY
*Det at Phil
*Chi at Wash
*Mia at Atl
Utah at Ind
Hou at Minn
*LAC at LAL
Den at GS

Tue Jan 17
SA at Bos
Char at Orl
Den at Phoe
Port at Sac
Cle at Sea

Wed Jan 18
Bos at Mia
SA at Char
Phil at Atl

Dennis Rodman led in technicals, ejections, rebounds.

Utah at Det
LAL at Ind
Mil at Chi
Orl at Dal
Cle at LAC

Thu Jan 19
Wash at Mil
Sea at Minn
NY at Hou
GS at Sac
Phoe at Port

Fri Jan 20
LAL at Bos
Phil vs Wash
    at Balt
SA at Mia
NJ at Char
Hou at Det
Atl at Ind
Minn at Chi
NY at Dal
Orl at Den
Cle at Utah
Port at LAC

Sat Jan 21
LAL at Phil
Bos at Atl
Det at Mil
Sea at Dal
Cle at Den
Sac vs LAC
    at Anaheim

Sun Jan 22
*Wash at NJ
NY at Mia
*SA at Ind
*Hou at Chi
*Char at Minn
*Orl at Phoe
Sac at Port

Mon Jan 23
LAL at Char
LAC at Cle
Dal at Utah

Tue Jan 24
Port at NY
Bos at Orl
Ind at Mia
Phil at Det

SA at Chi
Hou at Mil
Phoe at Minn
NJ at GS
Dal at Sac
Den at Sea

Wed Jan 25
LAC at Bos
Mil at Phil
Atl at Char
Sac at Utah
NJ at LAL

Thu Jan 26
LAC at NY
GS at Wash
Chi at Orl
Cle at Atl
Port at Det
Phoe at Ind
Hou at SA
Utah at Sea

Fri Jan 27
GS at Bos
Phoe at Phil
NY at Char
Port at Cle
Mia at Mil
Minn at Dal
NJ at Den

Sat Jan 28
LAC at Wash
Mil at Orl
Char at Atl
Mia at Det
Phil at Ind
Sac at Dal
Minn at Hou
Den at SA
NJ at Utah
*LAL at Sea

Sun Jan 29
*Phoe at NY
*GS at Chi

Mon Jan 30
Sea at Phil
Atl at Mia
Phoe at Cle
LAC at Det

Minn at Utah
NJ at Port

Tue Jan 31
GS at NY
Char at Wash
Dal at Mil
Den at Hou
Chi at LAL
SA at Sac

Wed Feb 1
Char at Bos
Mil at NJ
Wash at Phil
Det at Mia
GS at Atl
Cle at Ind
Dal at Minn
Den at Utah
LAL at Phoe
SA at Port

Thu Feb 2
Sea at Orl
Cle at Det
Utah at Hou
Chi at Sac

Fri Feb 3
NY at Phil
Mia at Wash
Mil at Char
Sea at Atl
Orl at Ind
Port at Minn
SA at Dal
Chi at Phoe
Den at LAL
LAC at GS

Sat Feb 4
Bos at NJ
Ind at Cle
Atl at Det
Phil at Mil
Utah at Dal
Sac at SA
LAL at LAC

Sun Feb 5
Minn at Bos
*NY at Orl
*Sea at Mia
*Wash at Char

*Hous at Phoe
*Chi at GS

Mon Feb 6
Det at NJ
Atl at Phil
Hou at Port

Tue Feb 7
Mil at NY
Ind at Char
Phil at Cle
GS at Minn
Phoe at Dal
LAL at Den
Utah at LAC
SA at Sea

Wed Feb 8
Cle at Bos
Dal at Orl
Wash at Mia
NJ at Atl
Char at Det
NY at Ind
Minn at Mil
Phoe at Utah
SA at LAL
Hou at Sac
Chi at Port

Thu Feb 9
GS at Den
Hou at LAC
Chi at Sea

Sun Feb 12
*ALL-STAR
GAME at
Phoe

Tue Feb 14
Char at NJ
Ind at Orl
Mil at Mia
NY at Det
Wash at Minn
Port at Dal
LAC at Hou
Utah at SA
Atl at Den
Bos at Sac
GS at Sea

Wed Feb 15
Min at Phil

Orl at Cle
Det at Ind
Wash at Chi
Port at Phoe
Sea at LAL
Bos at GS

Thu Feb 16
Den at NJ
NY at Mia
Hou at Char
Cle at Mil
SA at Utah
LAL at Sac

Fri Feb 17
Mia at NY
Hou at Wash
Phil at Orl
Det at Chi
Ind at Minn
Atl at Dal
GS at Phoe
Bos at LAC
Sea at Port

Sat Feb 18
Cle at NJ
Den at Phil
Det at Char
Chi at Mil
Atl at SA
Bos at Utah
Sea at GS
LAC at Sac

Sun Feb 19
*Hou at NY
Den at Wash
*Mia at Ind
*Orl at Minn
Utah at Phoe
Port at LAL

Mon Feb 20
Chi at Char
Mia at Cle
Sac at Det
Orl at Mil
Phil at GS
LAL at Sea

Tue Feb 21
Cle at NY
Dal at Wash

Chi at Atl
SA at Hou
LAC at Den
Bos at Phoe
Minn at Port

Wed Feb 22
Ind at NJ
Sac at Char
Wash at Mil
Phoe at SA
LAC at Utah
Phil at LAL
Port at GS
Minn at Sea

Thu Feb 23
Orl vs Bos
   at Hart
Sac at NY
Dal at Atl
Det at Hou
Phil at Den

Fri Feb 24
Dal at NJ
Atl vs Wash
   at Balt
Bos at Orl
Chi at Mia
Ind at Mil
Det at SA
LAC at Phoe
Char at LAL
Utah at Port
Den at Sea

Sat Feb 25
Sac at Wash
NJ at Cle
GS at Hou
LAL at LAC

Sun Feb 26
Phil at NY
*Chi at Orl
*Dal at Ind
Mia at Minn
GS at SA
*Utah at Den
*Char at Phoe

Mon Feb 27
Ind at Bos
Sac at Atl

Mil at Det
NJ at Chi
Cle at Hou
Utah at LAL
LAC at Port
Char at Sea

Tue Feb 28
Phil at Wash
NY at Orl
Mia at Mil
Hou at Dal
Cle at SA
Minn at Den
Phoe at LAC

Wed Mar 1
Wash at Bos
Ind at Det
Mia at Chi
Phoe at LAL
Utah at GS
Minn at Sac

Thu Mar 2
Chi at NY
Atl at Mil
Cle at Dal
Orl at Hou
Sea vs LAC
   at Anaheim
Char at Port

Fri Mar 3
Mil at Bos
Phil at NJ
Ind at Wash
Det at Atl
Hou at Minn
Orl at SA
Mia at Den
Sea at Phoe
Sac at LAL
Char at GS

Sat Mar 4
Chi at Phil
NY at Cle
Bos at Ind
Det at Dal
*Port at Utah
Den at LAC

Sun Mar 5
*Mil at NJ
Atl at Orl

*Wash at Mia
*Hou at SA
Minn at LAL
*Phoe at GS
Char at Sac

Mon Mar 6
Port at Chi
Minn at LAC
GS at Sea

Tue Mar 7
Bos at NY
LAL at Mia
Det at Cle
Port at Mil
Den at Dal
Phoe at Hou
Ind at SA
Utah at Sac

Wed Mar 8
NY at Bos
NJ at Phil
Det at Wash
LAL at Orl
Den at Atl
Sea at Minn
Dal at Utah
LAC at GS

Thu Mar 9
Port at Mia
Sea at Char
SA at Cle
Ind at Sac

Fri Mar 10
NJ at Bos
SA at Phil
Port at Orl
NY at Atl
Den at Det
Cle at Chi
LAL at Minn
Sac at Utah
Ind at Phoe
GS at LAC

Sat Mar 11
Sea at NY
NJ at Wash
Mia at Char
LAL at Chi
Dal at Hou

Sun Mar 12
*Atl at Bos
*Cle at Phil
*SA at Orl
Utah at Mia
Sea at Det
*Den at Mil
*Port at Minn
GS at Phoe
*Sac at LAC

Mon Mar 13
Wash at Char
Hous at Det
Ind at LAL
Dal at GS

Tue Mar 14
Den at NY
Hous at Phil
Chi at Wash
Utah at Orl
Char at Mil
Minn at SA
Det at Phoe
Dal at Sac
Mia at Port
Bos at Sea

Wed Mar 15
Orl at NJ
Mil at Ind
Atl at Chi
Det at LAC
LAL at GS

Thu Mar 16
Phoe at Char
Utah at Cle
Minn at Hou
Phil at SA
Sac at Den
Bos at Port
Mia at Sea

Fri Mar 17
Utah at NJ
NY at Wash
Orl at Ind
Mil at Chi
Cle at Minn
Phil at Dal
Mia at LAC
Bos at LAL
GS at Sac

Sat Mar 18
NJ at NY
Phoe at Atl
Dal at SA
Port at Den
*Det at Sea

Sun Mar 19
Cle at Wash
Phoe at Mia
*Utah at Char
*Chi at Ind
*Bos at Mil
*LAC at Minn
*Phil at Hous
Sac at LAL
*Det at GS

Mon Mar 20
LAC at Atl
Dal at Cle
Sea at SA
Den at Sac

Tue Mar 21
Char at NY
Phoe at Orl
Ind at Mia
NJ at Det
GS at Mil
Sea at Hou
Wash at Port

Wed Mar 22
Chi at Bos
SA at NJ
GS at Phil
Mia at Atl
Sac at Cle
LAC at Ind
Dal at Minn
Den at Utah
Port at LAL

Thu Mar 23
Char at Orl
Dal at Det
LAC at Mil
Utah at Hou
NY at Den
Wash at Sea

Fri Mar 24
Bos at Phil
GS at Mia

Atl at Cle
Sac at Ind
Orl at Chi
SA at Minn
Hou at Phoe
Wash at LAL
Sea at Port

Sat Mar 25
Ind at Phil
NJ at Mia
Cle at Char
Chi at Atl
Bos at Det
SA at Mil
Utah at Dal
NY at LAC

Sun Mar 26
*GS at Orl
*Sac at Minn
Hou at LAL
*Den at Port
NY at Sea

Mon Mar 27
SA at Det
NJ at Ind
LAC at Den
Wash at Utah

Tue Mar 28
Chi at NY
GS at NJ
Bos at Mia
Mil at Dal
LAL at Hou
Utah at Phoe
Orl at Sac
Atl at Port

Wed Mar 29
Char at Phil
Mia at Wash
NY at Det
Cle at Ind
LAL at SA
Minn at Sea

Thu Mar 30
Port at NJ
Dal at Char
Bos at Chi
Hou at LAC
*Atl at GS

Phoe at Sac

Fri Mar 31
Mia at Bos
Dal at NY
Port at Phil
Wash at Cle
Den at Ind
Mil at SA
Orl at Utah
Minn at Phoe
Atl at LAL
Sac at Sea

Sat Apr 1
Wash at Det
Phil at Chi
Mil at Hou
Utah vs LAC
   at Anaheim
Minn at GS

Sun Apr 2
Dal at Bos
*NY at NJ
Char at Mia
*Den at Cle
*Port at Ind
*Phoe at SA
Orl at LAL
*Atl at Sea

Tue Apr 4
Ind at NY
Phil at Mia
Bos at Cle
LAL at Den
Sea at Utah
SA at LAC
Phoe at GS
Hou at Sac
Minn at Port

Wed Apr 5
Chi at NJ
Det at Orl
Phil at Char
Cle at Atl
Wash at Ind
NY at Mil
LAL at Dal

Thu Apr 6
Sea at Den
Hou at GS
SA at Sac

Fri Apr 7
Phil at Bos
Char at Wash
Ind at Atl
Orl at Det
Cle at Chi
NJ at Mil
Minn at Dal
Utah at LAL
Hou at Port

Sat Apr 8
Det at NY
Mia at NJ
Orl at Phil
Sea at Dal
SA at GS
LAC at Sac

Sun Apr 9
*Bos at Wash
*Chi at Cle
*Char at Ind
*Atl at Mil
*Hou at Den
SA at LAL
*Phoe at Port

Mon Apr 10
Bos at Char
Den at Minn
GS at Dal

Tue Apr 11
Mia at NY
Atl at Phil
Cle at Orl
Ind at Chi
Det at Mil

Dal at Hou
Port at SA
LAL at Utah
Sac at LAC
Phoe at Sea

Wed Apr 12
NJ at Char
Wash at Atl
Chi at Det
GS at Minn
SA at Phoe
LAL at Sac

Thu Apr 13
Orl at Bos
Wash at NY
NJ at Phil
Cle at Mia
Port at Hou
GS at Utah
Den at LAC
Dal at Sea

Fri Apr 14
Atl at Cle
Char at Det
NY at Ind
Mil at Minn
Sac at SA
Phoe at Den

Sat Apr 15
Det at Bos
Phil at NJ
Mil at Wash
*Orl at Mia
Sac at Hou
LAC at Utah

LAL at Phoe
*Sea at GS
Dal at Port

Sun Apr 16
*Atl at Char
*Minn at Ind
*NY at Chi
*SA at Den
Dal at LAL

Mon Apr 17
NJ at Bos
Mil at NY
Char at Phil
Wash at Orl
Chi at Mia
LAC at Hou
Port at Sea

Tue Apr 18
Cle at Det
Utah at Minn
LAC at Dal
Den at SA
Sac at Phoe
Sea at LAL
Port at GS

Wed Apr 19
Atl at NJ
Orl at Wash
Mia at Cle
Phil at Ind
Bos at Mil
Minn at Den
Hou at Utah

Thu Apr 20
NY at Char
Det at Chi
SA at Dal
Sac at GS
LAL at Port
Hou at Sea

Fri Apr 21
NY at Bos
Wash at NJ
Mia at Phil
Ind at Orl
Det at Atl
Mil at Cle
LAC at SA
Minn at Utah
Dal at Phoe
Sea at Sac

Sat Apr 22
*Char at Chi
Port at LAL
*Den at GS

Sun Apr 23
*Orl at NY
Bos at NJ
*Phil at Wash
Det at Mia
*Cle at Char
*Atl at Ind
*Chi at Mil
*SA at Minn
*Utah at Hou
Sac at Den
*Sea at Phoe

1994-95 NBA ON NBC
GAME OF THE WEEK SCHEDULE
(Starting Times Eastern)

Day	Date	Game	Pre-Game	Game Time
Sun	Dec 25	Seattle at Denver	3:30	4:00
		New York at Chicago		6:30
Sun	Jan 22	Houston at Chicago	12:30	1:00
		Orlando at Phoenix		3:30
Sun	Jan 29	Phoenix at New York		Noon
		Golden State at Chicago		2:30
Sun	Feb 5	New York at Orlando	12:30	1:00
		Houston at Phoenix		3:30
Sun	Feb 12	45th NBA All-Star Game	6:00	6:30
		(America West Arena)		
Sun	Feb 19	Houston at New York	12:30	1:00
Sun	Feb 26	Chicago at Orlando	12:30	1:00
		Utah at Denver or		3:30
		Charlotte at Phoenix		
Sun	Mar 5	Houston at San Antonio or	12:30	1:00
		Milwaukee at New Jersey		
		Phoenix at Golden State		3:30
Sun	Mar 12	San Antonio at Orlando		Noon
Sun	Mar 19	Chicago at Indiana or		Noon
		Utah at Charlotte		
Sun	Mar 26	Golden State at Orlando		Noon
Sun	Apr 2	New York at New Jersey or		1:30
		Phoenix at San Antonio		
Sun	Apr 9	Chicago at Cleveland or	12:30	1:00
		Charlotte at Indiana or		
		Atlanta at Milwaukee		
		Houston at Denver or		3:30
		Phoenix at Portland		
Sat	Apr 15	Orlando at Miami or	3:00	3:30
		Seattle at Golden State		
Sun	Apr 16	Atlanta at Charlotte or		3:00
		San Antonio at Denver		
		New York at Chicago		5:30
Sat	Apr 22	Charlotte at Chicago or	3:00	3:30
		Denver at Golden State		
Sun	Apr 23	Orlando at New York	12:30	1:00
		Atlanta at Indiana or		3:30
		Cleveland at Charlotte or		
		Utah at Houston or		
		Seattle at Phoenix		

1994-95 NBA ON TNT SCHEDULE
(Starting Times Eastern)

Day	Date	Game	Air Time
Fri	Nov 4	Charlotte at Chicago	8:00
		Portland at LA Clippers (from Japan)	11:00
Tue	Nov 8	Houston at Cleveland	8:00
Fri	Nov 11	Charlotte at Milwaukee	8:00
Tue	Nov 15	San Antonio at Denver	8:00
Fri	Nov 18	Seattle at Indiana	8:00
Tue	Nov 22	Golden State at Charlotte	8:00
Fri	Dec 2	New York at Orlando	8:00
Tue	Dec 6	Houston at Seattle	8:00
Fri	Dec 9	Chicago at Detroit	8:00
Tue	Dec 13	LA Lakers at Dallas	8:00
Fri	Dec 16	New York at Phoenix	8:00
		Orlando at Golden State	10:30
Tue	Dec 20	New Jersey at New York	8:00
Fri	Dec 23	Indiana at Chicago	8:00
Tue	Jan 3	Phoenix at Sacramento	8:00
Fri	Jan 6	Seattle at Chicago	8:00
Tue	Jan 10	Indiana at New York	8:00
Fri	Jan 13	Utah at Boston	8:00
Tue	Jan 17	Denver at Phoenix	9:00
Fri	Jan 20	Orlando at Denver	8:00
Tue	Jan 24	San Antonio at Chicago	8:00
Fri	Jan 27	New York at Charlotte	8:00
Tue	Jan 31	Charlotte at Washington	8:00
Fri	Feb 3	Seattle at Atlanta	8:00
		Chicago at Phoenix	10:30
Tue	Feb 7	Golden State at Minnesota	8:00
Fri	Feb 10	All-Star Friday Night	10:00
Sat	Feb 11	NBA All-Star Saturday	7:00
Tue	Feb 14	Utah at San Antonio	8:00
Fri	Feb 17	Golden State at Phoenix	8:00
Tue	Feb 21	San Antonio at Houston	8:00
Fri	Feb 24	Chicago at Miami	8:00
Tue	Feb 28	New York at Orlando	8:00
Fri	Mar 3	Seattle at Phoenix	8:00
Tue	Mar 7	Phoenix at Houston	8:00
Mon	Mar 13	Houston at Atlanta	8:00
Tue	Mar 14	Denver at New York	8:00
Tue	Mar 21	Phoenix at Orlando	8:00
Tue	Mar 28	Chicago at New York	8:00
Fri	Mar 31	Orlando at Utah	8:00
Tue	Apr 4	Phoenix at Golden State	9:00
Fri	Apr 7	Indiana at Atlanta	8:00
Tue	Apr 11	Phoenix at Seattle	9:00
Fri	Apr 14	New York at Indiana	8:00
Tue	Apr 18	Denver at San Antonio	8:00
Fri	Apr 21	Indiana at Orlando	8:00

1994-95 NBA ON TBS SCHEDULE
(Starting Times Eastern)

Day	Date	Game	Air Time
Thu	Nov 10	Orlando at New York	8:00
Thu	Nov 17	Chicago at Houston	8:00
Thu	Nov 24	Golden State at Indiana	8:00
Wed	Nov 30	Phoenix at Chicago	8:00
Thu	Dec 8	Charlotte at Houston	8:00
Thu	Dec 15	Denver at Miami	8:00
Thu	Dec 22	Phoenix at Houston	8:00
Thu	Dec 29	Orlando at Charlotte	8:00
Thu	Jan 5	San Antonio at Utah	8:00
Thu	Jan 12	Miami at San Antonio	8:00
Thu	Jan 19	New York at Houston	8:00
Thu	Jan 26	Chicago at Orlando	8:00
Thu	Feb 2	Seattle at Orlando	8:00
Thu	Feb 9	Golden State at Denver	8:00
Thu	Feb 16	Houston at Charlotte	8:00
Thu	Feb 23	Philadelphia at Denver	8:00
Thu	Mar 2	Chicago at New York	7:30
		Orlando at Houston	9:45
Thu	Mar 9	San Antonio at Cleveland	8:00
Thu	Mar 16	Phoenix at Charlotte	8:00
Thu	Mar 23	Charlotte at Orlando	8:00
Thu	Mar 30	Atlanta at Golden State	8:00
Thu	Apr 6	Seattle at Denver	8:00
Thu	Apr 13	Golden State at Utah	8:00
Thu	Apr 20	New York at Charlotte	8:00

Ever a threat, Mitch Richmond is key to Kings' picture.

Revised and updated third edition!

THE ILLUSTRATED SPORTS RECORD BOOK
Zander Hollander and David Schulz

Here, in a single book, are more than 400 all-time—and current—sports records with 50 new stories and 125 action photos so vivid, it's like "being there." Featured is an all-star cast that includes Martina Navratilova, Joe DiMaggio, Joe Montana, Michael Jordan, Jack Nicklaus, Mark Spitz, Wayne Gretzky, Nolan Ryan, Muhammad Ali, Greg LeMond, Hank Aaron, Carl Lewis and Magic Johnson. This is *the* authoritative book that sets the record straight and recreates the feats at the time of achievement!
